Quechua Expressions of Stance and Deixis

Brill's Studies in the Indigenous Languages of the Americas

Series Editors

David Beck (*University of Alberta*)
Mily Crevels (*Leiden University*)
Hein van der Voort (*Museu Paraense Emílio Goeldi*)
Roberto Zavala (*CIESAS-Sureste*)

Editorial Board

Peter Bakker (*Aarhus University*)
Nora England (*University of Texas, Austin*)
Ana Fernández Garay (*Universidad Nacional de La Pampa*)
Michael Fortescue (*University of Copenhagen*)
Victor Golla (*Humboldt State University*)
Pieter Muysken (*Radboud University Nijmegen*)
Enrique Palancar (*CNRS*)
Keren Rice (*University of Toronto*)
Frank Seifart (*Max Planck Institute for Evolutionary Anthropology*)
Leo Wetzels (*CNRS/Sorbonne-Nouvelle, VU Amsterdam*)

VOLUME 11

The titles published in this series are listed at *brill.com/bsila*

Quechua Expressions of Stance and Deixis

Edited by

Marilyn S. Manley and Antje Muntendam

BRILL

LEIDEN | BOSTON

Library of Congress Cataloging-in-Publication Data

Quechua expressions of stance and deixis / Edited by Marilyn S. Manley and Antje Muntendam.
 pages cm. — (Brill's Studies in the Indigenous Languages of the Americas; 11)
 Includes bibliographical references and index.
 ISBN 978-90-04-28956-7 (hardback : alk. paper) — ISBN 978-90-04-29010-5 (e-book : alk. paper)
 1. Quechua language—Terms and phrases 2. Quechua language—Deixis. 3. Quechua language—Semantics.
 4. Quechua language—Etymology. 5. Indians of South America—Ecuador—Languages. 6. Indians of
 South America—Peru—Cuzco—Languages. 7. Indians of South America—Bolivia—Languages.
 8. Ecuador—Languages. 9. Peru—Cuzco—Languages. 10. Bolivia—Languages. I. Manley, Marilyn S., editor.
 II. Muntendam, Antje, editor.

PM6309.Q33 2015
498'.32301456—dc23

2015000207

This publication has been typeset in the multilingual 'Brill' typeface. With over 5,100 characters covering Latin, IPA, Greek, and Cyrillic, this typeface is especially suitable for use in the humanities. For more information, please see www.brill.com/brill-typeface.

ISSN 1876-5580
ISBN 978-90-04-28956-7 (hardback)
ISBN 978-90-04-29010-5 (e-book)

Copyright 2015 by Koninklijke Brill NV, Leiden, The Netherlands.
Koninklijke Brill NV incorporates the imprints Brill, Brill Hes & De Graaf, Brill Nijhoff, Brill Rodopi and Hotei Publishing.
All rights reserved. No part of this publication may be reproduced, translated, stored in a retrieval system, or transmitted in any form or by any means, electronic, mechanical, photocopying, recording or otherwise, without prior written permission from the publisher.
Authorization to photocopy items for internal or personal use is granted by Koninklijke Brill NV provided that the appropriate fees are paid directly to The Copyright Clearance Center, 222 Rosewood Drive, Suite 910, Danvers, MA 01923, USA. Fees are subject to change.

This book is printed on acid-free paper.

Printed by Printforce, the Netherlands

Contents

List of Tables and Figures   VI
Notes on Contributors   X

1 **Introduction**   1
   Marilyn S. Manley, Antje Muntendam and Susan E. Kalt

2 **Pointing in Space and Time: Deixis and Directional Movement in Schoolchildren's Quechua**   25
   Susan E. Kalt

3 **Demonstrative Deixis in Two Dialects of Amazonian Quichua**   75
   Janis Nuckolls, Tod Swanson and Belinda Ramirez Spencer

4 **Child Acquisition of Quechua Evidentiality and Deictic Meaning**   101
   Ellen H. Courtney

5 **Multidimensional Markers of Evidential, Epistemic and Mirative Stance in Cuzco Quechua**   145
   Marilyn S. Manley

6 **Discourse Deixis in Southern Quechua: A Case Study on Topic and Focus**   208
   Antje Muntendam

7 **From Nominal Predicate to Deictic Clausal Highlighter: The Development of *hina* 'like'**   259
   Pieter Muysken

8 **Right Peripheral Domains, Deixis and Information Structure in Southern Quechua**   287
   Liliana Sánchez

Index   323

List of Tables and Figures

Tables

1.1 Quechua pronominal system 7

1.2 Subject-verb agreement in English and Quechua present or unmarked tense 8

1.3 Object agreement in Quechua (singular forms only) 9

1.4 Chinchay Quechua intransitive future tense marking 12

2.1 Meanings and contingencies of *-mu* 37

2.2 Deictic and directional meanings of *-yku, -rqu, -ku, -pu* and *-mu* 39

2.3 Narrators' characteristics 46

2.4 Distribution of directional morphemes in narrative corpus 47

2.5 Complexity of derivation with directional suffixes by age group 48

2.6 Role of native speakers in this study 70

2.7 Derived verbs by level of complexity, nominalizations in parentheses 71

3.1 Occurrences of *kay, chi,* and *chay* in over 5,720 words of recorded data from the Pastaza dialect and their frequency of use with respect to the total number of words and demonstratives 94

3.2 Occurrences of *kay, chi,* and *chay* in over 5,720 words of recorded narrative data from the Tena dialect and their frequency of use with respect to the total number of words and demonstratives 94

3.3 Variants and instances of *kay, chi,* and *chay* used from Pastaza dialect 96

3.4 Variants and instances of *kay, chi,* and *chay* used from Tena dialect 98

4.1 Production of evidential morphemes, by age group 112

4.2 Functions of past inflections produced in conversations, by age group and type of verb 117

4.3 Sample pair of statements for each of three experimental contrasts 120

4.4 Mean percentages of predicted responses and standard deviations for each contrast, by age group 122

4.5 Ages in years and months of the 19 child story retellers 125

4.6 Excerpts from the adult narrative 127

4.7 Summary of adult-like and deviant production of 5 morphemes by 2- and 3-year-olds in narrative portions and direct quotations 129

LIST OF TABLES AND FIGURES   VII

4.8   Summary of adult-like and deviant production of morphemes by
      4-year-olds in narrative portions and direct quotations   132
4.9   Summary of adult-like and deviant production of morphemes by 5- and
      6-year-olds in narrative portions and direct quotations   135
4.10 Summary of production and comprehension data by age and type of
      data   137
5.1   Comparison of authors' accounts of Quechua evidentiality,
      epistemology and mirativity   157
5.2   Certainty ranking morphemic combinations   170
5.3   Average rankings and standard deviations for the six sentences   172
5.4   Tukey's HSD Post Hoc Test for Homogeneous Subsets for
      version 1   173
5.5   Tukey's HSD Post Hoc Test for Homogeneous Subsets for
      version 2   173
5.6   Multidimensionality of the combinations exemplified in this
      work   193
6.1   Characteristics of the participants   218
6.2   Frequencies and percentages of different word orders in three
      conditions: broad focus, contrastive focus on the subject (contrS) and
      contrastive focus on the object (contrO)   224
6.3   Frequencies and percentages of SOV and SVO in three conditions:
      broad focus, contrastive focus on the subject (contrS) and contrastive
      focus on the object (contrO)   226
6.4   Alignment of peak 1, peak 2, and peak 3 in SOV sentences   228
6.5   Frequencies and percentages of early versus late peak alignment
      for peak 1 in SOV sentences in three focus conditions: broad focus,
      contrastive focus on the subject (contrS) and contrastive focus on the
      object (contrO)   229
6.6   Alignment of peak 1, peak 2 and peak 3 in SVO sentences   230
6.7   Frequencies and percentages of early versus late peak alignment for
      peak 1 in SVO sentences in three conditions: broad focus, contrastive
      focus on the subject (contrS) and contrastive focus on the object
      (contrO)   230
6.8   Downstepped, even, and upstepped peaks in SOV sentences, comparing
      peak 1–2 and peak 2–3   233
6.9   Downstepped, even, and upstepped peaks in SVO sentences, comparing
      peak 1–2 and peak 2–3   234
6.10 Means of the duration of the subject, the object and the duration
      difference (subject – object) (in ms) in the three focus conditions for
      Speaker 6 (N = 6)   238

VIII LIST OF TABLES AND FIGURES

6.11 Means of the maximum intensity of the subject, the object and the difference (subject – object) (in dB) in the three focus conditions for Speaker 6 (N = 6) 239

6.12 Frequencies of the word orders used in the three focus conditions in the elicitation task (broad focus, contrastive focus on the subject (contrS) and contrastive focus on the object (contrO), per speaker 248

6.13 Downstepped, even, and upstepped peaks for SOV sentences, comparing peak 1–2 and peak 2–3, per speaker and condition 249

6.14 Downstepped, even, and upstepped peaks for SVO sentences, comparing peak 1–2 and peak 2–3, per speaker and condition 251

7.1 The entries for *hina* in three dictionaries; (-) marks when a particular usage is not found 264

Figures

2.1 Complexity of derivation with directional suffixes by age group 48

2.2 Frames 1–3 of instrument, read counter-clockwise 64

2.3 Frames 4–6 of narration instrument, read clockwise 65

4.1 Predicted responses obtained by contrast and age group 123

5.1 Appendix B, item 1 169, 196

5.2 Appendix B, item 2 197

5.3 Appendix B, item 3 198

5.4 Appendix B, item 4a 198

5.5 Appendix B, item 4b 199

5.6 Appendix B, item 4c 200

5.7 Appendix B, item 5 200

5.8 Appendix C, item 1 201

5.9 Appendix C, item 2 202

5.10 Appendix C, item 3a 203

5.11 Appendix C, item 3b 203

5.12 Appendix C, item 3c 204

6.1 Example of a sequence of pictures, used in the picture-story task 246

6.2 Example of a picture used in the question-answer task 247

6.3 Utterance with SOV order and contrastive focus on the object 253

6.4 Utterance with SOV order in broad focus 253

6.5 Utterance with SOV order and contrastive focus on the object 254

6.6 Utterance with SVO order in broad focus 254

6.7	Utterance with SOV order in broad focus	255
7.1	Schematic overview of the grammaticalization path of 'like' as proposed in Romaine and Lange (1991, 261)	261
7.2	The radial structure model for 'like' as proposed in Buchstaller (2001)	262
7.3	Radial structure model for *hina*	281
8.1	Overall frequencies of right dislocated constituents in the Quechua narratives	301
8.2	Frequency of sentences with RDCs according to main verb type	301
8.3	Number of RDCs per sentence	302
8.4	RDCs according to verb type	304
8.5	RDCs with intransitive verbs	308
8.6	Antecedents of oblique RDCs	310
8.7	Antecedents of Subject RDCs	311
8.8	RDCs with transitive verbs	312
8.9	Direct Object RDCs according to antecedent	313

Notes on Contributors

Marilyn S. Manley

is an Associate Professor of Spanish at Rowan University in Glassboro, New Jersey. She is also a Fully Certified Oral Proficiency Interview (OPI) Tester for Spanish through the American Council on the Teaching of Foreign Languages (ACTFL). At Rowan University, in addition to teaching Hispanic linguistics and Spanish language courses, she enjoys teaching basic Cuzco Quechua language within the context of two interdisciplinary Honors Program courses. Her recent publications include various journal articles and book chapters on Quechua language attitudes and maintenance, Quechua to Spanish cross-linguistic influence, and teaching Quechua as a less commonly taught language.

Antje Muntendam

is an Assistant Professor of Hispanic Linguistics in the Department of Modern Languages and Linguistics at Florida State University. Before joining Florida State University she was an Assistant Professor of Hispanic Linguistics at Middlebury College and an Assistant Professor of Linguistics at Radboud University Nijmegen. Her research focuses on language contact and bilingualism, in particular between Quechua and Spanish and Turkish and Dutch. Her research interests include information structure, the syntax-pragmatics interface and prosody. She has done fieldwork in Bolivia, Ecuador and Peru, and she has carried out research projects with heritage speakers of Turkish in the Netherlands.

Ellen H. Courtney

was an Associate Professor of Languages and Linguistics at the University of Texas at El Paso and is currently a Visiting Scholar at the University of Arizona. Her primary research interest is child acquisition of different varieties of Peruvian Quechua, with special focus on the development of morphosyntax. She has carried out fieldwork In the Peruvian Andes of Arequipa, Cuzco, and Ancash, including the collection of naturalistic speech samples as well as experimental data.

Susan E. Kalt

is Professor of Spanish at Roxbury Community College in Massachusetts and co-founder of Proyecto Yachay Q'ipi, a rural grassroots Andean curriculum initiative. Since 2008 she has received two National Endowment for the Humanities fellowships and a seed grant from the Foundation for Endangered

NOTES ON CONTRIBUTORS

Languages to document child Quechua morphosyntax and support revitalization efforts. Her team's collection of over a hundred interviews of rural Bolivian and Peruvian children is found at the Archive of the Indigenous Languages of the Americas. In 2013 she taught Field Methods in Linguistics with emphasis on the Quechua language at Boston College.

Janis Nuckolls
is Associate Professor in the Department of Linguistics and English Language at Brigham Young University. Her research has focused on various subcomponents within the grammar of the Pastaza dialect of Ecuadorian Quichua. Her published work has featured original analyses of the significance of ideophones in grammar, discourse and for Pastaza Quichua linguaculture: *Sounds Like Life* (1996), *Lessons from a Quechua Strongwoman* (2010). She has also studied the evidential subsystem in Pastaza Quichua from an interactional, pragmatic perspective: *Evidentiality in Interaction* (2014).

Pieter Muysken
is Professor of Linguistics at Radboud University Nijmegen. His research focuses on the ways human languages interact and the contact-induced language change that results from this interaction. Muysken was one of the first to study these processes of contact through different formal models of language. He has done fieldwork in the Andes, the Caribbean, as well as with bilingual groups in the Netherlands. He has also been involved in a number of projects trying to communicate research to a wider audience, most recently through the website "Stemmen van Afrika". He was also involved in producing a four volume series of grammars in Spanish on the indigenous languages of Bolivia, www.ru.nl/lenguasdebolivia. For more information on Pieter Muysken, please visit www.ru.nl/linc.

Belinda Ramirez Spencer
received her BA in Sociocultural Anthropology at Brigham Young University in 2013. She is currently pursuing a Masters Degree and PhD in Sociocultural Anthropology at the University of California, San Diego. Her main interests are religion, semiotics, and ontology, with a particular focus on the Ecuadorian Amazon region.

Liliana Sánchez
is a Professor of Spanish at Rutgers, The State University of New Jersey. She has published two monographs on Quechua languages *The Morphology and Syntax*

of Topic and Focus: Minimalist Inquiries in the Quechua Periphery (2010) and *Quechua-Spanish Bilingualism. Interference and Convergence in Functional Categories* (2003) as well as articles on Quechua-Spanish bilingualism in journals such as *Bilingualism: Language and Cognition, Lingua,* and *International Journal of Bilingualism,* among others. She has also co-edited the volume *Information Structure in Indigenous Languages of the Americas* (2010).

Tod Swanson

is Associate Professor of Religious Studies in the School of Historical, Philosophical, and Religious Studies at Arizona State University. His research uses Anthropological Linguistics to understand Andean/Amazonian philosophy of nature: *Singing to Estranged Relatives: Quichua Relations to Plants in the Ecuadorian Amazon* (2009). During the summer months he directs the Andes and Amazon Field School in Napo Province Ecuador where he is recording Amazonian Quichua oral tradition on plants and animals.

CHAPTER 1

Introduction

Marilyn S. Manley, Antje Muntendam and Susan E. Kalt

The primary goal of the present volume is to explore the semantics and pragmatics of a variety of expressions in Southern Quechua and Ecuadorian Quichua[1] that are considered here to be markers of stance, following Du Bois' (2007) notion of the "stance triangle", and communicate what some have alternately referred to as deixis. All of the subsequent chapters of this work investigate these stance-marking expressions through original fieldwork and experimental studies, many of which employ original methodologies. The expressions examined within this volume include the Cuzco Quechua verbal derivation markers, *-yku, -rqu, -ku, -mu* and *-pu* (Chapter 2), the Pastaza and Tena Quichua demonstratives, *kay, chi* and *chay* (Chapter 3), the Cuzco Quechua evidential enclitics, *-mi/-n, -chá,* and *-si/-s*, as well as the past tense suffixes, *-r(q)a-* and *-sqa-* (Chapters 4 and 5), the Southern Quechua markers of topic and focus, *-qa*, and *-mi/-n*, respectively, as well as syntactic and prosodic strategies for topic and focus marking (Chapter 6), the Puno, Lampa and Ayaviri Quechua postposition, *hina* (Chapter 7), and Cuzco, Apurimac and Arequipa Quechua morphologically unmarked right dislocated constituents, which may be used to introduce an element that is not part of the current topic structure or disambiguate the reference of null subjects (Chapter 8).

Upon first inspection of the range of expressions studied here, it may not be obvious how or why all of these should be considered as markers of stance (or deictic elements). Since theoretical discussions of stance and deixis are beyond the scope of each of the individual chapters, whose main objective is to examine their respective expressions in Quechua and Quichua, this Introduction aims to outline some of the most relevant aspects of the theoretical underpinnings of stance and deixis, thereby serving as a broad background for the chapters to follow. The Introduction is organized in the following way. First, we address aspects of some of the most influential theories of stance and deixis today. This is followed by a general outline of expressions of stance and

---

1 These languages form a large subgroup of the Amerindian languages spoken in the Andes, and are classified as QIIB-C or Chinchay Quechua (Torero 1964). Southern Quechua is also referred to as Cuzco-Collao Quechua.

© KONINKLIJKE BRILL NV, LEIDEN, 2015 | DOI 10.1163/9789004290105_002

deixis in Quechua. Finally, we provide information about the specific contributions in each chapter of this volume.

1 Indexicality, Stance and Deixis

Both stance and deixis fall within the realm of indexicality and serve to anchor utterances to the context of speech. As described below, this work supports the unification of the concepts of stance and deixis and suggests that deixis should be considered as a subtype of stance that serves a specifically referential function. Careful examination of the groundbreaking work of Du Bois (2007) in his conceptualization of the stance triangle, together with Hanks' (2005, 2011) influential description of his practice approach to deixis, reveals striking similarities between these preeminent theories of stance and deixis, respectively.

While this work is not the first to propose the unification of the two concepts of stance and deixis, to our knowledge, it is the first to address this topic at a level of detail beyond a simple, brief mention. For example, in his work on deixis, Hanks (2005, 205) states, "Deictics index a Spr's (speaker's) stance relative to the Adr (addressee) and the object...". Additionally, in her study of Kalapalo epistemology, Basso (2008, 246) states, "An approach that considers deictic functions within a stance model thus seems particularly useful for asking new questions about epistemic marking..." Furthermore, in reference to the work of Hanks and Du Bois, Williams (2009, 7) states, "...a comparison and potential unification of these frameworks deserves much attention." We undertake this comparison and unification as follows.

Fundamentally, Du Bois describes stance as: (1) a property of utterances "inherently embedded in their dialogic contexts" (2007, 148), (2) "the smallest unit of social action" (2007, 173), and (3) necessarily invoking an evaluation, with evaluation defined as "the process whereby a stancetaker orients to an object of stance and characterizes it as having some specific quality or value" (2007, 143). Du Bois also provides the following definition (2007, 163):

> Stance is a public act by a social actor, achieved dialogically through overt communicative means, of simultaneously evaluating objects, positioning subjects (self and others), and aligning with other subjects, with respect to any salient dimension of the sociocultural field.

This definition incorporates the three nodes of Du Bois' stance triangle, "the three key entities in the stance act, namely the first subject, the second subject, and the (shared) stance object" (2007, 164). Du Bois (2007, 163) further explains:

INTRODUCTION 3

The stance act thus creates three kinds of stance consequences at once. In taking a stance, the stancetaker (1) evaluates an object, (2) positions a subject (usually the self), and (3) aligns with other subjects.

Hanks' (2005, 205) statement mentioned above and repeated here, that "Deictics index a Spr's stance relative to the Adr and the object..." bears a striking resemblance to Du Bois' stance triangle.

Prior to drawing further parallels between Hanks' work on deixis and Du Bois' work on stance, some background information is in order regarding Hanks' theoretical position. Hanks presents his practice approach to deixis as an alternative framework to two contemporary theoretical traditions that he refers to as spatialist and interactionist. Hanks (2005, 196) describes these two traditions as "... two different background pictures of utterance context and particularly of deixis". According to the egocentric spatialist view, which Hanks (2005, 196) describes as "the standard default for most modern linguistic descriptions", "deictic acts take place when the Spr, the Adr, and the Object are physically copresent and perceptible". Furthermore, Hanks (2011, 319) explains that the spatialist view "... holds that relative contiguity (*this* = proximal, *that* = non-proximal and so forth) is fundamental...". Moreover, according to the spatialist position, "The situation may be interperspectival, but it is the Spr who produces the utterance and the Spr's body that serves as the anchor point..." (2005, 196).

Among Hanks' arguments against the egocentric spatialist view is the fact that it fails to account for the "many cases in which a deictic responds not to speaker accessibility, but to the addressee's access to the object, or to the relative symmetry of access between the co-participants" (2011, 320). Bühler (1934) was the first to describe this phenomenon, which he referred to as deictic transposition; rather than the speaker serving as the contextual anchor, the addressee, some other object or a narrative space may fulfill this function. Hanks additionally finds the spatialist view inadequate in that it "omits critical features of deictic practice, including the mutual orientation of interactants, all non-perceptual modes of access such as background knowledge, memory or anticipation, and all extra-physical aspects of social settings" (2011, 321). In other words, in addition to the fact that the speaker does not always serve as the deictic center in discourse practice, the spatialist view also falls short in that objects referenced by deictics need not always be physically present and perceptible.

According to the interactionist view of deixis, on the other hand, the emergent space of interaction serves as the core context for deictic expression, "and to study it, we must attend to sequential organization of talk, to situational variation and to the micro-ethnography of everyday usage " (Hanks 2011, 322). Furthermore, this view proposes that "Utterance meaning must be 'negotiated' or worked out by the co-engaged parties. It is not given in advance, nor is it fixed by the intentions of the Spr" (Hanks 2005, 196). Additionally, Hanks explains that according to this view, "In the course of deictic practice, interactants must jointly establish and display the relevance of spatial perceptual, discursive or other contextual frames" (2011, 322).

Hanks' (2005, 200) primary argument against the interactionist picture is that it fails to grasp:

> ... that the deictic field is partly structured by the *semantic field* of deixis, that is, the conventional linguistic array of oppositions and contrasts that defines the potentials of the forms for acts of referring.

Moreover, Hanks finds it "obviously implausible that... (deictic) meanings are entirely negotiated utterance by utterance" (2005, 200).

Drawing primarily from the work of Bühler, Goffman, and Bourdieu, Hanks' practice approach to deixis serves as a third, blended, compromise position between the spatialist and interactionist traditions. Hanks (2011, 323) explains, "We can grant interaction as the ordinary context of utterances, while still claiming that the semantics of deixis is egocentric and spatial." Hanks (2005, 197) further states, "the linguistic forms encode semantic values of the sort predicted by the spatialist picture (contiguity to ego), but the pragmatics is governed by interactional principles (including inference from relevance)." According to this alternative framework, the lexically encoded, default semantic values of deictic expressions are consistent with those proposed by the spatialist view, but the pragmatics of deictic expressions demonstrates the flexibility needed to shift the deictic center and refer to imperceptible objects located beyond the physical surround of the interactants.

An important way in which Hanks' practice approach to deixis theory differs from both the spatialist and the interactionist views is that according to Hanks' position (2005, 206), in order for interactants to interpret deictic meaning, in addition to having an understanding of the semantics of deictics and the local practical circumstances, they must also take into account the deictics' embedding in the broader social field. Hanks (2011, 323) explains that the broader social field, "includes the identities of participants, the genres of practice of which deixis is a part, the social definition of place and time and the values attaching to objects of reference." Hanks (2005, 211) further explains,

INTRODUCTION

... objects have value for the interactants and the social world around them. They are dirty, clean, evil, good, avoided, private, self-evident, secret, mine, yours, or someone else's. Such qualities and their evaluation may appear far removed from sheer indexicality, but they figure prominently in deictic practice... a Spr's evaluative stance in an utterance can help resolve the reference. At the same time, a Spr who refers to an object enters into a social relation with it and thereby engages with its value.

Thus, in his practice approach, Hanks recognizes that evaluation is central to deictic expression. As such, in recognizing that evaluation is unavoidable in deixis, Hanks' practice approach allows deictics to satisfy Du Bois' definition of stance, listed above and repeated here, as "an act of evaluation owned by a social actor" (2007, 173). Furthermore, within Hanks' practice approach, deictics are described in a way that is consistent with Du Bois' stance triangle, in which a stancetaker "(1) evaluates an object, (2) positions a subject (usually the self), and (3) aligns with other subjects" (Du Bois 2007, 163). For these reasons, it is proposed here that deixis should be considered as a subclass of stance.

If deictics are, in effect, markers of stance, the question arises as to what should distinguish deictics as a subclass within the larger category of stance. While the broad literature on deixis to date includes a variety of subtypes, including but not limited to, spatial deixis (*here, there*), temporal deixis (*now, later*, tense), personal deixis (pronominals), discourse deixis (reference to prior talk), and social deixis (honorifics), this work proposes that, within a model where deixis is considered as a subtype of stance, it would be terminologically useful to classify only referential deixis as "deixis" and to consider what has been called nonreferential deixis as "stance". In his work, Hanks (2011, 315) describes his focus on referential deixis as follows:

... those forms whose primary function is to individuate objects of reference (including events, material things, talk itself or any individuated concept). Referential deixis is found in all human languages and includes at least demonstratives, person markers, locative, directional and temporal markers, but excludes much 'social deixis' such as honorification (where social status is indexed but usually not singled out for comment) and standard sociolinguistic markers (where social factors are indexed but not singled out for comment).

Furthermore, Hanks (2005, 195) distinguishes referential deixis from nonreferential deixis as follows:

The fact of referentiality distinguishes these forms (referential deictic forms) from nonreferring indexicals such as regional or other accents, speech levels, or stylistic variants. All of these may index features of context, but they do so without shifting the reference. Second, deictics can usually be lexically expanded with further descriptors that characterize the object. Hence one could say simply 'this' or 'this old table with the broken leg,'...'here' or 'here in the East Bay,' 'you' or 'you my friend,' and so on.

Distinguishing referential deixis from nonreferential stance may prove difficult in practice due to the multidimensional nature of deictics and other markers of stance. Hanks (2005, 212) describes his concept of the deictic field as "a space of positions and position taking in relation to objects and their values in the embedding social field"; however, in his analysis of Yucatec Mayan examples, he finds that "there are multiple deictic dimensions in play in the actual field of utterance" (2005, 207). Hanks (2005, 207) sees the "multistranded makeup" of the deictic field to be problematic for deictic construal, since:

> At any moment in interaction, multiple dimensions of access (among participants, objects, and settings) are simultaneously available for interactants. The selection and understanding of deictics relies on the simultaneous articulation of space, perception, discourse, commonsense and mutual knowledge, anticipation, and the framework of participation in which Sprs and Adrs orient to one another. Any one of these factors can provide the basis for deictic construal according to the demands of the ongoing relevance structure in which it is produced.

Hanks (2005, 209) also finds that it is precisely this "simultaneity of alternate framings in the deictic field" that accounts for the variation that he has observed in Yucatec Mayan linguistic practice.

As Hanks has found for Yucatec Maya, the contributors to the present volume have also found rich variation in practice for Quechua expressions of stance and deixis. Since the primary focus of the chapters included here is on the semantics and pragmatics of Quechua expressions and not on theoretical considerations of stance and deixis, each chapter alternately refers to either "deixis" or "stance", following literary tradition. As further background for the chapters to come, the next section outlines categories of stance and deixis in Quechua as they have been described in the literature to date.

INTRODUCTION 7

2 Quechua Stance and Deictic Categories

The goal of this section is to provide a broad outline of the major stance/deixis categories in Quechua, including what has been referred to in the literature as person deixis, place deixis, time deixis, social deixis, discourse deixis and epistemological/evidential deixis/stance. All examples are presented in Southern Quechua, as it is the most-often studied in the present volume. The examples are by no means complete or exhaustive, serving only to provide illustrations of a portion of the deictic systems discussed in subsequent chapters of this volume.

2.1 *Person Deixis in Quechua*

The elements of person deixis outlined here include pronominals and inflectional marking. In marking person, languages generally distinguish between Speaker (S), Addressee (A) and other, based on the participants' roles in the speech event (Levinson 2004). Quechua marks person in pronouns and in inflectional marking. The Quechua pronominal system is provided in table 1.1.

TABLE 1.1 *Quechua pronominal system*

Singular		Plural	
+S, -A	*ñuqa*	+S, +A	*ñuqanchis*
		+S, -A, +AUG	*ñuqayku*
-S, +A	*qan*	-S, +A	*qankichis*
-S, -A	*pay*	-S, -A	*paykuna*

In singular, Quechua distinguishes between first person (+S, -A), second person (-S, +A) and third person (-S, -A). Regarding plural pronouns, a distinction is made between 'first person inclusive' (+S, +A) and 'first person exclusive' (+S, -A, +AUG). First person exclusive does not include the addressee, but it may include other individuals (AUG) (Levinson 2004, 113). Second person plural is (+A, -S) and third person plural is (-S, -A). Quechua pronouns are gender neutral and are frequently dropped, given that Quechua is a pro-drop language.

The following sentences adapted from Plaza (2005, 15) illustrate the exclusivity distinction for first person plural subjects. In (1) the first person plural

8   MANLEY ET AL.

exclusive is used, meaning that the addressee is not considered a participant, whereas in (2) the inclusive is used.

(1) *Ñuqa-yku-qa*   *jaqay*   *mayu-pi*   *llamk'a-chka-yku.*
    1-PL.EXCL-TOP   yonder   river-LOC   work-PROG-1.PL.EXCL
    'We (not including you) are working over yonder in the river.'

(2) *Ñuqa-nchik-qa[2]*   *jaqay*   *mayu-pi*   *llamk'a-chka-nchik.*
    1-PL.INCL-TOP   yonder   river-LOC   work-PROG-1.PL.EXCL
    'We (including you) are working over yonder in the river.'

The inflectional system spells out discourse roles through suffixes on nominal and verbal roots. Quechua verbal inflection marks the speaker and addressee roles more explicitly than it marks third persons, as shown in tables 1.2 and 1.3 below, in which English equivalents are included for comparison and ease of interpretation. Subject inflection is shown in table 1.2:

TABLE 1.2   *Subject-verb agreement in English and Quechua present or unmarked tense*

Person	Discourse role	English		Quechua	
		Sg	Pl	Sg	Pl
1	+S, -A	-∅	-∅	*-ni*	*-nchis* (+S, +A)
					-yku (+S, -A, +AUG)
2	-S, +A	-∅	-∅	*-nki*	*-nkichis*
3	-S, -A	-s	-∅	*-n* (optional)	*-nku*

Object inflection suffixes and their pronominal English equivalents are shown in table 1.3; only singular forms are included since the plural forms introduce unnecessary complexity:

---

2   *-nchis* and *-nkichis* are phonological and orthographic variants of *-nchik* and *-nkichik* in Cuzco-Collao Quechua (Howard 2013, 3–5).

INTRODUCTION 9

TABLE 1.3   *Object agreement in Quechua (singular forms only)*

Discourse role (Person)	English	Quechua
+S, -A	me	*-wa*
-S, +A	you	*-yki* 1 > 2 'I to you'
		-sunki 3 > 2 'he/she to you'
-S, -A	him, her, it	-∅

As is evident in table 1.3, subject and object person features are morphologically fused in the second person object suffixes. This is illustrated in the following examples from Plaza (1987, 195):

(3)   *Tapu-yki.*
      ask-1S2O
      'I ask you.'

(4)   *Tapu-sunki.*
      ask-3S2O
      'He asks you.'

Third person objects of transitive verbs are marked with a phonetically null inflectional affix, as argued in Plaza (1987, 202–203). These contrast with sentences in which the verb is used intransitively, as noted in examples (5) and (6), respectively (*ibid.*).

(5)   *Riku-ni.* (intransitive use)
      see-1
      'I see.'

(6)   *Riku-∅-ni.* (transitive use)
      see-3OBJ-1
      'I see him/her/it.'

Notice that the object in (6) can optionally have definite, specific anaphoric reference, which must be resolved in the discourse. First and second person objects, on the other hand, are always definite and specific, based on their correspondence to participant roles in the speech act. The presence or absence of third person objects is crucial to understanding the argument structure of verbs marked with directional morphemes, as noted by Torero (2005, 72–75).

2.2 *Place Deixis in Quechua*

Quechua examples of place deixis outlined here include demonstratives and directional morphemes. Bátori (1984) and Levinson (2004, 3) note that many of the world's languages have the option of placing both the speaker and addressee at the center of the deictic field. As shown above, the inflectional system in Quechua does this by marking first and second persons more explicitly than it does third persons. The option of emphasizing the addressee role is also seen in the fact that demonstrative elements may be indexed to proximity or perceptual availability to the addressee as well as the speaker, depending on the context of use. In Quechua, *kay* and *ankay* are equivalent ways of expressing proximity to the spatial or temporal deictic center 'here/now'; *chay, anchay* are distal demonstratives meaning roughly 'there/then'; and *haqay* plus its allomorphs means 'over yonder' or outside the perceptual field (Calvo 1993, 57–62).[3] Demonstrative pronouns are sometimes accompanied by gesture and the particle *aqna* 'like this' in order to identify the deictic center or establish shared attentional focus with the speaker.

The directional morpheme most frequently noted for its spatial deictic properties is the suffix *-mu*, which when added to a verb of motion indicates movement toward the speaker and/or hearer:

(7) *T'anta-ta*   *apa-mu-nqa.*
bread-ACC   carry-CIS-3FUT
'He will bring the bread.'

(8) *T'anta-ta*   *apa-nqa.*
bread-ACC   carry-3FUT
'He will take the bread.' (Bills 1972, 1, glosses ours)

---

3 According to an anonymous reviewer, demonstrative systems in the broader Quechua language family include two-term systems, three-term systems and, in a single case, a six-term system.

INTRODUCTION 11

When suffixed to a non-motion verb, *-mu* "indicates movement to a location distant from the speaker and hearer where the verbal action or concept takes place" (Bills, 1972, 2).

(9) *T'anta-ta   ranti-**mu**-nqa.*
     bread-ACC   buy-TRANS-3FUT
     'He will go buy some bread.'

(10) *T'anta-ta   ranti-nqa.*
     bread-ACC   buy-3FUT
     'He will buy some bread.'

A more comprehensive discussion of the properties of *-mu* and other directional morphemes is found in chapter 2.

2.3   Time Deixis in Quechua

In Quechua, time deixis is encoded in adverbs and is reflected in the tense system by suffixation. To express "a general truth, simple present tense, and in some contexts a recent past" (Howard 2013, 42), the person markings of the unmarked tense in table 1.2 are used. Two ways to express the past are by adding *-r(q)a-*[4] or *-sqa-*[5] immediately before the tense markings in table 1.2.[6] To express the future tense, the markings in table 1.4 are used.

As should be evident from this brief discussion of tense marking, the expression of tense is sometimes morphologically fused with the expression of verbal argument structure, verbal aspect, mood and evidentiality.

Time deixis is also marked in free-standing adverbs such as *kunan* 'now', *qhipaman* 'later' and *ñawpaqta* 'before' (Godenzzi & Vengoa 1994, 40). These interpretations are indexed to the deictic center. Demonstratives such as *chay* 'there', alone or in combination with numerous suffixes such as reportive *-si* (*chaysi* 'then they say') or adposition *-manta* 'from' (*chaymanta* 'from there, after that') can also serve a discourse deictic function, marking temporal sequence within a narrative.

---

4 In chapter 5 of the present volume, Manley finds *-r(q)a-* to be utilized as an evidentiality strategy to communicate direct information source and also with epistemic extension to indicate certainty.

5 In chapter 5 of the present volume, Manley analyzes *-sqa-* as an evidentiality strategy used to communicate indirect information source, with epistemic extension to indicate doubt, and as a mirativity strategy, indicating surprise and newsworthiness.

6 Cole (1982) includes an in-depth discussion of tense and aspect in Imbabura Quechua, an Ecuadorian variety.

TABLE 1.4   *Chinchay Quechua intransitive future tense marking*

		Ecuador	Bolivia/Peru
Singular	1	*-sha*	*-saq*
	2	*-ngi*	*-nki*
	3	*-nga*	*-nqa*
Plural	1 INCL	*-shun*	*-sun* or *-sunchik*
	1 EXCL		*-sqayku* or *saqku*
	2	*-ngichi*	*-nkichik*
	3	*-nga*	*-nganku*

(Hermon 1985, 22 for Ecuador; Howard 2013, 150–1 for Cuzco-Collao)

2.4   *Social Deixis in Quechua*

Social deixis is defined as the linguistic expression of the speech community's relationships, which Levinson (2004, 51) organizes along four axes:

Axis	*Honorific Types*	*Other encodings*
(1) Speaker to referent	Referent honorifics	Titles
(2) Speaker to addressee	Addressee honorifics	Address forms
(3) Speaker to non-addressed participant	Bystander honorifics	Taboo vocabularies
(4) Speaker to setting	Formality levels	Register

Examples from axes (1–2) in Cuzco-Collao Quechua are the honorific titles and forms of address, which include terms based on ritual relationships of friendship, such as *cumpariy*, '$godfather,[7] buddy' as well as those based on family roles such as *taytay* 'Sir (lit. father)', *mamay* 'Ma'am (lit. mother)', *wayqiy, turay* 'brother', uttered by males and females respectively, and *panay, ñañay* 'sister', uttered by males and females respectively. An example from axis (3) is the suppletive *na-*, which may substitute for almost any taboo word known to the interlocutors but unspoken (Hipólito Peralta, pers. comm.). *Na-* can also be used anaphorically, or to refer to an entity for which the speaker cannot immediately access the name. An example from axis (4) is the diminutive

---

7 Throughout this volume, the "$" symbol is used to represent Spanish borrowings.

INTRODUCTION   13

suffix, *-cha*, as in *mamacha* (lit. little mother), indicating informality. There are
no formality distinctions in the Cuzco Quechua inflectional system.

Cuzco Quechua depends heavily on the directional markers, *-yku, -rqu, -ku*
and *-pu*, in composition with the elements above, to fulfill social deictic functions, many of them as nuanced as the subjective evaluations that these suffixes have come to mean. *-Yku* (and its allomorph *-yu*) forms compositional
meanings with imperative voice, which express politeness and affection:

(11) *T'ika-yki-ta*   *raki-yu-wa-y.*
      flower-2POSS-ACC   share-INT-1OBJ-IMP
      'Share some of your flowers with me please.' (Cusihuamán 1976, 206)

When the verb is marked imperative, *-rqu* interacts with the addressee honorific system and with the formality register to express nuances of social relationship between speaker and hearer, for example, courtesy and respect:

(12) *Allichu,*   *mamá-y,*   *yanapa-rqu-ku-wa-y!*
      please   ma'am-VOC   help-DYN-REFL-1OBJ-IMP
      'Please, ma'am, kindly help me!' (Cusihuamán 1976, 208)

It also expresses the priority and urgency with which an action should be
realized:

(13) *Kuti-mu-na-yki-paq*   *papa-ta*   *wayk'u -rqu-chka-saq.*
      return-CIS-NOM-2POSS-GEN   potato-ACC   cook-DYN-PROG-1FUT
      'I'll be cooking potatoes for your return.' (Cusihuamán 1976, 207)

Similarly, reflexive *-ku* interacts with other softening elements such as the second person irrealis affix to produce meanings of "affection, courtesy or care in
the realization of an action" (Cusihuamán 1976, 212).

(14) *Lliklla-ta*   *ranti-ku-waq-chu?*
      shawl-ACC   buy-REFL-IRR-INTR
      'Would you like to buy yourself a shawl?' (*ibid.*)

Finally, benefactive *-pu* combines with first person object *-wa* to form the
meaning 'for me' which is often used to mean 'please':

(15) *Ni-pu-wa-y*   *waqya-mu-wa-chun.*
      say-BEN-1OBJ-2IMP   call-CIS-1OBJ-3IMP
      'Tell her to call me please/for me.' (Martín Castillo, pers. comm.).

In summary, speakers of Cuzco Quechua use the suffixes *-yku, -rqu* and *-ku* in combination with social deictic markers such as imperative voice to add social nuances to their requests such as affection, formality, politeness and urgency, as well as to indicate the degrees of attention, intention, intensity, affection, emotion or energy with which requested actions should be carried out. Additionally, the benefactive marker *-pu* acquires a social deictic function of request when combined with the first person object marker.

2.5   *Discourse Deixis in Quechua*

Discourse deixis refers to the use of expressions that signal a relationship between a specific utterance and the prior or subsequent discourse (Levinson 1983, 2004). There is a rich inventory of morphemes by which a Quechua speaker can encode reference to previously or subsequently expressed elements within a discourse. Many of these morphemes are independent suffixes or enclitics, which Cusihuamán (1976) groups in the following ways: topic markers, focus markers, relational markers and specification markers.

The topic marker in Quechua is *-qa*, which can either be used to refer to the topic of the sentence, or the topic of the larger discourse. By relating the element to the preceding or following discourse, *-qa* has a discourse deictic function. For example, it appears that the sentence below is a response to a comment asserting or implying that it snows in Chinchero. Both the verb and the place name are topicalized with the enclitic *-qa* here:

(16) *Mana-n*   *rit'i-mu-n-chu-qa*   *Chinchero-ta-qa.*
      no-DIREV   snow-CIS-3SUBJ-NEG-TOP   Chinchero-ACC-TOP
      'But it doesn't snow in Chinchero.' (Cusihuamán 1976, 238, gloss and
      translation ours)

In the next example, we see the interrogative conjunction *-ri*, which Cusihuamán also considers a topic marker. Here it seems that the conjunction makes a discourse link to a previous assertion on the part of the speaker.

(17) *Pi-taq*   *qan-ri*   *ka-sha-nki?*
      who-DISC   you-INTR   be-PROG-2SUBJ
      'And who are you?' (*ibid.*)

According to Levinson (1983, 88), morphological topic markers can be classified as discourse deictic elements, as

INTRODUCTION   15

> ...a major function of topic marking is precisely to relate the marked utterance to some specific topic raised in the prior discourse, i.e. to perform a discourse-deictic function.

Another group of enclitics considered by Cusihuamán is what he calls the focus markers, which include the evidential suffixes. These suffixes can be used to draw the attention to the new or non-presupposed information in a sentence, and are discussed in a separate section below.

Quechua speakers also have a variety of syntactic and prosodic means to mark information as new (focused) or presupposed (topic). Peruvian Southern Quechua speakers may use the evidential markers to mark new information on elements *in situ* or those that are fronted, and they use prosodic means to mark presupposed information that has been displaced to the right periphery (Sánchez 2010).

The third type of enclitics considered by Cusihuamán (1976, 249) is what he calls relational enclitics, which:

> ...mark one or more elements of a complementary utterance, be it declarative, imperative or interrogative, for the purpose of indicating that the references made by these elements maintain a tight relationship with the information contained in a previous utterance.

These include additive *-pis/-pas*, which have the meaning 'also, as well', and the contrastive *-taq,* which translates roughly as 'instead, in contrast'.

The fourth type of enclitics we are considering as encoders of discourse reference are what Cusihuamán (1976, 254–5, translation ours) calls the 'specification' enclitics, which "specify the state or frequency of the action, the actor or other element that intervenes in the realization of an action." For example, the limitative *-lla,* when attached to a noun, signifies that the effect of the action was limited to the noun mentioned:

(18) *Kuka-cha-lla-ta-n*   *hallpa-ku-sha-ra-ni.*
      coca-DIM-LIM-ACC-DIREV   chew-REFL-PROG-PST1–1SUBJ
      'I was only chewing coca, or (It was only coca that I was chewing)' (*ibid.*)

Another apparently discourse-relevant enclitic is the definitive *-puni* when used to specify that the person marked is 'precisely' the person one means to indicate as the actor, for example:

(19) *Kiki-nchis-**puni***   *ruwa-ku-nchis*   *chay-mi*   *ima-pis*
same-1INCL-CERT   do-REFL-1INCL   that-DIREV   what-ADD

ati-ku-n.
accomplish-REFL-3SUBJ
'We accomplish that very thing we hope to when we do it ourselves.'
(Cusihuamán 1976, 257)

Another such discourse specifier is the continuative morpheme -*raq*:

(20) *Para-sha-lla-n-**raq**-mi.*
rain-PROG-LIM-3SUBJ-CONT-DIREV
'It still keeps on raining.' (*ibid.*)

A final specifier is the discontinuative *ña*:

(21) *Ña-n*   *paqari-mu-sha-n-ña.*
DISC-DIREV   dawn-CIS-PROG-3SUBJ-DISC
'The day is already dawning.' (Cusihuamán 1976, 260)

The enclitics in the specifier class are discourse referent in the very narrowest sense; in the two examples above they function to specify reference of attributes within words and clauses rather than outside of them.

2.6 *Epistemological and Evidential Deixis/Stance in Quechua*
In the case of Quechua language varieties, there has been ongoing debate regarding: (1) which linguistic elements should be considered as communicating evidentiality, epistemology and mirativity, and (2) whether the relevant morphemes should be considered to be primarily evidential, epistemic or mirative in nature. Also, Quechua scholars have alternately referred to the evidential enclitics, -*mi/-n*, -*chá*, -*si/-s* and the past tense suffixes, -*r(q)a-* and -*sqa-*, as marking either evidential or epistemic deixis or stance. According to Mushin (2001, 33):

> Evidential markers are deictic because they index information to the conceptualiser who makes an epistemological judgment. In context, the choice of evidential categories (eg. witness or report) serves to select the deictic origin—the one from which all temporal, spatial and identifying information can be calculated.

In other words, the choice of evidential markers helps identify what has been referred to here as the deictic center.

There is general consensus in the literature that Cuzco Quechua -*mi/-n* expresses that the speaker has direct evidence for the information content, or believes it is highly reliable; in contrast, it is generally accepted that the marker -*si/-s* expresses that the speaker has indirect evidence for the information content, or feels less certain of its reliability. While some have found -*r(q)a*- and -*sqa*- to carry similar evidential connotations to -*mi/-n* and -*si/-s*, respectively, Manley (this volume) is the first to claim epistemic extensions for -*r(q)a*- and -*sqa*-, indicating certainty and doubt, respectively.

Additional senses for these markers, and their role in deictic transposition or shifts in perspective within narratives, have been developed for Ecuadorian Quichua and Central Peruvian Quechua by Nuckolls (2008) and Howard (2012) respectively. They show that deictic markers like -*mi/-m* and -*rqa*- are used in narratives to denote "the assertion making function of the speaking self" (Nuckolls 2008, 83), which can either be part of the story or observing the story, onstage or offstage in the sense of Langacker (1985, 121) and Mushin (2001, 8). Nuckolls (2008, 83) notes that "this assertion-making function may also mark such pragmatically significant notions as focus and illocutionary modifications of propositional content (promising, warning, and threatening)."

On the other hand, markers like -*si/-s* and -*sqa*- are often used in narratives for information or perspectives from which the narrator would like to distance himself. This distance can be for any number of reasons, including stylistic, such as the following (Nuckolls 2008, 83):

> assuming the voice of a traditional storyteller,... to express conventional wisdom (or)... puzzled ruminations that have an otherness because they are represented as outside of the speaking self's capacity for resolution.

In summary, evidential markers with epistemic meanings are used in oral narratives to distinguish between content with which speakers wish to identify themselves or from which they distance themselves and serve an important function in identifying shifts in the deictic center established by the speaker as a story progresses.

3   The Contributions of this Work

As stated above, the primary goal of the present volume is to investigate examples of stance/deictic phenomena in Southern Quechua and Ecuadorian

Quichua. Additionally, beyond providing a background context for the chapters to come, this Introduction has sought to make a meaningful contribution to the study of stance and deixis in general, in proposing that deixis should be considered as a subtype of stance, supported by a comparison and unification of Du Bois' (2007) stance triangle and Hanks' (2005, 2011) practice approach to deictic theory. To continue, this section includes additional details regarding each of the individual chapters and concludes by describing additional ways in which this volume serves as a valuable contribution to the field beyond what has already been mentioned above.

Kalt's work in Chapter 2 examines the encoding of person, place and time deixis through an investigation of the use of the Cuzco-Collao Quechua verb derivation suffixes, *-yku, -rqu, -ku, -mu* and *-pu*. Kalt explains that these five morphemes currently or historically express directional movement denoting that the verb's action moves toward, away from, inside/downward, and outside/upward in relation to either the speaker, hearer or a verbal argument. In addition to spatial and temporal/aspectual meanings, she also finds these morphemes to carry psychological (manner) and social (mood) meanings. Kalt's work is the first to document Quechua-speaking children's use of these morphemes through a unified discourse-level approach. She finds that children five to eleven years old from the rural highland communities of Ccotatóclla and Jayubamba in Cuzco, Peru demonstrate evidence of mastery of the full semantic range of uses for the directional markers as they are used productively within short narratives, in complex combinations with other affixes on a variety of types of verbal roots.

In Chapter 3, Nuckolls, Swanson and Ramirez Spencer also investigate place and time deixis, as they propose that a three-way contrast exists among the demonstratives of the Pastaza and Tena varieties of Ecuadorian Quichua, *kay* 'here', *chi* 'there' and *chay* 'way over there'. Their claim stands in opposition to the general consensus among grammarians of Ecuadorian dialects of Quichua that there is a two-way contrast between proximal and distal demonstratives. The authors hypothesize that, similar to the findings of some scholars of Peruvian Quechua varieties (e.g. Guardia Mayorga 1973, 103; Parker 1969, 36; Weber 1989, 38), the two forms *chay* and *chi* are not exact synonyms, but rather, one of them, *chay*, communicates a greater degree of spatial distance. In order to test their hypothesis, in addition to examining the distributions of the three demonstratives in narratives and informal conversations, the authors utilized sentence judgment tasks designed to elicit choices between the forms, observed naturally occurring speech, and analyzed metalinguistic comments made by speakers. Their data shows evidence for the hypothesized three-way

INTRODUCTION

contrast among the demonstratives. Furthermore, their results reveal different discourse functions for the three demonstratives.

Courtney's work in Chapter 4 sheds light on children's acquisition (starting at age two) of the Cuzco Quechua evidential enclitics, *-mi/-n* (DIRECT EVIDENCE), *-chá* (CONJECTURE), and *-si/-s* (REPORTATIVE) as well as the past tense suffixes, *-r(q)a-* and *-sqa-*, which Courtney classifies as 'experienced' and 'non-experienced' respectively. Based on the analysis of naturalistic data from recorded conversations between mothers and their children, results from an experimental comprehension task and data obtained through story retellings, she finds that the ability to understand and evaluate information source develops over time. As regards the evidential enclitics, she argues that children first reveal an understanding of these morphemes in focusing and establishing epistemological stance. In the case of the past tense inflections, she discovers that these are used first to distinguish between dynamic events (with *-r(q)a-*) and end states (with *-sqa-*). She concludes that it is not until the age of four years that children begin spontaneous production of the enclitics in their evidential function and the past-tense inflections to distinguish experience/ perception and lack of experience. Furthermore, in the story retelling task, Courtney found that the four-year-olds had clearly learned to make use of the enclitics and past-tense inflections to shift the deictic center back and forth from the real world of the narrator and audience to the characters in the story world. Courtney's work, like Kalt's, also serves as a valuable contribution to the field of Quechua first language acquisition.

In Chapter 5, Manley employs recent conceptualizations of evidentiality, epistemics and mirativity, especially as proposed by Aikhenvald (2004) and Aikhenvald and Storch (2013), in order to propose a new, multifaceted analysis of the semantics and pragmatics of the Cuzco Quechua enclitics, *-mi/-n*, *-chá* and *-si/-s*, and past tense morphemes, *-r(q)a-* and *-sqa-*. Her results are from an investigation of how these morphemes were used by two bilingual Quechua/Spanish communities in Cuzco, Peru in spontaneous conversation and in response to two elicitation tasks, role-playing and a certainty-ranking exercise. Based on a review of the relevant literature as well as her original data and analyses, she finds: (1) *-mi/-n* is a direct evidential which may be utilized with epistemic extension to indicate certainty, (2) *-chá* is a conjecture evidential which may be utilized with epistemic extension to communicate doubt, (3) *-si/-s* is an indirect evidential which may be utilized with epistemic extension to indicate doubt, (4) *-r(q)a-* may be utilized as an evidentiality strategy to communicate a direct information source and also with epistemic extension to indicate certainty, and (5) *-sqa-* may be utilized as an evidentiality strategy to communicate an indirect information source, with epistemic extension to indicate doubt, and as a mirativity strategy, indicating surprise. As such, she offers a coherent and inclusive compromise to the debate regarding the semantics and pragmatics of these morphemes that is long overdue in the case of Cuzco Quechua.

Muntendam, Muysken and Sánchez each investigate the communication of discourse deixis. In Chapter 6, Muntendam, presenting the results of a picture-story task and an elicitation study on topic and broad and contrastive focus, finds that although topic and focus are morphologically marked in some varieties of Quechua (-*qa* TOPIC and -*mi/-n* FOCUS) (see Muysken 1995, Sánchez 2010), in the Quechua spoken in the department of Cochabamba, Bolivia, the topic marker is less frequent and the focus marker has been lost. These aspects of discourse deixis are primarily encoded instead through syntax (marked *in situ* and fronted) and to some extent in prosody. Specifically, contrastive focus is correlated with a more prominent peak on the focused element. Also, some speakers infrequently use differences in Fo, intensity and duration to convey contrastive focus. No differences were found between focus conditions for the alignment of peaks; that is, the majority of peaks were aligned within the stressed syllable, regardless of focus type. Individual differences in morphological, syntactic and prosodic strategies to mark focus are addressed. In all, this chapter contributes to the understanding of topic and focus marking in Quechua and shows differences among Quechua varieties.

In his examination of data from Puno, Lampa and Ayaviri, Peru in Chapter 7, Muysken finds that the postposition, *hina*, has undergone distributional and grammatical changes and may now be used to mark discourse deixis. Beyond being a postposition used with nouns, Muysken observes that *hina* has also developed into a clausal complementizer with nominalized clauses, a postposition with finite clauses, a highlighter with adverbial (switch reference) clauses, a highlighting complementizer with some finite clauses, a verbal element, an independent adverbial element and a prepositional conjunction. In addition to outlining these uses for *hina*, he explores the possibility that its changes in distribution are due to Aymara substrate influence and compares *hina* with the Cuzco Quechua complementizer/highlighter, *chayqa*.

Finally, in Chapter 8, Sánchez examines the distribution of morphologically unmarked right dislocated constituents (RDCs) and their interaction with antecedents in the picture-based narratives of adult speakers of Southern Quechua. She finds that unlike their left peripheral counterparts that are morphologically marked for topic, focus or evidentiality, some RDCs are not marked for these features in Southern Quechua discourse. Following Sánchez (2010) and previous proposals on deixis (Cornish 2008, 2011), she analyses her

INTRODUCTION

data as representing two basic types of unmarked RDCs: (1) RDCs with a deictic function that introduce new objects in discourse and (2) RDCs that reintroduce referents that are not part of the main topic structure of discourse. Furthermore, she argues that unmarked RDCs are the result of a strategy that allows for the construal of deictic relations outside the scope of the narrow syntax and that both types may be used to introduce an element that is not part of the current topic structure or disambiguate the reference of null subjects.

As is clear from the above descriptions of the individual chapters contained within this volume, in addition to what has been presented above, this volume is significant in that, while the majority of existing cross-linguistic studies on deixis in both Indo-European and non-Indo-European languages (i.e. Weissenborn and Klein 1982) focuses on the three most traditional types of deixis as outlined by Bühler (1934), person, place and time deixis, this work includes chapters that go beyond these to include significant work on discourse deixis (coined by Fillmore 1975), epistemological/evidential stance/ deixis (Mushin 2000) and mirative stance.

Furthermore, while the majority of existing work on deixis across languages has examined free morphemes without meaningful consideration of the surrounding discourse environment, this volume primarily addresses the way in which bound morphemes embedded in discourse function strategically to communicate stance/deictic meaning as manifested through phonology, morphology and syntax.

Moreover, while this work is not the first to investigate stance and deixis in Quechua, unlike the existing literature, cited throughout this volume, this is the first to study a broad range of stance/deictic phenomena in Quechua and Quichua in-depth with examples that have been elicited as well as captured from natural discourse.

Finally, this volume stands as an important contribution to the study of an endangered language. Quechua language varieties are spoken today in regions of Peru, Bolivia, Ecuador, Argentina, Colombia and Brazil (FUNPROEIB ANDES 2009), nations whose territory includes land that once belonged to the Inca Empire. Despite being the most widely-spoken among the indigenous languages of the Americas, with over six million speakers (FUNPROEIB ANDES 2009, 517), Quechua is endangered, as Quechua speakers increasingly shift toward Spanish. Pastaza Quichua is listed in UNESCO's *Atlas of the World's Languages in Danger* as "definitely endangered", meaning that "children no longer learn the language as mother tongue in the home" (Moseley 2010). Quechua in Bolivia and Peru is listed as "vulnerable", meaning that "most children speak the language, but it may be restricted to certain domains (e.g., home)" (*ibid.*). Such factors as prevalent negative attitudes toward Quechua and the migratory trend of Quechua speakers from rural, Quechua-dominant areas to urban, Spanish-dominant areas, threaten the future of Quechua as a living, widely-spoken language. Our hope is that this volume serves to document the nuances of Quechua expressions of stance and deixis for those who value the language today and in the future.

Appendix A

$	borrowing from Spanish	INT	intensifier
1	first person subject	INTR	interrogative
2	second person subject	IRR	irrealis
3	third person subject	LIM	limitative
ACC	accusative	LOC	locative
ADD	additive	NEG	negative
BEN	benefactive	NOM	nominalizer
CERT	certainty	OBJ	object
CIS	cislocative	PL	plural
CONT	continuative	POSS	possessive
DIM	diminutive	PROG	progressive
DIREV	direct evidential	PST1	simple past
DISC	discontinuative	REFL	reflexive
EXCL	exclusive	SUBJ	subject
FUT	future	TOP	topic
GEN	genitive	TRANS	translocative
IMP	imperative	VOC	vocative
INCL	inclusive		

Bibliography

Aikhenvald, Alexandra Y. 2004. *Evidentiality.* Oxford: Oxford University Press.

Aikhenvald, Alexandra Y. and Anne Storch, eds. 2013. *Perception and cognition in language and culture.* Leiden/Boston: Brill.

Basso, Ellen B. 2008. "Epistemic deixis in Kalapalo." *Pragmatics* 18(2): 215–252.

Bátori, Istvan. 1984. "On verb deixis in Hungarian." In *Here and There: Cross-linguistic Studies on Deixis and Demonstration,* edited by Jürgen Weissenborn and Wolfgang Klein. 155–165. Philadelphia: John Benjamins.

Bills, Garland Dee. 1972. "The Quechua Directional Verbal Suffix." *Papers in Andean Linguistics* 1 (1): 1–15.

Bühler, Karl. 1934. *Sprachtheorie*. Jena-Stuttgart: Gustav Fischer.

Calvo, Julio. 1993. *Pragmática y gramática del quechua cuzqueño*. Cuzco: Centro Bartolomé de las Casas.

Cole, Peter. 1982. *Imbabura Quechua*. Amsterdam: Lingua Descriptive Series 5.

Cornish, Francis. 2008. "How indexicals function in texts: Discourse, text, and one neo-Gricean account of indexical reference." *Journal of Pragmatics* 40: 997–1018.

———. 2011. "'Strict' anadeixis, discourse deixis and text structuring." *Language Sciences* 33: 753–767.

Cusihuamán G., Antonio. 1976. *Gramática quechua: Cuzco-Collao*. Lima: Ministerio de Educación.

Du Bois, John W. 2007. "The stance triangle." In *Stancetaking in Discourse: Subjectivity, evaluation, interaction*, edited by Robert Englebretson. 139–182. Amsterdam/Philadelphia: John Benjamins Publishing Company.

Fillmore, Charles J. 1975. *Santa Cruz lectures on deixis* (delivered 1971). Bloomington: Indiana University Linguistics Club.

Fundación para la Educación en Contextos de Multilingüismo y Pluriculturalidad (FUNPROEIB ANDES). 2009. *Atlas sociolingüístico de pueblos indígenas en América Latina*. Cochabamba, Bolivia: FUNPROEIB ANDES.

Godenzzi, Juan Carlos and Vengoa Zúñiga, Janett. 1994. *Runasimimanta yuyaychakusun: manual de lingüística quechua para bilingües*. Cuzco: Asociación Pukllasuchis and Centro de Estudios Regionales Andinos Bartolomé de las Casas.

Guardia Mayorga, Cesar A. 1973. *Gramática Kechwa*. Lima: Ediciones Los Andes.

Hanks, William F. 2005. "Explorations in the deictic field." *Current Anthropology* 46(2): 191–220.

———. 2011. "Deixis and indexicality." In *Foundations of Pragmatics*, edited by Wolfram Bublitz and Neal R. Norrick. 315–346.

Hermon, Gabriella. 1985. *Syntactic modularity*. Dordrecht: Foris.

Howard, Rosaleen. 2012. "Shifting voices, shifting worlds: evidentiality, epistemic modality and speaker perspective in Quechua oral narrative." *Pragmatics and Society* 3 (2): 246–269.

———. 2013. *Kawsay Vida. A Multimedia Quechua Course for Beginners and Beyond*. Austin: University of Texas Press.

Langacker, Ronald W. 1985. "Observations and speculations on subjectivity." In *Iconicity in Syntax: Proceedings of a symposium on iconicity in syntax*, Stanford, June 24–26, 1983, edited by John Haiman. 109–150. Palo Alto, Stanford University.

Levinson, Stephen. 1983. *Pragmatics*. Cambridge: Cambridge University Press.

Levinson, Stephen C. 2004. "Deixis." In *The Handbook of Pragmatics*, edited by Laurence Horn. 97–121. Oxford: Blackwell.

Moseley, Christopher, ed. 2010. *Atlas of the World's Languages in Danger*, 3rd edition. Paris: UNESCO Publishing. http://www.unesco.org/culture/en/endangeredlanguages/atlas

Mushin, Ilana. 2000. "Evidentiality and deixis in narrative retelling." *Journal of Pragmatics* 32: 927–957.

———. 2001. *Evidentiality and Epistemological Stance: Narrative Retelling*. Philadelphia: John Benjamins.

Muysken, Pieter. 1995. "Focus in Quechua." In *Discourse Configurational Languages*, edited by Katalin É. Kiss. 375–393. New York: Oxford University Press.

Nuckolls, Janis. 2008. "Deictic Selves and Others in Pastaza Quichua Evidential Usage." *Anthropological Linguistics* 50 (1): 67–89.

Parker, Gary J. 1969. *Ayacucho Quechua grammar and dictionary*. The Hague: Mouton.

Plaza Martínez, Pedro. 1987. "Objetos Pronominales del Quechua" *Allpanchis* 29 (30): 179–226. Sicuani, Cuzco.

———. 2005. *Qallarinapaq: curso básico de quechua boliviano*. Unpublished manuscript, Cochabamba: ProEIBAndes, Universidad Mayor San Simón.

Sánchez, Liliana. 2010. *The morphology and syntax of topic and focus: Minimalist inquiries in the Quechua periphery*. Linguistik Aktuell Series. Amsterdam: John Benjamins.

Torero, Alfredo. 1964. "Los dialectos quechuas." *Anales Científicos de la Universidad Agraria* 2: 446–478.

Weber, David. 1989. *A grammar of Huallaga (Huanuco) Quechua*. Berkeley: University of California Press.

Weissenborn, Jürgen and Wolfgang Klein (eds.). 1982. *Here and there: Cross-linguistic studies on deixis and demonstration*. Philadelphia: John Benjamins.

Williams, Nicholas. 2009. "Toward a linguistic anthropological account of deixis in interaction: *ini* and *itu* in Indonesian conversation." *Colorado Research in Linguistics* 22: 1–23.

CHAPTER 2

Pointing in Space and Time: Deixis and Directional Movement in Schoolchildren's Quechua

Susan E. Kalt

1 Introduction

In this chapter I will consider the grammar of Quechua verbal derivation at the interfaces of pragmatics, semantics and syntax in the developing mind. In particular, I will study rural highlands Quechua-speaking children's oral mastery of five verbal suffixes, *-yku, -rqu, -ku, -pu* and *-mu*, all but one of which currently have directional movement among their meanings attested in the literature on adult usage by Adelaar (1997), Bills (1972, 1975), Calvo (1993), Cerrón-Palomino (1987), Cusihuamán (1976), van de Kerke and Muysken (1990), van de Kerke (1996) and Torero (2005).

More specifically, I will examine the interaction of directional suffixes with the syntax and semantics of verbal roots, with other directional affixes, and with extra-linguistic elements. I will demonstrate that children as young as five years old have mastered a highly-nuanced system for expressing a range of objective and subjective meanings, and show that the distribution and significance of directional suffixes in their stories resembles those of adults. These findings have implications for linguistic researchers as well as educators in the Andes, because they document systems of mental representation children have already mastered by the time they reach school, intellectual capital that is too often ignored or mischaracterized.

Data from the experiment reported here come from the elicited narratives of ten children ages 5–11 and two adults ages 17 and 36 in Ccotatóclla and Jayubamba, communities in rural Cuzco, Perú. These narratives were elicited as part of a larger study of Quechua-speaking children's oral comprehension and production of sentences containing third person and reflexive arguments conducted in Quechua and Spanish among more than 200 children, beginning in 2000.

The organization of this chapter is as follows: section 2 contains an overview of the pragmatics and semantics of utterances containing historically directional morphemes in the adult grammar, with a discussion of controversies and unanswered questions about them in the literature, particularly relating

© KONINKLIJKE BRILL NV, LEIDEN, 2015 | DOI 10.1163/9789004290105_003

them to recent findings about evidential morphemes and other deictic elements (Hintz 2007, Howard 2012, Nuckolls 2008, Mushin 2001). Where needed, newly elicited adult data is introduced, illustrating in particular the interpretation of these elements in clusters of derivational suffixes as well as appearing singly. Section 3 considers the aesthetics of Andean narrative discourse and the contribution of directional morphemes thereto. Section 4 presents an original experiment investigating the distribution and meaning of these morphemes in child narratives, with conclusions and implications for further research in section 5.

2 Directional Movement in Cuzco-Collao Quechua

2.1 *Overview of the Directional Movement Suffixes*

Verbal suffixes encoding directional movement, especially the suffix *-mu,* appear in texts dating back to 1584 (Durston, 298) and are mentioned in many works on Southern Quechua, including Adelaar (1997), Bills (1972, 1975), Calvo (1993), Cerrón-Palomino (1987, 2003), Cusihuamán (1976), Hintz (2011), van de Kerke and Muysken (1990), van de Kerke (1996) and Torero (2005), to name only those consulted most frequently for this study. Despite careful diachronic reconstruction and comparative synchronic work on some of these suffixes, a precise understanding of their multiple functions and meanings is extremely complex. As a class, derivational suffixes are considered to belong to the least understood part of Quechua morphosyntax (Hintz 2011, 8). Although Hintz' (2011) study is based on a Quechua I, Central Peruvian language variety which is mutually unintelligible with Cuzco-Collao Quechua, his insights on how derivational suffixes work within Quechuan languages can be applied productively here. Hintz (2011, 4) notes that the semantic features of Quechua derivational suffixes overlap with each other and with those of other suffixes. Similarly, there is no clear single meaning associated with a particular suffix.

Suffixes with current or historic directional meaning in Southern Quechua interact with the semantics of verb roots, other derivational, inflectional and evidential markers and with periphrastic elements to influence the interpretation of the verb's tense, mood, aspect and manner. No single one of these elements fully determines the expression of deictic and subjective meanings within a discourse, but rather, they act in concert with non-directional elements to do so. Although some of their meanings overlap, and they may appear in clusters with each other, affecting each other's phonological form, their meanings remain largely analytic. There are 31 logically possible combinations of the five morphemes under consideration, whose order is fixed thus: *-yku, -rqu, -ku, -mu, -pu*. In principle, there is no semantic or pragmatic restriction on the co-occurrence of these morphemes in clusters within the same word.

The five morphemes *-yku, -rqu, -ku, -pu* and *-mu* (along with their allomorphs) are given the label 'directional' because among their meanings are the notions that the verb's action moves inside/downward, outside/upward, away from or toward some entity.[1] The historically spatial meanings of *-yku* and *-rqu* (Cerrón-Palomino 1987, 283) have undergone semantic extension and are frequently used to express degrees of attention, intention, intensity, affection, emotion or energy with which actions are carried out (Cusihuamán 1976, 206–8). When interpreted in composition with first and second person inflectional elements, these latter meanings acquire what Levinson (2004) calls social deictic functions, such as heightening the urgency of a situation or softening commands, as well as describing the manner in which actions should be performed.

In the following sections I will examine the literature on each of these five morphemes, and add new insights from fieldwork and consultation with adult native speakers. A legend of abbreviations is found in Appendix A.

2.2 *Deixis, Directionality and the Morpheme* -yku

According to Peruvian Quechua native speaker linguist Cusihuamán (1976, 206–7) the intensifying suffix *-yku*, which he calls augmentative, has four allomorphs: *-yu, -yka, -ya* and *-y: -yku* and *-yu* stand in free variation but undergo a vowel change to *-yka* and *-ya* before inchoative *-ri*, assistive *-ysi*, causative *-chi* and before the morphemes *-mu* and *-pu;* the final allomorph *-y* is found before the dynamic *-ru* (see section 2.3) but not before *-ru*'s allomorphs *-rqu* and *-rqa*. Cusihuamán (ibid) states that the suffix *-yku* adds the following connotations: a) the intense manner in which an action is realized, b) the personal affection with which the realization of an action is offered or solicited, and c) the direction of an action toward something or someone, toward the interior or downward.

According to van de Kerke's (1996, 20) survey of the literature and his own fieldwork in Bolivia, *-yku*'s directional meaning of 'inward, toward, onto' is not restricted to verbs indicating directional motion. Moreover, *-yku* also has interpretations including 'completion' and 'decisiveness'.

---

1 *-Ku* is not typically considered a directional morpheme, but because of its semantic and phonological interaction with adjacent suffixes and its contribution to deictic and directional meanings, I consider it here.

An example of an intensifying affective interpretation of *-yku* is found in the following series of sentences elicited from and translated into Spanish by Janett Vengoa de Orós (JVO), a native speaker originally from Sicuani, Cuzco, Peru. All examples in this chapter are from JVO unless otherwise marked.[2]

(1) *Wallata-qa   apa-Ø-n*[3]
    goose-TOP   carry-3OBJ-3
    'The goose carries it.'

(2) *Wallata-qa   apa-yu-Ø-n*
    goose-TOP   carry-INT-3OBJ-3
    'The goose takes or brings it with emotion or conviction.'

Adults easily interpret and produce *-yku* in clusters of two, three, four and five derivational suffixes. Here *-yku* appears in a cluster of two:

(3) *Sinchi-ta-n   para-ya-mu-sha-n.*
    hard-ADVL-DIREV   rain-INT-CIS-PROG-3
    'It's raining really hard.' (Cusihuamán 1976, 206, my gloss)

Cluster of three:

(4) *Puñu-ya-ka-pu-sqa*
    sleep-INT-BEN-MAL-3PST2
    '(The duck) enjoyed sleeping deeply and I am/was not pleased by it.'

---

2 All examples in this chapter are presented in official 1985 Peruvian orthography with the modification that the progressive morpheme is spelled *-chka* regardless of its pronunciation, which is [-ʃa] in Cuzco and [-χa] or [-ʃa] in rural Chuquisaca. The spelling of this frequently used morpheme is part of a normalization effort promoted in Plaza (2005) and elsewhere among colleagues in the Andean education sector. Further discussion and detail is found in Howard (2013, 3–5).

3 Torero (2005, 71–4) argues that the silence of the third person object marker in Quechua can obscure important semantic details derivable from argument structure. Therefore, I add the symbol 'Ø' to represent third person object inflection to transitive verbs in the position where the first person marker is normally found, for all examples and analyses in this study.

POINTING IN SPACE AND TIME

Cluster of four:

(5) *Wallata-qa   apa-ya-ka-m-pu-∅-n*
    goose-TOP   carry-INT-REFL-CIS-REG-3OBJ-3
    'The goose brought it back here and fervently considered it her own.'[4]

Here *-yku* appears in sentences exhibiting clusters of five such morphemes:

(6) *Wallata-qa   apa-ya-ra-ka-m-pu-∅-n*
    goose-TOP   carry-INT-DYN-REFL-CIS-REG-3OBJ-3
    'The goose quickly/forcefully brought it back here and fervently considered it her own.'

(7) *Atuq-qa   mikhu-ya-ra-ka-m-pu-∅-n*
    fox-TOP   eat-INT-DYN-REFL-TRANS-MAL-3OBJ-3
    'The fox eats it intensely/thoughtlessly and fast and elsewhere with pleasure/for himself and the speaker disapproves.'

In sentences (6) and (7) above, the distinction in the type of verb, *apay* (allowing for directional motion) vs. *mikhuy* (a non-motion verb), forces different interpretations for the morpheme *-m(u)*, corresponding to 'here' in (6) and 'elsewhere' in (7), but the interpretation of *-yku's* allomorph *-ya* (intensity, fervor) is not affected by this distinction. It is also important to mention that the subtleties of interpretation of directional suffixes often do not get elaborated in initial translations from Quechua to Spanish by native speakers; this is relevant in that much of my own fieldwork and that of other linguists relies on the intuitions of Quechua-Spanish bilinguals such as JVO.

2.3   *Deixis, Directionality and the Morpheme -rqu*

The dynamic morpheme *-rqu* used to mean 'movement toward the outside' according to Cerrón-Palomino (1987, 283) and still does in some varieties of Quechua I, but this meaning is no longer among the interpretations mentioned by Cusihuamán (1976, 207–8) who lists the following for what he calls the hortative suffix: a) urgency or priority with which an action must be carried out, b) consummation of the action, c) sudden or unexpected realization

---

4   For all examples in this chapter, the fox's gender is assumed to be male and the duck and
    geese are female. This is purely for convenience of distinguishing among pronouns in
    English, since Quechua has no grammatical gender.

of the action, d) expression of courtesy or respect for the interlocutor. *-Rqu* has an allomorph *-ru*; these two become *-rqa* and *-ra* respectively when they occur before *-ri, -ysi, chi, -mu/-m,* and *-pu.*

Pedro Plaza (pers. comm.), a native speaker of the Norte de Potosí variety of Southern Quechua, offers the following observations about the semantic extension of the archaic outside/upward meanings of *-rqu* as it interacts with the semantics of verb roots (glosses mine):

(8) *apa-**rqu**-∅-y*
     carry-DYN-3OBJ-INF
     'take it out/finish taking it' (with some urgency and with the intention of pleasing someone, which could also be translated as 'honorably')

(9) *chuqa-**rqu**-∅-y*
     hurl-DYN-3OBJ-INF
     'throw out/away' (can imply with certain care or action which is subject to evaluation)

(10) *maqa-**rqu**-∅-y*
     fight-DYN-3OBJ-INF
     'beat someone once and for all, for a short time'

(11) *qhawa-**rqu**-∅-y*
     look-DYN-3OBJ-INF
     'look what's going on outside/glance' (implies rapid evaluation)

(12) *mikhu-**rqu**-∅-y*
     eat-DYN-3OBJ-INF
     'eat with pleasure or grace/spread out a feast' (implies honorably)

I offer the following examples of sentential uses of *-rqu* in order of levels of clustering with other derivational morphemes, provided by Vengoa:

Singleton use:

(13) *Wallata-qa   apa-**ru**-∅-n*
     goose-TOP   carry-DYN -3OBJ-3
     'The goose takes or brings it with force or speed.'

POINTING IN SPACE AND TIME

Cluster of two:

(14) *Puñu-**ra**-**pu**-lla-n-taq*
sleep-DYN-MAL-LIM-3-EMPH
'She has fallen asleep again! (and I don't like it).'

Cluster of three:

(15) *Atuq-qa*   *mikhu-**ra**-**m**-**pu**-∅-n*
fox-TOP   eat-DYN-TRANS-MAL-3OBJ-3
'The fox eats it fast and elsewhere and for his own egotistical benefit /
speaker disapproves.'

Although I do not have an example of *-rqu* in a cluster of four, *-rqu* participates
in a cluster of five in examples (6) and (7) above. I assume that the contribution of *-rqu* to the interpretation of those utterances is that of an adverb of
manner, with the values of speed and forcefulness.

2.4   *Deixis, Directionality and the Morpheme* -ku

The morpheme *-ku*, which is the reflexive marker and indicator of middle
voice (van de Kerke 1996, 30–31), has also acquired the modal meanings of
heightened intensity, affection, and emotion in Cuzco-Collao Quechua. In (16)
-ku can have both benefactive and modal meanings. For example:

(16) *Atuq-qa*   *mikhu-**ku**-∅-n*
fox-TOP   eat-BEN-3OBJ-3
'The fox eats it with pleasure/for himself.'

(17) *Waswa-qa*   *puñu-**ku**-chka-n*
duck-TOP   sleep-BEN-PROG-3
'The duck is sleeping and I am pleased by it/she is pleased by it.'

Example (18) below, which contains the morpheme traditionally recognized as
benefactive in Quechua, *-pu*, can be compared with *-ku* in examples (16) and
(17) above.

(18) *Wallata-qa*   *apa-**pu**-∅-n*
goose-TOP   carry-BEN-3OBJ-3
'The goose took it and considered it her own/ took it for herself.'

Thus, it is clear that *-ku* has come to overlap with the benefactive and modal meanings of the suffix *-pu*, which will be considered next.

2.5 *Deixis, Directionality and the Morpheme* -pu

The morpheme *-pu* indicates that the verb's action is carried out "to or for another; another place, time or person" (Torero 2005, 71). Torero's view loosely captures the meanings attributed to *-pu* elsewhere in the literature, corresponding to the benefactive/malefactive, stative and regressive meanings (van de Kerke 1996, 32–3). The meaning 'toward another place' that Torero refers to is further specified by Cusihuamán as "toward the point of origin of the sentential subject or object" (1976, 215). The temporal meaning that Torero alludes to is further specified by van de Kerke (1996, 33): "The result of an action, or a certain state of affairs is considered to prevail for a least a relatively long period, or even to be irreversible." It is difficult to distinguish whether the speaker intends a regressive or stative meaning when affixing *-pu* to a verb, and in this corpus I have often glossed them as ambiguous. Regressive and stative meanings are found with both transitive and intransitive motion verbs, as in the following two examples from my query of Vengoa:

(19) *Wallata-qa   apa-pu-⊘-n*
     goose-TOP   carry-REG/STAT-3OBJ-3
     'The goose took it/returned it.'

(20) *Puri-pu-n*
     walk-BEN/REG/STAT-3
     'He walked for someone else's benefit/walked back to where he came from/ left for good.'

When *-pu* attaches to a non-motion verb, its interpretation tends to be benefactive or malefactive, regardless of whether the verb is transitive, as in (21), or intransitive, as in (22) below:

(21) *Atuq-qa   mikhu-pu-⊘-n*
     fox-TOP   eat-MAL-3OBJ-3
     'The fox eats it for his own egotistical benefit/speaker disapproves.'

(22) *Waswa-qa   puñu-pu-chka-n*
     duck-TOP   sleep-MAL-PROG-3
     'The duck is sleeping and I am not pleased by it.'

POINTING IN SPACE AND TIME

Benefactive *-pu* attains the illocutionary force of a request when used with a first person object marker, as in the following example:

(23) *Alli-chu*   *unu-man*   *ri-rqa-**pu**-wa-y*
    good- INTR   water-DAT   go-DYN-BEN-1OBJ-IMP
    'Please go get water for me' (Cusihuamán 1976, 215)

There is controversy in the literature as to whether *-pu* should be considered a translocative suffix in complementary distribution with *-mu*, meaning 'away from the speaker'. Calvo claims that while *-mu* implies involvement of the speaker's perspective, *-pu* is "focused on the location of the (argument), the separation of the ego or its lack of accompaniment" (Calvo 1993, 66, translation mine). Torero (2005, 72–74) argues that Calvo's presentation of the data misses important detail, so I will be careful to clarify here the restricted contexts in which Calvo's claim is true. Bills (1976, 71–4), by his own admission "somewhat hesitantly", presents data in favor of a translocative meaning for *-pu.* He notes that a verb marked *-pu* may co-occur with the distal but not proximal demonstrative, as in (24) and (25) below:

(24) *Haqay-man*   *kuti-**pu**-nku*
    yonder-DAT   return-REG/STAT-3PL
    'They returned to over there.'

(25) **Kay-man*   *kuti-**pu**-nku*
    here-DAT   return-REG/STAT-3PL
    'They went back to here.' (Bills 1976, 73, glosses mine)

The incompatibility of the proximal demonstrative *kay* with *kuti-pu* leads Bills to assert that "The translocative *-pu*, then, seems to function exactly like the translocative *-mu,* except it occurs with [+ Motion] verbs" (*ibid.*). This example may be problematic because the meaning of the verb overlaps completely with the meaning of regressive *-pu*; however, Vengoa (pers. comm.) confirms that the same restriction occurs with another intransitive verb of motion, *puriy* 'to walk/travel'. In other words, at least two verbs of motion marked with *-pu* are incompatible with the proximal demonstrative, suggesting that *-pu* contributes an interpretation of 'elsewhere' from the deictic center.

The following type of opposition with transitive motion verbs also seems to indicate a cislocative/translocative opposition for verbs marked with *-pu*:

(26) *Apa-**mu**-∅-y!*
carry-CIS-3OBJ-IMP
'Bring it here!'

(27) *Apa-**pu**-∅-y!*
carry-REG/STAT-3OBJ-IMP
'Take it back/return it for me!'

Nevertheless, close examination of example (27) reveals that speaker-related reference could be established here not via the suffix *-pu* but rather by the imperative marker *-y*. Here, *-pu* could plausibly indicate nothing more than movement of the object back to its point of origin, which corresponds to the regressive interpretation established by Cusihuamán (1976, 215). I conclude that *-pu*, when combined with verbs of motion, should be considered a distancing element in the inventory of Quechua deictic devices, but only in the absence of first or second person object marking, and in the absence of imperative mood.

2.6 *Deixis, Directionality and the Morpheme* -mu

The directional morpheme most commonly associated with the deictic center in Quechua is the verbal modifier *-mu*. Van de Kerke (1996, 165–6), building on an extensive literature, including Adelaar (1997), Bills (1972, 1975), Cusihuamán (1976) and especially van de Kerke and Muysken (1990), summarizes the essential character of *-mu* in the following way:

> The suffix expresses the concept that two different locations are relevant in the speech act, one of which coincides with speaker.... The semantic content of *-mu* is sensitive to the distinction motion/non-motion verbs, since one of the Locations linked in the conceptual structure...coincides with the Direction argument of a motion verb. It is this location which results in the cis-locative interpretation. With non-motion verbs *-mu* introduces a second Location different from the one where 'ego' is located.

Below in examples (28)–(31) are two pairs of sentences with and without *-mu*, elicited to demonstrate the cislocative and translocative interpretations when *-mu* is affixed to the motion verb *apay* 'to carry' and the non-motion verb *mikhuy* 'to eat', respectively:

(28) *Wallata-qa   apa-∅-n*
goose-TOP   carry-3OBJ-3
'The goose carries it.'

POINTING IN SPACE AND TIME

35

(29) *Wallata-qa   apa-**mu**-∅-n*
     goose-TOP   carry-CIS-3OBJ-3
     'The goose brings it to me/here.'

(30) *Atuq-qa   mikhu-∅-n*
     fox-TOP   eat-3OBJ-3
     'The fox eats it.'

(31) *Atuq-qa   mikhu-**mu**-∅-n*
     fox-TOP   eat-TRANS-3OBJ-3
     'The fox eats it elsewhere.'

The spatial meanings of *-mu* have been noted above. The implication of spatial displacement is strong, such that if the action of a non-motion verb derived by *-mu* is reported to have occurred in a particular location, the speech act must be happening in a different location, as in (32):

(32) *Wasimasi-y-pa*   *wasi-n-pi*   *wayk'u-**mu**-rqa-ni*
     neighbor-1POSS-GEN   house-3POSS-LOC   cook-TRANS-PST1–1
     'I cooked at my neighbor's house.' (and I am not there now)

In certain cases, *-mu* can have a temporal interpretation as well. When the location of the speech act and that of a non-motion event are known to coincide, then the implied spatial displacement must happen at a different time from the speech act, either in the past, future or in the habitual present, as the multiple meanings of example (33) demonstrate:

(33) *Wasimasi-y-pa*   *wasi-n-pi*   *wayk'u-**mu**-ni.*
     neighbor-1POSS-GEN   house-3POSS-LOC   cook-TRANS-1
     'I came to cook at my neighbor's house.' (where speech act is now occurring)
     'I will come cook at my neighbor's house.' (where speech act is now occurring)
     'I habitually come cook at my neighbor's house.' (where speech act is now occurring)

I have illustrated with new data that translocative *-mu* can force a 'not now' interpretation on a sentence otherwise unmarked for tense. This only happens when the place of the speech act and the verbal event are known to be the same.

As noted in Cusihuamán (1976, 213–14) and developed in van de Kerke and Muysken (1990), the [± motion] distinction is not the only one relevant to the interpretation of verbs derived with *-mu*. Atmospheric verbs and verbs indicating emergence from inside either a human body, object, the earth or a body of water all receive cislocative interpretations, which van de Kerke and Muysken attribute to the notion that "something that is happening in another place... comes into the perception field of the speaker" (1990, 160). For example:

(34) *Para-mu-chka-n*
rain-CIS-PROG-3
'It's raining.' (speaker/hearer is affected) (Bills et al. 1969, 206)

(35) *Yarqa-mu-wa-n*
hunger-CIS-1OBJ-3
'I was getting hungry.' (van de Kerke and Muysken 1990, 154)

(36) *Pampa-manta-n   k'allampa-qa   phata-mu-n*
earth-ABL-DIREV   mushroom-TOP   sprout-CIS-3
'The mushrooms sprout from the earth.'

A final type of verb which triggers the cislocative interpretation with *-mu* also entails emergence into the perceptual field of the speaker. These verbs are described by Adelaar (1997, 141) as those which "imply some sort of a psychological approach to the speaker... (so that) the subject... becomes more visible or otherwise perceptible than it was before the event took place"; such verbs include *pacarimuy* 'to come into existence', *causarimuy* 'to revive', *yurimuy* 'to be born', *rimarimuy* 'to speak up', among others.

I have shown that spatial meanings of *-mu* extend to temporal and psychological meanings, contingent upon situational context and the semantics of the verb to which it attaches. The following table is a composite of insights about the meanings and contingencies associated with *-mu*, taken mainly from Cusihuamán (1976, 213–14) but also Adelaar (1997, 141) and van de Kerke and Muysken (1990); the latter attributed as K&M in the table.

Some intransitive verbs of motion, such as *riy* 'to go', do not allow a cislocative interpretation with *-mu* according to Cusihuamán (1976, 213) or allow both cislocative and translocative interpretations, as with *puriy* 'to walk, to move':[5]

---

5 Recall from example (20) above that the verb *puriy* also elicits multi-valued interpretations when suffixed with *-pu*.

POINTING IN SPACE AND TIME

TABLE 2.1   *Meanings and contingencies of* -mu

Verb types with *-mu*	Meaning
Verbs of motion, transfer, communication, shifting and projection, except *riy* 'to go'	Action originates elsewhere and moves toward the speaker or the verbal object
Non-motion verbs	Action takes place elsewhere from speech act
Atmospheric verbs	Condition originates elsewhere and moves toward the speaker, affecting him (K&M 1990, 153)
Verbs expressing actions which originate inside the body, an object, the earth or water, or imply a transition from less perceptible to more perceptible state	Action originates inside or outside the speaker's perceptual field and enters it, making the speaker aware (Adelaar 1997, K&M 1990, 158–160)

(37) *Puri-mu-n*
walk-CIS/TRANS-3
'She will walk towards us here, she will walk around elsewhere, she will go elsewhere to walk.'

The suffix *-mu* also functions in contexts of perspectival shift and deictic transposition. Transposition allows the speaker to change the domain of reference of the deictic center *I, here now* to some other set of coordinates relevant to a narrative or discourse. Example (38) from van de Kerke and Muysken (1990, 160) shows contemporary, adult usage of *-mu* in a context of deictic transposition. They note that the deictic center in the utterance is not indexed to the speaker's actual location at time of speech, but rather to one within the story.

(38) *Sukri-pi   ka-chka-qti-y   chaya-mu-rqa*
Sucre-LOC   be-PROG-SEQ-1POSS   arrive-CIS-3PST1
'When I was in Sucre he arrived there.'

Adelaar (1997, 143–6) contains a detailed account of deictic directional movement and multiple shifts in perspective signaled by *-mu* within the Huarochirí manuscript, an early colonial document dating back to 1608. He claims that uses of *-mu* remain essentially unchanged from contemporary usage. An example of simple cislocative use is found as follows (glosses mine):

(39) *Cocha   pata-pi   chaya-spa-ca...   Pachacamac-ñic-man*
     ocean   top-LOC   arrive-GER-TOP   Pachacamac-APPR-DAT

*cuti-**mu**-rca-n*
return-CIS-PST1-3
'Having reached the seashore, he turned back toward Pachacamac
(*writer's direction*).' (Adelaar 1997, 144)

An example of deictic transposition in the Huarochirí manuscript, or adoption
of a vantage point within the story, is found after the orientation point changes
to the spot where the character Huatyacuri is resting, and two foxes approach
from either side (Adelaar 1997, 145, glosses mine):

(40) *Huc   hatoc-ca   ura-manta   **amu**-sca   hoc-ri*
     one   fox-TOP   below-ABL   come.CIS-PST2   another-ADD

*hanac-manta   **amu**-sca-tac...*
above-ABL   come.CIS-PST2- CONTR
'A fox came from below and another one came from above...'

In summary, I have presented examples from the literature demonstrating that:
(1) the directional marker *-mu* fulfills deictic functions related to person, place
and time in adult Cuzco-Collao Quechua, serving to anchor the utterance's referential indices to the immediate or transposed center *I* (*and you*), *here*, *now*;
(2) *-mu* has cislocative readings with transitive motion verbs and verbs indicating emergence from a physical or metaphysical body into the perceptual field,
including atmospheric phenomena and phenomena such as birth; and (3) *-mu*
has translocative readings when attached to some intransitive verbs and transitive verbs lacking a meaning of directional motion.

2.7   *Summary of Deixis and Directionality among these Five Suffixes*
In table 2.2, I present a summary of the meanings attributed to *-yku*, *-rqu*, *-ku*,
-pu and *-mu* in the literature (Cusihuamán 1976, 206–7; Hintz 2011, 128, 130, 150;[6]
van de Kerke 1996, 31–33) as well as those based on the new data presented above.

---

6   Although Hintz' book focuses on a Quechua I dialect, I have only included information
    which he identified specifically as pertaining to Cuzco Quechua.

POINTING IN SPACE AND TIME 39

TABLE 2.2 *Deictic and directional meanings of* -yku, -rqu, -ku, -pu and -mu

	Spatial meanings	Temporal/Aspectual meanings	Psychological/Social meanings (Manner and Mood[7])
-yku	into downward onto toward ingesting or taking in	completely decisively	thoughtfully thoughtlessly affectionately politely special attention or care, intensity intentional with imperative: affectionate or polite request
-rqu	(archaic) out of upward	completely fast abruptly unexpectedly	forcefully with conviction with urgency honorably politely with imperative: urgent request request that action be carried out with care
-ku	toward the subject		self-serving affectionate polite special attention or care intensity done of own free will with imperative: affectionate or polite request

---

7 Examples and further discussion of social deictic uses of directional suffixes are found in chapter 1.

TABLE 2.2   *Deictic and directional meanings of* -yku, -rqu, -ku, -pu and -mu (*cont.*)

	Spatial meanings	Temporal/Aspectual meanings	Psychological/Social meanings (Manner and Mood)
-pu	away toward the point of origin	toward or attaining a permanent or enduring state	distant from speaker perspective doing something for another egotistical for another's benefit to the detriment of another self-serving
			with 1 OBJ–*wa* plus imperative: polite request 'for me'
-mu	toward the speaker/ hearer/object from elsewhere occurring elsewhere	emerging gradually or continuously into the perceptual field	speaker is affected personal involvement

Selection from among these shades of meaning, some of which are mutually exclusive, depends highly on the verb root as well as on other elements in the utterance, especially subject and object person inflection. In particular, the interpretation of *-mu* and *-pu* is determined primarily by whether the verb encodes movement or not, which is not always transparent. The transitivity distinction also affects interpretation in some cases.

All of the suffixes include a meaning which grammaticalizes affect or expresses the degree of speaker/hearer involvement (see table 2.2 above, under Manner and Mood). It is interesting to note that the grammaticalization of affect is found elsewhere in the literature on Quechua discourse. Hintz (2007) finds that speakers of South Conchucos Quechua use tense markers in narrative contexts to express distance and proximity not only in terms of time and position within the narrative structure, but also in terms of positive and negative affect.

Finally, many of the meanings associated with directional suffixes in table 2.2 above fulfill what Hanks (1992, 48) calls the communicative, characterizing, relational and indexical functions of deictic elements. In other words, they signal speech act value (as in 'polite request'), describe referents (as in 'abruptly'), signal the relation referent-to-origo (as in 'emerging gradually into the speaker's perceptual field') and/or ground reference to the origo in a speech event (as in 'distant from speaker perspective').

I now turn to a discussion of the broader characteristics of Andean narrative discourse contexts in which these elements are used.

3   Subjectivity and Aesthetics in Andean Rhetorical Traditions

Speakers of Cuzco-Collao Quechua are heirs not only to a rich linguistic system for expressing subjective meanings, but also to a remarkably resilient narrative tradition that has persisted in the face of a colonial experience bent on its subordination or eradication. There is evidence that even in the delivery of historical accounts and social reckoning, Quechua-speaking communities traditionally value multiple rather than singular voices. This comes from anthropologist Frank Salomon in his study of modern day practices of the descendants of expert community storytellers in Tupicocha, a tiny community in the Huarochirí province of the department of Lima, Peru. The community has preserved many ancient traditions related to the Andean pre-alphabetic system for record-keeping and storytelling that are claimed to have directly influenced the Huarochirí manuscript mentioned in Adelaar's (1997) analysis of narrative uses of -*mu* in section 2 above. Salomon notes that the *khipus*, or knotted cords used in the system, are never handled in solitude (2004, 145–6). Because the locals no longer speak Quechua, *khipus* are known as 'quipocamayos' in Tupicocha (*ibid.*):

> Quipocamayo work is always done four-handed: one person holds the ends of the main cord while another arranges the pendant cords. If this continues an ancient practice, the practice seems a testimony to the profoundly social, rather than individually authorial, work of the quipocamayo master.

Multiple storytellers and shifts in perspective appear confusing or even undesirable to some Western audiences familiar with a different aesthetic. Scholars familiar with the 'Mexican annals', a Nahuatl rendition of history, considered them "disorderly", "confusing," "repetitive" and "choppy" until they were discovered to be intentional retellings of the same event, multiple times but from different perspectives (Townsend 2011, 6).

Adelaar (1997, 143) states that in the Huarochirí document mentioned above,

> ... the author is still very conscious about his 'place of writing' and seems confused as to which place should be chosen as an orientation point in individual instances. The use of *-mu* in relation to shifting orientation points is in fact quite inconsistent and unpredictable. This is symptomatic of an incipient literary tradition in which the role of the narrator cannot yet be duly disposed of.

I would like to suggest instead that shifts in orientation points may be intentional and even aesthetically pleasing to a native speaker audience for whom subjectivity and multiple perspectives add veracity, depth and a sense of contextually grounded participation. This is supported by the work of Nuckolls (2008) and Howard (2012), who offer accounts of the philosophical and aesthetic underpinnings of shifts in speaker perspective in Andean oral narratives. Both authors also mention the use of frequent dialogue and asides to the audience. It seems no accident that when written Quechua literature experienced its "golden age" between the late 17th and late 18th centuries, the primary literary genre was theatrical (Adelaar 1997, footnote 2, Mannheim 1991, 71–74), as theater allows for maximal subjective experience of a story and shifts in perspective.

In summary, dramatic dialogue and multiple shifts in perspective seem to be persistent aesthetic preferences in adult Andean narrative traditions. It remains to be seen whether children perceive this aesthetic and reproduce it in their own narratives, and to what extent directional morphemes play a role in their encoding the expression of subjective content.

4   Child Acquisition of Directional Morphemes

4.1   *Rationale*

Increasing attention has been paid to the pragmatics interface with syntax and semantics in the acquisition of grammar (see Rothman and Guijarro-Fuentes 2012 for a review of recent literature). The current study of schoolchildren's use of directional morphemes breaks new ground investigating the acquisition of deictic elements in Quechua, complementing work on the acquisition of evidential morphemes by Courtney (this volume). Courtney's work suggests that Quechua-speaking children have acquired perspectival meanings of the evidential and tense/aspect markers *-mi, -ra, -si* and *-sqa* by the time they are four years old, although they have not yet learned to make distinctions of reliability of information source by age six, as adults do when using evidential and epistemic markers.

Courtney's finding that perspectival uses of evidential morphemes are acquired by the time children reach school age would lead me to predict that spatial uses of the directional morphemes, including uses in contexts of deictic transposition, should also be available to children, since these do not depend on assessments of reliability of information source.

However, the question remains as to whether schoolchildren have mastered the full semantic and pragmatic range of these suffixes, including abstract psycho-social meanings such as the 'egotistical' meaning of malefactive *-pu*. An additional question is whether children are able to derive verbs with directional markers at the same level of complexity as adults, as measured by level of suffix clustering.

If the answers to the above two questions are yes, then this study should offer a measure of first language vitality among schoolchildren in rural communities. There is concern about attrition in the use of Quechua by Andean children. In fieldwork since 2000, I have observed that communities are increasingly sending their elementary school-aged children away to study in towns and cities so that they can acquire Spanish and access more stable formal education conditions. The Peruvian national census (INEI 2007, 2.4.1) indicates that declaration of Quechua as the language learned in childhood declined from 16.6 to 13.2 percent nationally, a 3.3 per cent drop since 1993. Late mastery of these suffixes might signal that the nuances of Quechua discourse would be vulnerable to attrition; conversely, early acquisition would offer the hope of vitality.

4.2   *Methods*

The experimental instrument consists of a six frame comic strip created specifically to elicit an original narrative from each participant. I drew initial sketches and planned speech content of the strip in consultation with indigenous research partners Hipólito Peralta, Martín Castillo, Rocío Macedo and well-known illustrator, Jaime Aráoz, whose final illustration is reproduced in Appendix B. The story line does not belong to the genre of local myths and legends, although the characters and sensibilities are Andean. In the first frame, an Andean goose sets up the story context by telling a duck via a speech bubble that she is going swimming and asks the duck to watch her eggs. The benefactive marker *-pu* is used honorifically in combination with first person object marker *-wa* to soften the request. Speech bubble content is as follows:

(41) *Qucha-man-mi*   *hayku-saq*   *runtu-cha-y-ta*
lake-DAT-DIREV   go-1FUT   egg-DIM-1POSS-ACC

qhawa-ri-pu-wa-nki
watch-INCH-BEN-1OBJ2
'I'm going to the lake; please watch my little eggs for me.'

The duck falls asleep on her own nest in the second frame, and a fox can be seen running away with an egg in the third frame. In the fourth frame, the duck exclaims via another speech bubble that there are only two eggs left:

(42) *¡Iskay*   *runtu-lla-ña-taq!*
two   egg-LIM-DISC-EMPH
'Only two eggs left!'

The duck puts one of her tiny eggs into the goose's nest in the fifth frame. The goose returns in the last frame and observes the scene; the story is open-ended. The sun and a nearby mountain are depicted as sentient beings with facial expressions that change in reaction to events in each frame, in keeping with the local belief that they embody life-giving and ancestral spirits (Allen 2002, team members pers. comm.).

It was hoped that this instrument would allow participants to reveal the role of derivational morphology in creating complex meanings within a discourse context larger than single sentences, which it did.

The research team arrived in each community and made contact with the school teachers and community leaders; usually at least one team member had a prior relationship with at least one member of the school or community beforehand. At morning assembly we engaged in games and introductions with the entire school community. Children were then sent by their teachers one by one to meet briefly with an interviewer in an empty room or school office during the school day.

Each interview consisted of three parts: elicitation of a brief sociolinguistic profile, administration of a picture selection and description task modeled after Deutsch, Koster and Koster (1986) and described in Kalt (2002, 2009), and finally, the narrative task.

The research partners who assisted with this inquiry are all fluent speakers of both Quechua and Spanish, known in the Andes as expert intercultural educators, researchers and curriculum developers who learned Quechua in infancy from parents or caregivers and continue to speak it regularly in their personal and professional lives. All of them assisted with community liaison and orien-

POINTING IN SPACE AND TIME

tation to the rural Andean context, and consulted on key issues of task design, as well as interpretation of results. Their roles are listed in Appendix D.

4.3 *Participants*

Narratives were selected from recordings of 105 interviews carried out in July and September of 2009 in four Peruvian and Bolivian communities. All experimental participants were Quechua-dominant, living in agro-pastoralist communities of less than 120 households, more than ten kilometers from the nearest town or city. Videos, permissions from regional and local community authorities, experimental instruments and transcripts related to each interview have been deposited at the Archive of the Indigenous Languages of Latin America (Kalt 2012) and the portions dedicated to narratives selected for this study constitute about 30 minutes of video-recorded speech out of the 17 hours archived in total.

Of 75 children and 5 adults given the narrative task in Bolivia and Peru, only 10 children from the two Peruvian communities succeeded in the creation of a narrative. These were from Ccotatócclla (elevation circa 3,679 m) and Jayubamba (elevation circa 3,475 m) in the department of Cuzco. The high number of unsuccessful narratives is hypothesized to be the result of the task being administered directly after a picture description task, in which there was a one-to-one correspondence between interviewer questions and child responses. Successful narratives were chosen by Vengoa and verified by Kalt; the criterion for success was that the interviewer limited his interventions to infrequent prompts rather than long explanations and frequent questions, and that the child did most of the talking. Unsuccessful narratives were characterized by long silences and a near one-to-one correspondence between the number of interviewer questions and child responses.

A summary of the narrators' characteristics, as well as the age group I assigned their observations to, is found in table 2.3. In keeping with local convention (Pedro Plaza, pers. comm.) pseudonyms are not used for participants.

4.4 *Results*

In this section I will present four types of results. First, I will give an overview of distribution and frequencies by suffix, comparing children and adults. Second, I will examine complexity of derivation by age group. Next, I will present sentences which exemplify the semantic and pragmatic range of directional morphemes in the corpus as compared to uses attested in the literature. Finally, I will present a portion of a child's narrative which illustrates the interplay of directional morpheme -*mu* and other non-directional deictic elements in the negotiation of perspectival shifts, and in the maintenance of joint attentional

46   KALT

TABLE 2.3   *Narrators' characteristics*

Narrator	Age (years)	Grade	Age group	Sex	Community	Length of narrative	Archive location
Nando	5	first	5–7	M	Jayubamba	1:39	MUL028R044I002.mp4 8:26–10:05
Yenni	5	first	5–7	F	Jayubamba	2:07	MUL028R045I002.mp4 7:53–10:00
José Luis	7	second	5–7	M	Jayubamba	2:01	MUL028R049I002.mp4 6:24–8:25
Yuselki	8	third	8–9	F	Jayubamba	4:15	MUL028R051I002.mp4 5:18–9:33
Verónica	8	third	8–9	F	Jayubamba	2:13	MUL028R053I002.mp4 5:30–7:43
Clara Luz	9	fourth	8–9	F	Jayubamba	1:42	MUL028R056I002.mp4 5:22–7:04
Adriel	10	fourth	10–11	M	Ccotatócclla	2:56	MUL028R054I002.mp4 5:10–8:04
Sudith	10	fifth	10–11	F	Ccotatócclla	1:50	MUL028R029I002.mp4 5:28–7:18
Hugo	10	fifth	10–11	M	Ccotatócclla	1:37	MUL028R031I002.mp4 7:14–8:51
Abelardo	11	sixth	10–11	M	Ccotatócclla	1:29	MUL028R038I002.mp4 5:50–7:19
Luz Marina	17	sixth[8]	17–36	F	Ccotatócclla	2:08	MUL028R039I002.mp4 5:38–7:46
Justino	36	finished sixth	17–36	M	Ccotatócclla	1:22	MUL028R043I003.mp4 0–1:22

---

8 The age range in Andean rural schools is greater than in city schools and sometimes reflects the labor needs of families.

POINTING IN SPACE AND TIME   47

TABLE 2.4   *Distribution of directional morphemes in narrative corpus*

Suffix	Adults' use (n=2)	Children's use (n=10)	Total tokens
-yku/-yu/-yka/-ya/-y	0	38	38
-rqu/-ru/-rqa/-ra	3	55	58
-ku	3	10	13
-mu/-m	8	10	18
-pu	9	78	87
Grand totals	23	191	214

focus. These findings particularly relate to narrators' mastery of the discourse
conventions discussed in section 3 of this chapter.

4.4.1   Distribution and Frequency of Directional Morpheme Use
Narrators produced 214 tokens of directional suffixes on 142 derived verb roots
in the narrative corpus as a whole, outlined in table 2.4.

I have excluded from these counts any instances of suffixes found on verbs
in the speech bubble of the comic strip, including *qhawa-ri-pu-wa-y* 'please
watch for me' and any suffixes obligatorily included within the verb, such as
haykuy 'to go', *hamuy* 'to come' and *urquy* 'to remove'. I included nominalized
verbs in the count, such as *baña-ku-q* 'bather' and *wacha-pu-y-ta* 'for egg-laying'.

Given the open-ended nature of the task and the lack of comparable cor-
pora, it is difficult to draw any conclusions about the distribution of tokens,
other than to note that the suffix *-pu* was greatly favored.

Complexity of derivation proved more conclusive. Child narrators produced
126 verbs derived by the suffixes *-yku, rqu, -ku, -mu* and *-pu*; with 48% occurring
singly, another 46% in clusters of two, 6% in clusters of three and zero clusters
of four. Adults produced 16 derived verbs; 44% occurring singly, 38% in clusters
of two, 6% in clusters of three and 13% clusters of four. Complexity of clusters
was remarkably stable across age groups, considering the small sample size,
but no children produced four-part clusters. The distribution and frequencies
are found in table 2.5:

TABLE 2.5 *Complexity of derivation with directional suffixes by age group*

Level of complexity	5–7 yrs (n=3) N	%	8–9 yrs (n=3) N	%	10–11 yrs (n=4) N	%	17–36 yrs (n=2) N	%	Total derived verbs in corpus
Singletons	10	45	38	52	12	39	7	44	67
Clusters of two	11	50	32	44	15	48	6	38	64
Clusters of three	1	5	3	4	4	13	1	6	9
Clusters of four	0	0	0	0	0	0	2	12	2
Total derived verbs by age group	22		73		31		16		142

A graphic representation of the table 2.5 results is found in figure 2.1 below.

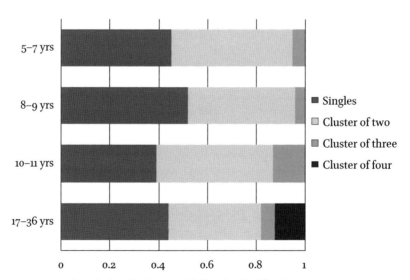

FIGURE 2.1 *Complexity of derivation with directional suffixes by age group*

POINTING IN SPACE AND TIME

Multiple occurrences of the same clusters on different verbs tended to be made by the same speakers, lending structural parallelism within narrations. According to Durston (2007, 233), semantic and structural parallelism is deeply characteristic of traditional Quechua poetics. An example of such parallelism is found below with the sequence *-ya-pu-sqa*:

(43) *Anchay   patu-qa   qhawa-ya-pu-sqa   may-taq*
     there $duck-TOP   look-INT-REG/STAT-3PST2   where-CONTR

    huk   runtu-y-ri   ni-spa   ni-ya-pu-sqa
    one   egg-1POSS-INTRCONJ   say-GER   say-INT-REG/STAT-3PST2
    'That duck looked intently and 'where is my egg' saying she said intently'
    (Adriel, age 10)

A table of all of the derived verbs found in the corpus, with the exception of those excluded because of their appearance in the speech bubbles, is found in Appendix E.

The most popular two-morpheme combination in the corpus was *-ra-pu*, especially on the directional verbal root *apay* 'to carry', with the connotations of suddenness and forcefulness for *-rqu* and malefactive (or possibly regressive) for *-pu* 'snatch (away) greedily.' Another popular use of the *-ra-pu* combination was on the non-directional verb root *mikhuy* 'to eat', with the connotations for *-rqu* of 'eat with pleasure or grace/spread out a feast' and malefactive 'to feast at another's expense.'

The second most popular two-morpheme combination was *-ya-pu*, with the first suffix (derived from *-yku*), signaling inward motion/attentiveness and *-pu*, signaling that the verb's action marks either a return or an entry to a long-lasting state. An example of regressive/stative *-pu* is found in the following sentence:

(44) *Chay-si   na q'isa-pi   uqlla-ya-pu-∅-sqa*
     DIST.DEM-INDEV uh nest-LOC   incubate-INT-REG/STAT-3OBJ-3PST2
     'And they say uh she went back to warming it in her nest.' (Adriel, age 10)

Among the derived verb roots is the Quechua nonce or wildcard root *na-*, "a declinable and conjugatable root used to take the place of a forgotten or deleted word" (Hornberger 2008, 65). This appears in the corpus twice as *na-rapusqa*. In example (45), *na-* appears as a topicalized noun (*na-qa*), and as a conjugated verb derived with the suffixes *-ra-pu*:

(45) *Ankiy*   *na-qa*   *qucha-lla-qa*   *anchay*
PROX.DEM   uh-TOP   lake-LIM-TOP   DIST.DEM

na-ra-pu-∅-sqa
do.something-DYN-MAL-3OBJ-3PST2
'This one (points at the duck in frame 2) uh from the lake, that one did something really bad to her.' (Adriel, age 10)

The same child assumes the duck's perspective in his next utterance and demonstrates the use of derivational morphology on the borrowed verb root *cuida-* ($to care for) in (46) below:

(46) *Imana-saq-taq*   *kunan-qa*   *yanqa-paq*
what.do-1FUT-CONTR   now-TOP   in.vain-BEN

cuida-lla-∅-y-man   *ka-rqa-n;*   *ima-lla-paq*
$care-LIM-3OBJ-1POSS-IRR   be-PST1-3POSS   what-LIM-BEN

mana   *cuida-yu-ra-ni-chu*   *ni-spa*   *ni-chka-n*
no $care-INT-PST1-1-NEG   say-GER   say-PROG-3
'And what will I do now? In vain (I was careless), I should have just taken care of it. Why didn't I take good care of it? She said.'

In example (46) above, the Spanish borrowing *cuida-* '$to.take.care.of' is derived with the derivational suffix *-yku*'s allomorph *-yu*. Although the vast majority of derived verbs in the corpus are of Quechua origin, six Spanish borrowings are also derived, with instances of all four suffixes found on borrowings: *alcanza-pu-sqa-chu* '$to.reach', *cuida-yu-ra-ni-chu* '$to.take.care', *iskapa-ra-ka-pu-sqa* '$to.escape', used transitively as in 'to make an egg disappear', *pasa-pu-sqa* '$to.go', *queda-pu-qtin* '$to.stay', *tira-mu-chka-ra* '$to.shoot,go.fast'. Quechua equivalents of most of these roots are also found with directional suffixes: *qhawa-ya-pu-n* 'to look: take.care', *chinka-yu-sqa* 'to disappear', *ri-pu-sqa* 'to go', *tiya-ya-pu-sqa* 'to stay', *phala-ri-ka-pu-sqa* 'to fly'. These findings relate to the vitality of Quechua verbal derivation and show that complex clusters of derivations are found even on borrowed roots, and that in rural areas Quechua roots still compete with Spanish borrowings.[9]

---

9   Van de Kerke (1996, 73) analyzed a corpus of oral narratives by adult monolingual Quechua speaking city dweller Gregorio Condori Mamani and found that in sentences with verb roots borrowed from Spanish, he omitted Quechua derivational affixes 49% of the time, while

POINTING IN SPACE AND TIME   51

4.4.2   Semantic and Pragmatic Range of Directional Morphemes in the
         Corpus
Now I will give examples of sentential uses of each directional suffix, touching
on the syntactic and semantic characteristics of the verb root when these have
been mentioned as relevant in section 2. The composition of deictic interpretations in relation to other elements in the discourse is discussed where relevant as well. In choosing examples, I tried to find exemplars of as many of
the types of uses of directional morphemes discussed in the adult literature as
possible, and when choosing among multiple occurrences, to present uses by
the youngest narrators.
     I begin by examining the speaker-oriented suffix -*mu*.

(47) *Chay-si*   *apa-ra-pu-qti-n-si*   *pay-qa*
      DIST.DEM-INDEV   carry-DYN-REG/STAT-SEQ-3-INDEV   3-TOP

      waqa-yu-ku-spa   *supay*   *apa-mu-y*   *chay*   *atuq-ta*
      cry-INT-REFL-GER   devil   carry-CIS-IMP   DIST.DEM   fox-ACC
      'They say after he snatched it away she was crying: 'Devil, bring it to me'
      to that fox.' (Clara Luz, age 9)

The verb *apay*, 'to carry', is +transitive, +directional, requiring a cislocative
interpretation.
     The child's use of cislocative -*mu* in example (47) and use of the imperative
voice on the same verb indicates she has merged her perspective with that of
the duck who is speaking to the fox inside the story. This is immediately preceded by an introduction in the narrative voice using evidential -*si*, highlighting a shift in perspective.
     In (48), below, -*mu* is used with a literally spatial-deictic interpretation,
although from within the perspective of two imaginary interlocutors:

(48) *Ka-sqa-n-man*   *kuti-ra-m-pu-sqa*
      be-PST2-3POS-DAT   return-DYN-CIS-REG/STAT-3PST2

      runtu-cha-n-ta   *chay*   *ka-pu-chka-sqa*   *iskay-lla-ña*
      egg-DIM-3POSS-ACC DIST.DEM   be- STAT-PROG-3PST2   two-LIM-DISC
      'Having returned her little egg finally here to its own place, there were
      only two left.' (Sudith, age 10)

_____

     omitting them with Quechua verbs only 28% of the time. I have not yet completed a similar
     comparison within this corpus.

52   KALT

The verb *kutiy*, 'to return', is +transitive, +directional in this context, requiring a cislocative interpretation. Because all of the verbal arguments are third person, the cislocative cannot be fulfilling a spatial deictic function in relation to the speaker. Instead, the child's use of *–mu* could indicate movement toward a place previously referred to, or to the goal of movement of the verb's object, the egg's own place. She uses *-sqa* on the same verb as *-mu*, a narrative past tense marker.

-Mu is used on a verb of communication in the following example:

(49) *Hina-s*   *khuya-y-ta*   *anchay*   *mama-n-ta*
     like-INDEV   pity-INF-ADVL   DIST.DEM   mother-3POSS-ACC

*pusa-ra-**mu**-spa*
guide-DYN-CIS-GER
'So they say, that one pitifully was calling her mother to come to her.'
(Veronica, age 10)

The verb *pusay*, 'to guide', is used here as a verb of communication (JVO, pers. comm.), which is +transitive and +directional, requiring a cislocative interpretation. The target of directionality for *-mu* is most likely the baby's mother and the intended hearer of her call, the accusative object of *pusay*. Alternatively, *-mu* could indicate strong identification by the narrator with the character (verbal subject), who is crying in the story, or that the narrator hopes the listener will share the character's perspective. This emotional engagement adds a layer of subtlety and contrast with the use of indirect evidential *-s* at the beginning of the sentence, a distancing device, and with the distal demonstrative pronoun *anchay*.

(50) *Phawa-ya-ru-chka-n*   *na,*   *na*   *surru-ña-taq*   *phawa-y-lla*
     run-INT-DYN-PROG-3   uh,   uh $fox-DISC-EMP   fly-INF-LIM

*tira-**mu**-chka-ra-n*
$shoot-CIS-PROG-PST1-3
'She was flying hard and fast, uh, uh and already the fox also was shooting towards them rapidly.' (Yuselki, age 8)

The verb *tiray* ('$to shoot:run') in this context is -transitive, +directional. The child's use of the experienced past tense marker, *-ra*, indicates the narrator's identification with the duck's perspective, and the fox, marked third person subject on the verb, is presented as running towards the duck because of

POINTING IN SPACE AND TIME

cislocative *-mu*. There is no first person object marked on the verb, so motion toward the narrator/audience is merely implied.

The next example shows a series of perspectival shifts in a very young speaker's narrative:

(51) *Mama-n-wan*   *tupa-∅-sqa-ku*   *hinaspa*   *chay-pi*
     mother-3POSS-COM   meet-3OBJ-PST2-3PL   then   DIST.DEM-LOC

     umm   *mama-n-mi*   *patu*   *chay-pi*   *inti*
     umm   mother-3POSS-DIREV $duck   DIST.DEM-LOC   sun

     k'ancha-ri-mu-chka-n
     shine-INCH-CIS-PROG-3
     'They met up with their mother, and then there umm, their mother is the duck umm, there the sun is beginning to shine on them' (Yenni, age 5)

The verb *k'anchay*, 'to shine', is +transitive, +directional, and also atmospheric, which is a special class that selects cislocative *-mu* and has an affected reading for its object, meaning that the experiencer is affected by the atmospheric condition (van de Kerke 1996, 31). The child shifts in perspective phrase by phrase, from a narrative perspective marked by the suffix *-sqa*, to an aside to the audience marked by direct evidential *-mi*, and then re-engaging inside the story with progressive aspect *-chka* on the same verb that is marked with the cislocative.

The following example displays a creative use of cislocative *-mu* to indicate heightened sensory awareness of a continuous outgrowth:

(52) *Chay-sis*   *surru-qa ni-n pay-ta-wan mikhu-ra-pu-∅-saq*
     DIST.DEM-INDEV $fox-TOP say-3 3-ACC-COM eat-DYN-STAT-3OBJ-1FUT

     wiksa-ra-ka-mu-sqa   *pay-wan*
     belly-DYN-REFL-CIS-3PST2   3-INS
     'So (they say) the fox says 'I will also eat her up!' He made a belly full of her.' (Yuselki, age 8)

I have classified *wiksay*, 'to make a belly', as +transitive, +directional because it implies growth outward of the belly and it also belongs to the class of verbs which connote a development which comes into the perceptual field of the speaker (Adelaar 1997, 141; van de Kerke and Muysken 1990, 159). This kind of verb relates semantically to verbs which describe what Cusihuamán calls "actions that proceed from the interior, whether from the body, an object, the earth or the water" (1976, 214). I would like to note that the action depicted in such verbs is perceived as continuous and imperfective rather than perfective, in harmony with a cislocative interpretation (toward the perceptual field of the self) rather than a translocative one (after completion of displacement).

This sense of continuous movement or welling up into perceptual salience may explain why Vengoa commented during the analysis of a different task (picture description) that a different child's use of *-mu* in the context of sheep-shearing was to indicate the action was 'continuous, like the rain.' One need only visualize wool welling up from the sheep and the naked skin emerging to understand Vengoa's emphasis on continuous aspect:

(53) *Q'ala-cha-**mu**-chka-∅-n*
naked-VBLZ-CIS-PROG-3OBJ-3
'She's leaving him naked.' (Gregorio, age 6)

All of the examples above have demonstrated cislocative uses of *-mu* by children. Translocative uses of *-mu* in the narrative corpus were relatively few in number. Here is an example:

(54) *Hina-s   atuq-qa   kunan   mikhu-ra-**mu**-saq-puni*
like-INDEV   fox-TOP   now   eat-DYN-TRANS-1FUT-CERT

llapan-ta-puni-n   tuku-ru-saq   ni-spa   ni-n
all-ACC-CERT-DIREV   finish-DYN-1FUT   say-GER   say-3
'So the fox said 'Now I will surely take it elsewhere and feast on it; I definitely will finish every bit', he says.' (Adriel, age 10)

The verb *mikhuy* is +transitive, -directional. The lack of directionality forces a translocative interpretation, meaning that the action takes place elsewhere. Displacement to elsewhere is a perfective event implied by *-mu*.

In summary, I have provided examples from the corpus, demonstrating that speakers use transitive, intransitive, motion and non-motion verbs, as mentioned in section 2. Children use *-mu* with a cislocative interpretation with transitive motion verbs and verbs indicating emergence from a physical or metaphysical body into the perceptual field, including the atmospheric phenomenon of the sun shining, and phenomena such as birth or hatching. They use *-mu* to express a translocative meaning by attaching it *mikhuy*, 'to eat', a

POINTING IN SPACE AND TIME

transitive verb lacking the meaning of directional motion according to the judgment of native speaker adults Vengoa and Plaza.

Now I turn to uses of -*yku* in the narrative corpus. A classic example of intensifying or attentive usage is the following:

(55) *Chay-manta*   *chay-pi*   *qhawa-yu-chka-n*
DIST.DEM-ABL   DIST.DEM-LOC   look.at-INT-PROG-3
'Then she's looking there intently.' <pointing at the duck in frame 5> (José Luis, age 7)

Conversely, -*yku* is used to denote an intense lack of attention or consciousness, which is reinforced by the choice of *puñuy* 'to sleep' as well as the morpheme cluster -*ka-pu* indicating a benefit to the self while causing offense to another in the following example:

(56) *Chay-qa*   *ankay-qa*   *puñu-ya-ka-pu-sqa*
DIST.DEM-TOP   PROX.DEM-TOP   sleep-INT-BEN-MAL-3PST2
'And then this one (points at the duck) had neglectfully fallen fast asleep.' (Adriel, age 10)

-*Yku* is also used to indicate intensity of physical movement, as on both the verbs *asiy* 'to laugh' and *chinkay* 'to disappear' in (57):

(57) *Chay-si*   *chay*   *atuq-qa*   *asi-yku-spa-s*
DIST.DEM-INDEV   DIST.DEM   fox-TOP   laugh-INT-GER-INDEV

chinka-yu-sqa
disappear-INT-3PST2
'Then that fox disappeared laughing heartily, so they say.' (Clara Luz, age 9)

Additionally, -*yku* is used in polite requests, or to signify affection toward the hearer. In the following example from the corpus, the adult storyteller reads the phrase *qhawaripuway* from the speech bubble and adds -*yku* to the verb, increasing the politeness or affection of the request, even though the morpheme -*ri* directly precedes it and also indicates politeness, and -*pu-wa* 'for me/please' directly follows it. No similar example is uttered by a child in this corpus.

(58) *Huk   kutin-si   patu-cha-qa   runtu-cha-y-ta*
one   time-INDEV $duck-DIM-TOP   egg-DIM-1POSS-ACC

qhawa-ri-ya-pu-wa-y   ni-sqa   wallata-ta
look.at-INCH-INT-BEN-1OBJ-IMP   say-3PST2   goose-ACC
'Once upon a time, the little duck said to the goose, please watch my little egg for me.' (Justino, age 36)

In sum, we see that *-yku* is used in this corpus to express an intensification of attention, consciousness or unconsciousness, energetic movement and (by an adult) polite requests. These are all subjective uses attested in the literature and discussed in section 2.

Next, I consider *-rqu*, which historically has the directional meaning 'to produce from inside' and is used to describe the production of an egg in the following example:

(59) *Patu-s   runtu-ta   runtu-ru-sqa   hina-s   anchay*
$duck-INDEV   egg-ACC   egg-DYN-3PST2   like-INDEV   DIST.DEM

baña-ku-q   ri-pu-sqa
$bathe-REFL-AG   go-BEN-3PST2
'They say that the duck had laid an egg, so they say, then she went swimming.' (Veronica, age 10)

Another directional usage with the added connotation of intensity is the following:

(60) *Kunan   yacha-nqa   p'ana-yu-∅-saq-puni   ucha*
now   know-3FUT   beat-INT-3OBJ-1FUT- CERT   or

ñawi-n-ta   urqu-ru-∅-saq   ni-spa   ni-sqa
eye-3POSS-ACC   extract-DYN-3OBJ-1FUT   say-GER   say-3PST2
'Now he'll know I will always beat him or poke out his eyes,' she said.'
(Clara Luz, age 9)

I found no uses of *-rqu* on verbs in imperative mood in this particular corpus. When *-rqu* is not used by a speaker addressing a second person directly, it often indicates speed, suddenness, unexpectedness or completion of an action (Cusihuamán 1976, 207–8). *-Rqu* was used frequently to describe the fox's eating or stealing of the egg in these stories, as in the following two examples:

POINTING IN SPACE AND TIME   57

(61) *Surru-s*   *runtu-ta*   *mikhu-ra-pu-∅-sqa*
     $fox-INDEV   egg-ACC   eat-DYN-MAL-3OBJ-3PST2
     'They say the fox greedily gobbled up the egg.' (Yenni, age 5)

(62) *Hina-s*   *allqu*   *runtu-n-ta*   *qichu-ra-pu-∅-sqa*
     like-INDEV   dog   egg-3POSS-ACC   seize-DYN-MAL-3OBJ-3PST2
     'So they say the dog seized her egg.' (Veronica, age 10)

In sum, *-rqu* is used in this corpus to express directionality of movement from inside to outside, as well as sudden, forceful and completive action.

The reflexive suffix *-ku* plays some of the same semantic roles in the corpus as the directional morphemes. In (63) below, it is used on the noun *runtu* 'egg' as *-rqu* was in example (59) above, meaning to lay eggs. In the following example, the narrator appears to assume that the duck is an offspring of the goose, hence the notion that a parent is laying eggs with her child:

(63) *Wawa-n-kuna-wan*   *runtu-ku-sqa*
     child-3POSS-PL-COM   egg-REFL-3PST2
     'With their children they laid eggs.' (Clara Luz, age 9)

Most uses of *-ku* in the corpus are reflexive. However, in the following example, *-ku*'s allomorph *-ka* is used in a function that cannot be reflexive because the verb's subject (*surru* '$the fox') and object (*runtunta* 'her egg') are clearly two distinct entities. The transcriptionist noted that the narrator seemed to omit causative *-chi* from the verb *iskapay* 'to escape':

(64) *Surru*   *iskapa-ra-(chi)-ka-pu-sqa*   *runtu-n-ta*
     $fox $escape-DYN-(CAUS)-REFL-MAL-3PST2   egg-3POSS-ACC
     'The fox quickly and nastily made her egg disappear.' (Luz Marina, age 17)

It could be that in (64) *-ku* indicates that the action of making the egg disappear was completed for the fox's own benefit, or directionally toward himself.

Finally, I turn to a discussion of the uses of *-pu* in the corpus. In examples (61), (62) and (64) above, it is possible to observe malefactive uses of *-pu*, which are frequent in these narratives. In this final section delineating the interaction of directional morphemes with the semantics of verbal roots, I return to the consideration of spatial and perspectival deictic meanings, which are particularly found when the suffix *-pu* is attached to a verb indicating movement. In the following example, *-pu* is used with transitive verbs of movement *hap'iy* 'to grab' and *apay* 'to carry', to indicate directional movement away from the protagonist's point of reference. The protagonist occupies the speaker's center of attention and is the object of both of these verbs; she is the one being grabbed and carried away. Despite being the center of attention, marking the verbs with -*pu* rather than -*mu* shows the speaker's intent to distance herself from the protagonist, which is supported by the use of indirect evidential -*s* on *hina* 'like', and by the use of the narrative rather than experienced past.

(65) *Askha-ta*   *wacha-yu-sqa*   *hina-s*   *huk*   *kundur-wan*
a.lot-ADVL   give.birth-INT-3PST2   like-INDEV   one   condor-INS

hap'i-chi-ka-pu-sqa   *hina-s*
capture-CAUS-REFL-REG/STAT-3PST2   like-INDEV

apa-chi-ka-pu-sqa
carry-CAUS-REFL-REG/STAT-PST2
'She had nurtured it for a long time and in that way they say she had allowed herself to be trapped by a condor, so they say, she allowed it to carry her away.'[10] (Veronica, age 10)

Children also used -*pu* together with first person object -*wa* in the grammaticalized form of the benefactive to indicate an entreaty ('for me/please') along with the honorific address form *cumpari, cumpariy* '$godfather, buddy' and inflection indicating direct address to a second person:

(66) *Chay-manta*   *surru,*   *cumpari-y*   *surru*   *cumpari-y*
DIST.DEM-ABL $fox $godfather-1POSS $fox $godfather-1POSS

surru   *mana-chu*   *riku-pu-wa-ra-Ø-nki*   *mana-chu*
$fox   no-INTR   see-BEN-1OBJ-PST1-3OBJ-2   no-INTR

riku-pu-wa-ra-Ø-nki
see-BEN-1OBJ-PST1-3OBJ-2
'Then fox, my friend fox, my friend fox, haven't you watched it for me? Haven't you watched it for me?' (Yuselki, age 8)

Thus, in this and previous sections, children and adults use -*pu* to express a nearly complete range of benefactive, malefactive, regressive and stative meanings as well as socially deictic meanings.

---

10   Use of causative –*chi* connotes a meaning stronger than 'allowing' as I have glossed it, indicating that the child believes the duck was fully responsible for her own misfortune.

POINTING IN SPACE AND TIME

4.4.3   Interaction of Directional Markers with other Deictic Elements
As discussed in section 3, directional elements are used by adults in composition with evidential suffixes, demonstrative pronouns and gesture to produce shifts in perspective and engage the listener according to an especially Andean aesthetic. In this corpus, the open-ended nature of the task led to the creation of narratives, which differ from each other stylistically; some employ slapstick humor, others are quite earnest, yet all share an engaging and multi-vocalic aesthetic. One narrative is found in its entirety in Appendix C; I selected it as an exemplar because it offers a clear illustration of the use of directional morphemes and the other elements mentioned to create a dramatic deictic space in which the listener is led through a series of shifts in perspective. This story was created by a seven-year-old named José Luis. He was one of four children ranging from ages 5–10 (and no adults) to use gesture as an integral part of the story, and only he created a spatio-temporal path through the frames of the story, even venturing with his index finger outside the frame into the world of the story teller and listener. Directional morphemes -pu and especially -mu played a key role in expressing this path. Here I will repeat only excerpts from the beginning and end of his narrative to analyze the interaction of directional morphology with other deictic elements in his usage.

In concordance with the observations of Hintz (2007), Nuckolls (2008) and Howard (2012), evidential and tense morphemes are used here to mark stylistic distance and proximity rather than truth value or information source; the interviewer knows that the child is creating this story himself, and yet the child introduces it as if it had been told to him, using the indirect evidential morpheme -s and the narrative past marker -sqa to report events from a perspective of personal distance.

Although there is no car depicted in the comic strip, the child decides to begin this story with his own innovation:

(67) *Karru-pi-s*   *puri-sqa*
     $car-LOC-INDEV   move-3PST2
     'They say she traveled by car' <points at the goose>. (José Luis, age 7)

After he has nearly finished the story, when the interviewer asks how it ends, the child uses a pointing and tracing gesture to bring the goose outside the frame of the comic strip and move her towards himself. Cislocative -mu combined with his gesture indicates that the narrator has become the deictic center:

(68) *Ankay*   *lluqsi-**mu**-chka-n*
PROX.DEM   exit-CIS-PROG-3
'Here she's coming out.' <traces out of the frame towards himself from the nest in frame 6>

He then reintroduces his initial innovation in the story as a way of introducing its summary and conclusion:

(69) *Karru-pi-s*   *puri-sqa*
$car-LOC-INDEV   move-3PST2
'They say she traveled by car.'

Then, with a combination of gesture and the regressive morpheme *-pu*, the child indicates a return to the deictic world inside the perspective of the comic strip, adding his own witness (direct evidential *-mi*) to a proximal demonstrative morpheme (*ankay*), which lends immediacy to the story's perspective. In other words, the child uses both distancing directional and approximating evidential morphemes as well as distancing gesture and an approximating demonstrative pronoun to add depth within the deictic field, seen in the following excerpt:

(70) *Ankay-mi*   *chaya-**pu**-sqa*
PROX.DEM-DIREV   arrive-BEN-3PST2
'I see she arrived back here.' <traces an arc up to stop at the nest in frame 4>

After being prompted once more by the interviewer, the child finishes the story by moving sequentially through the frames of the comic strip, using the sequential morpheme *-qti* and cislocative *-mu* plus gesture; at this point, his perspective and the perspective of the protagonist of his story are aligned and yet maintain their depth of distance:

(71) *Queda-**pu**-qti-n-mi*   *ankay-man*   *kuti-chi-**mu**-n*
$stay-REG/STAT-SEQ-3-DIREV   PROX.DEM-DAT   return-CAUS-CIS-3

aqna   *kuti-ya-m-**pu**-sqa*
like.this   return-INT-CIS-REG/STAT-3PST2
'I see when she stayed she made this one return toward here, she returned back home toward here like this.'

POINTING IN SPACE AND TIME   61

In his final statement above, the child reinforces the sense of alignment in perspective by combining cislocative *-mu* (towards here) with regressive *-pu* (towards the place of origin). At this point the child has used the cislocative four times in the course of six utterances, a device that can be considered to engage the listener by orienting the action in his direction. Thus we see that a seven year old has spontaneously created a summary to his story, which operates in multiple dimensions. He engages the listener on a journey in which the listener is made aware of the narrator's own contributions to the story as well as the perspectives of its protagonists, combining directional morphemes *-mu* and *-pu* with other devices to highlight shifts in space onstage, narrative time and vantage point. The cislocative renders this telling extremely compelling in terms of attentional focus, and works in conjunction with the evidential marker *-mi* plus gesture to shift the perspective clearly. Within this corpus, I have found no clearer illustration of the use of directional markers as contributors to the expression of spatio-temporal path and the highlighting of shifts in perspective, as well as of the negotiation of shared attentional focus. It stands to reason that verbally placing the speaker and hearer at the center of action and indicating that events or arguments are moving toward or away from them should engage the listener's attention, yet this claim is hard to illustrate without video that includes gesture. The URL to view this video, along with a glossed transcript of the child's entire narrative, is found in Appendix C.

5   Conclusions

This chapter fulfills the dual purpose of presenting a systematic view of derivational marking as it relates to directionality and deixis in adult uses of Cuzco-Collao Quechua, as well as documenting the use of the suffixes *-yku, -rqu, -ku, -pu* and *-mu* and other deictic elements within the elicited narratives of rural schoolchildren's speech. I have shown that the complexity and semantic range of children's use of these morphemes is remarkably comparable to that of adult usages attested in the literature. Children use directional suffixes to express spatial and temporal relations, signal their vantage point and negotiate joint attentional focus, and to evaluate and induce a variety of psychological states and social roles. Within the corpus, *-pu* (benefactive/malefactive, regressive, stative) was the directional morpheme that appeared most frequently, accounting for 40% of usage of such morphemes. The suffixes *-rqu* (dynamic) and *-yku* (intensifier) occurred 18% and 27% of the time that directionals were used. *-Mu* (cislocative, translocative) and -*ku* (reflexive) were least frequent. The complexity of clusters of these morphemes was remarkably stable across all age groups.

This work complements recent findings of other linguists, most recently the insight of Hintz (2011) that complex derivational morphology must be viewed holistically as part of an array of devices for expressing related and overlapping meanings in the domain of manner, aspect, tense and mood, and the work on shifting perspectives in Quechua narrative as explored within the realm of tense-marking and evidentiality by Hintz (2007), Howard (2012) and Nuckolls (2008). This study also supports and extends the Quechua child language acquisition findings of Courtney (this volume) from the evidential domain to that of the directional suffixes, suggesting that there are no obvious maturational delays in school-age children's use of Quechua directional morphemes to convey deictic, perspectival and social meanings.

I have demonstrated that by the time Quechua speaking children reach school and during their elementary school years, they have mastered all of the characteristics of a highly nuanced deictic system for representing a range of objective and subjective meanings in discourse. This system is part of the intellectual foundation upon which their subsequent acquisition and schooling in their native and non-native languages may build. Language acquisition in any context requires the interaction of pragmatic, semantic and syntactic systems; in a bilingual context this interaction is more complex. It is my hope that the current study contributes to an increased awareness of the rich linguistic system that rural Quechua speaking children bring to the mix.

As a next step for this research, comparable data should be collected from a larger population of children and adults, with particular attention to including Bolivian participants. The documentation of Bolivian children's acquisition of their L1 Quechua in rural areas is inadequate, considering the large number of communities that would benefit from their language being represented accurately in written and video form.

Acknowledgments

I am indebted to the children, families, and teachers of Ccotatócclla and Jayubamba, Peru for creating the narratives studied here. Thank you to Pedro Plaza Martínez for key discussions of directional movement, and for connecting me to research partners through ProEIBAndes at the Universidad Mayor San Simón: Hipólito Peralta Ccama and Martin Castillo Collado; other key partners were Jaime Aráoz Chacón, Rocio Macedo Portillo, Maria Cristina Parackahua Arancibia, Alfredo Quiroz Villarroel and Janett Vengoa de Orós.

POINTING IN SPACE AND TIME

Boston College students Bryan Fleming, Jonathan Geary, Katherine O'Keefe and Matthew Schlanger assisted with glosses. Funding for various phases of work came from the National Endowment for the Humanities Documenting Endangered Languages Program (FN50091–11), Foundation for Endangered Languages, Roxbury Community College and the Community College Humanities Association. Finally, I thank the editors, co-authors and anonymous reviewers of this volume for many fruitful insights. Errors and omissions remain my own.

Appendix A

$	borrowing from Spanish	EMP	emphatic
1	first person subject	EUPH	euphonic
1FUT	first person future	GEN	genitive
1OBJ	first person object	GER	gerund
1POSS	first person possessive	IMP	imperative
2	second person subject	INCH	inchoative
3	third person subject	INDEV	indirect evidential
3FUT	third person future	INF	infinitive
3OBJ	third person object	INS	instrumental
3POSS	third person possessive	INT	intensifier
ABL	ablative	INTR	interrogative
ACC	accusative	IRR	irrealis
ADD	additive	LIM	limitative
ADVL	adverbalizer	LOC	locative
AG	agentive	MAL	malefactive
APPR	approximative	NEG	negative
BEN	benefactive	OBL	obligative
CAUS	causative	PL	plural
CERT	certainty	PROG	progressive
CIS	cislocative	PST1	simple past
COM	comitative	PST2	narrative past
CONJ	conjunction	REFL	reflexive
CONTR	contrastive	REG	regressive
DAT	dative	SEQ	sequential
DIM	diminutive	STAT	stative
DIREV	direct evidential	TOP	topic
DISC	discontinuative	TRANS	translocative
DYN	dynamic	VBLZ	verbalizer

64 KALT

Appendix B

Narration instrument illustrated by Jaime Aráoz Chacón

FIGURE 2.2 *Frames 1–3 of instrument, read counter-clockwise*

Speech bubble in frame 1 reads:

qucha-man-mi   *hayku-saq*   *runtu-cha-y-ta*   *qhawa-ri-pu-wa-nki*
lake-DAT-DIREV   go-1FUT   egg-DIM-1POSS-ACC   watch-INCH-BEN-1OBJ-2
'I'm going to the lake, please watch my little eggs for me.'

POINTING IN SPACE AND TIME 65

FIGURE 2.3 *Frames 4–6 of narration instrument, read clockwise*

Speech bubble in frame 4 reads:

¡iskay   runtu-lla-ña-taq!
two   egg-LIM-DISC-EMPH
'Only two eggs left!'

66   KALT

Appendix C

Transcript of interview with José Luis, age 7

Hipólito Peralta Ccama (HPC) interviews José Luis (JL), Jayubamba, Cuzco, Peru, Sept. 28, 2009, video *www.ailla.utexas.org* MUL028R049, 6:24–8:25. Parenthesis indicates that SK has added a meaning to the gloss not found explicitly in Vengoa's Spanish translation of the Quechua.

HPC: *Kunanqa kayta qhawasunchis, kaymi huk willakuycha kachkan. Kaypi kachkan waswa, kaytaq kachkan wallata. Chaymanta paqarirachiwaqchu huk riy-, huk willakuyta umallaykimanta.* 'Now we're going to look at this. This is a little story. This is the duck <points> and this, the goose <points>. From that you could produce a . . . a story right from your head.'

JL: *Arí.* 'Yes.'

HPC: *A ver paqarirachiy.* '$Let's $see, make it up fast.'

JL:

Karru-pi-s	*puri-sqa*	*hina-s*	*sayk'u-sqa-ña*
$car-LOC-INDEV	move-3PST2	LIKE-INDEV	tire-3PST2-DISC

naq'u-y-ta-lla-ña		*puri-sqa*
exhaust-INF-ADVL-LIM-DISC		walk-3PST2

'They say she traveled by car' <points at the goose> 'Then already tired, exhausted, she walked.'

HPC: *Chayrí?* 'And after that?'

JL:

Puri-qti-n	*unu-ta*	*tari-spa*	*puytu-pi*	*nada-sqa*
move-SEQ-3	water-ACC	find-GER	hollow-LOC	$swim-3PST2

'After walking, finding water she swam in the pond.'

HPC: *Chaymantarí?* 'And then?'

POINTING IN SPACE AND TIME   67

JL:

Chay　　　*nada-qti-n*　　　　*kuti-**ya**-**pu**-sqa*　　　　　　　*wasi-n-man*
DIST.DEM　　$swim-SEQ-3　　return-INT-REG/STAT-3PST2　　house-3POSS-DAT
'Then after swimming she returned (intently) to her house.'

HPC: *Chaymantarí?* 'And from there?'

JL:

Chay-manta　　*runtu-ta wacha-sqa*　　　*chay-manta*　　*wacha-spa-ña*　　　*mm*
DIST.DEM-ABL egg-ACC give.birth-3PST2 DIST.DEM-ABL give.birth-GER-DISC mm
'Then she produced an egg, after producing it mm. . .' <he expressed all of this
pointing at the goose>

HPC: *Kaypi iman, ima kasqa chaymanta?* 'Here what, what happened next?' <Points
at the other drawings to show the story should go on>

JL:

*Phala-ri-**ka**-**pu**-sqa*
fly-INCH-REFL-REG/STAT-3PST2
'She started to fly away.'

HPC: *Umm chaymantarí?* 'Umm and then?'

JL:

*Phala-ri-**ya**/-**lla**[11]-q-ni-n*　　　　　　　　*pampa-man*　　*tiya-**ya**-**pu**-sqa*
fly-INCH-INT/LIM?-GEN-EUPH-3POSS　　earth-DAT　　sit-INT-REG/STAT-3PST2
'She sat her flyer (right) down on the ground. (meaning her behind)'Alt 'The one who
had started to fly and kept hovering around her sat right down on the ground.'

HPC: *Umm*'Umm'

11　An anonymous reviewer notes that analyzing *-ya* as an allomorph of *-yku* in the word *phalar-iyaqnin* is ungrammatical since there is no subsequent suffix that would condition this sound change. Based on video review and correspondence with native speakers JVO and MCC, I would offer the following alternatives: a) child said *-ya* meaning *-yku* and hasn't mastered sound change rule, or b) the child said *phala-ri-lla-q-ni-n* with the limitative *-lla*; in any event JVO and MCC both find the construction creative, pleasing and difficult to analyze.

JL:

Chay-taq-si   *puri-sqa*   *puri-sqa*   *luma-lla-n-ta.*
DIST.DEM-CONTR- INDEV   move-3PST2   move-3PST2 $hill-LIM-3POSS-ACC

puri-sqa   *ankay-wan*   *tupa-pu-sqa*
move-3PST2   PROX.DEM-COM   meet-REG-3PST2

'Then she walked and walked among the hills. <points to the hills> She walked and she ran into this one.' <points to the fox>

HPC: *Imatan chayrí sutin*? 'What is this one's name?'

JL: < no response >

HPC: *Imata ima-, imata chayrí rurasqa*? 'What, what, what did this one do?'

JL: *Surru.* '$The fox.'

HPC: *Imata rurasqa*? 'What did he do?'

JL:

Runtu-ta   *apa-ra-pu-sqa*
egg-ACC   carry-DYN-REG/STAT-3PST2
'He snatched away the egg.'

HPC: *Ah, chaymantarí*? 'Ah, and then?'

JL:

Simi-n-pi-ri   *ni-yu-chka-n*   *Pin-mi*   *apa-ru-n*
mouth-3POSS-LOC-INCH   say-INT-PROG-3   who-DIREV   carry-DYN-3
'In her mouth she's saying Who took it without my noticing?! <roaring voice>'

Chhayna   *qapari-chka-n*
like.this   shout-PROG-3
'That's what she's shouting.'

HPC: *Ya chaymantarí*? 'OK. And then?' <shows him figure 2.3 frame 5>

POINTING IN SPACE AND TIME

JL:

Chay-manta	*chay-pi*	*qhawa-yu-chka-n*
DIST.DEM-ABL	DIST.DEM-LOC	look.at-INT-PROG-3

'Then she's looking there intently.' <pointing at the duck in figure 2.3 frame 5>

HPC: *Umm chaymantarí imapi tukupun?* 'Umm and then, how did it end?'

JL:

Ankiy	*ankay-cha-pi*	*run-,*	*q'isa-cha-lla-pi*	*ka-chka-n*
PROX.DEM	PROX.DEM-DIM-LOC	egg	nest-DIM-LIM-LOC	be-PROG-3

'Here, right here the egg-, is right in the little nest.'

HPC: *Umm chaypi tukupun?* 'Umm does it end there?'

JL:

Chay-man xxx		*ankay*	*lluqsi-mu-chka-n.*
DIST.DEM-DAT	(unintelligible)	PROX.DEM	exit-CIS-PROG-3

'Afterwards …' <unintelligible> 'Here she's coming out.' <traces out of the frame towards himself from the nest in figure 2.3 frame 6>

Karru-pi-s	*puri-sqa.*	*Ankay-mi*	*chaya-pu-sqa*
$car-LOC-INDEV	move-PST2	PROX.DEM-DIREV	arrive-REG/STAT-PST2

'They say she traveled by car. I see she arrived back here.' <traces an arc up to stop at the nest in figure 2.3 frame 4>

HPC: *Chaymantarí?* 'And then?'

JL:

Queda-pu-qti-n-mi	*ankay-man*	*kuti-chi-mu-n*
$Stay-REG/STAT-SEQ-3-DIREV	PROX.DEM-DAT	return-CAUS-CIS-3

'I see when she stayed she made this one return toward here,'

aqna	*kuti-ya-m-pu-sqa*
like.this	return-INT-CIS-REG/STAT-PST2

'she returned back home toward here like this.'

HPC: *Kusa wawqiy, munay.* 'Excellent my brother, nice.'

Appendix D

TABLE 2.6   *Role of native speakers in this study*

Community	Ccotatóclla, Peru	Jayubamba, Peru
Interviewer	HPC	HPC
Videographer	SK	RMP
Transcriber	RMP	RMP
Translator to Spanish	JVO	JVO
Glossing	JVO, SK and students	JVO, SK and students
Verification, translation to English and data analysis	SK	SK

Native speakers of Quechua are marked with an asterisk.
*Hipólito Peralta Ccama (HPC) originally from Paruro, Peru
*Jaime Aráoz Chacón (JAC) originally from Cuzco, Peru
*Janett Vengoa Zúñiga de Orós (JVO) originally from Sicuani, Peru
Rocio Macedo Portillo (RMP) originally from Cuzco, Peru
Susan Kalt (SK) originally from Greenwich, Connecticut

Bolivian portion of the study and further consultation involved the following native speakers:
*Alfredo Quiroz Villarroel (AQV) originally from Valle Alto, Bolivia
*Martin Castillo Collado (MCC) originally from Apurímac, Peru
*Maria Cristina Parackahua Arancibia (MCP) originally from Chuquisaca, Bolivia
*Pedro Plaza Martínez (PPM) originally from Siglo XX, Bolivia

Appendix E

TABLE 2.7 *Derived verbs by level of complexity, nominalizations in parentheses*

Level of complexity	Clusters	Numbers found	Derived verbs
Clusters of four	*ra-ka-m-pu*	2	chaskirakampusqa, tarirakampusqa
Clusters of three	*ya-m-pu*	1	kutiyampusqa
	ra-m-pu	3	kutirampu-, mikhurampusqa, kutirampusqa
	ra-ka-mu	1	wiksarakamusqa
	y-ka-pu/ya-ka-pu	2	laqaykapusaku, puñuyakapusqa
	ra-ka-pu	2	churarakapusqa, iskaparakapusqa
Clusters of two	*y-ru*	3	phawayruchkan, tirayruchkan, (urayruspa)
	ya-ku/yu-ku	1	(waqayukuspa)
	ya-mu	2	kutiyamuchkallasqa, kutiyamusqa
	ya-pu	15	qhawayapusqa, niyapusqa, uqllayapusqa, waqayapusqa x 3 mikhuyapusqa x 2, saqiyapusqa, qhawayapun, waqayapuqtin, tiyayapusqa, chanqayapusaku, waqayapuqtin
	ra-mu	3	mikhuramusaqpuni, (pusaramuspa), pusaramusqa
	ra-pu	33	qichurapusqa, wañurapusqa, aparapusqa x 12, aparapuchkan x 3, aparapuqtin, puñurapusqa x 2, mikhurapusaq, aparapuran, puñurapuranmi, mikhurapusqa x 7, aparapun, narapusqa, tukurapusqa
	ka-pu	6	phalarikapusqa, phiñarikapusqa, puñukapusqaku, hap'ichikapusqa, apachikapusqa, iskaparakapusqa
	m-pu	1	hampuchkannan

TABLE 2.7 *Derived verbs by level of complexity, nominalizations in parentheses (cont.)*

Level of complexity	Clusters	Numbers found	Derived verbs
Singletons	-yku/-yu/-yka/-ya	15	(asiykuspas), saqiyusqa, wachayusqa, wachayusqa, chinkayusqa, p'anayusaq, hap'iyusqa, chinkayusqa, cuidayuranichu, niyuchkan, qhawayuchkan, chinkayachin, phalapayasqa, pikalayasqa, yarqayuwachkan, yarqayuwachkan
	-rqu/-ru/-rqa/-ra	13	urqurusaq, urqurusaq, runturusqa, wacharusqa, (rikuruspa), waturukun, (riruspa), phawayruchkan, tukurusaq, aparusqa, aparun, (urayruspa), (qhawarukunanpaq)
	-ku/-ka	4	tiyakusqaku, runtukusqa, (manchakuspa), (bañakuq)
	-mu/-m	8	tiramuchkaran, apamuy, k'ancharimuchkan, kutimusqa, (uqarimuspa), willamusqa, lluqsimuchkan, kutichimun
	-pu	27	ripusqa x 2, kawsapuchkasqa, kapuchasqa, alcanzapusqachu, pasapusqa, apusqa, pasapusqa, kapuchkasqa, mikhupusqañachu, kapunchu, kapusqachu, rikupuwaranki, rikupuwaranki, kapusqachu, qhawapusqachu, kapuchkasqa, kapuchkasqa, kapusqachu, tapusqa, kapunchu, kapunchu, kapuchkasqa, uqllapun, kapusqa, quedapuqtinmi, (wachapuyta)

Bibliography

Adelaar, Willem. 1997. "Spatial reference and speaker orientation in early colonial Quechua." In *Creating context in Andean Cultures*, edited by Rosaleen Howard-Malverde. 135–148. Oxford: Oxford University Press.

Allen, Catherine. 2002. *The Hold Life Has: Coca and Cultural Identity in an Andean Community*. 2nd edition. Washington, DC: Smithsonian Institution Press.

Bills, Garland Dee. 1972. "The Quechua Directional Verbal Suffix." *Papers in Andean Linguistics*, 1 (1): 1–15.

———. 1975. "On Case in Quechua." *Papers in Andean Linguistics*, 2 (2): 1–130.

Bühler, Karl. 1934. *Sprachtheorie. Die Darstellungsfunktion der Sprache*. Jena: Fischer.

Calvo, Julio. 1993. *Pragmática y gramática del quechua cuzqueño*. Cuzco: Centro Bartolomé de las Casas.

Cerrón-Palomino, Rodolfo. 1987. *Lingüística quechua*. Cuzco: Centro Bartolomé de las Casas.

Cusihuamán G., Antonio. 1976. *Gramática quechua: Cuzco-Collao*. Lima: Ministerio de Educación.

Deutsch, Werner, Koster, Charlotte, and Koster, Jan. 1986. "What can we learn from children's errors in understanding anaphora?" *Linguistics* 24: 203–225.

Durston, Alan. 2007. *Pastoral Quechua: the history of Christian translation in colonial Peru, 1550–1650*. Notre Dame: University of Notre Dame Press.

Hanks, William. 1992. "The indexical ground of deictic reference." In *Rethinking Context, Language as an Interactive Phenomenon*, edited by Charles Goodwin and Alessandro Duranti, 43–77. Cambridge: Cambridge University Press.

Hintz, Daniel J. 2011. *Crossing Aspectual Frontiers. Emergence, Evolution, and Interwoven Semantic Domains in South Conchucos Quechua Discourse*. UC Publications in Linguistics 146. Berkeley: University of California Press.

Hintz, Diane. 2007. *Past tense forms and their functions in South Conchucos Quechua*. Pacific Rim Research Program. Santa Barbara: University of California.

Hornberger, Esteban and Hornberger, Nancy. 2008. *Diccionario trilingüe Quechua de Cusco: Qhiswa, English, Castellano*. Cuzco: Centro Bartolomé de las Casas.

Howard, Rosaleen. 2012. "Shifting voices, shifting worlds: evidentiality, epistemic modality and speaker perspective in Quechua oral narrative." *Pragmatics and Society* 3 (2): 246–269.

———. 2013. *Kawsay Vida. A Multimedia Quechua Course for Beginners and Beyond*. Austin, University of Texas Press.

Instituto Nacional de Estadística e Informática. 2007. *Censo Nacional de Población y Vivienda*. Lima, Peru.

Kalt, Susan. 2002. *Second language acquisition of Spanish morphosyntax by Quechua-speaking children*. PhD diss., Los Angeles: University of Southern California. http://suekalt.files.wordpress.com/2014/01/tesis-kalt.pdf

————. 2009. "Bilingual Children's Object and Case Marking in Cusco Quechua." *University of British Columbia's Working Papers in Linguistics*, edited by Heather Bliss and Raphael Girard. 26: 126–142. Vancouver: University of British Columbia.

————. 2012. "The Speech of Children from Cusco and Chuquisaca." *The Archive of the Indigenous Languages of Latin America.* www.ailla.utexas.org. Media: video, text.

Lardiere, Donna. 2009. "Some thoughts on a contrastive analysis of features in second language acquisition." *Second Language Research* 25 (2): 173–227.

Levinson, Stephen. C. 2004. "Deixis." In *The Handbook of Pragmatics*, edited by Laurence Horn. 97–121. Oxford: Blackwell.

Mannheim, Bruce. 1991. *The Language of the Inka Since the European Invasion.* Austin: University of Texas Press.

Mushin, Ilana. 2001. *Evidentiality and Epistemological Stance: Narrative Retelling.* Philadelphia: John Benjamins.

Nuckolls, Janis. 2008. "Deictic Selves and Others in Pastaza Quichua Evidential Usage." *Anthropological Linguistics* 50 (1): 67–89.

Plaza Martínez, Pedro. 2005. *Qallarinapaq: curso básico de quechua boliviano.* Unpublished manuscript, Cochabamba: ProEIBAndes, Universidad Mayor San Simón.

Rothman, Jason and Guijarro-Fuentes, Pedro. 2012. "Linguistic interfaces and language acquisition in childhood: Introduction to the special issue." *First Language* 32 (1–2): 3–16.

Salomon, Frank. 2004. *The Cord Keepers: Khipus and Cultural Life in a Peruvian Village.* Durham: Duke University Press.

Sánchez, Liliana. 2003. *Quechua-Spanish Bilingualism. Interference and Functional Categories.* Language Acquisition and Language Disorders 35. Amsterdam: John Benjamins.

Torero, Alfredo. 2005. *Idiomas de los Andes. Lingüística e Historia.* 2nd edition Navarro de Torero, Ana. Lima: Editorial Horizonte.

Townsend, Camilla. 2011. "The Political Language of the Aztec Histories." Paper presented at the Symposium on Teaching and Learning Indigenous Languages of Latin America, Oct. 30–Nov. 2, 2011. South Bend, University of Notre Dame.

van de Kerke, Simon. 1996. *Affix Order and Interpretation in Bolivian Quechua.* PhD diss., Amsterdam: University of Amsterdam.

van de Kerke, Simon and Muysken, Pieter. 1990. "Quechua *-mu* and the perspective of the speaker." *Unity in Diversity, papers presented to Simon C. Dik on his 50th birthday,* edited by Harm Pinkster and Inge Genee. 151–165. Dordrecht: Foris.

CHAPTER 3

Demonstrative Deixis in Two Dialects of Amazonian Quichua[1]

Janis B. Nuckolls, Tod D. Swanson, and Belinda Ramirez Spencer

1 Introduction

Deixis is a universal category in the world's languages, found in forms that shift their reference to time, space, and person. Examples of deictic forms include pronouns, demonstratives, tense and evidential categories (Nuckolls 2012), discourse markers (Fraser 1999), and honorific forms (Irvine 1998). Following Peirce (1955), Roman Jakobson (1971) considered deictic forms to be shifters that combine both conventionally symbolic as well as indexical modes of meaning. For example, if we encounter in discourse a personal pronoun such as 'I', we understand that it both refers by a conventional rule, as well as points to a context-specific speaking subject of the speech event or of a narrated speech event. If we expand our consideration of deixis to such discourse entities as contextualization cues, especially rising or falling intonation, and the kinds of expressive performances involving analogical gestures that occur in ideophonic simulations (Nuckolls 1996), however, we are forced to see the conventionalized meanings of deixis along a continuum from extremely conventionalized to minimally conventionalized.

Demonstrative usage in Quichua is, for the most part, concerned with communicating, by a conventional rule, notions of physical proximity and distance (e.g. 'this'/'that', 'here'/ 'there'), as well as related discourse notions such as anaphora (e.g. 'this'/'that' already referred to) and backchanneling (e.g. is 'that' so?). However, Quichua demonstratives may, at times, exhibit speaker-specific contextualizing and expressivity that would place them a bit farther away from the conventionalized end of a hypothetical continuum. For example, expressive lengthening would allow speakers to communicate personal perceptions

---

[1] Ecuadorian Quichua is now officially written as *Kichwa* in materials produced by the Ecuadorian Ministry of Education. In that context, the term *Kichwa* generally refers to the standardized *Kichwa Unificado*. We retain the older spelling 'Quichua' both because of its long history of use and because materials written in the Pastaza and Tena dialects have traditionally used the spelling 'Quichua'.

© KONINKLIJKE BRILL NV, LEIDEN, 2015 | DOI 10.1163/9789004290105_004

of greater duration or spatial expanse. As will become apparent in our paper, some demonstrative usages do exploit the possibilities for intonationally-communicated, subjective perceptions of distance by using expressive lengthening to communicate an idea of greater distance from a speaker. Although there is a growing literature on the discourse characteristics of demonstratives in a variety of languages, and even one attempt to typologize the discourse use of demonstratives (Himmelman 1996), there has, as yet, been no study of the discourse characteristics of demonstratives in Ecuadorian Quichua.

This paper, then, will examine a form of referential deixis, that of demonstratives, in two dialects of Ecuadorian Quichua, both of which are spoken in Amazonian Ecuador. These two dialects are quite similar, mutually intelligible, and spoken in contiguous provinces. When attempting to identify a text as belonging to either one of these dialects, the most obvious indicators are the past tense suffixes. Additionally, there are some differences in lexical usage and in phonological inventories. (See Nuckolls, Stanley, Nielsen and Hopper (forthcoming), and O'Rourke and Swanson 2013.)

We refer to these dialects as the Pastaza dialect, after the province in which it dominates, and the Tena dialect, after the capital city of the adjacent province in which this dialect is spoken. However, we must be extremely cautious about assuming that these dialect divisions are unproblematic. Because they are geographically contiguous, speakers are related to each other through complex kinship networks. In fact, identifying our own consultants as belonging to one dialect versus another is complicated by the fact that one person may have a spouse, a parent or grandparents from another dialect. The term 'dialect' as used here, therefore, is shorthand for a complex and dynamic sociolinguistic environment.

Following Diessel (2006, 464), we note the intrinsically interesting qualities of demonstratives, which not only indicate the location of something relative to a speaker, but also "serve to coordinate the interlocutors' joint attentional focus" (2006, 469). This and other discourse functions of demonstratives in Quichua have not been given any attention by grammarians, who tend to focus on their spatial, locative functions. Consider, for example, that there is a general consensus among many grammarians of Ecuadorian dialects of Quichua that there is a two-way contrast between proximal and distal demonstratives. Such claims have been made in Catta Quelen (1994, 55), Cole (1982, 132), Lema Guanolema (1997, 42), Múgica (1967, 24), Ross (1979, 14–15) and Vásquez Suárez (1992, 62–64). Ross (1979, 14–15), for example, states the following:

> There are only two commonly used demonstratives in Quichua:
> *Cai* "this" used to describe anything fairly close to the speaker
> *Chai* "that" used to describe anything not quite close to the speaker

Ross also mentions *chi* as a dialectal variant of *chai*, used in the communities of Calderón and Salasaca. There is no mention of any possible discourse functions.

Our data from Pastaza and Tena varieties, however, reveal a three-way contrast between *kay* 'this', *chi* 'that' and *chay* 'that'. Contra Orr and Wrisley (1981, 52–53), who label *chi* as a Tena dialectal variant of *chay* in their *Vocabulario* and translate its meaning as equivalent to the Spanish forms *aquel* and *ese*, we have found that *chi* is used by speakers of both Pastaza and Tena dialects. We find, moreover, that the two forms, *chi* and *chay*, are somewhat synonymous and overlapping in their usage, but have different discourse functions, which are identifiable in narratives as well as in conversation. We argue, then, that speakers of both dialects use the three forms, *kay, chi* and *chay*, to communicate proximal/distal contrasts as well as discourse functions. *Kay* 'this' encodes proximal meaning and functions in discourse to focus interlocutors' attention on newly introduced topics. *Chi* 'that' is the 'workhorse' demonstrative for these two varieties, and is used abundantly in discourse to refer to what is not spatially immediate and to what has already been mentioned. Its reference is therefore anaphoric and it functions to build coherence within texts. *Chay* 'that' is used much less frequently than either *kay* or *chi*. It points to a 'that' which may be spatially farther than *chi*, to something that someone may not have previously mentioned, or to an entity or place that is unknown.

2 Methodology

We base our claims for *kay, chi* and *chay* upon data from transcribed narratives, interviews with speakers from both dialects, and by observing naturally occurring conversations.[2] Each occurrence of *kay, chi,* and *chay* in the transcriptions was distinctively color-coded to make visual scanning and numerical calculations more convenient. Since *chi* and *chay* have so often been treated as mere dialectal variants, we not only observed their occurrence in transcribed narratives but also decided to focus our attention upon their usage in everyday discourse, by means of sentence elicitation and speaker judgment tasks where speakers were given spatially situated stimuli and asked to specify which of the deictic demonstratives was most appropriately used. We interviewed a total of

---

2   The narratives we used have been transcribed by Nuckolls and Swanson. Nuckolls' narratives may be accessed at The Archives of Indigenous Languages of the Americas: ailla.utexas.org. Both Tena and Pastaza narratives were examined by Ramirez Spencer, who color-coded each instance of *kay, chi* and *chay*, occurring in several hundreds of pages of transcribed narratives of over 50 hours of recordings.

14 different speakers from both Pastaza and Tena dialects, the details of which are explained in a subsequent section. Our analyses also make use of speakers' metalinguistic commentary, which revealed some awareness of the subtle differences between *chi* and *chay*. We will discuss each demonstrative separately, analyzing its proximal/distal functions as well as its discourse functions.

Since the demonstratives *kay, chi,* and *chay* rarely occur without some kind of suffixal elaboration, we noted each occurrence of a demonstrative, whatever suffix it had.[3] Demonstratives may occur prenominally as well as adverbially, and are marked with a variety of suffixes, including the accusative *-ta/-ra*, the instrumental *-wan*, the dative *-ma*, the ablative *-manda*, the locative *-i/pi*, and the limitative *-lʲa*. These suffixes may then be further affixed with any of the enclitic suffixes, including the topicalizing *-ga*, epistemically modal *-mi/ -chu*, and the evidentials *-mi/-shi*.[4] We proceed by analyzing each of the three demonstratives, *kay, chi,* and *chay*, showing with examples of usage for each, how a three-way distinction involving spatial as well as discourse functions works for the Pastaza and Tena dialects.

3 The Proximal Demonstrative *kay* 'this'

Following Hanks (2012, 176–77), we distinguish between three aspects of any demonstrative act. First there is an origo, or deictic center, expressed by an individual who is pointing and referring. Second, there is an access relation, such as spatial proximity or perceptibility. And third, there is an object, location, or concept that is being pointed to. We first discuss the demonstrative *kay*, using evidence primarily from narratives.

3.1 *Immediate Spatial/Conceptual Access with* kay
The demonstrative *kay* is the form used to point to what is closest in space to interlocutors, whether that space is in an imagined narrative world of reported discourse, or in an actual speech event. Examples (1) and (2) from Pastaza Quichua both express an access relation of immediate spatial proximity within a narrative space. Example (1) consists of reported speech in a mythic narrative.

---

3 The lists of the varieties of suffixes that may be affixed to the demonstratives are provided in our appendices B and C.

4 Although much has been written about the differences between evidentials *-mi* and *-shi*, we will not be marking their distinctive semantics in our glosses. Nuckolls (1993, 2008, 2012) has argued that their meanings encode speaker perspective, and that direct or indirect evidence may be implied.

DEMONSTRATIVE DEIXIS IN TWO DIALECTS OF AMAZONIAN QUICHUA

(1) **Kay-bi** *ñuka* *mama* *kay* *ñambi* *tiya-w-n.*
this-LOC my mother this path live-DUR-3SG
'**Here** (literally: 'in this'), along this path, is where my mother lives.'

Example (2) consists of reported speech within a personal narrative, from an early childhood experience:

(2) *Kan-guna=ga* *kay-lʸa-y* *a-u-ngichi.*
you-PL=TOP this-LIM-LOC be-DUR-2PL
'As for you-all, stay **right here**.' (literally: 'just in this')

Closely related to its use for pointing to immediate spatial proximity is the use of *kay* to foreground a comparison that may require speakers to use their own bodies, which are immediately accessible, as a referential field. One such usage occurs in example (3) below. It is taken from a tale describing a forest spirit that appeared to have a very large head. The speaker uses the gesture space immediately in front of her upper body to arrange her open hands in a way that illustrates a larger than life head:

(3) **Kay** *uma* *ruku-yuk=shi* *a-shka.*
this head large-POSS=EV be-PRF
'His head, apparently, was **this** big.' (more literally: 'he was this-much-of-a-big-head-possessor.')

Another expression using *kay* for bodily comparison is *kay-wan pariu-lʸa akcha-yuk* 'a with-this-much hair-possessor', which is always used to describe a woman with very long hair.

An interesting observation about these formulaic expressions featuring a *kay* that depends on comparing something with a speaker's own body or immediate spatial field is that they are so well understood that they may be used without gestures. On the other hand, when speakers are not making use of idiomatic expressions, they may use demonstratives that are crucially dependent on prolific bodily gestures. What is noteworthy about these kinds of gestures, moreover, is that speakers often use their hands to point, by directly touching their own bodies. This differs from Anglo-cultural, English speaking traditions which feature a gestural space that is not in direct contact with speakers' own bodies (see, for example, McNeill 1992).

The next example features just such a demonstration that uses *kay* by tracing a line along the speaker's upper body to describe the way people living in an earlier time draped beaded necklaces across their chests. The speaker's gesture traces the line across her chest.

(4) **Kay-gama** *apari-shka-una* *walʸka.*
here-until wear-PRF-3PL necklace
'**As far as here** (they) wore necklaces.'

3.2 *Joint Focus with* kay

In addition to its use for expressing spatial proximity, *kay* also functions to help interlocutors jointly focus on concepts that are of immediate topical importance, a function also noted by Mithun (1987, 188). In the following example, we observe the use of *kay* at the beginning of a narrative to demarcate a conceptual space. The narrator is telling Nuckolls about shamans who live along the Napo River. At the time she was relating this, Nuckolls and the narrator were not, however, anywhere near that river, nor even in the Napo province. Moreover, Nuckolls had never been to this area and did not know anything about it. Yet, the demonstrative *kay* is used several times in this orientational introduction to a narrative about how young men acquire shamanic abilities by apprenticing themselves to established shamans in another province.

(5) *Payguna* *malta-manda=shi* **kay-ma=shi** *puri-nawn.*
they young-from=EV this-DAT=EV travel-3PL
'They, from a young age, apparently, travel **here** (literally: 'to this').'

It is clear that the narrator is using *kay* to introduce a topic—the Napo River—that will continue to be relevant in subsequent discourse. It is not unlike uses of 'this' in English, where a speaker will say something like 'and there was this guy who…', in order to demarcate a new conversational terrain that is meant for the joint attention of interlocutors.

The next example demonstrates this very same function of *kay* within the Tena dialect. Taken from a personal account recorded by Swanson, the narrator uses *kay* 'this' to focus listeners' attention upon an individual who has not yet been mentioned, but is the person upon whom the entire narrative is focused, since it is a story about his disappearance:

(6) *Ñuka-ga* *a-k* *a-ni* *segundo* *grado,* *pay=ga,* **kay** *ñuka* *tío*
I-TOP be-AG be-1SG $second $grade he=TOP this I $uncle

Manuel-ba *churi* *Bartolo Andi* *pay* *a-ka* *primer* *grado.*
Manuel-POSS son Bartolo Andi he be-PAST $first $grade
'As for me, I am in the second grade (at this time); as for him, **this** (one who is) my uncle Manuel's son, Bartolo Andi, he was in the first grade.'

DEMONSTRATIVE DEIXIS IN TWO DIALECTS OF AMAZONIAN QUICHUA 81

In sum, in this section the meanings of the demonstrative *kay* have been examined and it has been shown to have a variety of functions, all of which are related to immediate spatial access. In conversations and narratives, *kay* points to a 'here' that is in close spatial proximity to a speaking origo, or, by analogy, to a concept that is intended as an immediate focus for joint attention among interlocutors.

4 The Distal Spatial Demonstrative *chi* 'that'

We turn now to a discussion of *chi*. Before discussing the distal functions of *chi*, we will examine its interesting discourse functions, which are somewhat overlapping, semantically, with *kay*.

4.1 *The Discourse Functions of* chi

Chi is also used to establish a joint focus of attention for interlocutors. The main difference between *kay* and *chi* is that *chi* is used to point to something that has already been referred to in previous discourse. In pointing to what is temporally antecedent, *chi* may point to a referent that is immediately antecedent in discourse time. In example (7), from Tena Quichua, the speaker mentions a bilingual school, and then refers to it as 'that school', using *chi*:

(7)   *Shina-kpi*   *ñukanchi*   *ñawpa,*   *kay-bi*   *kawsaw-shka-y,*   *kay*
     like-SWRF   we   earlier   this-LOC   live-PRF-LOC   this

     comunidad-pi   *chari-k*   *a-nchi*   *shu*   *eskwela*   *bilingüe*
     $community-LOC   have-AG   be-1PL   one $school $bilingual

     tiya-ka.   *Shina-kpi*   *ñukanchi*   ***chi***   *eskwela-y*   *a-k*   *a-nchi...*
     dwell-PAST   Like-SWRF   we   that $school-LOC   be-AG   be-1PL
     'And so, at an earlier time when we lived here, in this community, we had one bilingual school which was here. And so, we were in **that school. . .**'

In the Pastaza dialect as well, we can easily find numerous examples of *chi*, all of which refer to something that has already been mentioned. In example (8), the narrator of a traditional story uses *chi* to refer to an ax that had just been described.

(8) *Ima hacha kiru-ruku-yuk=shi a-shka!* **Chi-wan=shi** *pay=ga ruya*
   what $ax teeth-big-POSS=EV be-PRF That-INS=EV he=TOP tree

   angu-ta=ga taka-sha puri-k a-ra.
   vine-ACC=TOP hit-COR walk-AG be-PAST
   'What a big blade-possessing-ax it was! **With that** he would walk hitting tree vines.'

Besides pointing to a referent that is immediately antecedent in discourse time, *chi* may also refer to something that has not been mentioned for a while. In the next example, it is used to refer to something going all the way back to an earlier reference, 15 sentences earlier, in our transcription, to a particular school that was mentioned by another speaker (see example (7) above). By way of context, there were two speakers present, a husband and wife, each telling their own version of a traumatic, early life experience, involving the disappearance of the wife's young cousin, to Swanson, who elicited and recorded the narrative. The husband and wife each listened to the other relate this experience. The wife, named Carmen, was the first narrator. Example (9) is taken from the beginning of her husband's version of the experience. In the following example, he is talking about having gone to the same bilingual school as his wife when they were both children. The reference to the school was made by his wife at the very beginning of her narrative, but never mentioned again. Her husband then used *chi* to refer all the way back to that earlier usage, tying it anaphorically, to its first mention by Carmen:

(9) *Ñuka-s shina-ĺa-ra* **chi** *eskwela-y a-ka-ni, ñuka warmi*
   I-INCL like-LIM-ADV that $school-LOC be-PAST-1SG I wife

   tukuna Carmen Andi, pai-wa pariju shina-ĺa-ra.
   to.become Carmen Andi she-COM $equal like-LIM-ADV
   'I, also, just like that, I was in **that** school, just the same as my wife-to-be, (at the time), Carmen Andi.'

In addition to its use for referring to already-mentioned referents, *chi* has other important discourse functions, especially in Pastaza Quichua. In narratives, *chi* combines with the topicalizing enclitic *-ga*, to form *chiga*, which functions like a conjunction, meaning approximately 'and then', or 'so then'. *Chiga* relates an utterance that has just been spoken with one that is about to be articulated.

DEMONSTRATIVE DEIXIS IN TWO DIALECTS OF AMAZONIAN QUICHUA   83

Typically, utterances introduced with *chiga* coincide with a shift in narrative topic or events.[5]

In example (10), from a traditional Pastaza narrative, *chiga* signals a break in the narrative from actions described, to words spoken. The men in this story have just returned from hunting and when they come home, they immediately head for a fermented manioc beverage, called *aswa*, not realizing that it has been tainted. The woman who knows that it has been tainted tells them how she was warned by someone else not to let them drink it. Her words are introduced with *chiga*:

(10) *Aswa-ta   wa   wa   wa   paska-k-guna, yayta upi-shka-una.*
     aswa-ACC IDEO IDEO IDEO open-AG-PL   lots   drink-PRF-PL

     Chiga   *"Chasna=mi shuk runa   shamu-sha=ga rima-n*
     And then Like then=EV one person come-COR=TOP speak-3SG

     'Ama   upi-naw-chun'   ni-sha."
     NEG   drink-3PL-SBJV say-COR
     'Opening up the *aswa wa wa wa*, the openers drank lots of it.[6] **And then**, (she said) "That's what one man, having come here, said not to do, saying 'let them not drink it."

One final function of *chiga* in discourse must be mentioned. It is often used in casual conversations for phatic communication (Jakobson 1960, 355), as a back-channel cue, when one speaker is holding the floor. In such a situation, the speaker holding the floor will pause slightly at periodic intervals and wait for the other speaker to simply say *chiga* 'and then. . .', which indicates that they are ratifying that person's rights to continue speaking.

---

5 In Tena Quichua, *chiga* is not used with the same frequency as it is in Pastaza Quichua. Alternative expressions such as *shinakpi* 'like-that-being-so' fulfill similar functions for Tena speakers, however.

6 *Wa* is an ideophone that simulates an idea of something being opened, exposed, or otherwise revealed. Here, the image of opening refers to the opening of the storage jars holding the *aswa* pulp, by lifting off the leaves tied over their tops.

4.2 *The Distal Spatial meaning of* chi

In order to analyze the spatial meaning of *chi*, we decided to ask speakers to focus on possible differences between *chi* and *chay* (which has yet to be discussed). At this point in our investigation, we were hypothesizing that *chi* 'that' would be used for objects that were not close to the deictic center, but not very far away. We thought there might be a three-way, gradient distinction between *kay* 'this', *chi* 'that', and *chay* 'that', with *chay* being used for something very far from the deictic center. We therefore conducted short interviews consisting of two questions.

First of all, we asked about something that was far away but still visible. As trees are very salient in everyday Quichua life, and are easy to locate in space, we used a tree as the object of our locational queries. One tree in particular, *Erythrina poeppigiana* in the *Fabaceae-Papil* family, is quite easy to pick out from other trees because it blooms periodically, with bright orange-red flowers and is therefore easy to focus upon, even from far away. We were interested in determining whether speakers would use *chi* or *chay* for a tree that was visible but quite far away. We hypothesized that *chay* would be used by most speakers because of the distant location of the tree.

We conducted a series of short interviews with seven speakers of Pastaza Quichua and another set of seven different speakers of Tena Quichua. We asked them to judge the acceptability of two sentences, differing only in their use of demonstratives. We stood near the shore of the Napo River and pointed to one of these trees situated on the opposite side of its banks, about one half kilometer away, that was easily distinguished from its surroundings as the only bright red flowering tree. This tree, called the *chuku* tree by both Tena and Pastaza speakers, was pointed to as we asked in Quichua, 'What will I say? "Is it way over there" or "Is it over there?"' The Quichua script we used was as follows:

Chuku ruya tiya-n, mana=chu? Ima-ta ni-sha? "Chay-ma
chuku tree be.located-3SG not=NEG What-INT say-1FUT There-DAT

tiya-n"   o "chi-ma tiya-n?"
be.located-3SG $or there-DAT be.located-3SG
'There is a *chuku* tree (pointing across the river), right? What will I say?: "It's located **way over there**" or "it's located **over there?**"'

DEMONSTRATIVE DEIXIS IN TWO DIALECTS OF AMAZONIAN QUICHUA   85

Of our 14 speakers, the majority, ten altogether, answered that *Chi-ma tiyan* 'It's located over there' was the correct choice.[7] Examples that follow are a sample of the participants' responses. Each participant is given an initial derived from the first letter of their name:

(11) R: (Pointing) Ñuka   chuku   yura-ra   riku-sha   rima-ni
                     I   chuku   tree-ACC   see-COR   say-1SG

                  "chi-ma   shaya-w-n."
                  there-DAT   stand-DUR-3SG
                  'Seeing the *chuku* tree, I say, "**over there** it stands".'

(12) E: (pointing with arm extended)   *Chi-ma.*
                                        there-DAT
                                        '(It's) **over there**.'

(13) J: (pointing) **Chi-bi**   shaya-w-n   yura, o   **chi-ma**
                there-LOC   stand-DUR-3SG   tree $or there-DAT

                shaya-w-n. (pointing with chin)
                stand-DUR-3SG
                '**There** (literally: in that place) the tree stands or **over there** it stands.'[8]

(14) B: **Chi -ma**   tiya-n   chimba-ma   chi   chuku   ruya.
           there-DAT   be.located-3SG across-DAT   that   chuku   tree
           'It's **over there** (pointing with arm), across (the river) that *chuku* tree.'

Given the majority of responses from speakers of both Pastaza and Tena Quichua, in favor of *chi*, and the unequivocal way in which our question was answered, we feel confident in asserting that the demonstrative *chi*, when used

---

7 Only one speaker, a young female speaker of the Tena dialect, gave *chayma* as the correct answer. Two speakers rephrased the answer in a way that avoided using either of the given choices. One woman from Pastaza said that both *chi* and *chay* were possible answers.

8 We are translating *chibi* as 'there' (literally 'in that') and *chima* as 'over there' (literally 'toward that') because of the locative and dative suffixes with which they occur.

with dative or locative suffixes, expresses the distal meanings of 'there' or 'over there', in contrast with the proximal meanings of *kay* 'here'.

5 The Distal Spatial Demonstrative *chay* 'that'

We now turn to the demonstrative *chay*. Our expectation was that the differences encoded by the demonstratives *chi* and *chay* would involve gradience, and that *chay* would be used comparatively, for distances greater than *chi*. The next question in our interview was therefore built upon the first question, but this time we asked about a hypothetical tree which was so far downriver that it could not even be seen. We expected *chay* to be used by everyone for this much farther away tree. Instead, we discovered that only seven of our interviewees answered with *chayma*, which we translate as 'way over there', while the rest continued to say that it was just *chima* 'over there', and pointed in the downriver direction with an extended arm.[9] Our script for this question follows:

Chi-manda=ga,	*shuk*	*chuku*	*ruya*	*tiya-n-ma*		*yaku*
then-ABL=TOP	one	chuku	tree	be.located-3SG-COND		water

uray-bi		*mana*	*rikwi-bak=chu*	*tiya-n.*		*Ima-ta*	*ni-ni:*
downriver-LOC		NEG	see-BEN=NEG	be.located-3SG		What-INT	say-1SG

"Chuku	*ruya*	*tiya-n*		*chay-ma"*	*o*	*"chuku*	*ruya*	*tiya-n*
Chuku	tree	be.located-3SG		there-DAT	$or	chuku	tree	be.located-3SG

chi-ma?"
there-DAT
'Well then, another *chuku* tree might be downriver—not visible, it (might) be there. What do I say? "The *chuku* tree is **way over there**" or "the *chuku* tree is **over there?**"'

Sample responses from those who gave *chi-ma* 'over there' as their answer, include the following:

---

9 These results are complicated by the fact that two of these seven respondents gave *chayma* for an answer to Nuckolls' interview, and then gave *chima* for an answer to Ramirez Spencer when she conducted the same interview.

DEMONSTRATIVE DEIXIS IN TWO DIALECTS OF AMAZONIAN QUICHUA 87

(15) B: *Mana   rikwi-bak,   "chi-ma"   tiya-n.*
        NEG   see-BEN   that-DAT   be.located-3SG
        '(If) not see-able (we say) it's **over there**.'

(16) E: (pointing)   ***Chi-ma,   uray-ma.***
        there-DAT   downriver-DAT
        'It's **over there**, downriver.'

It is, however, possible that an inherent design flaw in our questioning procedure resulted in *chima* being given as an answer by so many of our consultants. In other words, it is possible that, by referring to a place downriver where
another tree was standing, but not visible, we unwittingly laid the groundwork
for *chi*, since its anaphoric usage depends upon what has already been referred
to. This is not a question that could easily be resolved by eliciting metapragmatic commentary from speakers. However, this design flaw in our procedure
needs to be acknowledged as a constraint. In the next section we turn to a
discussion of *chay*, beginning with those who gave *chay* for an answer to our
question.

5.1   *The Distal Spatial Use of* chay

What is interesting about those who responded to our question about the
not visible tree with *chay*, is that most of them were Tena speakers. Only two
Pastaza speakers that we spoke with used *chay* in answer to this question.
Examples of speakers' responses using *chayma* 'way over there' follow:

(17) J: *Mana   rikwi-bak,   "chay-ma."*
        NEG   see-BEN   that-DAT
        '(If) not visible, (we say) "**way over there**".'

Another speaker who used *chayma* included a rare metalinguistic reflection:

(18) R: (pointing)   ***"Chayyy-ma   shaya-w-n,"   mana   rikwi-bak;   Mana***
        thaaat-DAT   stand-DUR-3SG   NEG   see-BEN   NEG

        serto-ra   rima-nchi,   "chay-ma"   ni-nchi.
        $certain-ADV   speak-1PL   that-DAT   say-1PL
        '"**Waaay over there** it is standing" (we say when) it isn't
        visible; (When) we don't speak with certainty we say "**way
        over there**".'

This example is also significant as it reveals that *chay* undergoes expressive lengthening of the first syllable to communicate an idea of greater distance. Furthermore, its expressive lengthening is congenial with statements made by other Tena speakers, and observed by Swanson. For example, an airplane flying overhead at night was described by one woman as *chayyyma* 'waaay over there'. In another instance, a deer that was spotted at the outermost edges of an extensive property was described by a man as being *chayyyma* 'way over there'.

It seems obvious that speakers who used *chay* were clear about its spatial, distal meaning. Yet, there was an equal number of speakers, from both Pastaza and Tena, who chose *chima* 'over there' as their answer to the question about the not visible tree. In addition to the possibility of a design flaw in our questioning, resulting from the fact that *chi* has an anaphoric function, and that it refers to a 'that' or a 'there' which has already been mentioned, another problem with our interviews was the small sample size of our speakers, which could not possibly have given us an adequate picture of the uses of *chay*.

We therefore consulted our narrative transcripts of Pastaza and Tena dialect speakers, where we found examples of *chay* to express spatial, distal meanings. These usages of *chay* involved either an instance of something located in an unknown place, or in a far away place, or simply in a place that had not already been referred to. The next example, from a Pastaza narrative, illustrates the use of *chay* to point to a spatially unknown location. It is from a traditional narrative that relates how a man was followed by a forest spirit. In this extract, the man has just been examined by the curious forest spirit as he pretends to sleep. Finally, he can endure it no longer, and jumps up from his prone position and runs away, while at the same time throwing his ax. The place that he throws the ax is described as *chay*, most probably *not* because it was thrown a great distance, but more likely because it was thrown to an unknown location. Although the word *chay* is not expressively lengthened here, it is pronounced louder and followed by a noticeable pause:

(19) *Pay-ba   hacha pulʸu-ta   chay* (pause) *ichu-sha=shi   kalʸpa-shka.*
      he-POSS $ax   piece-ACC that   abandon-COR=EV run-PRF
      'Abandoning his piece of ax **over there** (pause), he ran off.'

The narrator uses *chay*, we believe, because it would not be appropriate to use either *kay* or *chi*. The protagonist is throwing the ax away from his deictic center, which eliminates *kay* as a possible demonstrative. He is, moreover, throwing the ax to a location that has not yet been referred to in the narrative.

DEMONSTRATIVE DEIXIS IN TWO DIALECTS OF AMAZONIAN QUICHUA 89

This means that *chi* cannot be used either. Not only has the location of the thrown ax not yet been mentioned in the narrative, it has also not been explicitly identified by the narrator. Nor is it even important to know where it was thrown. Once the throwing of the ax is mentioned, however, its exact location is still unknown and unknowable. It simply does not matter exactly where it was thrown, just as it did not matter exactly where in the sky the airplane was flying, exactly where on a property, a deer was spotted, or exactly where downriver a flowering tree was located.

An additional example demonstrating the use of *chay* for unknown locations follows. It is taken from a narrative that is traditional for both Pastaza and Tena speakers, called the *Tihiras anga* or 'Scissortail hawk' story, although the extract comes from a Pastaza version of the story. We translate *chay-bi*, which literally would mean 'in that location' or 'there', with our own 'there-ever' to communicate the uncertainty of the location.

(20) *Chi-ga   runa-guna   may   chari   chagra-shka,   sara   chagra*
     then   person-PL   where perhaps field-PRF   corn   field

     ***chay-bi**=shi   pay-ba   sara-ta   shuwa-sha=shi   miku-g   a-ra.*
     there-LOC=EV she-POSS corn-ACC steal-COR=EV eat-AG be-PAST
     'So then, wherever, perhaps, people made cornfields, **there-ever**, they say, stealing their corn, she would eat.'

In this example, it is not great distance, but rather, the unknown location that is pointed to with *chay*.

The next example from a Tena narrative features the use of *chay* to point to a distant location. It is taken from a flood narrative and describes how people escaped the rising waters by fleeing to a far away, treeless mountain:

(21) *Tuta   manzhari-sha   tuta   urku-ra   kalʲpa-ja-sha   **chay-ma***
     night   afraid-COR   night   mountain-ACC run-DUR-COR that-DAT

     lʲushti   urku.
     bare   mountain
     'At night, being scared, they were running to a mountain **over there**, to a bare mountain (literally: naked mountain, or treeless mountain).'

The spatial, distal functions of *chay* encompass the interrelated meanings of unknown location, distant location, or previously unspecified location. It is not difficult to understand how these three different aspects of the meaning of *chay* might shade imperceptibly into each other. What is extremely distant is also likely to be not very well known. What is foregrounded in discourse because it is unknown is also not likely to have been previously specified. We turn now to a discussion of the discourse functions of *chay*, functions that exploit its complex semantics in everyday conversation as well as in narrative.

5.2 *The Discourse Functions of* chay

In discourse, there are two main functions for the demonstrative *chay*. Both functions use the semantics of *chay*, especially the aspect of its meaning involving unknown location, to communicate an awareness of something startling or surprising. This is the fundamental notion underlying the concept of mirativity (DeLancey 1997). However, we are not certain whether we can claim that mirativity is encoded in *chay*, or whether it is an implicature. More research is called for. In casual conversation, when one speaker upsets the previously held understandings of another, then *chay* will be uttered by the startled party (as if to say 'Wow!' or 'That's amazing!' or 'That's completely different from what I thought was the case.'). As an example of this function, one evening in the summer of 2011, two Pastaza speakers were sitting with Nuckolls by the shores of the Napo River at dusk, and we all suddenly heard a high-pitched sound coming from the water. Both Pastaza speakers suddenly exclaimed *chay!* and speculated about the source of the sound.

A similar use of *chay* to indicate a startled or surprised reaction can be observed in a traditional Pastaza horror story about a spirit called the *Huri huri* spirit, who eats all of the greenery in the forest right before the really horrific forest spirit called *Amasanga* comes. At the narrative moment in which the following extract occurs, the first *Huri huri* spirits have begun to make their sounds uncomfortably near the people. Once these sounds are heard, the woman who tried to warn everyone earlier exclaims *chay!* and then tells them they should have believed her:

(22) *Ña   unanig chishi-lʸay=shi   "huri   huri   huri   huri   huri   huri*
    then later   afternoon-LIM=EV IDEO   IDEO   IDEO   IDEO   IDEO   IDEO

    huri   huri   huri   huri=shi" ni-ra   kay-ma   shuk   kay-ma
    IDEO   IDEO   IDEO   IDEO=EV say-PAST this-DAT one   this-DAT

    Shukshi ni-ra;   "Chay-ga! Kunan-ga uya-y!   Pay   ni-k-ta
    one-EV   say-PAST That-TOP Now-TOP listen-IMP He   say-AG-ACC

DEMONSTRATIVE DEIXIS IN TWO DIALECTS OF AMAZONIAN QUICHUA 91

kasna-ta   *kan-guna*   *mana*   *kiri-wa-ra-ngichi=chu."*
like.this-ADV   you-PL   NEG   believe-1ACC-PAST-1PL=NEG
'Then, later, just in the afternoon, they say, it said: '*huri huri huri huri huri huri huri huri huri huri*'; one here, another here (as they fell on the ground), apparently, it said (like that). '**There!**' (said the woman) 'Now listen! You-all didn't believe that he said (it would happen) like this'.'

Although we have not found any evidence for the exclamative *chay* in Tena narrative, we have observed its use in everyday contexts. What follows is an example of *chay*, which may indicate surprise or far away distance or both simultaneously. It is from a casual conversation observed by Swanson:

(23) K: *Kam-ba*   *wawa-una*   *may-bi-ra*   *estudia-nun?*   *Quitu-y?*
       you-POSS   child-PL   where-LOC-ADV $study-3PL   Quito-LOC
       'Where are your children studying? In Quito?'

      S: *Mana.*   *Arizona-y*   *estudia-nun.*
       NEG   Arizon-LOC $study-3PL
       'No, in Arizona.'

      K: *Chay-ma!*
       that-DAT
       '(Oh!) **Over there!**'

Although it is not certain whether the above usage of *chay* is expressing extreme distance or surprise, or possibly both, it is certainly true that our Tena narratives reveal only scant use of *chay*, compared to our Pastaza narratives. One Tena speaker claimed to not use it at all, saying that it was something used by Pastaza speakers. The demonstrative *chay* is the most different in terms of its rate of usage, between the two dialects, if we are only looking at narrative data, an issue to be addressed in our conclusions.

In order to determine whether speakers could spontaneously think of examples where *chay* would be used only for surprise, Swanson asked speakers if they could think of situations where *chay* would be used this way. He elicited the following response:

(24) *Maykan*   *auto*   *takari-kpi*   *"Chay=ga*   *ni-sha*   *rima-nchi.*   *Ima-shina*
     which $car   hit-SWRF   That=TOP   say-COR   speak-1PL   What-how

     takari-huna-ra-y!"
     hit-RECP-ACC-NML
     'When some car crashes we say "**There!** (Look) how they were crashing!"'

In addition to *chay*, another exclamative, *ching!* is also used by Tena speakers. It is not exactly the same as *chay*, however, and we are certain that it is unrelated to *chi*, despite its appearance.[10] For Tena speakers, it is used to express surprise at the appearance of something that has been foretold or warned about. In the case of *ching*, the speaker is transferring his or her surprise, and projecting it onto a listener, as if to say, 'Aren't you surprised that this has happened (although I, myself, am not)!' An English speaker might express the same sentiment with "See, I told you so!" A situation where *ching* might be used is described below:

(25) *Kari wawa muntun puglʸa-y kachari-nu-kpi rima-nchi "Ama*
       boy   little group   play-NML   send-3PL-SWRF speak-1PL NEG

     shina puglʸa-ychi=chu. Susuri-ngichi=mi." Chi rima-shka washa
     like   play-IMP.PL=NEG   Mess-2PL=EV   That speak-PRF after

     kungaylʸay waka-sha kapari-nun. Chi-ta uya-sha ñukanchi
     suddenly   cry-COR   scream-3PL That-ACC hear-COR we

     rima-nchi "Ching! Shina=mi susuri-ngichi ni-kpi   mana
     speak-1PL Ching   like=EV   mess-1PL   say-SWRF NEG

     uya-ka-ngichi."
     hear-PAST-2PL
     'When we send a group of boys out to play we say "Don't play (i.e. roughly) like that. You will get hurt!" Then after we have said that they suddenly shout out crying. When we hear that we say, "**Ching!** You get hurt like that because you don't listen".'

6 Discussion and Conclusions

The main contribution of this paper has been to elucidate a three-way distinction for the demonstrative systems of Pastaza and Tena Quichua. We conclude, based on evidence from narratives, informal conversations, and structured elicitations, that both dialects use all three demonstratives, in both proximal/

---

10   *Ching* is most certainly related to an ideophone widely used in Pastaza Quichua, *dzing*, which expresses a surprised, sudden awareness of something, especially something that causes fright (see Nuckolls 1996).

distal as well as discourse functions. *Kay* encodes proximal meaning and functions in discourse to focus interlocutors' attention on newly introduced topics. *Chi* is the 'workhorse' demonstrative for these two varieties, and is used abundantly in discourse to refer to what is not spatially immediate and to what has already been mentioned. Its reference is therefore anaphoric and it functions to build coherence within texts.

The other demonstrative glossed as 'that', *chay*, is used much less frequently than either *chi* or *kay*, and in particular, it is used much less frequently in Tena narratives than in Pastaza narratives. It points to a 'that' which may be spatially farther than *chi*, or, alternatively, it points to something that someone may not have previously mentioned, or it points to an entity or place that is unknown. In discourse, *chay* indicates an unprepared mind on the part of a speaker or narrator, which probably carries an implicature of surprise. The mirative meaning of *chay* is more often found in Pastaza than in Tena narratives. Some metapragmatic commentary also supports these observations from narratives. This may, however, have more to do with our small narrative samples from Tena speakers, than with the actual facts of narrative usage.

An additional finding has to do with the two dialects themselves, and their status as dialects. We wondered whether demonstrative usage in narratives was different enough between the two dialects to be statistically significant. Before addressing this problem, however, we must admit at the outset, that although we have a good number of Tena consultants, our Tena speakers are mostly from one large extended family living on the South bank of the Napo River between Tena and Ahuano. Our Pastaza speakers come from somewhat more diverse backgrounds, mainly two different communities along the Bobonaza River, Puka Yaku and Canelos. We cannot, therefore, claim a representative sample.[11] Nevertheless, if we look at tables 3.1 and 3.2, we can see that there are some stark percentage differences between uses of the demonstrative *chay* in Pastaza and in Tena, namely that *chay* accounts for about 10% of all demonstratives used by Pastaza narrators, while Tena narrators' use was far below that figure, at 0.24%.

---

11   We have extensive Pastaza narratives from many different speakers, although our featured examples from the narratives and interviews are drawn from seven different speakers. We have drawn from seven Tena speakers for our narratives and interviews, however, our total pages of Tena narratives are fewer.

94   NUCKOLLS ET AL.

TABLE 3.1   *Occurrences of* kay, chi, *and* chay *in over 5,720 words of recorded data from the Pastaza dialect and their frequency of use with respect to the total number of words and demonstratives*

Demonstrative	Occurrences	Percentage of total words	Percentage of total demonstratives
kay	102	1.78%	22.37%
chi	306	5.35%	67.10%
chay	48	0.84%	10.53%
Total	456	7.97%	

TABLE 3.2   *Occurrences of* kay, chi, *and* chay *in over 5,720 words of recorded narrative data from the Tena dialect and their frequency of use with respect to the total number of words and demonstratives*

Demonstrative	Occurrences	Percentage of total words	Percentage of total demonstratives
kay	94	1.64%	23.54%
chi	317	5.54%	76.94%
chay	1	0.02%	0.24%
Total	412	7.20%	

If we attempt to evaluate these differences with a measure of their significance, using chi-square as a tool, we find that the two dialects vary enough in demonstrative usage as a whole, to be considered statistically significant ($\chi^2(2)$ = 43.5, p <.001). Therefore, there is a relationship between the dialect spoken and the frequency of the use of the demonstratives *kay, chi,* and *chay*.

Tables 3.1 and 3.2 also reveal the interesting finding that demonstratives, whatever their function, amount to a very small percentage of the total number of words in our texts. They account for only about 8% of total words in Pastaza, and about 7% of all words in Tena narratives. Yet, these closed-class function words make incalculably large contributions to Pastaza and Tena speakers' abilities to refer, to expressively point to, to comment on, and to jointly focus upon, a variety of spatial and conceptual aspects of their experience. Our findings suggest that future research is needed on the syntactic behavior of demonstratives, which has not been examined within this study. Further work on the interconnections between the mirative use of demonstratives and other expressions of mirativity within Quichua grammar could shed additional light on the complex features and workings of Quichua's demonstrative system.

Appendix A

1	first person	ICH	inchoative
2	second person	IDEO	ideophone
3	third person	IMP	imperative
$	borrowed from Spanish	INCL	inclusive
AA	accusative OR adverbializer	INS	instrumental
	(the suffix -ta could be either	INT	interrogative
	and is contextually determined)	LIM	limitative
ABL	ablative	LOC	locative
ACC	accusative	NEG	negation
ADV	adverbializing suffix	NML	nominalizer
AG	agentive	PAST	past
BEN	benefactive	PL	plural
COM	comitative	POSS	possessive
COND	conditional	PRF	perfect
COR	coreference	RECP	reciprocal
DAT	dative	SBJV	subjunctive
DUR	durative	SG	singular
EV	evidential	SWRF	switch reference
FUT	future	TOP	topicalizer

Appendix B

List of *kay*, *chi*, and *chay* and the variants of each of these included in our calculations, as well as the total number of instances of each variant over the 5,720 words of recorded narrative data from the Pastaza dialect.

TABLE 3.3   *Variants and instances of* kay, chi, *and* chay *used from Pastaza dialect*

Kay and its variants	Total # of instances	*Chi* and its variants	Total # of instances	*Chay* and its variants	Total # of instances
kay this	50	*chi* that	146	*chay* that	19
kay-bi this-LOC	1	*chi=ga* that=TOP	89	*chay-bi* that-LOC	1
kay=ga this=TOP	2	*chi-gama* that-until	1	*chay=ga* that=TOP	8
kay-gama this-until	1	*chi-gama=ga* that-until=TOP	1	*chay-gama-lʲa* that-until-LIM	1
kay-guna this-PL	1	*chi-guna* that-PL	2	*chay-lʲa-y* that-LIM-LOC	2
kay-guna=ga this-PL=TOP	1	*chi-guna=ga* that-PL=TOP	1	*chay-lʲa-y-ta* that-LIM-LOC-AA	3
kay-guna-ta this-PL-AA	1	*chi-guna-ta* that-PL-AA	1	*chay-ma* that-DAT	3
kay-guna-was this-PL-INCL	1	*chi-guna-wan* that-PL-INS	1	*chay-manda-lʲa* that-ABL-LIM	2
kay-lʲa this-LIM	2	*chi-lʲa* that-LIM	1	*chay-pi* that-LOC	5
kay-lʲa-y this-LIM-LOC	1	*chi-lʲa-y* that-LIM-LOC	4	*chay-ta* that-AA	3
kaylʲa-ya-shka near-ICH-PRF	1	*chi-lʲa-n* that-LIM-INS	1	*chay-wan* that-INS	1
kay-ma this-DAT	11	*chi-lʲa-wan* that-LIM-INS	3		
kay-manda this-ABL	4	*chi-lʲa-ta* that-LIM-AA	2		
kay-manda=chu this-ABL=NEG	6	*chi=mi* that=EV	4		

DEMONSTRATIVE DEIXIS IN TWO DIALECTS OF AMAZONIAN QUICHUA   97

Kay and its variants	Total # of instances	*Chi* and its variants	Total # of instances	*Chay* and its variants	Total # of instances
kay=mi this=EV	2	*chi-ma* that-DAT	1		
kay-pi this-LOC	6	*chi-ma-y* that-DAT-LOC	1		
kay-pi=chu this-LOC=NEG	2	*chi-ma=ga* that-DAT=TOP	1		
kay-ta this-ADV	8	*chi-manda* this-ABL	9		
kay-wan this-INS	1	*chi-manda=ga* that-ABL=TOP	1		
		chi-manda-lˠa that-ABL-LIM	1		
		chi-pi that-LOC	1		
		chi-ta that-AA	16		
		chi-ta-ga that-AA=TOP	4		
		chi-ta-s that-AA-INCL	1		
		chi-ta=mi that-AA=EV	2		
		chi-ta-was that-ACC-INCL	1		
		chi-wan that-INS	10		
Total	102	Total	306	Total	48

Appendix C

List of *kay*, *chi*, and *chay* and the variants included in our calculations, as well as the total number of instances of each variant over the 5,720 words of recorded narrative data from the Tena dialect.

TABLE 3.4 *Variants and instances of* kay, chi, *and* chay *used from Tena dialect*

Kay and its variants	Total # of instances	*Chi* and its variants	Total # of instances	*Chay* and its variants	Total # of instances
kay this	64	*chi* that	221	*chay-ma* that-DAT	1
kay-bi this-LOC	4	*chi-bi* that-LOC	32		
kay-bi=mi this-LOC=EV	1	*chi-bi=ga* that-LOC=TOP	1		
kay=ga this=TOP	2	*chi-bi=mi* that-LOC=EV	2		
kay-ma this-DAT	11	*chi-bi-mari* that-LOC-EV	1		
kay-ma-ɓa-ra this-DAT-LIM-ADV	3	*chi=ga* that=TOP	9		
kay-manda this-ABL	2	*chi-gama* that-until	1		
kay-manda-ɓa-ra this-ABL-LIM-ADV	2	*chi-gama-s* that-until-INCL	1		
kay-ta this-AA	4	*chi-guna=mi* that-PL=EV	1		
kay-ta=mi this-AA=EV	1	*chi-kuna* that-PL	1		
		chi-ɓa-y that-LIM-LOC	4		
		chi-ma that-DAT	9		
		chi-ma-ɓa that-DAT-LIM	1		
		chi-ma-ɓa-ra that-DAT-LIM-ADV	1		

Kay and its variants	Total # of instances	Chi and its variants	Total # of instances	Chay and its variants	Total # of instances
		chi-manda that-ABL	13		
		chi-manda=ga that-ABL=TOP	1		
		chi-manda=mi that-ABL=EV	2		
		chi-manda-wa that-ABL-INS	1		
		chi-mari that-EV	1		
		chi-ma-s that-DAT-INCL	1		
		chi=mi that=EV	1		
		chi-ta that-AA	7		
		chi-wa that-INS	5		
Total	94	Total	317	Total	1

Bibliography

Catta Quelen, Javier. 1994. *Gramática del Quichua Ecuatoriano*. Third edition. Quito: Abya-Yala.

Cole, Peter. 1982. *Lingua Descriptive Studies: Imbabura Quechua*. Amsterdam: North-Holland Publishing Company.

DeLancey, Scott. 1997. "Mirativity: The Grammatical Marking of Unexpected Information." *Linguistic Typology* 1: 33–52.

Diessel, Holger. 2006. "Demonstratives, Joint Attention, and the Emergence of Grammar." *Cognitive Linguistics* 17(4):463–89.

Fraser, Bruce. 1999. "What are discourse markers?" *Journal of Pragmatics* 31(7):931–52.

Hanks, William F. 2012. Foreword "Evidentiality in Social Interaction" to *Evidentiality in Interaction*, edited by Janis B. Nuckolls and Lev Michael. *Pragmatics and Society*, Special Issue 3(2):169–80. Amsterdam/Philadelphia: John Benjamins Publishing Company.

Himmelman, Nikolaus. 1996. "Demonstratives in Narrative Discourse: A Taxonomy of Universal Uses." In *Studies in Anaphora*, edited by Barbara Fox, 206–54. Amsterdam/Philadelphia: John Benjamins Publishing Company.

Irvine, Judith T. 1998. "Ideologies of Honorific Language." In *Language Ideologies: Practice and Theory*, edited by Bambi Schieffelin, Kathryn Woolard, and Paul Kroskrity, 51–68. New York: Oxford University Press.

Jakobson, Roman. 1960. "Closing Statement: Linguistics and Poetics." In *Style in Language*, edited by Thomas A. Sebeok, 350–77. New York: John Wiley & Sons, Inc.

———. 1971. "Word and Language." Vol. 2 of *Selected Writings*, edited by Stephen Rudy. The Hague: Mouton.

Lema Guanolema, Segundo Francisco. 1997. *Gramática del Quichua*. Quito: Abya-Yala.

McNeill, David. 1992. *Hand and Mind*. Chicago: University of Chicago Press.

Mithun, Marianne. 1987. "The Grammatical Nature and Discourse Power of Demonstratives." Proceedings of the Thirteenth Annual Meetings of the Berkeley Linguistics Society, 184–94. http://elanguage.net/journals/bls/article/view/2499/2466.

Múgica, P. Camilo. 1967. *Aprenda el Quichua: Gramática y Vocabularios*. Aguarico: Edita CICAME, Prefectura Apostólica del Aguarico, Ecuador.

Nuckolls, Janis B. 1996. *Sounds Like Life: Sound-Symbolic Grammar, Performance and Cognition in Pastaza Quichua*. New York: Oxford University Press.

———. 2012. "From Quotative Other to Quotative Self in Pastaza Quichua Evidential Usage." In *Evidentiality in Interaction*, edited by Janis B. Nuckolls and Lev Michael. *Pragmatics and Society* Special Issue, 3(2):226–42. Amsterdam/Philadelphia: John Benjamins Publishing Company.

Nuckolls, Janis B., Joseph Stanley, Elizabeth Nielsen, and Roseanna Hopper. forthcoming. "The Systematic Stretching and Contracting of Ideophonic Phonology in Pastaza Quichua." International Journal of American Linguistics.

O'Rourke, Erin and Tod Swanson. 2013. "Tena Quichua." *Journal of the International Phonetic Association* 43(1):107–20.

Orr, Caroline and Betsy Wrisley. 1981. *Vocabulario Quichua del Oriente*. Quito: Abya-Yala.

Peirce, Charles S. 1955. "Logic as Semiotic: The Theory of Signs." In *Philosophical Writings of Peirce*, edited by Justus Buchler, 98–119. New York: Dover.

Ross, Ellen. 1979. *Introduction to Ecuador Highland Quechua*. Madison: Foundation for Inter-Andean Development.

Vásquez Suárez, P. Víctor. 1992. *Aprendamos Quichua: Runa Shimita Yachacushun*. Quito: Abya-Yala.

CHAPTER 4

Child Acquisition of Quechua Evidentiality and Deictic Meaning

Ellen H. Courtney

1   Introduction

This investigation presents data that shed light on the development of the evidential system in Peruvian children acquiring Cuzco Quechua[1] as their first language. Quechua-speaking children are faced with a daunting acquisitional challenge because the evidential morphemes encode several related but distinct deictic meanings. Acquisition of these morphemes is difficult to investigate because they express often subtle distinctions in the ways we perceive and think about events; these cognitive processes are not directly observable. Therefore, to explore the acquisition of this complex system, three types of data were gathered: naturalistic speech, experimental data and elicited story retellings. The logical starting point entailed examination of children's spontaneous production of the morphemes. Naturalistic data have limitations that hinder straightforward analysis, but even tentative analysis of naturalistic data yields useful working hypotheses. Thereafter, an experimental procedure and a story-retelling task were developed to fine-tune these working hypotheses by observing different aspects of children's comprehension and production of the morphemes.

Previous studies investigating the development of evidential systems in a number of languages yield the same outcome: the path to full understanding and adult-like production of evidential morphemes is a protracted process involving early production of forms with delayed and gradual acquisition of the associated meanings and functions. It is not surprising that the development of evidential competence should be a protracted process, since the acquisition of grammatical forms encoding information source relates to cognitive development, specifically children's theory of mind. As noted by Papafragou (2002, 62), "the ability to reason evidentially about the origins ... of our beliefs is part of our ability to reason about mental states in general." Insofar as belief is a mental state, understanding the sources of information underlying one's

---

1   In the remainder of this chapter, 'Cuzco Quechua' will be referred to simply as 'Quechua.'

© KONINKLIJKE BRILL NV, LEIDEN, 2015 | DOI 10.1163/9789004290105_005

beliefs and those of others is an essential milestone in the development of theory of mind.

This study begins with a review of the ongoing debate among linguists regarding the essential nature of evidential morphemes (section 2), followed by a brief presentation of previous investigations of the development of evidential systems in children acquiring different languages (section 3). Thereafter, the highlights of the Quechua evidential system will be briefly discussed (section 4). Section 5 presents the naturalistic, experimental, and story-retelling data. The final goal of this study is to sketch a picture of the acquisitional process observed in Quechua-speaking children by comparing, contrasting and consolidating the findings obtained through the three investigations.

2 Evidentiality: Information Source and Epistemic Modality

Willett (1988) discussed the basic evidential distinctions observed across languages. He asserted that the overarching semantic contrast in evidential systems distinguishes direct and indirect information source, and indirect information source, in turn, may be hearsay or observed results, etc. Languages differ widely in the formal means available for conveying evidentiary information (Aikhenvald 2004, Plungian 2001). In many languages, evidential distinctions are encoded in the morphology; that is, morphemes such as evidential enclitics and distinct verb forms indicate the source of the speaker's information. Korean and Turkish, for example, rely on a pair of contrasting past-tense morphemes used to express several evidential distinctions. Quechua exhibits distinct evidential enclitics in addition to contrasting past-tense inflections. Given this variety of morphemes, Quechua is an ideal candidate for investigating the acquisition of evidential meaning.

There are three evidential enclitics available to Quechua speakers: DIRECT EVIDENCE *-mi* (allomorph: *-n*), CONJECTURE *-chá*, and REPORTATIVE *-si* (allomorph: *-s*), and these perform double duty as markers of different deictic contrasts and sentence focus (Muysken 1995, Sánchez 2010). Additionally, there are two distinct past-tense inflections in Quechua, herein labeled EXPERIENCED PAST *-r(q)a* [PST] and NON-EXPERIENCED PAST *-sqa* [NX], following Cerrón-Palomino (1994) and Faller (2004). These labels aptly capture the important spatiotemporal deictic distinction encoded in the two morphemes, which will be discussed in section 4, describing the Quechua evidential system.

Whereas evidentials encode the speaker's source of information for particular statements, epistemic modality indicates relative speaker certainty, i.e., the speaker's degree of commitment to the truth of a proposition. Information source (evidentiality) and certainty of knowledge (epistemic modality) are related. Matsui and Fitneva (2009, 4) aptly characterize the relationship:

> If you hear someone claim that something *must be* the case, you may infer that he has strong evidence to support the claim. Conversely, if someone says that she witnessed an event directly, you may infer that she is certain about the truthfulness of the report.

While acknowledging a relationship between evidentiality and epistemic modality, linguists offer conflicting proposals regarding the precise nature of this relationship. Some claim that epistemic modality is a broad category, with evidentiality falling within the semantic scope of modality (e.g., Palmer 2001, Trask 1999). Many others assert that information source and certainty are distinct conceptual categories or that certainty is merely an epistemic extension of the primary, evidential meaning (e.g., Aikhenvald 2004, DeLancey 2001). For Quechua, this position is supported by Faller (2002).

The view that certainty is an extension of evidential meaning is upheld by de Haan (2005), who claims that evidentiality is a deictic category whereby evidential morphemes fundamentally encode the relative distance between speakers and the events they describe. He compares evidentiality to spatial deixis (physical distance between speaker and object) and temporal deixis (time). He refers to evidentiality as propositional deixis because it relates to the distance between a speaker and an entire proposition. Accordingly, a speaker will make use of an indirect evidential when a particular event occurs outside his/her deictic sphere or if he/she wishes to represent it as such; in like manner, direct evidentials are reserved for events that are expressed as taking place within the speaker's deictic sphere. Arguing that evidential deixis pertains to distance in terms of information source, de Haan claims that epistemic modality is not the essential meaning encoded in evidential morphemes.

Mushin (2000) advocates a broader approach, whereby evidential morphemes serve the additional deictic function of indicating the speaker's epistemological stance or point of view; in this regard, she characterizes evidential coding as epistemological deixis. This pragmatic-deictic function is especially noteworthy in narrative discourse, where the speaker's repertoire of evidential morphemes allows him/her to shift perspective—the deictic center—from the storyteller and audience in the real world to the characters in the story world. According to this view, evidential marking serves not merely to encode information source but also to shift perspective, and, consequently, narrative discourse yields instances of mismatches between actual information source and evidential marking. For Quechua, a similar approach is adopted by Nuckolls (2008).

3 Child Acquisition of Evidential Systems: Antecedents

In her groundbreaking study of children's acquisition of the Turkish evidential system, Aksu-Koç (1988) noted that children do not make consistently appropriate use of the evidential suffixes until after the age of four years, even though they start producing them by the age of two. In subsequent work, Aksu-Koç and her colleagues observed that the earliest suffixes used appropriately are those denoting direct observation and inference from physical evidence, with the hearsay suffix emerging later (Aksu-Koç 2000, Aksu-Koç, Ögel-Baladan and Alp 2009).

In fact, the observation that children start off with the evidential morpheme encoding direct evidence is a robust finding across languages, perhaps because children's earliest nonlinguistic understanding of information source is that seeing leads to knowing (Matsui and Miura 2009, for Japanese; Fitneva 2009, for Bulgarian; Choi 1995, for Korean; Ifantidou 2009, for Greek; de Villiers et al. 2009, for Tibetan).

The only previous investigation of evidential competence in Quechua-speaking children (Courtney 1999) yielded the observation that the direct evidence morpheme, -mi, emerges at the end of the third year exclusively as a focus marker in affirmative answers to direct questions. The analysis relied primarily on spontaneous speech produced by three children who were acquiring the variety of Quechua spoken in the highlands of Arequipa, Peru.

A number of studies have centered on the development of non-linguistic source reasoning abilities, an aspect of theory of mind, as it relates to the acquisition of the corresponding linguistic forms. Non-linguistic source reasoning tasks involve identifying the source of remembered information without relying on evidential morphemes or other linguistic means. Some of these studies have shown that linguistic evidentiality emerges after, or in tandem with the development of non-linguistic source monitoring abilities (Papafragou et al. 2007, for Korean; Ozturk and Papafragou 2008, for Turkish). These studies further show that children acquiring languages with evidential systems do not outperform those acquiring languages without them (e.g., English) in source-monitoring tasks. By contrast, Ögel (2007) found that four-year-old Turkish speakers surpassed their English-speaking counterparts in a source-monitoring task, an outcome reminiscent of the Sapir-Whorf hypothesis (Whorf 1956) whereby the structure of a language is thought to influence speakers' con-

CHILD ACQUISITION OF QUECHUA EVIDENTIALITY & DEICTIC MEANING 105

ceptualization of the world. In like manner, Aksu-Koç, Őgel-Baladan and Alp (2009, 25) propose that "implicit knowledge and early use of the obligatory evidential markers in discourse sensitizes attention to information source before children reach explicit understanding of this domain."

Two studies suggest that along the way to full mastery of the morphemes encoding epistemic modality (speaker certainty) and evidentiality (speaker's information source), children develop understanding of certainty contrasts before evidential distinctions (de Villiers et al. 2009, for Tibetan; Matsui, Yamamoto and McCagg 2006, for Japanese). De Villiers et al. observed that Tibetan children initially use the direct evidential morpheme *'dug* to indicate certainty rather than personal (direct) observation. Noting that speakers who produce this morpheme are likely committed to the truth of their assertions, they propose that children may initially assign the meaning of certainty to the evidential form. They explain this preference as follows (de Villiers et al. 2009, 35):

> ... what may be more salient for the child may not be information regarding the perceptual evidence available to the speaker but the certainty of the speaker's claims.

However, they also suggest that *'dug* may have two meanings, marking either direct evidence or certainty, especially since Tibetan adults make use of the morpheme to express certainty even in the absence of direct evidence.

Matsui, Yamamoto and McCagg (2006) had Japanese children perform a task requiring them to make decisions regarding the whereabouts of different hidden objects, based on statements containing different markers of certainty and evidentiality (direct evidence vs. hearsay). The authors found that the five- and six-year-olds outperformed the three- and four-year-olds in understanding the evidential contrasts. They also discovered that children's comprehension of the certainty contrasts surpassed their understanding of the evidential contrasts. Matsui and colleagues have attributed this finding to the greater cognitive processing demands involved in the comprehension of evidentiality as compared with that of certainty. They argue that assessing the relative reliability of evidential contrasts entails extra steps in processing (Matsui and Miura 2009, 66):

> ... one needs to understand not only the quality of evidence (direct versus indirect) encoded in the linguistic indicators ... but also how the quality of evidence is likely to affect the speaker's commitment to the truthfulness of the content of the proposition.

However, they also acknowledge the possibility that toddlers may have trouble determining the reliability of information when the stated source is hearsay. Along the lines of de Villiers et al.'s (2009) proposal, they further mention the possibility that hearers may attribute non-belief to a speaker whose assertion indicates that the information source is indirect evidence such as hearsay.

To this writer's knowledge, no one has yet investigated child production of the evidential morphemes as a means of shifting perspective in narrative. The present study explores this issue through the elicitation of story retellings. Before turning to child language data, relevant highlights of the Quechua evidential system are presented. As seen in section 4, the previously discussed debate regarding the essential meanings of the evidential morphemes extends to Quechua.

4 The Quechua Evidential System

4.1 *Evidential Enclitics*

4.1.1 Information Source, Sentence Focus, Degree of Certainty
As illustrated in (1), there are three evidential enclitics available to Quechua speakers for indicating information source (e.g., Calvo Pérez 1993; Faller 2002a; Floyd 1996); Quechua allows only one evidential suffix per main clause. In (a–c), the subject *Xwan* bears different evidential suffixes, underlined in each example.

(1) a. *Xwan-mi* *chaya-mu-n.*
   Juan-DIREV arrive-TRANS-3
   '(SPEAKER has witnessed that) Juan has arrived.'

  b. *Xwan-chá* *chaya-mu-n.*
   Juan-CONJ arrive-TRANS-3
   '(SPEAKER infers/supposes that) Juan has arrived.'

  c. *Xwan-si* *chaya-mu-n.*
   Juan-REP arrive-TRANS-3
   '(SPEAKER has been told that) Juan has arrived.'

In (a), the speaker uses the suffix *-mi* (DIRECT EVIDENCE) in its evidential function to indicate that the statement about Juan's arrival is based on direct observation; that is, the speaker's information is first-hand. According to Faller, *-mi* is licensed when the speaker has the most direct evidence possible,

CHILD ACQUISITION OF QUECHUA EVIDENTIALITY & DEICTIC MEANING   107

or "best possible grounds" (2002a, 21). The speaker's use of the suffix *-chá* (CONJECTURE) in (b) serves to express an inference regarding Juan's arrival, based on reasoning and indirect evidence. Finally, the speaker employs the suffix *-si* (REPORTATIVE) in (c) to note that the source of information regarding Juan's arrival is what someone else has said (Faller 2002a).

Overt evidential marking is not obligatory in Southern Peruvian Quechua as it is in other languages such as the Colombian language Tuyuca (Lazard 2001) and, possibly, other varieties of Quechua. In fact, in informal discourse, Cuzco Quechua speakers often produce sentences lacking evidential morphology (Faller 2002b, 15–16):

> *-mi* in normal conversation is primarily used in situations of real or anticipated argument—in situations in which the speaker wants to make a particular strong point

According to Faller, hearers rely on the context to recover the evidential value of unmarked utterances. However, with respect to Quechua narrative, Mannheim and Van Vleet (1998) assert, without further comment or explanation, that the absence of *-si* or *-mi* generally indicates that the speaker is hedging. Perhaps speakers sometimes wish to conceal their relationship to narrated events.

It is important to note that the Quechua enclitics also serve to mark sentence focus. Following Muysken (1995, 381), when the evidential enclitic appears on the sentence-initial constituent, as in (1a) above, *Juan-mi chayamun*, there is focus ambiguity. Accordingly, there are two possible glosses for this sentence: 'It is JUAN who has arrived' (contrastive focus) and 'Juan has arrived' (non-contrastive focus). Quechua speakers frequently produce *-mi* on the verb *ni-* 'say' in direct quotations, in equi-statements[2] lacking the copula *ka-*, on wh-question words and in affirmative responses to direct questions. It is likely that the suffix is a focus marker in these conventional contexts.

In his work on Tarma Quechua, Adelaar (1977) claims that the use of *-mi* in questions has little if any meaning at all. By contrast, Floyd (1996) proposes that the presence of *-mi* on wh-words in Wanka Quechua indicates the speaker's assumption that the addressee knows the answer and has direct evidence for the requested information. Sample wh-questions in (2), both from Cuzco

---

2   As it is used in this study, the term 'equi-statement' refers to a sentence in which the copula links the subject with a predicate complement (nominative, adjectival, adverbial), e.g.,

    Xwan   *chakra-pi-n*   *ka-sha-n*
    Juan   field-LOC-DIREV   be-PROG-3
    'Juan is in the field.'

Quechua, were produced by adults during the adult-child conversations discussed in section 5.1.

(2) a. *Pi-n̲*   *jardin-pi*   *maqa-sunki?*
     who-FOC $kindergarten-LOC   hit-3S2O
     'Who hits you in kindergarten?'

     b. *Ima-n̲*   *haqay*   *orqo-q*   *suti-n-qa?*
     what-FOC   that   hill-GEN   name-3POSS-TOP
     'What is the name of that hill?'

It has been claimed that the Quechua enclitics also have an epistemic function: they serve to indicate relative speaker certainty or degree of commitment to the truth of particular statements (Floyd 1996; Nuckolls 1993). Linguists largely concur that CONJECTURE *-chá* has both evidential and epistemic import, while REPORTATIVE *-si* serves only the evidential function of marking information as hearsay. In this regard, Faller notes the following:

> The meaning of *-chá* is not purely evidential, indicating that the speaker arrived at his or her statement by reasoning, but also encodes that the speaker is less than 100% certain. (2002a, 177)

> *-si* ... is a true evidential, indicating the speaker's source of information, and ... it does not encode an epistemic modal value. (2002a, 204)

Where linguists diverge is in the characterization of *-mi*. Faller (2002a) maintains that the morpheme is purely evidential, while Nuckolls (1993) has asserted that the primary function of *-mi* is epistemic. According to Nuckolls (1993, 239), "personal conviction or belief rather than direct experience is the Gesamtbedeutung of *-mi*"; that is, *-mi* indicates certainty, particularly in contrast to *-chá*, which is used in its epistemic function to express uncertainty. Nuckolls buttressed her position by presenting situations in which Quechua speakers use *-mi* without any possibility of access to direct evidence, as in sentences with future verb forms. Examples of *-mi*-marked first-person future statements produced by Cuzco Quechua-speaking adults in the current study (section 5.1) are presented in (3).

(3) a. *Apa-ra-m-pu-saq-m̲i̲.*
     take-EXH-TRANS-REG-1FUT-AF
     'I'll bring it back.'

b. *Anchay   ura-s-ta-n*   *pasa-saq   wichay-ta.*
  that $hour-$PL-ACC-AF   go-1FUT   up-ACC
  'I'll go up there at that hour.'

For Floyd, *-mi* has an epistemic function in statements such as these (Floyd 1996, 85):

> ... the speaker's commitment to a proposition may be justified to the extent that s/he construes his/her own subsequent actions as being particularly subject to his/her initiation and control.

If this is true, Quechua speakers may add the *-mi* suffix to assure the addressee that they will complete the future action, based on personal conviction of ability and intention. Noting that the speaker may use *-mi* to express strong personal commitment to the truth of a statement without any evidentiary justification, Floyd further proposes that *-mi* actually encodes two independent notions: direct evidence as information source (evidential) and commitment (epistemic). This proposal represents a departure from both Faller's (2002) assertion that *-mi* is purely evidential and Nuckolls's (1993) claim that the morpheme serves primarily to express commitment or certainty.

4.1.2   Different Voices and Perspectives

More recently, Nuckolls (2008) presents a reinterpretation of the Quechua enclitics in line with Mushin's (2000) proposal that evidential morphemes primarily serve the deictic function of indicating the speaker's epistemological stance or point of view. Nuckolls (2008) argues that *-mi* and *-si* serve to differentiate the voice of the 'speaking self' from the voice of 'the other', respectively. Accordingly, in storytelling, the narrator uses *-si* to establish the perspective of 'the other', a voice reflective of traditional wisdom. When storytellers shift perspective to a character in the story, as when a character speaks, they use the speaking self *-mi* to represent the protagonist's voice. When this occurs, following Mushin's application of Deictic Center Theory, "narrative information is deictically centered somewhere within the story world, independent of the actual teller and audience" (Mushin 2000, 939). In light of this new proposal, Nuckolls (2008, 84) offers the following critique of linguists who consider the intrinsic component of evidential meaning to be perceptual field:

> In reality, the immediate perceptual field of evidential usage is tied to the deictic, perspectival nature of evidentials, rather than to their meaning as such.

For Nuckolls, the debate regarding the essential meaning of -*mi* as direct evidence for a proposition or commitment to a proposition is a futile enterprise.

4.2 Past Tense Inflections

Like Korean and Turkish, Quechua exhibits distinct past-tense inflections, each illustrated in (4): EXPERIENCED PAST -*ra* (allomorph: -*rqa*) in (a) and NON-EXPERIENCED PAST -*sqa* in (b).

(4) a. *Xwan   chaya-mu-ra-n.*
       Juan   arrive-TRANS-PST-3
       'Juan arrived.' (directly perceived)

   b. *Xwan   chaya-mu-sqa-Ø.*
       Juan   arrive-TRANS-NX-3
       'Juan arrived.' (not directly perceived)

In Cuzco Quechua, -*ra* indicates that the speaker has direct perceptual evidence that John arrived, whereas -*sqa* marks the absence of direct perceptual evidence (Cusihuamán 1976; Faller 2004). According to Faller, -*sqa* is "a spatio-temporal deictic which specifies that the described eventuality *e* is not located within the speaker's perceptual field at topic time" (Faller 2004, 2). On this account, -*sqa* is not a true evidential morpheme; nonetheless, if a speaker has not perceived an event, his or her evidence is necessarily indirect. Faller (2004) also discusses the mirative function of -*sqa* as encoding surprise or unexpectedness. In like manner, Cusihuamán (1976) observes that Quechua speakers make use of this form, labeled "sudden discovery" by Adelaar (1977, 96), to remark on new situations or newly discovered phenomena, as in *Ruphan kay kafiyqa ka-sqa* (Cusihuamán 1976, 171) 'This coffee (turned out) to be hot!'

As in other languages (Aikhenvald 2004), NON-EXPERIENCED PAST -*sqa* exhibits a cluster of interrelated functions. For instance, -*sqa* is appended to verb stems to form past participles that highlight the results or observed end states of actions or processes, as in change-of-state verbs. One example is the verb *rikch'a-sqa* [*rikch'a-* 'awaken' + -*sqa*], meaning 'he/she is awake', the expression of a resulting state. In like manner, the contrasting meanings of *ri-sqa* (go-NX with null third-person marking) and *ri-ra-n* (go-PST-3) might be glossed respectively as 'he is gone' (resulting state) and 'he went' (dynamic event). The morpheme serves a reportative function in Quechua narrative: narrators make use of -*sqa* in recounting stories, myths, and legends to indicate that they have neither witnessed nor participated in the narrated events. Additionally, storytellers generally combine -*sqa* with REPORTATIVE -*si* to characterize narrated events as reported information. In her analysis of corresponding morphemes in Pariarca Quechua narratives, Howard-Malverde (1988) notes that a speaker typically uses -*si* co-occurring with the NON-EXPERIENCED PAST morpheme in the first two utterances to establish non-personal knowledge, thereafter dropping -*si* and sustaining the non-personal mode exclusively through consistent use of the NON-EXPERIENCED PAST.

It is noteworthy that Quechua speakers typically produce sentences lacking both evidential morphology and past-tense marking in narratives about recent past events, with relevance to the present. In (5), the verb is NON-PAST, and in some contexts may refer to action already completed, as in the following example from Calvo Pérez (1993, 159). An English translation has been substituted for Calvo Pérez's original Spanish.

(5) *Wayna   iskay   ch'ayña-ta   hap'i-n.*
    youth   two   linnet-ACC   catch-3
    'The young man has caught two linnets.'

In this regard, Howard-Malverde (1988) further observes that narrators prefer NON-PAST verb forms in the "personalized" mode, especially where the verb is first-person. The personalized mode discussed by Howard-Malverde corresponds to Mushin's shifting of the deictic center from the narrator's perspective to the story world.

It is not the intention of this investigation to favor one analysis over others. However, the three types of production and comprehension data reported in the following sections suggest that Quechua-speaking children acquire distinct functions of the evidential morphemes and past tense inflections, including their use in the expression of different deictic relations, one-by-one over a protracted period. In what immediately follows, I present the highlights of an analysis of naturalistic speech, reported elsewhere (Courtney 2014). I then summarize essential findings of a previously reported experimental procedure (Courtney 2011), and, subsequently, I present new data collected through the elicitation of story retellings. As previously mentioned, these different types of data were gathered as a means of developing a working theory of the acquisitional process in Quechua-speaking children.

Both child and adult participants were recruited for the three investigations. In each study, data collection was conducted in participants' home communities, all rural villages situated in the province of Paruro in Cuzco, Peru. Because the socioeconomic status of all these children is low, even by Peruvian standards, the children lack toys, books, and television, and they are not acquainted with the lifestyle of mainstream Peruvians. The younger children spend their days with their mothers, generally tending the family livestock out in the fields. The older children attend kindergarten or elementary school, where they typically struggle to learn Spanish. Although the parents of the children may be bilingual in Spanish and Quechua, particularly the fathers, Quechua is spoken at home; it is the children's first language.

5 Quechua Child Language: Three Investigations

5.1 *Naturalistic Data: Mother-child Conversations*

Mothers were asked to tape-record conversations with their children in familiar settings for 30 to 60 minutes. The topics of conversation were remarkably similar across mother-child dyads. Typically, mothers and their children talked about chores to be done (cooking, attending to animals, working in the fields, gathering firewood and fodder), about school and getting ready for school, and about the whereabouts and activities of different family members. In all, recordings were obtained of conversations with thirteen children between the ages of 2;3 and 4;4 (mean age = 3;3), including 7 girls and 6 boys.

The recordings were later transcribed by native speakers of Quechua who had interacted with the mothers and children in other settings. Utterances which merely acknowledged what was said with responses such as *ya, ha, aha, hay, han, uhu, a* were eliminated. The remaining utterances were coded for instances of the evidential enclitics *-mi, -si,* and *-chá,* as well as for occurrences of the past tense inflections *-sqa* and *-ra.* The *-mi* utterances underwent further pruning: instances of the filler *ima-n* (*ima* 'something'/ 'what' + *-mi*) were eliminated from the analysis, as well as tokens of the negative form *mana-n* (*mana* 'not' + *-mi*), because there is no way of telling whether or not the children produced the form as an unanalyzed amalgam. The mothers' utterances were also coded for these morphemes. Table 4.1 presents the total number of utterances and tokens of each evidential enclitic produced by the children and adults.

TABLE 4.1   *Production of evidential morphemes, by age group*

	2 years (N = 5)	3 years (N = 5)	4 years (N = 3)	Adult (N = 13)
utterances	731	577	482	1978
-mi	35	21	39	78
-chá	10	3	13	64
-si	—	—	9	19

CHILD ACQUISITION OF QUECHUA EVIDENTIALITY & DEICTIC MEANING   113

It is important to note that the following analysis of these naturalistic data is only suggestive and not conclusive. The multifunctional nature of the suffixes and the dearth of tokens in the corpus are the main obstacles to clear-cut analysis. Moreover, even when forms are contextualized in natural conversations, it is often difficult to discern a speaker's intended message. Finally, a child's failure to produce a particular form does not necessarily mean than s/he has not yet acquired it. Nonetheless, examining spontaneous speech is a good first step, as it provides insights and observations that are useful in subsequent investigations.

5.1.1 Analysis: Emergence of Enclitics

Analysis of the naturalistic data suggests that the earliest occurrences of *-mi* produced by the two-year-olds, starting at age 2;6, serve primarily to mark focus, both in conventional grammatical contexts (i.e., *wh*-questions, answers to questions, equi-statements, on *ni-* 'say' in direct quotations) and in contrastive focus. Examples from the data are presented in (6)–(10). Two-year-olds also mark constituents in first-person future sentences with *-mi*, most likely to express their firm intention to do something, as illustrated in (11) below. That is to say, in these statements it is likely that *-mi* indicates commitment to a proposition, especially as contrasted with CONJECTURE *-chá*, which emerges productively in the late two's. Therefore, the data suggest that early uses of *-mi* and *-chá* may be confined to focus-marking and epistemic expressions of certainty/probability.

Examples (6)–(10) present two-year-old child utterances from the conversations in which *-mi* is used to mark focus, while (11) illustrates the occurrence of *-mi* in a first-person future statement. Example (7) includes the mother's (M) utterance.

(6) 2;6   (wh-question)

     Ima-<u>n</u>   *ankiy-pa*   *suti-n-qa?*
     what-FOC   that-GEN   name-3POSS-TOP
     'What's the name of that?'

(7) M   *Waqra-yu-sunki-chu,*   *mana-chu?*
     butt-INT-3S2O-INTR   NEG-INTR
     'It butts you with its horns, doesn't it?'

2;11 (response to direct question)

Waqra-yu-wa-n-mi
butt-INT-1OBJ-3-FOC
'It butts me with its horns.'

(8) 2;8 (direct speech with *ni-* 'say')

Kicha-ra-pu-wa-y   *qhawa-na-y-paq*   *ni-yki-n.*
open-EXH-BEN-1OBJ-IMP   look.at-NMLZ-1-DAT   say-1S2O-FOC
'I say to you, "Open it for me so I can have a look."'

(9) 2;8 (equi-statement without *ka-* 'be')

Kay-qa   *papa-yki-q-mi.*
this-TOP   dad-2POSS-GEN-FOC
'This is your dad's.'

(10) 2;11 (contrastive focus)

Ama, ama, ama! Nuqa-paq-mi, nuqa-paq-mi, yaw!
PROH   I-BEN-FOC   I-BEN-FOC, hey
'Don't, don't, don't! It's for ME, it's for ME. Hey!'

(11) 2;11 (first-person future statement)

Pintula   *apa-ku-saq,*   *apa-ku-saq-mi.*
$paint   carry-REFL-1FUT   carry-REFL-1FUT-AF
'I'll take paint.'

As previously mentioned, by the late two's, children begin producing CON-JECTURE *-chá* in utterances that appear to express a lack of certainty, as contrasted with *-mi*. This is illustrated in (12), in which *-chayki*, a free variant of *-chá* in Paruro Quechua, expresses both uncertainty and contrastive focus.[3]

---

3 Local informants claim that there is no difference in meaning between *-chá* and *-chayki*. In Ayacucho Quechua, another Southern Peruvian variety, the evidential suffixes are commonly followed by the independent suffix *-ki* (Cerrón-Palomino, 1987). I thank one reviewer for pointing out that speakers of this variety of Quechua can append the independent suffix *-ki* to the evidential suffixes to appeal to knowledge shared with the addressee; additionally, the shape of the suffix is *-iki*, appearing as *-ch-iki* in Ayacucho Quechua when combined with the

CHILD ACQUISITION OF QUECHUA EVIDENTIALITY & DEICTIC MEANING   115

(12) 2;11   *Kay-rí*   *nuqanchis-pa-<u>chayki</u>;*   *haqay-rí,*   *ankay-rí,*
             this-RESP   us-GEN-CONJ   that-RESP   that-RESP

             chay-rí,   *qan-kuna-q-chu*
             that-RESP   you-PL-GEN-INTR
             'This might/must be OURS; and that, and that, and that, is it YOURS?'

For the most part, the linguistic behavior of three-year-olds with respect to the production of *-mi* and *-chá* is very similar to that of the children in their late two's. The only noteworthy development is the occurrence of *-mi* on a wider variety of focused constituents. As shown in (13), children continue to use *-mi* to express commitment to a proposition rather than direct evidence. Additionally, there are no instances of REPORTATIVE *-si* in the utterances of the three-year-olds.

(13) 3;8   (*Child tells her mother about the existence of a ghost.*)

            Margus-cha   *riku-ru-ra-n-<u>mi</u>.*
            Margus-DIM   see-EXH-PST-3-AF
            'Marguscha SAW it.'

At the age of four years, in addition to these functions, it is possible that children make use of *-mi* as an evidential indicating direct evidence, as shown in the mother-child dyads in (14)–(15). In these examples, it is plausible that the children wish to convey that they have first-hand evidence of the money in (14) and the egg in (15).

(14) 4;2   *Qolqe-ta-wan*   *erqe-kuna*   *tari-ru-ku-rqa-n-ku.*
            money-ACC-INS   child-PL   find-EXH-REFL-PST-3-PL
            'The children found themselves (some) money.'

      M   *Han.* ('Really.')

      4;2   *Qolqe-ta-<u>n</u>.*
            money-ACC-DIREV
            'Money.'

---

conjecture suffix. One may speculate that the *-chá/-chayki* variation observed here in Paruro-Cuzco Quechua has been influenced by the Ayacucho variety.

(15) M   *Wallpa-nchis*   *untu-ru-ra-n-chus*   *mayna-chá?*
          hen-IPL   lay.egg-EXH-PST-3-DUB   how-CONJ
          'Could our hen have laid an egg?'

    4;4   *Ka-sha-n-mi.*
          be-PROG-3-DIREV
          'There is (one).'

    M   *Runtu.*
          egg
          'An egg.'

It must be noted that, for two reasons, there is no way of establishing conclusively from spontaneous production data whether or not children actually assign evidential meaning to -*mi*. First, the suffix is ambiguous in many contexts. Additionally, perhaps because the evidential enclitics are optional elements in Quechua conversation, very few exemplars of -*mi* were encountered in both child and mother speech. However, it is at the age of four years that children first produce REPORTATIVE -*si*, from which we may infer that children have developed an understanding of information source as a linguistic category.

In the total corpus of child utterances, there were only 9 in which -*si* or its allomorph -*s* were encountered, all produced by children aged 4;2 and older. In fact, in the corpus of child-directed speech, the mothers produced only 19 instances of -*si* in three functions: (a) so-called "delayed" mandates (7 tokens); (b) reported information/hearsay (3 tokens); and (c) questions formed either with *wh*-words or in combination with INTERROGATIVE -*chu* (9 tokens).[4] Delayed mandates are directives from third parties, transmitted by the speaker through use of -*si* (Cusihuamán 1976). The four-year-olds produced -*si* in both delayed mandates and reported information, as shown in (16)–(17).

---

4 There were so few instances of -*si* in the child-mother conversations that the parents of one of the children were asked to record their own adult conversation. This is because the mothers might have avoided using the enclitic in child-directed speech during their talks with their children. The adult conversation, 3793 words in length, consisted of 445 exchanges between husband and wife. These spouses produced utterances with -*si*-marked constituents in only 21 of their conversational exchanges.

CHILD ACQUISITION OF QUECHUA EVIDENTIALITY & DEICTIC MEANING   117

(16) 4;2 *Kuti-mu-nki-s.*
            return-TRANS-2-REP
            '(S/he says) for you to come back.'

(17) 4;4 *Hamu-sha-n-si.*   *Seqa-mu-sha-n-ña.*
            come-PROG-3-REP   climb-TRANS-PROG-3-DISC
            '(They say) he's coming.'   He's already climbing.'

5.1.2   Analysis: Emergence of Past Tense Morphemes
As mentioned earlier, Quechua speakers use Past *-ra* when they have direct
perceptual evidence of a past event (Cusihuamán 1976; Faller 2004); lacking direct perceptual evidence, they employ NON-EXPERIENCED PAST *-sqa*.
Additionally, in the resultative function, *-sqa* serves to focus on the observed
end state of an action or process such as a change of state. Table 4.2 presents a
summary of the past-tense forms produced by the children and adults.

    In the two-year-olds' speech, *-sqa* occurs exclusively on verbs expressing
changes of state and existence, as well as on unaccusative movement verbs
equivalent in meaning to *go, come, enter*, etc., when the intention is to focus on
the observed end state of the movement. The two-year-olds did not produce
-sqa on any agentive verbs. However, since movement verbs can also be con-
strued as agentive, they occurred quite frequently with *-ra*. The 4 two-year-olds
produced 20 past-inflected verb forms, including 15 tokens of *-ra* on agentive
verbs and 5 tokens of *-sqa* on unaccusative/existence verbs. Example (18) presents utterances produced by one of the two-year-olds. The child produced the
utterance in (18a) after shooting a marble and observing the outcome of its

TABLE 4.2   *Functions of past inflections produced in conversations, by age group and type of verb*

| | *-sqa* (NON-EXPERIENCED PAST) | | | *-ra* (EXPERIENCED PAST) | | |
	unaccus/ existence	agentive activity	auxiliary *ka-*	unaccus/ existence	agentive activity	auxiliary *ka-*
Two years	5	—	—	9	6	---
Three years	12	2	1	3	21	1
Four years	16	6	1	2	15	2
Adult	73	46	---	33	114	24

trajectory. Since the understood subject of this sentence is the marble, an inanimate object lacking volition, *-sqa* is used to focus on the result or end state of the movement (*ri-* 'go'); there is no agentive role in this sentence.

(18) a. M *Ch'uchu-ta-chu*   *hap'i-y-ra-mu-nki?*
              marble-ACC-INTR   hold-INT-EXH-TRANS-2

              Awer, tira-y.
              $A ver, $throw-IMP
              'Will you grab (pick.up) the marble? Let's see, shoot it.'

      2:11 (unaccusative verb)

              (h)aqay-manta-má   *ri-sha-sqa,*   *(h)aqay-man.*
              that-ABL-IMPR   go-PROG-NX   that-ILLA
              'It was going from over there to over there!'

      b. 2:11 (agentive verb)
              Mama-y,   *anchay*   *naranja-ta*   *qo-ku-ra-ni.*
              mom-1POSS   that $orange-ACC   give-REFL-PST-1
              'Mommy, I gave (him/her) that orange.'

Thus, at age two years, children's verbs exhibit the basic distinction between *-sqa* for expressing end states or results and *-ra* for expressing agentive action. Since the 40 past-tense forms produced by the 4 three-year-olds yielded only 2 instances of agentive verbs marked with *-sqa*, it appears that two- and three-year-olds are not yet aware of the semantic distinction between perceived and unperceived past events; otherwise, they might produce agentive verbs with *-sqa* to indicate that the corresponding events were not directly experienced. While the basic pattern (*-sqa* for unaccusatives; *-ra* for agentives) is also observed in the past-tense verb forms produced by the 3 four-year-olds, children at this age produce a few more agentive verbs bearing *-sqa*. Given this, it is plausible that they have begun to attribute to *-sqa* the notion of past events not directly experienced or perceived.

    As previously mentioned, the present analysis of naturalistic data is suggestive and not conclusive. While it seems likely that children first acquire the focus functions and epistemic meanings of the suffixes before arriving at evidential meaning, this working hypothesis must be further tested. For this purpose, the experimental procedure explained in section 5.2 was employed to investigate children's interpretation of the Quechua morphemes as denot-

CHILD ACQUISITION OF QUECHUA EVIDENTIALITY & DEICTIC MEANING 119

ing either certainty or information source. In addition to children, adults were tested as a basis of comparison.

5.2 *Experimental Data: Hidden Objects*

In the experimental task, adapted from procedures developed by Matsui, Yamamoto and McCagg (2006), participants were required to judge the relative reliability of contrasting statements about the whereabouts of hidden objects. In all, 10 adults and 63 children were tested, the latter divided into two age groups: three- and four-year-olds (N = 30; mean age = 3;11) and five- and six-year-olds (N = 33; mean age = 6;0). The tests were conducted in participants' rural home communities.

5.2.1 Materials and Procedures

At the beginning of the experiment, the research assistant, a native speaker of Quechua and well-known educator in the Province of Paruro, invited participants to play a game with two puppets, a dog and a sheep, manipulated by a second assistant. After explaining that a particular object was hidden in one of two differently colored boxes, he asked each puppet a question, *Mayqen kaq cajapitaq kashan____? '*Which box is the ____ hidden in?' There were no real objects hidden in the boxes, so the game involved pretending. The two puppets gave different answers to the question, equivalent to English statements such as "Maybe it's in the red box", and "It's definitely in the blue box." In these English sentences, the contrasting forms are the adverbs, *maybe* and *definitely*, and the predicted response would be indicated as *definitely* > *maybe* because *definitely* indicates a higher degree of certainty than *maybe*; hence, the statement with *definitely* is more reliable. The Quechua counterparts to these statements are presented in what immediately follows. The participant was then asked to indicate which box the object was in, based entirely on the conflicting answers provided by the puppets, by stating the whereabouts of the hidden object.

Three Quechua contrasts were considered in this experiment, as indicated in table 4.3. With respect to the epistemic and evidential values of -*chá* and -*si*, I adopt Faller's (2002a) analysis: -*chá* encodes both uncertainty and reasoning as information source, while -*si* is purely evidential. The left column of table 4.3 shows the pairs of contrasting suffixes as well as the predicted responses in terms of relative reliability. Sample contrasting test items are provided in the middle and right columns, each a statement indicating the color of the box in which the object is hidden. In the first contrast, -*chá* is contrasted with -*puni*, a suffix which unambiguously expresses certainty (CERT). The suffix -*puni* serves only to indicate a high degree of certainty and not information source,

TABLE 4.3 *Sample pair of statements for each of three experimental contrasts*

Contrasts	DOG	SHEEP
-puni > -chá	*Papa q'omer caja-pi-chá ka-sha-n.* potato green $box-LOC-CONJ be-PROG3 'The potato is in the green box.'	*Papa q'ello caja-pi-puni* *ka-sha-n.* potato yellow $box-LOC-CERT be-PROG-3 'The potato is in the yellow box.'
-mi > -chá	*Papa puka caja-pi-n ka-sha-n.* potato red $box-LOC-DIREV/AF be-PROG3 'The potato is in the red box.'	*Papa yuraq caja-pi-chá* *ka-sha-n.* potato white $box-LOC-CONJ be-PROG-3 'The potato is in the white box.'
[-mi + -ra] > [-si + -sqa]	*Alex-mi puka caja-man chura-ra-n* *papa-ta.* Alex-DIREV red $box-ILLA put-PST-3 potato-ACC 'Alex put the potato in the red box.'	*Xwan-si yuraq caja-man* *chura-sqa papa-ta.* Juan-REP white $box-ILLA put-NX-3 potato-ACC 'Juan put the potato in the white box.'

and it may co-occur with evidential suffixes (Cusihuamán 1976; Faller 2002a). This epistemic contrast was included in an effort to determine whether children understand that *-chá* encodes a lesser degree of certainty than *-puni*; the predicted response is *-puni > -chá*. In the second contrast, *-chá* is contrasted with *-mi*, with *-mi*-statements predicted as more reliable than *-chá*-statements (*-mi > -chá*). In the third contrast, *-mi* is paired with EXPERIENCED PAST *-ra*, and *-si* is paired with NON-EXPERIENCED PAST *-sqa* in statements indicating where a particular individual has put the object in question. The pairings in this contrast serve to reinforce the evidential distinction between directly observed past events [*-mi + -ra*] and reported, unperceived events [*-si + -sqa*], and the predicted reliability judgment is [*-mi + -ra*] > [*-si + -sqa*]. The second and third contrasts are included in an effort to observe whether children assign both epistemic and evidential meanings to *-mi* and understand *-si*, a purely evidential morpheme.

Suppose that children successfully interpret *-mi*-statements as more reliable than *-chá*-statements in the second contrast but fail to evaluate *-mi*-state-

CHILD ACQUISITION OF QUECHUA EVIDENTIALITY & DEICTIC MEANING   121

ments as more dependable than *-si*-statements in the third, purely evidential contrast. This outcome would suggest that children have acquired only an epistemic, non-evidential interpretation of *-mi*. That is, they construe *-mi*, like *-puni*, as an epistemic marker indicating greater certainty than *-chá* in its epistemic function. (It is highly unlikely that 3- to 6-year-olds would assign to *-chá* an evidential value, i.e., information source as inference based on reasoning. As noted by de Villiers et al. (2009), before the age of 9 or 10 years, children are not yet capable of understanding the inferences of others.) Without an understanding of the evidential contrast between *-mi* and *-si*, they are not equipped to judge the reliability of the third set of contrasting statements.

The test comprised a total of 16 experimental trials, with trials for each contrast grouped together in a block. The three blocks were presented in different orders. The colors used to describe the boxes were red, green, white, and yellow, and the hidden objects were familiar to the children (e.g., potato, corn, stone, stick), although children never actually saw these objects. Predicted responses were evenly distributed between colors and between puppets. Before commencing the experimental trials, the investigator had participants perform two practice trials to make certain they understood the game. In the first practice trial, one of the puppets stated the participant's name correctly and the other, incorrectly. The participant was then asked to indicate which puppet had provided the correct response. In the second practice trial, more directly related to the game, the participant was asked in which box a potato was hidden, with two options provided by the puppets: *Mana yacha-ni-chu* [NEG know-1-NEG] 'I don't know' and *Puka caja-pi ka-sha-n* [red $box-LOC be-PROG-3] 'It's in the red box.'

5.2.2   Results and Discussion

Table 4.4 presents the mean percentages of the previously-discussed predicted responses that were obtained for each contrast by age group.

A mixed, within-between subjects ANOVA was conducted to examine the performance of the three age groups for each category of contrast (i. e., *-puni* > *-chá*; *-mi* > *-chá*; *-mi/-ra* > *-si/ -sqa*), based on the percentages of predicted responses. In this analysis, age group was the between-subjects variable and contrast type was the within-subjects variable. With respect to the between-subjects analysis, there was a main effect of age group (F $(2, 70)$ = 11.42, p = 0.000). A Bonferroni post hoc test revealed that the adults and the five- and six-year-olds both performed significantly better overall than the three- and four-year-olds (p = 0.001 and p = 0.000, respectively). When examining the within-subjects factor of contrast type, there was also a main effect (F $(2, 140)$ = 23.45, p = 0.000). However, this effect was qualified by a significant interaction

TABLE 4.4 *Mean percentages of predicted responses and standard deviations for each contrast, by age group*

Contrast and predicted response	Age group	Mean %	Std. deviation
-puni > -chá	3 to 4 years (N = 30)	71.33	20.13
	5 to 6 years (N = 33)	85.45	14.38
	Adults (N = 10)	80.00	16.33
-mi > -chá	3 to 4 years (N = 30)	70.67	25.59
	5 to 6 years (N = 33)	83.64	16.92
	Adults (N = 10)	78.00	28.98
-mi/-ra > -si/-sqa	3 to 4 years (N = 30)	36.60	23.72
	5 to 6 years (N = 33)	51.03	25.96
	Adults (N = 10)	76.60	21.03

between contrast type and age group ($F_{(4, 140)}$ = 3.33, p = 0.012). As shown in table 4.4 and figure 4.1, the means for the first two contrasts, *-mi > -chá* and *-puni > -chá*, were similar for each age group; however, the mean percentage obtained by the adults for the third contrast, *-mi/-ra > -si/-sqa*, was higher than those obtained by both groups of children. Adult performance on the three contrasts was similar. By contrast, both groups of children achieved adult-like performance on the first two contrasts, while, on the third contrast, the five- and six-year-olds performed at chance and the three- and four-year-olds actually favored *-si/-sqa* over *-mi/-ra-*.

The older children outperformed the younger children overall; that is, across contrasts, the three- and four-year-olds produced lower percentages of predicted responses than the five- and six-year-olds. Beyond this result, there were no noteworthy age-related differences among the children.

As in Matsui, Yamamoto and McCagg's (2006) Japanese study, children appeared to have greater success interpreting certainty contrasts than evidential contrasts. First, the outcome suggests that neither age group of children has yet captured the evidential import of *-mi* as contrasted with *-si*. In fact, the mean for the younger group of children shows that, overall, the three- and four-year-olds actually judged *-si/-sqa* to be more reliable than *-mi/-ra*. Possibly, absent discourse context, children in the age range of 3 to 4 years rely, not on the evidential distinction encoded in *-mi* and *-si*, but on a construal of *-sqa* in its mirative function as expressing sudden discovery (Adelaar 1977; Faller 2004).

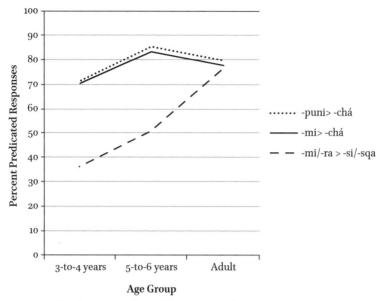

FIGURE 4.1 *Predicted responses obtained by contrast and age group*

Second, the results for both age groups yielded adult-like reliability judgments for *-puni > -chá* and *-mi > -chá*. As mentioned previously, if children successfully interpret *-mi*-statements as more reliable than *-chá*-statements but fail to judge *-mi*-statements as more dependable than *-si*-statements (a purely evidential contrast), it is likely that they have acquired only an epistemic, non-evidential meaning of *-mi*, akin to that of *-puni* (high certainty). It must be noted, however, that this was a challenging task because the contrasting statements were not contextualized in discourse. The task also entailed heavy cognitive demands: it required participants not only to interpret the degree of certainty and the information source encoded in each of the puppets' statements but also to evaluate the merits of their statements.

Nonetheless, based on the composite findings of these two previously reported studies—the analysis of naturalistic production and the experimental comprehension task—it is possible to develop a working hypothesis:

- Quechua-speaking children first acquire (a) the focusing and epistemic functions of the evidential enclitics and (b) the distinction encoded in the past tense inflections between end states and dynamic events.
- Only at the age of four years do children begin sorting out the evidential meanings of the Quechua enclitics as well as the spatiotemporal deictic

distinction between experienced/perceived vs. non-experienced events in past time.

This preliminary analysis gains support from two comments offered by deVilliers et al. in their discussion of children's acquisition of Tibetan evidentiality (2009, 36):

> Though little is known about how children develop the capacity to understand others' inferences, it appears from our work that these skills mature much later than theory of mind—perhaps around nine to ten years of age.

> Fixing...a direct evidential requires establishing it as part of a system of evidentials encoding source information and contrasting its meaning with that of other evidentials, such as the inferential or indirect evidentials (whose acquisition poses even greater developmental challenges) ... Without the contrast between correlative members of the same linguistic system, the correct meaning of the evidential cannot be represented.

The first comment relates to the difficulty even older children have understanding inference. Considering that the source of information encoded in *-chá* is inference, it is not surprising that children should acquire the epistemic meaning first. DeVilliers et al.'s second comment makes the very important point that children cannot assign evidential meaning 'in a vacuum.' That is, there can be no direct evidence without indirect evidence, and these contrasting notions of information source must be available to children before they can assign the meaning of direct evidence to a morpheme such as *-mi*. Without the knowledge that *-chá* or *-si* indicates indirect evidence, children will probably interpret *-mi* as expressing certainty rather than direct evidence.

In light of this drawn-out acquisitional process, one might predict that children would fail to produce the appropriate enclitics and past-tense forms in narrative discourse. To begin with, as noted by Stromqvist and Day (1993, 137), children "have to spend a lot of time acquiring the knowledge and skills relevant to the production of a coherent narrative." Until at least the age of five years, children have difficulty telling cohesive stories because they present events out of sequence, and their stories lack coherence because of unclear pronoun reference, etc. It would seem unlikely, then, that young Quechua-speaking children could make use of the evidential enclitics and past-tense

CHILD ACQUISITION OF QUECHUA EVIDENTIALITY & DEICTIC MEANING 125

morphemes as stance-shifting devices, following Mushin (2000) and Nuckolls (2008). To explore this issue, children were asked to retell stories they had just heard. Although the adult storyteller modeled appropriate use of the enclitics and past-tense suffixes in Quechua narration, it is not the case that children's production of these morphemes in their own retellings was merely imitative. Lust, Flynn and Foley (1998, 56) note:

> In order for the child to 'imitate' a structure, the structure must apparently be part of the child's grammatical competence ... Again, imitation is not a passive copy; it reflects cognitive competence.

I now turn to the story-retelling task.

5.3 Story Retellings

A native speaker of Quechua assembled small groups of children for storytelling. The group included the target participant and other children, often older siblings, who accompanied the participant. After considerable practice, the storyteller told each participant the same version of a traditional Andean tale about a fox and a condor while enacting the events with toy figures of people and animals. He then invited the child to retell the story with the toy figures. In total, 19 retellings were collected, all produced by children aged 2;6 to 6;4 (mean age = 4;4). Table 4.5 presents the exact ages of all the participants.

In the story, a condor takes a fox to a party in the sky. Later, the fox cannot get back down to earth when the condor flies away without him. The fox decides to make a rope and begins climbing down the rope to the ground. On the way down, he repeatedly insults a parrot, who retaliates by cutting the rope in two.

TABLE 4.5 *Ages in years and months of the 19 child story retellers*

Two-year-olds	Three-year-olds	Four-year-olds	Five-year-olds	Six-year-olds
2;6	3;8	4;1	5;0	6;0
2;9	3;9	4;2	5;1	6;1
	3;10	4;6	5;8	6;4
	3;10	4;6		6;4
		4;6		
		4;7		

In spite of the fox's cries for help as he falls to earth, none of the people below come to the fox's aid because he is a thief. The researcher embellished the story with dialogue, and in his narrative of 47 sentences, he used all the morphemes appropriately, i.e., the evidentials *-mi, -si, -chá,* and the past tense suffixes, *-sqa* and *-ra*. All of the renditions of the children's retellings were recorded and transcribed by native speakers of Quechua. Thereafter, the retellings were coded for instances of the five morphemes: *-mi, -si, -chá, -sqa,* and *-ra*.

In table 4.6, three segments of the story (a, b, c) are presented as it was told by the researcher to the children, each comprising both straightforward narrative and direct quotations. The noteworthy aspects are underlined in both the original Quechua and the English glosses. For example, the first two words, *huk pacha-s,* literally, 'one time-REP' are underlined because they present a conventional beginning in Quechua stories, akin to English 'once upon a time'. Reportative *-si* is appended to this expression to identify the narrative as a report. There are two other salient characteristics in the adult story telling: verb form and evidential marking. In each case, a clear distinction is observed between the straight narrative portions of the story and the dialogues (direct quotations). Accordingly, this narrative presents clear evidence for the employment of the evidential enclitics and past-tense morphemes in perspective-shifting. The adult storyteller shifts the deictic center back and forth from the real world of the speech act of reporting to the characters in the story world (Mushin 2000)—from the narrator's voice to the speaking-self of the protagonists (Nuckolls 2008).

With respect to the verb inflections, the different uses of three forms are particularly noteworthy: NON-EXPERIENCED PAST *-sqa* (NX), EXPERIENCED PAST *-ra* (PST), and NON-PAST. Whenever verbs occur in straightforward narrative, they are marked either in NON-EXPERIENCED PAST or in NON-PAST. Quechua speakers may use the NON-PAST in the narrative to make the account more vivid; accordingly, this form produces an effect similar to that of the English historical present, e.g., *qaparimun kay suwa atoq* 'shouts this thieving fox,' by means of a shift in temporal deixis. In this regard, Mushin (2001, 187) notes the following:

> The well-documented 'historical' present . . . marks a shift in temporal deictic origin from time of narration to time of the narrative . . . The narrative information is thus presented as if the teller and her audience had direct experience of the events for the rhetorical purpose of telling a more vivid and interesting story.

CHILD ACQUISITION OF QUECHUA EVIDENTIALITY & DEICTIC MEANING 127

TABLE 4.6 *Excerpts from the adult narrative*

---

a. *Huk pacha-s kay atoqcha huyaylla*　　*tiyakusha-sqa ka-ra-n wank'a patachapi.*
One time-REP this fox sadly　　　　　sit-NX be-PST at the top of a crevice.

Chaymantataq-sis huk kuntur　volaspa rihurimu-sqa.　Hinaspa tapu-sqa kay atoqta,
And then-REP a condor　　　$flying appear-NX　　Then he ask-NX this fox,

"Compadre, imamantataq huyayri kashankiri?"　nispa-s tapu-n.
"$Friend, why are you so sad?"　　　　saying-REP he ask.

Kay atoqchataq-si kutichi-sqa,　　"Cielupi-s fiesta kashan.
This fox-REP reply-NX　　　　"They say there's a $party in the $sky.

Chayman-mi mana riyta atinichu,　chayrayku huyay kashani."
There-DIREV I can't go.　　　That's why I'm sad."

Phawaylla-s　　askhata ichhuta huñuramu-n-ña.　Chaywan-si waskhata k'uyuyu-n;
Quickly-REP　　lots of grass he gather　　With that-REP a rope he make;

chayqa warkuyamu-n-si waskhata.
then he hang-REP the rope.

b. *Chay-si kay lorochataq kutiramu-n,　　"Yaw atoq!　Imamantataq k'amiwashankiri?*
then-REP the parrot reply,　　　"Hey, fox!　Why do you insult me?

Nuqari imana-ra-yki-taq?　Ya sichus hukpi k'amiwanki　chayqa k'uturusaq-mi waskhaykita,"
And what I do-PST to you? If you insult me again,　　then I will cut-DIREV your rope,"

nispa-s kay lorucha nimu-n.
saying-REP the parrot say

"Chayta ruwaruwanki chayqa urma-ya-pu-y-man-chá, riki,　wañurapuyman. Ama wayqey!"
"If you do to that me,　then I would fall-CONJ　　　and I would die. Don't, my brother!"

c. *"Qhawariy! Auxilio! Socorro!　　Pampaman mast'aychis ponchuta, llikllata.*
"Look! $Help! $Help!　　　On the ground lay out $ponchos and blankets.

128 COURTNEY

TABLE 4.6   *Excerpts from the adult narrative (cont.)*

Taytachaykichis-mi urmaymushani,"	*nisparaqtaq-si qaparimu-n kay suwa atoq*
I, your <u>Father-DIREV</u> am falling,"	<u>saying-REP</u> <u>shout</u> this thieving fox.
Runakuna wasinmanta phawari-sqa-ku;	*chayqa runakunaqa rikuru-sqa-ku.*
People from their houses <u>run-NX</u>;	then the people <u>see-NX</u> (him).

The only verb form inflected in EXPERIENCED PAST appears in directly quoted material: *imana-ra-yki* 'what did I do to you?' The direct quotations also include NON-PAST, future, and conditional verb forms.

A similar dichotomy is observed in the evidential marking. DIRECT EVIDENCE -*mi* appears only within direct quotations, e.g., *k'uturusaq-mi waskhaykita* 'I will cut your rope' and *Taytachaykichis-mi urmaymushani* 'I, your Father, am falling'. CONJECTURE -*chá* occurs rarely and only in direct quotations, i.e., *urma-ya-pu-y-man-chá* 'I would probably fall'.[5] By contrast, REPORTATIVE -*si* occurs throughout the actual narrative, including fixed forms such as *chay-si, chaymanta-s* 'then' and *hinaspa-s* 'and so'. To sum up, there is a clear demarcation between actual narrative and directly quoted material, which reveals the distinct stances assumed by the storyteller. The storyteller is a reporter of events not actually witnessed, whereas each character speaks from direct experience.

5.3.1   Retellings by Two- and Three-year-olds

Table 4.7 presents a summary of the tense and evidential suffixes produced by the two- and three-year-olds in their story retellings. The table shows adult-like (✓) uses of these morphemes for each participant in the (N)arrative portions and direct (Q)uotations, as well as those that deviate from adult usage (x).

As shown in the table, the youngest child invited to retell a story was aged 2;6. The child produced a total of six sentences, with a great deal of coaxing and scaffolding from older children who were listening. The child produced only 6 verbs, including 2 in NON-PAST and 4 uninflected roots or stems. There were no evidentials in the retelling, although the last word uttered was *chaychis* (for *chaysi* 'then-REP'), occurring at the end of a sentence where it made

---

5 This suffix will not be further discussed because it occurs only twice in directly quoted material cited by two children, aged four- and five-years.

CHILD ACQUISITION OF QUECHUA EVIDENTIALITY & DEICTIC MEANING 129

TABLE 4.7 *Summary of adult-like and deviant production of 5 morphemes by 2- and 3-year-olds in narrative portions and direct quotations*

	-sqa		*-ra-*		NON-PAST		*-mi*		*-si*	
	N	Q	N	Q	N	Q	N	Q	N	Q
2;6						✓				
2;9	✓					✓	✓	x	✓	
3;8	✓					✓				
3;9	✓					✓			✓	
3;10	✓		x		✓				✓	
3;10	✓		x				x		✓	

no sense. The excerpt from the retelling presented in (19) shows the child's utterances as well as his brother's intervention (B).

(19) 2;6 *Comi-__ aha-y-ta   atoq.*
         \$eat   chicha-1POSS-ACC fox
         'The fox eat_ my chicha.'

   B   *"Urma-yu-<u>sqa</u> atoq"   ni-y   wayqe-y.*
        fall-DIR-NX   fox   say-IMP   brother-1POSS
        'Say "the fox fell" my brother.'

   2;6 *Atoq urma-yu-n anchay.*
        fox   fall-DIR-3 that
        'The fox falls, that.'

It is clear from this exchange that, even when the NON-EXPERIENCED PAST is modeled by his brother, the child does not produce it.

The second two-year-old, aged 2;9, produced a longer retelling—14 sentences—although he, too, required some coaxing. In the narrative portions of the retelling, the child used the NON-EXPERIENCED PAST consistently for both unaccusative and agentive verbs except for two instances of NON-PAST, but there were no REPORTATIVE forms. The child marked 5 constituents with DIRECT EVIDENCE *-mi*, twice in the actual narrative (fixed form *chaymanta-n* 'then-DIREV' and *nanukuna-n* for *runakuna-n* 'people-DIREV'). The three

130 COURTNEY

mi-marked constituents in the directly quoted material included two instances of *mana-n* (NEG-DIREV 'no; not'), in addition to the utterance shown in (20).

(20) 2;9   *May-ta*   *tatichiski-<u>mi</u>*   *urma-y-mu-sha-ni?*
                     (for *tata-yki-chis-mi*)
         where-ADVL   father-2-PL-DIREV   fall-DIR-TRANS-PROG-1
         'Where am I, your Father, falling?'

The verb forms produced in the narrative portion of this retelling are adult-like, whereas the child has not yet sorted out the evidential morphemes.

The retellings produced by the 4 three-year-olds averaged 15 sentences in length (range: 9 to 18 sentences). Although none of the children required any coaxing, the sequencing of events is muddled in all of the narratives; that is, the children recall the most important events in the story, but they present them out of sequence. The two youngest of the four children, aged 3;8 and 3;9, produced -*sqa* consistently in the actual narrative for both unaccusative and agentive verbs, and produced just a few NON-PAST and future forms in directly quoted material. There were no instances of -*ra* in their retellings. While the younger of these two children produced no evidential morphemes, the older of the two produced *chaychis* (for *chaysi* 'then-REP') five times during the narrative. This child also marked a single constituent with -*si* in combination with -*sqa*, although the corresponding sentence did not reflect events in the original story: *Punchukunata-s apaymusha-sqa* 'They say he was taking ponchos'.

There were two children aged 3;10. The retelling produced by one of these children, which began with the word *atoqsi* ('fox-REP'), was entirely narrative—no dialogue—and all the verbs but one were appropriately -*sqa*-inflected; one sentence in the narrative contained a verb marked in -*ra*. This child produced one other constituent with -*si* as well as one instance of *chaymi* ('then-DIREV'). In (21), two consecutive sentences are presented from the child's narrative, which illustrate his inconsistent use of the past tense and evidential suffixes, i.e., -*mi* and -*ra* in the first sentence and -*si* and -*sqa* in the second.

(21) *Chay-<u>mi</u>*   *ichhu-manta*   *waskha-ta*   *ruwa-ku-<u>ra</u>-n.*
     that-DIREV   grass-ABL   rope-ACC   make-REFL-PST-3
     'Then he made himself a rope from straw.'

     Loro-<u>s</u>   *kuchu-ra-pu-<u>sqa</u>*   *waskha-n-ta.*
     $parrot-REP   cut-EXH-REG-NX   rope-3-ACC
     'The parrot cut his rope.'

CHILD ACQUISITION OF QUECHUA EVIDENTIALITY & DEICTIC MEANING   131

The second child aged 3;10 also produced the two Past Tense inflections, *-sqa* and *-ra*, in free variation in the narrative portion of her retelling. Her only *-si*-marked constituent was the opening convention, *huk pacha-s* 'once upon a time'. Thereafter, she used *-mi* only in self-directed wh-questions, which were not actually part of the retelling. Four sentences from her retelling are presented in (22).

(22) a. *Chay-manta-qa   urma-yu-mu-ra̱-n.*
        that-ABL-TOP   fall-DIR-TRANS-PST-3
        'Then he fell.'

    b. *Tayta-cha-manta   hina-ku-sqa̱.*
        Father-DIM-ABL   do.as-REFL-NX
        'He acted like the Father.'

    c. *Estaka-ta   taka-ra̱-n-ku;   rumi-ta-pu-wan   chura-sqa̱-n-ku.*
        $stake-ACC   nail-PST-3-PL   stone-ACC-REG-INS   put-NX-3-PL
        'They nailed stakes; and they put stones.'

    d. *Chay-manta-taq* ... *ima ni-n-ku-ṉ?*   *Ima ni-n-ku-mi̱?*
        that-ABL-CNT   what say-3-PL-FOC   what say-3-PL-FOC
        'And then ... What did they say? What did they say?'

Examples (a)–(c) show the child's inconsistent use of the past tense alternatives, while (d) includes self-directed wh-questions marked with *-mi*.

5.3.2   Retellings by Four-year-olds

On average, the retellings produced by the 6 four-year-olds are the same length (range: 9 to 18 sentences) as those produced by the three-year-olds. Table 4.8 presents a summary of the use of the tense and evidential suffixes by the four-year-olds. Once again, the table shows adult-like (✔) uses of these morphemes for each participant in the (N)arrative portions and direct (Q)uotations, as well as those that deviate from adult usage (x). As shown in the table, nearly all the four-year-olds used NON-EXPERIENCED PAST or NON-PAST in the narrative portions of their retellings, with production of other verb forms, such as future and conditional, confined to directly quoted material. One child, aged 4;6, produced a single instance of EXPERIENCED PAST *-ra*, occurring in a direct quotation, while another, aged 4;7, produced two, one in the narrative and one in reported speech. Most of the four-year-olds produced very few constituents

132 COURTNEY

TABLE 4.8   *Summary of adult-like and deviant production of morphemes by 4-year-olds in narrative portions and direct quotations*

	-sqa		-ra-		NON-PAST		Future; Conditional		-mi		-si	
	N	Q	N	Q	N	Q	N	Q	N	Q	N	Q
4;1	✓										✓	
4;2	✓								✓		✓	
4;6	✓				✓		✓	x		✓		
4;6	✓		✓		✓		✓			✓		
4;6	✓					✓				✓	✓	
4;7	✓	x		✓	✓			✓		✓	✓	

marked with -*si*: four of the children did not use the suffix at all or produced only one instance in the narrative portion.

The remaining two children, aged 4;1 and 4;6, produced -*si* on several constituents in the narrative, as illustrated in (23), which presents portions of their retellings. These narrative sequences demonstrate competent use of -*si* and -*sqa*, and, in the retelling produced by the child aged 4;6, appropriate use of -*mi* in reported speech.

(23) a. 4;1 *Atoq-si, uu,   tiya-sha-sqa.*
              fox-REP, um,   reside-PROG-NX
              'The fox was staying [there].'

              Hinaspa   aha-ta   tuma-spa   macha-ra-pu-sqa.
              then   chicha-ACC $drink-SR   get.drunk-EXH-REG-NX
              'Then when he drank chicha he got drunk.'

              Hinaspa-s   kuntur   rihuri-ra-mu-sqa.
              then-REP   condor   appear-EXH-TRANS-NX
              'Then the condor suddenly appeared.'

     b. 4;6 *Waskha-n-ta-s   hayku-m-pu-sqa,   loritu*
              rope-3-ACC-REP   fall-TRANS-REG-NX $little.parrot

CHILD ACQUISITION OF QUECHUA EVIDENTIALITY & DEICTIC MEANING   133

> *k'utu-ru-<u>sqa</u>,*   *"pun"*   *ni-spa.*
> cut-EXH-NX $pun   say-SR
> 'The parrot cut his rope and it fell below with a "pun" sound.'

> *Atoq-<u>si</u>*   *waskha-ntin*   *urma-y-pu-<u>sqa.</u>*
> fox-REP   rope-INCL   fall-DIR-REG-NX
> 'The fox fell along with the rope.'

> *Urma-yu-spa-taq*   *qapari-ka-mu-<u>sqa</u>*   *"wayqe"...*   *ni-spa,*
> fall-DIR-SR-CNT   shout-REFL-TRANS-NX brother   say-SR
> 'And falling, he shouted, saying, brother...'

> *"Runa-kuna,*   *pasara-ta*   *mast'a-y-chis."*
> person-PL   blanket-ACC extend-IMP-PL
> 'People, lay out blankets.'

> *"Tayta-yki-<u>n</u>*   *urma-y-mu-sha-n."*
> father-2-DIREV   fall-DIR-TRANS-PROG-3
> 'Your Father is falling.'

There were 5 other instances of DIRECT EVIDENCE *-mi*, produced by three different four-year-olds, all but one occurring in directly quoted material.

The retellings of the four-year-olds are cohesive insofar as the story events are correctly sequenced. They also show quite competent use of the enclitics and past-tense morphemes for perspective-shifting, even though there is evidence of difficulty in making their narratives coherent through accurate referencing. For example, in attempting to produce sentences with subordinate clauses, one child, aged 4;6, confused the same-reference and switch-reference morphemes. To express sequential action through subordination of the earlier event, Quechua speakers make use of two affixes: SAME REFERENCE *-spa* (SR) indicates that the subject of both actions is the same entity, while SWITCH REFERENCE *-qti* (SWR) indicates that the subjects are different. Example (24) presents errors produced by this child, together with the intended versions.

(24) a. *Hinaspa macha-ru-qti-n-taq,*   *seku-ta*   *puñu-ya-pu-sqa.*
        then   get.drunk-EXH-SWR-3-CNT $dry-ADVL sleep-INT-REG-NX
        'Then, after he$_1$ got drunk, he$_2$ slept soundly.'

Intended:

Hinaspa macha-ru-spa-taq,   seku-ta   puñu-ya-pu-sqa.
then   get.drunk-EXH-SR-CNT $dry-ADVL   sleep-INT-REG-NX
'Then, after he₁ got drunk, he₁ slept soundly.'

b. *Hinaspa-n   rikch'a-ru-qti-n,   may,   huyay-lla   waqa-yu-sqa*
   then-DIREV   awaken-EXH-SWR-3   where   sad-LIM   cry-INT-NX

   chay-pi.
   that-LOC
   'Then, when he₁ woke up, where, he₂ cried there very sadly there.'

Intended:

Hinaspa-s   rikch'a-ru-spa,   may,   huyay-lla   waqa-yu-sqa
then-REP   awaken-EXH-SR   where   sad-LIM   cry-INT-NX

chay-pi.
that-LOC
'Then, when he₁ woke up, where, he₁ cried there very sadly there.'

c. *K'utu-ra-m-pu-spa   urma-y-mu-n.*
   cut-EXH-TRANS-REG-SR   fall-DIR-TRANS-3
   'After he₁ cut it, he₁ fell.'

Intended:

K'utu-ra-m-pu-qti-n   urma-y-mu-n.
cut-EXH-TRANS-REG-SWR-3   fall-DIR-TRANS-3
'After he₁ cut it, he₂ fell.'

The other four-year-olds did not exhibit problems with these morphemes, perhaps because they made few attempts at subordination.

5.3.3   Retellings by Five- and Six-year-olds

Compared to the retellings of the younger children, the narratives produced by the 7 five- and six-year-olds are longer (average length: 17 sentences; range 9 to 23), and more coherent: the events are well-sequenced, reference in subordinate clauses is clear, and the actors and speakers are adequately identified.

CHILD ACQUISITION OF QUECHUA EVIDENTIALITY & DEICTIC MEANING   135

Table 4.9 presents a summary of the use of the tense and evidential suffixes by these children.

With respect to the production of evidential morphemes, the retellings of the five-year-olds pattern with those of the four-year-olds: there is very limited but largely adult-like use of -*mi* and -*si*. It is the retellings produced by the six-year-olds that exhibit use of -*si* on a variety of constituents. Sample excerpts from the retellings produced by 2 six-year-olds are presented in (25)–(27). Examples (25), (26a) and (27b), from the narrative portions of the retellings, exhibit adult-like use of -*si* and -*sqa* as well as successful attempts at subordination. In the sentences shown in (26b) and (27a), -*mi* is used appropriately in direct quotations. It is thus clear from these examples that six-year-olds can manipulate the verb forms required for narrative and direct quotations and produce the appropriate evidential markers.

(25) 6;0   *Kuntur-sis   apa-sqa   atoq-ta   cielo-man,   fiesta   ka-qti-n.*
           condor-REP   take-NX   fox-ACC $sky-ILLA $party   be-SW-3
           'The condor took the fox to the sky, there being a party.'

(26) 6;1 a. *Apa-ri-ka-pu-qti-n-si   aha-ta   tuma-yu-sqa*
             take-INCH-REFL-REG-SWR-3-REP   chicha-ACC $drink-INT-NX

             askha-ta,   mikhuna-kuna-ta
             a.lot-ACC   food-PL-ACC
             'After he₁ had carried him [there], he₂ drank a lot of chicha, and food.'

TABLE 4.9   *Summary of adult-like and deviant production of morphemes by 5- and 6-year-olds in narrative portions and direct quotations*

	-*sqa*		-*ra*-		NON-PAST		future; conditional		-*mi*		-*si*	
	N	Q	N	Q	N	Q	N	Q	N	Q	N	Q
5;0	✓					✓		✓				✓
5;1	✓			✓	✓	✓				x		
5;8	✓			✓								✓
6;0	✓					✓		✓			✓	✓
6;1	✓					✓		✓			✓	✓
6;4	✓					✓		✓			✓	✓
6;4	✓			✓		✓		✓		x	✓	✓

b. *Chay-si̱, noqa allin-mi̱ ka-ku-sha-ni ni-spa ni-sqa̱.*
that-REP I good-DIREV be-REFL-PROG-1 say-SR say-NX
'Then he said, "I'm doing well".'

(27) 6;4 a. *"Noqa-qa kama-y-pi-ṉ trankilo puñu-ku-sha-ni"*
I-TOP $bed-1-LOC-DIREV $peaceful sleep-REFL-PROG-1

ni-sqa̱.
say-NX
'He said, "I'm sleeping peacefully in my bed".'

b. *Chay-si̱ "Compadre" ni-spa waha-kacha-ku-sqa̱.*
that-REP $compadre say-SR call-SIM-REFL-NX
'Then he kept calling out, "Compadre".'

These data reveal that, by the age of six years, Quechua-speaking children are fully adept at making their narratives vivid and interesting by using the evidential enclitics and past-tense suffixes to shift perspective from the narrator's world to that of the characters.

6   Final Remarks: Consolidating Results in a Working Theory

This section considers the composite findings of the three studies with particular respect to the development of the Quechua evidential system in children aged two to four years. Table 4.10 presents a summary of the major observations regarding the production and comprehension of the past tense inflections and evidential enclitics.

Taken together, the next two sections present a working theory of child acquisition of the Quechua past-tense inflections and evidential morphemes, one which will inform future research in this area.

6.1   *Past Tense Inflections*

The most noteworthy observation from the story retellings is children's early acquisition of the deictic function of the past tense morphemes as a means of establishing epistemological stance (Mushin 2000). In their retellings, two- and three-year-olds manifest some difficulty in sorting out the use of the two past-tense morphemes. Nonetheless, by the late two's, they appear to understand that the storyteller uses *-sqa* to narrate past events, including agentive/

CHILD ACQUISITION OF QUECHUA EVIDENTIALITY & DEICTIC MEANING   137

TABLE 4.10 *Summary of production and comprehension data by age and type of data*

		Past tense suffixes: -*sqa* and -*ra*-	Evidential enclitics: -*mi*, -*chá* and -*si*
Conversations	2 and 3 yrs	– Use of -*sqa* confined to unaccusatives to express end states – Use of -*ra* for expressing agentive action	– Use of -*mi* to mark focus – Epistemic use of -*mi* in statements to express commitment to a proposition – Emergence of -*chá*; absence of -*si*
	4 yrs	– Use of -*sqa* on a few agentive verbs	– First use of -*mi* to indicate direct evidence – Limited use of -*si* in delayed mandates and reported information
Expt	3 and 4 yrs	– Comprehension of epistemic contrast: – No comprehension of evidential contrast:	-*mi* vs -*chá* -*mi*/-*ra* vs -*si*/-*sqa*
Retellings	2 yrs	– Consistent use of -*sqa* on both unaccusative and agentive verbs in narrative segments – No instances of -*ra*	– Use of -*mi* in both narrative segments and direct quotations – Absence of -*si*
	3 yrs	– Mostly consistent use of -*sqa* on both unaccusative and agentive verbs in narrative segments – Instances of -*ra* and -*sqa* in free variation in narrative segments	– Emerging use of -*si* in narrative segments, mostly in fixed form *chaysi* – Just 1 token of -*mi* inappropriately produced in narrative portion: *chaymi*
	4 yrs	– Consistent use of -*sqa* in narrative portions and limited use of -*ra* in direct quotations	– Use of -*mi* in direct quotations – Increased use of -*si* in narrative segments

dynamic verbs, because this is the appropriate form for establishing the narrator's perspective. This outcome is surprising because, in spontaneous conversations, two- and three-year-olds generally confine production of *-sqa* to unaccusative/ existence verbs and *-ra* to agentive verbs. Children at this age may not yet have a full understanding of *-sqa* as a spatio-temporal deictic used to mark an event as outside the speaker's perceptual field (Faller 2004). Although they may know that storytellers use *-sqa* to establish the role of narrator, they may not yet have captured the distinction between experienced (perceived) and non-experienced (unperceived) past. It is probably not until the age of four years that children begin to use the past-tense inflections to distinguish experience/perception and lack of experience.

6.2   *Evidential Enclitics*

With regard to children's acquisition of the evidential enclitics, the data suggest a developmental sequence. In spontaneous production, *-mi* emerges the earliest, probably as a marker of focus or commitment to a proposition. Children begin producing *-chá* by the late two's, and the data suggest that the first values assigned by two- and three-year-olds to *-mi* and *-chá* are epistemic: in the conversations of these children, the two morphemes likely indicate degree of certainty/commitment rather than information source, especially considering that *-si* is absent in their spontaneous speech. REPORTATIVE *-si* does not emerge until the age of four years in the naturalistic data. Since *-si* is purely evidential (Faller 2002a), it is probably at this age that children begin producing the enclitics in their evidential function. Thus, only at the age of four years is there evidence that children have begun to express propositional deixis (de Haan 2005), whereby a Quechua speaker would make use of *-si* for events occurring outside his/her deictic sphere and *-mi* for those that take place within his/her deictic sphere.

The above findings are supported by the experimental results. The experiment yielded the finding that children between the ages of three and six years judge *-mi*-statements as (a) more reliable than *-chá*-statements and (b) equally reliable as, or less reliable than *si*-statements. This suggests that, in isolated, decontextualized statements, children interpret *-mi* as indicating certainty, paralleling *-puni*, while they do not show understanding of the evidential import of *-mi* and *-si*. Even the six-year-olds had difficulty judging the relative reliability of direct evidence and hearsay perhaps because of the cognitive demands of the task and the absence of discourse context. Clearly, the acquisition of evidential meaning, specifically propositional deixis, is a protracted process.

Nonetheless, the story retellings show that the use of *-si* for establishing the narrator's perspective is a relatively early development, with three-year-olds already *si*-marking constituents in their narratives. By the age of four years, children have clearly learned to make use of the enclitics to shift the deictic center back and forth from the real world of the narrator and audience to the characters in the story world (Mushin 2000). This is an impressive accomplishment considering the difficulties children continue to have making their narrations coherent through adequate referencing of clausal subjects.

6.3   Past and Future Investigations

It is tempting to argue that the early development of epistemological stance favors the proposal that the Quechua evidential enclitics serve fundamentally to mark speaker perspective rather than source of information (Nuckolls 2008). In the same vein, one might interpret the results as also supporting the claim that epistemic modality encompasses information source (Nuckolls 1993) or that *-mi* encodes two independent notions: direct evidence as information source and commitment/certainty (Floyd 1996). However, a second interpretation is more likely: the acquisition of the various functions of the Quechua morphemes relies on different aspects of non-linguistic cognitive development, especially theory of mind. It is no coincidence, for example, that the understanding of the linguistic distinction between direct and indirect evidence emerges across languages at four years, the age at which children manifest the ability to reason about mental states in general (Papafragou 2002). In like manner, it is plausible that children initially assign the meaning of certainty to *-mi* because speaker certainty is more salient to children than information regarding perceptual evidence (de Villiers et al. 2009). Accordingly, the findings for the Quechua-speaking children converge with those of studies of the development of evidential systems in other languages. Crosslinguistically, acquisition of evidentiality is a protracted process because children's understanding of inference and indirect evidence is delayed (Aksu-Koç 1988; de Villiers et al. 2009). Along the route to full mastery of evidential encoding, children assign epistemic values to these morphemes (de Villiers 2009 et al.; Matsui, Yamamoto and McCagg 2006).

Although this preliminary analysis of the three data sets converges with findings from other studies, further research is necessary, especially considering the impossibility of straightforwardly interpreting children's use of the evidential morphemes in spontaneous production. Older children might be asked to explain their use of particular evidential enclitics and past tense inflections in their story retellings; however, metalinguistic tasks are often problematic (Robinson 2009).

With respect to experimental procedures, the hidden objects task should be repeated with more contrasts. Aydin and Ceci's (2009) experimental approach could be used to probe Quechua-speaking children's evidential understanding.

They tested Turkish children's interpretation of direct evidence and hearsay markers by observing their level of suggestibility when hearing information presented from a hearsay perspective followed by conflicting information presented from a direct witness perspective. In this case, children's level of suggestibility—their willingness to accept conflicting information marked as direct evidence—indicated their sensitivity to the evidential markers.

Finally, one of deVilliers et al's (2009) experiments could be adapted for Quechua to determine children's interpretation of certain evidential morphemes. In their study, they presented Tibetan children with a situation in which an inference was required to answer a direct question about the whereabouts of an individual. The question would always contain the direct evidence morpheme. In Quechua, the direct evidence enclitic may occur in wh-questions such as *May-pi-n Mama?* [where-LOC-DIREV mom] 'Where is Mom?' Recall Floyd's (1996) assertion that the use of the DIRECT EVIDENCE morpheme in such questions indicates the speaker's assumption that the addressee knows the answer and has direct evidence for the requested information. However, in this scenario, the child, lacking direct evidence, must rely on reasoning and conjecture to infer the mother's whereabouts. If the child's response, 'Mom is at home,' is marked as conjecture, i.e., *Mama wasi-pi-chá* [mom house-LOC-CONJ] he/she demonstrates understanding of the direct evidence and conjecture morphemes. If, however, the response is marked with the direct evidence morpheme, i.e., *Mama wasi-pi-n* [mom house-LOC-DIREV], the child understands *-mi* as encoding certainty rather than direct evidence. Procedures such as these represent promising approaches to further exploration of the working theory presented in this study.

Appendix A

ABL	ablative	INT	intensifier
ACC	accusative	INTR	interrogative
ADVL	adverbial	LIM	limitative
AF	affirmation	LOC	locative
BEN	benefactive	NEG	negative
CERT	certainty	NMLZ	nominalizer
CNT	contrastive	NX	non-experienced Past
CONJ	conjecture	OBJ	object
DAT	dative	PL	plural
DIM	diminutive	POSS	possessive

DIR	directional	PROG	progressive
DIREV	direct evidence	PROH	prohibitive
DISC	discontinuative	PST	experienced past
DUB	dubitative	REFL	reflexive
EXH	exhortative	REG	regressive
FOC	focus	REP	reportative
FUT	future	RESP	responsive
GEN	genitive	SIM	simulative
ILLA	illative	SR	same reference
IMP	imperative	SWR	switch reference
IMPR	impressive	TOP	topic
INCH	inchoative	TRANS	translocative
INCL	inclusive	1S2O	1 subject - 2 object
INS	instrumental	3S2O	3 subject - 2 object

Bibliography

Adelaar, Willem. 1977. *Tarma Quechua: Grammar, texts, dictionary.* Lisse: De Ridder.

Aikhenvald, Alexandra. 2004. *Evidentiality.* Oxford, UK: Oxford University Press.

Aksu-Koç, Ayhan. 1988. *The acquisition of aspect and modality: The case of past reference in Turkish.* Cambridge, UK: Cambridge University Press.

———. 2000. "Some aspects of the acquisition of evidentials in Turkish." In *Evidentials: Turkic, Iranian and neighboring languages*, edited by Lars Johanson and Bo Utas, 15–28. Berlin: de Gruyter.

Aksu-Koç, Ayhan, Hale Ögel-Balaban and I. Ercan Alp. 2009. "Evidentials and source knowledge in Turkish." In *Evidentiality: A window into language and cognitive development, New Directions for Child and Adolescent Development, 125*, edited by Stanka A. Fitneva and Tomoko Matsui, 13–28. San Francisco: Jossey-Bass.

Aydin, Çağla and Stephen Ceci. 2009. "Evidentiality and suggestibility: A new research venue." In *Evidentiality: A window into language and cognitive development, New Directions for Child and Adolescent Development, 125*, edited by Stanka A. Fitneva and Tomoko Matsui, 79–93. San Francisco: Jossey-Bass.

Calvo Pérez, Julio. 1993. *Pragmática y gramática del quechua cuzqueño.* Cuzco, Peru: Centro de Estudios Rurales Andinos "Bartolomé de las Casas".

Cerrón-Palomino, Rodolfo. 1987. *Lingüística quechua.* Cuzco, Peru: Centro de Estudios Rurales Andinos "Bartolomé de las Casas".

———. 1994. *Quechumara.* La Paz, Bolivia: Centro de Investigación y Promoción del Campesinado.

Chafe, Wallace and Janet Nichols, editors. 1986. *Evidentiality: The linguistic coding of epistemology.* Norwood, NJ: Ablex.

Choi, Soonja. 1995. "The development of epistemic sentence-ending modal forms and functions in Korean children." In *Modality in grammar and discourse,* edited by Joan Bybee and Suzanne Fleischman, 165–204. Amsterdam: Benjamins.

Courtney, Ellen H. 1999. "Child acquisition of the Quechua affirmative suffix." *Santa Barbara Papers in Linguistics. Proceedings from the Second Workshop on American Indigenous Languages,* 30–41. University of California, Santa Barbara.

———. 2011. "The Acquisition of Evidentiality: Insights from Quechua." Paper presented at the Workshop on Technological Approaches to Collaborative Research and Distance Learning in Quechua. Rutgers University, New Brunswick, NJ, November 5.

———. 2014. "The acquisition of evidential meaning: Insights from Quechua conversations." In *Peaches and Plums,* edited by C.T. James Huang and Feng-his Liu, 287–310. Taipei: Academia Sinica.

Cusihuamán, Antonio. 1976. *Gramática quechua Cuzco-Collao.* Lima, Perú: Ministerio de Educación/ Instituto de Estudios Peruanos.

De Haan, Ferdinand. 2005. "Encoding speaker perspective: Evidentials." In *Linguistic diversity and language theories,* edited by Zygmunt Frajzyngier and David Rood, 379–397. Amsterdam: Benjamins.

DeLancey, Scott. 2001. "The mirative and evidentiality." *Journal of Pragmatics* 33(3): 369–382.

de Villiers, Jill, Jay Garfield, Harper Gernet-Girard, Tom Roeper and Margaret Speas. 2009. "Evidentials in Tibetan: Acquisition, semantics, and cognitive development." In *Evidentiality: A window into language and cognitive development, New Directions for Child and Adolescent Development, 125,* edited by Stanka A. Fitneva and Tomoko Matsui, 29–47. San Francisco: Jossey-Bass.

Faller, Martina. 2002a. "Semantics and Pragmatics of Evidentials in Cuzco Quechua." PhD diss., Stanford University.

———. 2002b. "The evidential and validational licensing conditions for the Cusco Quechua enclitic *-MI." Belgian Journal of Linguistics* 16(1): 7–21.

———. 2004. "The Deictic core of 'Non-Experienced Past' in Cuzco Quechua." *Journal of Semantics* 21(1): 45–85.

Fitneva, Stanka A. 2009. "Evidentiality and trust: The effect of informational goals." In *Evidentiality: A window into language and cognitive development, New Directions for Child and Adolescent Development, 125,* edited by Stanka A. Fitneva and Tomoko Matsui, 49–61. San Francisco: Jossey-Bass.

Floyd, Rick. 1996. "Experience, certainty and control, and the direct evidential in Wanka Quechua questions." *Functions of Language* 3(1): 69–93.

CHILD ACQUISITION OF QUECHUA EVIDENTIALITY & DEICTIC MEANING 143

Howard-Malverde, Rosaleen. 1988. "Talking about the Past: Tense and Testimonials in Quechua Narrative Discourse." *Amerindia* 13: 125–55.

Ifantidou, Elly. 2009. "Evidentials and metarepresentation in early child language." *Functions of Language* 16(1): 89–122.

Lazard, Gilbert. 2001. "On the grammaticalization of evidentiality." *Journal of Pragmatics* 33: 359–367.

Lust, Barbara, Suzanne Flynn and Claire Foley. 1998. "What children know about what they say: Elicited imitation as a research method for assessing children's syntax." In *Methods for Assessing Children's Syntax*, edited by Dana McDaniel, Cecile McKee and Helen Smith Cairns, 54–76. Cambridge, MA: MIT Press.

Mannheim, Bruce and Krista Van Vleet. 1998. "The dialogics of Southern Quechua narrative." *American Anthropologist* 100(2): 326–346.

Matsui, Tomoko and Stanka A. Fitneva. 2009. "Knowing how we know: Evidentiality and cognitive development." In *Evidentiality: A window into language and cognitive development, New Directions for Child and Adolescent Development, 125*, edited by Stanka A. Fitneva and Tomoko Matsui, 1–11. San Francisco: Jossey-Bass.

Matsui, Tomoko, Taeko Yamamoto and Peter McCagg. 2006. "On the role of language in children's early understanding of others as epistemic beings." *Cognitive Development* 21: 158–173.

Matsui, Tomoko and Yui Miura. 2009. "Children's understanding of certainty and evidentiality: Advantage of grammaticalized forms over lexical alternatives." In *Evidentiality: A window into language and cognitive development, New Directions for Child and Adolescent Development, 125*, edited by Stanka A. Fitneva and Tomoko Matsui, 63–77. San Francisco: Jossey-Bass.

Mushin, Ilana. 2000. Evidentiality and deixis in narrative retelling. *Journal of Pragmatics* 32: 927–957.

———. 2001. *Evidentiality and Epistemological Stance: Narrative Retelling*. Amsterdam: Benjamins.

Muysken, Pieter. 1995. "Focus in Quechua." In *Discourse configurational languages*, edited by Katalin Kiss, 375–393. Oxford, UK: Oxford University Press.

Nuckolls, Janis. 1993. "The semantics of certainty in Quechua and its implications for a cultural epistemology." *Language in Society* 22: 235–255.

———. 2008. "Deitic selves and others in Pastaza Quichua evidential usage." *Anthropological Linguistics* 50(1): 67–89.

Ögel, Hale. 2007. "Developments in source monitoring and linguistic encoding of source." Master's thesis, Bogazici University, Istanbul, Turkey.

Ozturk, Ozge and Anna Papafragou. 2008. "The acquisition of evidentiality and source monitoring." *BUCLD 32 Proceedings* 2: 363–377. Somerville, MA: Cascadilla Press.

Palmer, Frank R. 2001. *Mood and Modality* (2nd edition). Cambridge, UK: Cambridge University.

Papafragou, Anna. 2002. "Mindreading and verbal communication." *Mind & Language* 17: 55–67.

Papafragou, Anna, Peggy Li, Youngon Choi and Chung-hye Han. 2007. "Evidentiality in language and cognition." *Cognition* 103: 253–299.

Plungian, Vladimir. 2001. "The place of evidentiality within the universal grammatical space." *Journal of Pragmatics* 33: 349–357.

Robinson, Elizabeth. 2009. "Commentary: What we can learn from research on evidentials." In *Evidentiality: A window into language and cognitive development, New Directions for Child and Adolescent Development, 125,* edited by Stanka A. Fitneva and Tomoko Matsui, 95–103. San Francisco: Jossey-Bass.

Sánchez, Liliana. 2010. *The Morphology and Syntax of Topic and Focus: Minimalist inquiries in the Quechua periphery.* Amsterdam: Benjamins.

Stromqvist, Sven and Dennis Day. 1993. "On the development of narrative structure in child L1 and adult L2 acquisition." *Applied Psycholinguistics* 14: 135–158.

Trask, Robert L. 1999. *Concepts in Language and Linguistics.* London and New York: Routledge.

Whorf, Benjamin L. 2012. *Language, thought and reality* (2nd edition), edited by John B. Carroll, Stephen C. Levinson and Penny Lee. Cambridge, MA: MIT Press.

Willett, Thomas. 1988. "A cross-linguistic survey of the grammaticization of evidentiality." *Studies in Language* 12(1): 51–97.

CHAPTER 5

Multidimensional Markers of Evidential, Epistemic and Mirative Stance in Cuzco Quechua

Marilyn S. Manley

1 Introduction

This chapter aims to fill important gaps in the broader literature on stance and deixis as well as in the study of Quechua specifically. The primary focus of this chapter is on the Cuzco Quechua[1] enclitics, *-mi/-n*, *-chá* and *-si/-s*, and the past-tense morphemes, *-r(q)a-* and *-sqa-*.[2] Based on the groundbreaking work of both Du Bois (2007), in his conceptualization of the stance triangle, and Hanks (2005, 2011), in his practice approach to deixis, these five Cuzco Quechua morphemes are referred to here as multidimensional markers of stance, which may simultaneously communicate evidentiality (information source), epistemology (degree of certainty/doubt) and, in the case of *-sqa-*, mirativity (surprise or newsworthiness). According to DeLancey (1997, 2001) and Aikhenvald (2004), mirativity is a category in its own right which has at its core the expression of surprise and an 'unprepared mind'.

While Jakobson (1957), building on Jespersen (1923), was the first to classify evidentials as a type of deictic 'shifter', anchoring utterances to the context of speech and shifting reference, depending on the context, the vast majority of the cross-linguistic literature fails to recognize the status of evidential, epistemic and mirative markers as markers of stance or of deixis and this work aims to fill this gap. Most cross-linguistic studies of deixis (i.e. Weissenborn and Klein 1982) focus on the three most traditional types of deixis as outlined by Bühler (1934), person, place and time deixis. Where the special status of evidential/epistemic/mirative markers as markers of stance or of deixis has been recognized, there is inconsistency in the literature, with some referring to these as markers of stance and others referring to these as deictic expressions. For example, Du Bois (2007) refers to 'epistemic stance' while Mushin (2000),

---

1   Cuzco Quechua, also known as Cuzco-Bolivian Quechua or Southern Quechua, is a subdialect of the Chinchay (QII-C) branch according to Torero's (1964) classification.
2   In Cuzco Quechua, *-mi* and *-si* follow a consonant and their allomorphs, *-n* and *-s*, follow a vowel; the past tense form, *-ra-*, occurs in free variation with *-rqa-*.

© KONINKLIJKE BRILL NV, LEIDEN, 2015 | DOI 10.1163/9789004290105_006

in her description of epistemic markers, alternately refers to either 'epistemo-logical stance' or 'epistemological deixis' with the same meaning. According to Mushin (2000, 932), "Evidentiality is a deictic category because it indexes some information to the source and/or epistemological status of that informa-tion". Following the Introduction to this volume, and as explained in section 2 below, this work supports the unification of the concepts of stance and deixis, with deixis being considered as a subclass of stance that serves a specifically referential function.

A second gap addressed here is that while the majority of existing work on stance/deixis across languages has examined free morphemes, this chapter addresses the way in which bound morphemes function strategically within discourse. Mushin (2000, 928–929) points out that there has been little study of the distribution and function of grammaticalized evidential forms in discourse and that "The lack of systematic study of evidential variation in the literature represents one gap in our knowledge of evidential systems". Despite the fact that epistemic markers play an important role in discourse, functioning to claim, diffuse or evade responsibility for knowledge (Hill and Irvine 1993), relatively few studies have carried out ethnographically-grounded research on epistemics and evidentials (Sidnell 2005); by the means of a thorough exami-nation of the ethnographic details of a speech situation, it is often possible to discover subtle nuances in the semantics and pragmatics of these markers. According to Bendix (1993, 243), the ethnography of the use of epistemics is a "...fertile corner of research within the larger study of responsibility and evidence in strategic interaction". Although, cross-linguistically, speakers have been found to manipulate chosen evidential and epistemic devices to convey their attitudes and perspectives toward knowledge, as in Chafe and Nichols' (1986) edited volume, even for languages that have been relatively well-described, there is still a need for more detailed studies (Aikhenvald 2004).

While it is true that substantial work has been carried out on Quechua, there is ongoing debate regarding the expression of evidentiality, epistemic meaning and mirativity in Quechua language varieties. In the case of Cuzco Quechua, the relevant morphemes, the enclitics, -*mi/-n*, -*chá* and -*si/-s*, and the past-tense morphemes, -*r(q)a-* and -*sqa-*, have been claimed to function as evidentials, markers of epistemic modality, mirative markers or a combination of these three categories (Cusihuamán 2001; Faller 2004; Hurtado de Mendoza Santander 2001). The present study employs recent conceptualizations of evi-dentiality, epistemics and mirativity, especially as proposed by Aikhenvald (2004) and Aikhenvald and Storch (2013), in order to propose a new, multi-faceted analysis of Cuzco Quechua -*mi/-n*, -*chá*, -*si/-s*, -*r(q)a-* and -*sqa-* that sheds light on the current debate. The analysis put forward here is new to the

MARKERS OF EVIDENTIAL, EPISTEMIC AND MIRATIVE STANCE 147

field in that it is the first to make this particular set of claims and it is new to the author as it represents a reanalysis of data gathered previously (Feke 2004, Manley 2007). As described below, this analysis is supported by the data presented here as well as a review of recent work on evidentiality, epistemics and mirativity across Quechua language varieties.[3]

More specifically, this work analyses the five morphemes of interest as follows: (1) *-mi/-n* is a direct evidential which may be utilized with epistemic extension to indicate certainty, (2) *-chá* is a conjecture evidential which may be utilized with epistemic extension to communicate doubt, (3) *-si/-s* is an indirect evidential which may be utilized with epistemic extension to indicate doubt, (4) *-r(q)a-* may be utilized as an evidentiality strategy to communicate direct information source and also with epistemic extension to indicate certainty, and (5) *-sqa-* may be utilized as an evidentiality strategy to communicate indirect information source, with epistemic extension to indicate doubt, and as a mirativity strategy, indicating surprise or newsworthiness. This analysis offers a coherent and inclusive compromise to the debate that is long overdue in the case of Cuzco Quechua and this work is the first to claim epistemic extensions for *-r(q)a-* and *-sqa-*, indicating certainty and doubt, respectively. Thus, as described here, each of these five morphemes is multidimensional and allows the speaker to simultaneously take more than one type of stance, including evidential stance, epistemic stance and mirative stance.

The results are drawn from an investigation of how the relevant morphemes were used by the members of two bilingual Quechua/Spanish communities in the city of Cuzco, Peru in spontaneous conversation (carried out in 2003) as well as in response to two different elicitation tasks: role-playing (carried out in 2002 with 62 participants) and a certainty-ranking exercise (carried out in 2003 with 61 participants). Examples are presented within this work from 17 participants of the 2002 role-playing elicitation task, who ranged in age from 10 to 25 years old (mean age 16.5 years old). The 61 participants of the certainty-ranking exercise in 2003 were between 11 and 58 years of age (mean age 21.5 years old); those participants who engaged in spontaneous conversation were a subset of these 61 participants. As detailed below in section 7.1, the certainty-ranking exercise yielded statistically significant results which inform the analysis of the participants' use of the relevant morphemes in response to the role play scenarios as well as during spontaneous conversation.

The remaining sections of this chapter are organized as follows: a discussion of the multidimensional nature of stance and deixis across all languages

---

3 The claims made here for *-chá* are based only on a review of the recent literature rather than original experimental data.

(section 2), an examination of the variation that exists in the literature regarding definitions of evidentiality and epistemology (section 3), a presentation of key terminological concepts from Aikhenvald (2004) and Aikhenvald and Storch (2013) (section 4), a description of the Quechua debate regarding evidentiality, epistemology and mirativity (section 5), and a presentation of this work, including the methodology (section 6), results (section 7), and conclusion (section 8).

2 Multidimensional Stance and Deixis

Both Du Bois (2007) and Hanks (2005, 2011), preeminent theorists of stance and deixis, respectively, have described these phenomena as being multifaceted. Du Bois (2007, 145) suggests that a single stance act may be "seen as encompassing multiple facets at once"; for example, he states, "The predicate *amazed* can be understood as incorporating, in addition to its affective dimension, a salient epistemic dimension as well" (2007, 175); in other words, a speaker who uses the predicate, *amazed*, may simultaneously communicate both his affective stance (positive affect in this case) and his epistemic stance (ignorance in this example) (Du Bois 2007, 143).

Fundamentally, Du Bois (2007, 163) defines stance in the following way:

> Stance is a public act by a social actor, achieved dialogically through overt communicative means, of simultaneously evaluating objects, positioning subjects (self and others), and aligning with other subjects, with respect to any salient dimension of the sociocultural field.

This definition incorporates the three nodes of Du Bois' stance triangle, "the three key entities in the stance act, namely the first subject, the second subject, and the (shared) stance object" (2007, 164). Du Bois (2007, 163) further explains:

> The stance act thus creates three kinds of stance consequences at once. In taking a stance, the stancetaker (1) evaluates an object, (2) positions a subject (usually the self), and (3) aligns with other subjects.

As presented in the Introduction to the current volume, Hanks' (2005, 2011) practice approach to deixis describes deictics in a way that is consistent with Du Bois' stance triangle, thus paving the way for a reanalysis of deixis as a subclass of stance. For example, in his practice approach, Hanks recognizes

MARKERS OF EVIDENTIAL, EPISTEMIC AND MIRATIVE STANCE

that evaluation is central to deictic expression. As such, in recognizing that evaluation is unavoidable in deixis, Hanks' practice approach allows deictics to satisfy Du Bois' definition of stance as "an act of evaluation owned by a social actor" (Du Bois 2007, 173).

Hanks' practice approach builds on two robust traditions in deictic theory, which he refers to as the spatialist and the interactionist traditions. According to the egocentric spatialist view, which Hanks (2005, 196) describes as "the standard default for most modern linguistic descriptions", "deictic acts take place when the Spr [Speaker], the Adr [Addressee], and the Object are physically copresent and perceptible". Moreover, according to the spatialist position, "The situation may be interperspectival, but it is the Spr who produces the utterance and the Spr's body that serves as the anchor point..." (2005, 196). According to the interactionist view of deixis, on the other hand, the emergent space of interaction serves as the core context for deictic expression, "and to study it, we must attend to sequential organization of talk, to situational variation and to the micro-ethnography of everyday usage" (Hanks 2011, 322). Furthermore, the interactionist view proposes that "Utterance meaning must be 'negotiated' or worked out by the co-engaged parties. It is not given in advance, nor is it fixed by the intentions of the Spr" (Hanks 2005, 196). Finding that neither the spatialist nor the interactionist views could adequately account for his discourse data in Yucatec Maya, Hanks proposed his practice approach as a third, blended, compromise position. Hanks (2011, 323) explains, "We can grant interaction as the ordinary context of utterances, while still claiming that the semantics of deixis is egocentric and spatial."

Additionally, Hanks (2005, 212) describes his concept of the deictic field as "a space of positions and position taking in relation to objects and their values in the embedding social field"; however, in his analysis of Yucatec Mayan examples, he finds that "there are multiple deictic dimensions in play in the actual field of utterance" (2005, 207). Hanks (2005, 207) sees the 'multistranded makeup' of the deictic field to be problematic for deictic construal, since:

> At any moment in interaction, multiple dimensions of access (among participants, objects, and settings) are simultaneously available for interactants. The selection and understanding of deictics relies on the simultaneous articulation of space, perception, discourse, commonsense and mutual knowledge, anticipation, and the framework of participation in which Sprs and Adrs [Speakers and Addressees] orient to one another. Any one of these factors can provide the basis for deictic construal according to the demands of the ongoing relevance structure in which it is produced.

In other words, as deictic expressions are multidimensional and, as such, may simultaneously access more than one dimension, determining which dimension(s) is/are being accessed with any particular use of a deictic expression may prove challenging. Hanks (2005, 209) also finds that it is precisely this "simultaneity of alternate framings in the deictic field" that accounts for the variation that he has observed in Yucatec Mayan linguistic practice.

Similar to Hanks' findings for Yucatec Maya, as will be explained in the present chapter, the variation that exists in the use of the Quechua enclitics, *-mi/-n, -chá* and *-si/-s*, and the past tense morphemes, *-r(q)a-* and *-sqa-*, may be accounted for by appealing to the inherent, multidimensional nature of markers of stance, including deictic expressions. As Hanks found for Yucatec Maya, each of the five Cuzco Quechua morphemes examined here has the potential to simultaneously access more than one deictic dimension at a time or, stated differently, may communicate more than one type of stance, including evidential stance, epistemic stance and mirative stance.

3 Defining Evidentiality and Epistemology

> What is knowing? What kinds of beings have knowledge? What sorts of things are known? ... For two thousand years philosophers have asked and attempted to answer these questions. This ongoing discussion constitutes the subject matter of the philosophical area called the theory of knowledge, or Epistemology (Lucey 1996, 9).

The notion of 'epistemology' has its origins in the field of philosophy. Relatively recently, its application to the field of linguistics has been explored. In the linguistic literature, there is debate as to the exact definition and nature of the terms, 'epistemic' and 'evidential'. While the present work finds evidentiality and epistemology to be separate linguistic categories, indicating information source and degree of certainty/doubt, respectively, others, such as Chafe (1986), have asserted that epistemology falls under the broader category of evidentiality. In the introduction to their often-cited work, *Evidentiality: The Linguistic Coding of Epistemology* (1986, vii), Chafe and Nichols describe the heterogeneous perspectives of the authors published in their volume as representing a stage of exploration in the study of evidentials and explain:

> The term 'evidential' ... now covers much more than the marking of evidence per se. We do not wish, for the moment at least, to suggest what the boundaries of evidentiality in the broad sense are.

Chafe (1986, 262) maintains that epistemic markers are subsumed by the broader category of evidentials and further states, "... everything dealt with under this broad interpretation of evidentiality involves attitudes toward knowledge". In Chafe and Nichols' volume, Anderson (1986) identifies twenty distinct examples of evidential meanings.

According to Escobar (2000, 213), on the other hand, epistemology may be considered to be the broader category, including two subsystems, one of judgment, which makes reference to the knowledge, opinions, and attitude of a speaker toward his/her utterance, and one of evidentials, which makes reference to the information source for an utterance (e.g. first-hand information, second-hand information, etc.).

Over two decades later, Brugman and Macaulay (2010) find that there continues to be a great deal of disagreement regarding the definition of evidentials. The authors compiled a list of thirty-eight definitions or characterizations of evidentials in the literature and from these, they created a preliminary list of several proposed parameters for the evaluation of evidentials. The only property not found by the authors to be contradicted in the literature is that evidentials mark the source of evidence (such as visual, sensory, inference, assumption, reported, and quotative). Brugman and Macaulay (2010) state that while some have defined evidentiality as the source of information the speaker has for his/her statement, shifted uses of evidentials have also been described for a few languages, where it is not the speaker who perceives the evidence identified by the evidential particle but rather a second or third person.[4] Additional examples of inconsistencies include: (1) while some authors treat obligatoriness as criterial, Brugman and Macaulay found that for others, evidentials may be optional, (2) while some authors assume that evidentials are mutually exclusive, Brugman and Macaulay observed that for other authors, terms in an evidential system may be complementary or overlapping, and (3) although the canonical set of evidentials consists of a closed class of grammatical morphemes, Brugman and Macaulay, among others, such as Aikhenvald (2004), have found that the expression of evidential meaning in the literature may range from lexical to grammatical.

In the following section, key concepts from Aikhenvald (2004) and Aikhenvald and Storch (2013) pertaining to evidentiality, epistemic modality and mirativity are presented that will be utilized throughout the remainder of this chapter.

---

4   Such shifted uses of evidentials have been noted for Quechua varieties and are described below.

4 Terminology from Aikhenvald (2004) and Aikhenvald and Storch (2013)

Based on the analysis of evidential/epistemic/mirative systems in 500 languages from around the world, Aikhenvald's (2004) typology offers much needed clarity to the understanding of these stance categories; Aikhenvald and Storch (2013) offer further description. Within this chapter, key concepts defined within these two works are applied to the case of Quechua and for this reason, it is necessary to first explore these concepts in depth, thereby providing the necessary background for the later discussion of the particulars of the debate as they pertain to Quechua.

This work agrees with Aikhenvald and Storch (2013, 4) that source of information is the primary meaning for the grammatical category of evidentiality, and the point of view here is that the enclitics, *-mi/-n* (direct evidential), *-chá* (conjecture evidential) and *-si/-s* (indirect evidential), have information source as their primary, lexically-encoded meaning. This is also the general sense among Quechua speakers who, when asked, will first point to information source meanings for these enclitics.

Aikhenvald and Storch (2013, 6) also state that evidentials may have epistemic extensions "...to do with probability and speaker's evaluation of the trustworthiness of information". Aikhenvald (2004, 153) explains:

> Individual terms in evidentiality systems may acquire various semantic extensions, including attitude to information, its probability, a speaker's certainty of the truthfulness of their statement, and their responsibility for it.

To a large extent, there is semantic overlap between the meaning of an evidential and its epistemic extensions.

The analysis put forth here is that all three of the Quechua evidential enclitics, *-mi/-n*, *-chá* and *-si/-s*, may be utilized with epistemic extensions of their meaning. The data presented below and a review of the relevant literature across Quechua language varieties support the claim that *-mi/-n* may be utilized with epistemic extension in order to indicate a high level of certainty. In this way, Quechua falls in line with other languages for which the visual evidential, communicating information that the speaker obtained through sight, may be extended to "...relate generally known facts, and sometimes even to facts the speaker is sure of" (Aikhenvald 2004, 20). Aikhenvald (2004, 187) further explains that across languages:

The VISUAL evidential may have epistemic extensions of certainty and commitment to the truth of the proposition. It also carries overtones of the speaker's conviction, and their responsibility for the statement, and is used to talk about generally known facts.

In general, it follows that speakers have a greater degree of certainty regarding information that they have acquired directly.

While the present work does not include original data on the use of *-chá*, an examination of the recent literature, presented below, suggests that this evidential may also be utilized with epistemic extension in order to communicate doubt, among other related meanings.

Furthermore, the data presented below as well as literature review support the argument that *-si/-s* may be utilized with epistemic extension of its meaning, indicating doubt. Across languages, Aikhenvald (2004, 158) has found that common meaning extensions for non-firsthand evidentials include a lack or denial of responsibility and overtones of doubt, among other meanings; this has been found for the reported evidential in Estonian, which carries overtones of doubt according to Aikhenvald and Storch (2013, 6). Aikhenvald (2004, 193) further explains:

> A reported evidential can develop an epistemic extension of unreliable information, as a means of 'shifting' responsibility for the information to some other source one does not vouch for.

It is also generally true that speakers have a lesser degree of certainty regarding information that they have acquired indirectly.

Aikhenvald and Storch (2013, 9) also describe the way in which evidential-like meanings may emerge as secondary for a variety of forms, in which case they may be referred to as evidentiality strategies. Aikhenvald (2004, 149) explains:

> ...a grammatical technique is an evidentiality strategy if, in addition to its primary meaning, it can acquire one or more semantic features characteristic of evidentiality proper.

Cross-linguistically, Aikhenvald (2004, 144) has found such grammatical categories as past tenses, non-indicative moods, perfects, resultatives, passives, nominalizations, complementation strategies, and person-marking to develop into evidentiality strategies. However, across languages, "The maximum number of evidential specifications is found in past tenses, and in perfective aspect" (Aikhenvald and Storch 2013, 6).

The viewpoint proposed here is that -$r(q)a$- and -sqa-, which have the communication of past tense as their primary, lexically-encoded meaning, may be used as evidentiality strategies: -$r(q)a$- may be used to communicate a direct information source and -sqa- may communicate an indirect information source. In this way, Quechua is similar to the Balkan Slavic languages, for which "The simple preterite acquired the 'firsthand' meaning and the old perfect became associated with the array of non-firsthand meanings..." (Aikhenvald 2004, 280).

Similar to the way in which it is claimed here that the evidential enclitics, -$mi/-n$, -$chá$ and -$si/-s$, are used with epistemic extensions of their meaning, it is also put forward here that -$r(q)a$- and -sqa-, identified here as evidentiality strategies, also have epistemic extensions. Specifically, -$r(q)a$- may also indicate a high level of certainty and -sqa- may indicate doubt. This work is the first to propose epistemic extensions of any kind for -$r(q)a$- and -sqa-. Aikhenvald (2004, 105) explains:

> Just like evidentials themselves, evidentiality strategies may, or may not, have 'epistemic' extensions of their meanings (that is, refer to the probability or possibility of something happening).

In addition to serving as an evidentiality strategy, it is also argued here that -sqa- serves as a mirativity strategy, communicating surprise and other related meanings, such as newsworthiness and unconscious and unintentional actions. Across languages, Aikhenvald (2004, 195) has found that "...evidentiality strategies may also acquire mirative nuances...". Aikhenvald and Storch (2013, 11), following (DeLancey 2001), describe mirativity and note:

> Many languages of the world have a grammatical form or construction expressing information which is new or surprising to the 'unprepared mind' of the speaker, or the hearer.

In this way, Quechua is similar to Jaqi, for which "...the remote past reported marker which typically occurs in myths and legends of all sorts may also indicate surprise" (Aikhenvald 2004, 203, citing Hardman 1986, 130).

As presented below, the data gathered for the present work include examples in which the Quechua enclitics, -$mi/-n$, -$chá$ and -$si/-s$, are combined with the past tenses, -$r(q)a$- and -sqa-. Therefore, within single utterances, both evidentiality and epistemic meaning may be marked twice, both on the evidential enclitics and on the past tenses, serving as evidentiality strategies. Aikhenvald (2004, 88) argues that such repetition of evidential meaning is not semantically redundant:

> Marking evidentiality more than once is different from the multiple expression of any other category: it is never semantically redundant. Having several evidentiality markers in one clause allows speakers to express subtle nuances relating to types of evidence and information source, either interrelated or independent of one another.

In Quechua, lexical items such as *rikuy* 'to see' or *niy* 'to say' may further reinforce the communication of information source, such as in the case of a speaker who explicitly states that he/she 'saw' an event or that someone 'told' him/her about an event. The Quechua suffix *-puni* also indicates certainty and may be combined along with the evidential enclitics and past tenses.[5]

Similarly, across languages, mirative meaning may be strengthened or reinforced by the addition of other markers or lexical items; this has been found for Abkhaz, which employs an emphatic particle or an emphatic interjection (Aikhenvald 2004, 199, citing from Chirikba 2003, 249). In Quechua, the suffix, *-má*, may also indicate surprise and appear in combination with the past tense morpheme, *-sqa-*, utilized as a mirativity strategy (Aráoz and Salas 1993, 74).[6]

The following section describes the current debate among Quechua scholars regarding the communication of evidentiality, epistemic modality and mirativity. With so much inconsistency in the cross-linguistic literature regarding evidentials, as noted by Brugman and Macaulay (2010) and described above, it comes as no surprise that the literature on Quechua specifically also contains much disagreement.

5   The Quechua Debate: Evidentiality, Epistemology and Mirativity

In the case of Quechua language varieties, there has been ongoing debate regarding: (1) which linguistic elements should be considered as communicating evidentiality, epistemology and mirativity, and (2) whether the relevant morphemes should be considered to be primarily evidential, epistemic or mirative in nature. By presenting a relatively recent sample of the varying viewpoints here that are representative of the various claims made in the literature,

---

5   The participants of this work did not produce *-puni* in the data analyzed here.
6   The participants of this work did not produce *-má* in the data analyzed here.

156   MANLEY

it will be possible to discern how this chapter compares with the literature to date. Table 5.1 below categorizes the viewpoints of nine different Quechua language scholars, in addition to the viewpoint of the present work, regarding the meanings and uses of the enclitics, *-mi/-n*, *-chá*, and *-si/-s*, as well as the past tense morphemes, *-r(q)a-* and *-sqa-*.[7] Furthermore, in table 5.1, the corresponding name of the variety of Quechua studied and its classification according to Torero (1964) are listed; these include QI: Central Peruvian Quechua, QII-C: Southern Peruvian Quechua, and QII-B: Quichua from Amazonian Ecuador. While these nine authors may not use the specific definitions and terminologies adopted in the present work and described above (for evidential meaning, epistemic meaning, evidentiality strategy, epistemic extension and mirativity strategy), it is possible to compare and categorize their claims according to the definitions and terminologies used here. As presented in table 5.1:

(1)   Some of these authors find *-mi/-n*, *-chá* and *-si/-s* to communicate evidential meaning, epistemic meaning, or both evidential and epistemic meaning.
(2)   Two of these authors find *-si/-s* to be used as a mirativity strategy.
(3)   Some of these authors find *-r(q)a-* and/or *-sqa-* to be used as evidentiality strategies.
(4)   The present work, alone, finds *-r(q)a-* to be used with epistemic extension of its meaning.
(5)   The present work, alone, finds *-sqa-* to be used with epistemic extension of its meaning.
(6)   Some of these authors find *-sqa-* to function as a mirativity strategy.

Each of the nine authors included in table 5.1 makes a particular set of claims regarding Quechua evidentiality, epistemology and mirativity that differs from the claims of the present work. For the sake of clarity, in the sections that follow, each author's claims are presented as a set. In presenting these claims author-by-author, rather than in a combined summary, it is possible to keep separate the different Quechua varieties represented; as described below, depending on the language variety, the morphemes of interest may have alternate realizations. Furthermore, presenting these sets of claims one author at a time allows for a more complete, nuanced understanding of each

---

7   As these nine scholars have examined different Quechua language varieties, these morphemes may have other, corresponding forms in the respective Quechua language varieties.

TABLE 5.1 *Comparison of authors' accounts of Quechua evidentiality, epistemology and mirativity*

Work	Variety name	Variety code	EV -mi/-n	EP -mi/-n	EV -chá	EP -chá	EV -si/-s	EP -si/-s	MIR -si/-s	EV -r(q)a-	EP -r(q)a-	EV -sqa-	EP -sqa-	MIR -sqa-
Manley (present work)	Cuzco Quechua	QII-C	x	x	x	x	x	x		x	x	x	x	x
Adelaar (2013)	Tarma Quechua	QI		x	x		x							x
Cusihuamán (2001)	Cuzco Quechua	QII-C	x		x		x			x		x		x
Faller (2004)	Cuzco Quechua	QII-C	x		x		x					x		x
Floyd (1999)	Wanka Quechua	QI	x	x	x	x	x	x	x					
Hintz (2007)	South Conchucos Quechua	QI	x	x	x	x	x			x		x		x
Hintz (2011)	South Conchucos Quechua	QI					x					x		x
Howard (2012)	Huamalíes Quechua	QI	x	x	x		x	x		x		x		
Hurtado de Mendoza Santander (2001)	Cuzco Quechua	QII-C	x	x	x	x	x	x		x		x		
Nuckolls (2008, 2012)	Pastaza Quichua	QII-B		x		x		x	x					

158   MANLEY

author's claims regarding each element of the set in comparison with all other elements of the set.[8]

5.1 Adelaar (2013)

According to Adelaar (2013, 102), "Tarma Quechua has a transparent system of evidentials consisting of three mutually exclusive categories: Certainty, Reported and Conjectural." Therefore, as indicated by its chosen label, the Tarma Quechua morpheme corresponding to *-mi/-n* is found to be primarily epistemic (indicating certainty) rather than evidential (indicating information source); Adelaar (2013, 102) continues:

> The 'Certainty' evidential implies a firm conviction on the side of the speaker. It does not always mean that the speaker has witnessed the communicated state or event in person, but the utterance contains information that (s)he can vouch for.

On the other hand, Adelaar (2013, 102) describes the morphemes corresponding to *-si/-s* and *-chá* as evidential in nature, and categorizes them as 'Reported', referring to hearsay, and 'Conjectural', indicating a guess, respectively.

While Adelaar (2013, 96) does not recognize any evidential or epistemic meanings or uses for *-r(q)a-* and *-sqa-*, he does find the Tarma Quechua affix *-na-*, which corresponds to *-sqa-*, to be mirative.

5.2 Cusihuamán (2001)

Cusihuamán (2001) recognizes only evidential (information source) meanings for *-mi/-n*, *-chá* and *-si/-s* in Cuzco Quechua. For example, he states that *-mi/-n* indicates that a speaker has seen or has personally participated in the realization of a described event, or that a speaker knows by direct means that an event is happening or will occur in the near future (2001, 229). For Cusihuamán (2001, 230–233), *-chá* indicates supposition or speculation by the speaker regarding an event and *-si/-s* denotes that a speaker has obtained information regarding an event from another person or an information source such as books, newspapers, letters, the radio, television, stories, conversations, etc.

Cusihuamán (2001, 159–161) also finds *-r(q)a-* and *-sqa-* to be used as evidentiality strategies, where *-r(q)a-* refers to concrete, completed past actions realized with the direct participation of or under the conscious control of the

---

8 Thus, presenting these claims in this way, below, also provides the reader with a clearer rationale for listing the authors' claims as they appear in table 5.1.

MARKERS OF EVIDENTIAL, EPISTEMIC AND MIRATIVE STANCE   159

speaker and -*sqa*- indicates past actions realized without the direct participation of the speaker or realized by the speaker in an unconscious state, as when drunk or in dreams.

Furthermore, Cusihuamán (2001, 160–161) finds -*sqa*- to be used as a mirativity strategy, to describe new situations or phenomena that the speaker has just discovered.

5.3   Faller (2004)

Like Cusihuamán (2001), Faller (2004), also studying Cuzco Quechua, finds -*mi/-n*, -*si/-s* and -*chá* to be evidential in nature, communicating information source. Faller (2004, 47) refers to these three enclitics as "... proper evidentials ... for best possible, reportative and conjectural evidence ...".

The past tense morpheme, -*sqa*-, is analyzed by Faller (2004, 80) as a deictic element that:

> ... encodes that the event is located outside the speaker's perceptual field at topic time from which it follows that the speaker cannot have had direct evidence for it. We may therefore speak of deictically induced evidential interpretations.

Therefore, in this way, Faller (2004) finds the use of -*sqa*- as an evidentiality strategy to follow from its use as a deictic element. Faller (2004, 55–60) also explains that "... -*sqa* is not an evidential proper" and "... does not carry epistemic modal force ...". In addition to serving as an evidentiality strategy, Faller (2004, 53) finds -*sqa*- to serve as a mirativity strategy.

No evidential or epistemic meanings are recognized by Faller for -*r(q)a*-; however, she indicates that linguistic work remains as far as analyzing the opposition between -*sqa*- and -*r(q)a*- (2004, 82).

5.4   Floyd (1999)

Floyd's (1999) investigation of evidentiality in Wanka Quechua examines the three morphemes corresponding to Cuzco Quechua -*mi/-n*, -*chá* and -*si/-s*; while no claims are made regarding the morphemes corresponding to -*r(q)a*- and -*sqa*-, Floyd (1999, 36) states that there are "... strong co-occurrence tendencies and restrictions ..." in the communication of tense and aspect along with information source (evidentiality) and validation (epistemology). While Floyd (1999) finds the three Wanka Quechua morphemes corresponding to -*mi/-n*, -*chá* and -*si/-s* to be deictic and primarily evidential in nature, he also notes epistemic extensions of their meaning as well as a mirative extension for -*si/-s*. Furthermore, in the case of -*si/-s*, Floyd (1999, 193) finds its evidential meaning to be primary, followed in importance by its mirative extensions, and its epistemic extensions to be the least frequent of its uses:

> I have showed that...each evidential involves some notion of data source at its semantic core, and that the prominence of validation is not the same for each evidential.

More specifically, in the case of -*mi/n*, Floyd (1999, 57) states that this direct evidential may communicate "...that a speaker's statement is based on personal experience with the concomitant conviction that what he is saying is true." However, Floyd (1999, 74) also explains that this morpheme may be used with epistemic extension of its meaning as follows:

> ...even in cases where it is clear either pragmatically or contextually that there is no direct experience involved, a speaker may nevertheless mark a statement with -*m(i)* and thus convey the certainty construal that is characteristic of directly perceived or experienced events.

Furthermore, in the case of the direct evidential, "...some rudimentary concept of spatial proximity is evoked..." since those who have witnessed an event directly must have been relatively close to the location of the event (1999, 184).

The Wanka Quechua morpheme corresponding to -*chá* is found by Floyd (1999, 93) to prototypically function "...as a marker of information source indicating that the utterance is an inference". As far as the epistemic extensions of -*chá* are concerned, in addition to the noncommitment to the truth of a proposition, this conjecture evidential may also contribute "...a sense of psychological distance or separation between the speaker and the proposition" (1999, 93). Also, as was the case for the direct evidential, the conjecture evidential may be used exclusively to communicate its epistemic extensions in the absence of its prototypical information source meaning (1999, 187).

The prototypical meaning for the Wanka Quechua morpheme corresponding to -*si/-s* is that of hearsay, "...in which the speaker serves as a conduit through which information from another source passes" (1999, 123). While Floyd (1999, 124) does acknowledge the use of the reportative evidential to communicate "...the speaker's uncertainty over the information in the utterance", unlike the direct evidential and the conjecture evidential, the reportative evidential is not found by Floyd to be used with epistemic extension, in the absence of its information source meaning (1999, 158):

I have no examples in my data base where -*sh(i)* is used strictly to indicate validation; any validational sense emerges only as a side effect. Mirativity, on the other hand, is what DOES pervade the extensions of the reportative...

Floyd finds the mirative extension of the reportative evidential to be used especially in the case of riddles and challenge questions, which "...evoke circumstances of 'impending revelation' and the potential for the subjective reaction of surprise on the part of the speech act participants" (1999, 126–127). Floyd further explains that in the case of riddles, there is addressee-based mirativity, since "...the speaker tells a riddle already knowing the answer, assuming, furthermore that the addressee does not know" (1999, 146–147).

5.5   *Hintz (2007)*

Hintz (2007) examines a variety of means for expressing evidentiality, epistemology and mirativity in South Conchucos Quechua.[9] With regard to the direct evidential, the conjecture evidential and the reportative evidential, Hintz (2007, 69–70) states:

> The use of the direct evidential -*mi* implies that the speaker has direct evidence of what is being stated (an evidential function), or that s/he is convinced that what s/he is stating is true without any doubt (a validational function). Speakers use the reportative -*shi* to pass on secondhand information (an evidential function), generally making no claims as to its reliability. The conjectural -*chi* is used primarily to indicate the speaker's attitude that the statement s/he is making is probably true (a validational function). It can also be considered to have an evidential function, in which the speaker's *assumption* is the source of evidence. In the use of -*chi*, speakers assume that what they are saying is probably true, based on their own reasoned analysis of generally known facts. This is a type of inference (an evidential function).

Therefore, it is clear from the above excerpt that Hintz (2007) finds both the direct evidential and the conjecture evidential to express both evidential and

---

9   In addition to the morphemes corresponding to Cuzco Quechua -*mi/-n*, -*chá* and -*si/-s*, Hintz (2007) notes the presence of additional evidential enclitics. As these additional enclitics do not have equivalent forms in Cuzco Quechua, as far as this author is aware, they will not be discussed here.

epistemic meaning. Even beyond information source and level of certainty, Hintz (2007, 70) also claims a variety of additional pragmatic functions for both the direct evidential and the conjecture evidential. In the case of the reportative evidential, however, the above citation states that this morpheme may communicate information source but not level of certainty.

With regard to the past tense morphemes equivalent to -*r(q)a*- and -*sqa*- (these are -*r(q)a*- and -*na:* in South Conchucos Quechua), Hintz (2007, 96–97) finds these to primarily communicate past tense. Hintz (2007, 36) explains that -*na:* is referred to as the 'narrative past' since "...it can be used to narrate a complete folktale or legend". Also, she finds both past tense morphemes to function as evidentiality strategies. Furthermore, she makes the claim that the morpheme corresponding to -*sqa*- may be used as a mirativity strategy. Regarding their use as evidentiality strategies, Hintz (2007, 96–97) explains:

> The past -*r(q)a* is used when the source of evidence is firsthand or when the situation is being talked about from the speaker's perspective. The narrative past -*na:* is used when the source of evidence is secondhand or when the speaker would like to give a reported perspective.

In terms of the use of the past tense morpheme corresponding to -*sqa*- as a mirativity strategy, Hintz (2007, 170) states, "The narrative past -*na:* by itself may also indicate surprise...".[10, 11]

5.6   *Hintz (2011)*

In his study of South Conchucos Quechua, Hintz (2011) finds -*na:*, the morpheme corresponding to Cuzco Quechua -*sqa*-, to be used as an evidentiality strategy and a mirativity strategy in addition to communicating imperfective aspect and past tense (2011, 85); in this way, this morpheme may present information, "....as outside the experience or expectation of discourse participants, whether interlocutors in a conversation or participants within the narrative itself" (2011, 142).

---

10   In addition to this past tense morpheme, Hintz (2007, 170) also finds the recent past that came from a perfect, -*sh((q)a)*, and the former past perfect, -*sh ka-shqa*, to be used to indicate surprise.

11   Additionally, Hintz (2007, 110–114) finds -*r(q)a*- to communicate affective neutrality and -*na:* to convey "...shame, distress or other feelings that could be classified as negative" (2007, 110).

MARKERS OF EVIDENTIAL, EPISTEMIC AND MIRATIVE STANCE   163

While no claims are made regarding the direct evidential, the conjecture evidential and the *-r(q)a-* past tense morpheme, Hintz (2011, 142) notes the following with regard to the reportative evidential:

> In keeping with its non-firsthand or indirect reporting function, *-na:* sometimes occurs with the reportative evidential marker *-shi* which further specifies that the source of information is someone other than the interlocutors.

Thus, Hintz (2011) recognizes an evidential (information source) meaning for the reportative evidential.

5.7 *Howard (2012)*

In her study of Huamalíes Quechua, Howard (2012) states that speaker perspective may be communicated through the use of the morphemes corresponding to *-mi/-n, -chá, -si/-s, -r(q)a-* and *-sqa-*;[12, 13] she finds all of these to communicate information source, with the enclitics serving as evidentials and the past tense morphemes serving as evidentiality strategies. Additionally, she finds the morphemes corresponding to *-mi/-n* and *-si/-s* to be used with epistemic extension of their meaning.

Regarding the communication of evidentiality, Howard (2012, 249) finds the morpheme corresponding to *-mi/-n* to mark 'personal knowledge' and the morpheme corresponding to *-si/-s* to mark 'non-personal knowledge'; these two morphemes are also found to correlate with the relevant past tense morphemes: "Thus *-mi* may co-occur with *-rqa-* (past tense, personal perspective) while *-shi* may co-occur with *-naa* (reportive past, non-personal perspective)" (2012, 249–250). Furthermore, regarding the correlation of these morphemes, Howard (2012, 250) explains:

> Neither is it essential for *-mi/-rqa-* and *-shi/-naa* systematically to co-occur in speech . . . In a given utterance, tense marking may do the job of establishing speaker perspective without evidential marking being present.

---

12   Howard (2012, 265) states, "In its function as reportive past in Huamalíes, *-naa*, is the semantic equivalent of *-sqa-* in Bolivian and Southern Peruvian varieties . . .".

13   Howard (2012) also observes the use of additional evidential enclitics that mark 'co-constructed knowledge'; since these do not have equivalent forms in Cuzco Quechua, as far as this author is aware, they are not discussed here.

In other words, the morphemes corresponding to *-r(q)a-* and *-sqa-* may communicate information source in their role as evidentiality strategies even when the evidential enclitics are not present.

As far as the epistemic extension of *-mi/-n* and *-si/-s* is concerned, Howard (2012, 249–259) states that the morpheme corresponding to *-mi/-n* may affirm a proposition and that the morpheme corresponding to *-si/-s* may be used to distance oneself from recounted events.

5.8 *Hurtado de Mendoza Santander (2001)*

Also working with Cuzco Quechua, Hurtado de Mendoza Santander (2001) recognizes both evidential and epistemic meanings for *-mi/-n, -chá,* and *-si/-s.* According to Hurtado de Mendoza Santander (2001, 134–135), *-mi/-n* communicates both direct experience and certainty, *-chá* indicates conjecture and a lack of responsibility toward the message conveyed, and *-si/-s* indicates a second-hand information source as well as doubt and a lack of responsibility regarding what is communicated. Additionally, Hurtado de Mendoza Santander (2001, 90) finds both past tense morphemes, *-r(q)a-* and *-sqa-,* to serve as evidentiality strategies, indicating direct and conscious participation and a lack of direct and conscious participation, respectively.

5.9 *Nuckolls (2008, 2012)*

In her examination of Pastaza Quichua, a dialect of Quechua spoken in Amazonian Ecuador, Nuckolls (2008, 83) identifies the morphemes corresponding to Cuzco Quechua *-mi/-n, -chá* and *-si/-s* as primarily indicating perspectival stance; these meanings are considered here as falling under the category of epistemic. Additionally, she finds the morpheme corresponding to *-si/-s* to be used miratively. Nuckolls (2008) makes no claims regarding the morphemes corresponding to *-r(q)a-* and *-sqa-.* Nuckolls (2012) echoes the claims of Nuckolls (2008) with regard to the morphemes corresponding to Cuzco Quechua *-mi/-n* and *-si/-s.*

While Nuckolls (2008, 67) does mention that the morphemes corresponding to *-mi/-n, -chá* and *-si/-s* may communicate direct experience, conjecture and reporting someone else's words, respectively, she argues: "... that a source-based characterization of these morphemes cannot be supported by the data". Nuckolls (2012, 237) further emphasizes:

> The enclitics *-mi* and *-shi* are not distinguishing between direct and indirect experience; rather, they signal the perspectives, whether self or other, from which utterances are articulated.

MARKERS OF EVIDENTIAL, EPISTEMIC AND MIRATIVE STANCE   165

More specifically, in the case of the morpheme corresponding to *-mi/-n*, she states (2008, 68):

> I argue that for the Pastaza Quichua dialect, at least, information source is best understood as a conventional implicature of what has been called the 'direct experience' morpheme.

According to Nuckolls (2008, 83), speakers primarily use the enclitic corresponding to *-mi/-n*, "... to voice the assertion-making perspective of the speaking self, who may belong to the speech event or to the narrated event." She states that the morpheme corresponding to *-chá* "... indicates conjectural knowledge" (2008, 84). The morpheme corresponding to *-si/-s* may be used (2008, 83):

> ... to adopt a stance of 'otherness' regarding what a speaker says, as when it is used by people who are speaking words that they themselves authored, but that they wish to distance themselves from for a variety of reasons ...

Finally, with regard to the mirative uses found for the morpheme corresponding to *-si/-s*, she states (2008, 79):

> Perhaps one of the most interesting uses of *-shi* occurs when a speaker expresses bewilderment or wonder about something ... This use of *-shi* can be understood as based in otherness because speakers represent that which is not known as outside their capacity for understanding.

5.10   *Summary*

Throughout this section, varying viewpoints have been presented regarding the communication of evidentiality, epistemology and mirativity through the use of five different morphemes, including the evidential enclitics, *-mi/-n, -chá* and *-si/-s*, as well as the past tense morphemes, *-r(q)a-* and *-sqa-*, and their corresponding counterparts, in several Quechua language varieties examined by nine different scholars. As outlined above, five of these scholars examine varieties of Central Peruvian Quechua, one studies Ecuadorian Quichua and three investigate Cuzco Quechua of Peru. By applying the definitions and terminologies proposed in the present work (following Aikhenvald (2004) and Aikhenvald and Storch (2013) for evidential meaning, epistemic meaning, evidentiality strategy, epistemic extension, and mirativity strategy) to the claims made by these nine authors, it has been possible to compare them with each other and also with the present work.

The viewpoint of the present work shares much in common with the claims made by the nine authors described above; however, the specific claims made here also differ in important ways from those made by these nine authors. For example, the present work, alone, finds -r(q)a- and -sqa- to be used with epistemic extension of their meanings. In general, the set of claims described in the present work is coherent and inclusive, unifying the majority of the varied claims of the literature to date: (1) -mi/-n serves as a direct evidential which may be utilized with epistemic extension of its meaning to indicate a high level of certainty, (2) -chá is a conjecture evidential which may be utilized with epistemic extension to communicate doubt, (3) -si/-s serves as an indirect evidential which may be utilized with epistemic extension of its meaning to indicate doubt, (4) -r(q)a- may be utilized as an evidentiality strategy to communicate direct information source and also with epistemic extension of its meaning to indicate a high level of certainty, and (5) -sqa- may be utilized as an evidentiality strategy to communicate indirect information source, with epistemic extension of its meaning to indicate doubt, and as a mirativity strategy, indicating surprise and newsworthiness.

6   Methodology

6.1   *Participants*
The participants of this work include bilingual, Quechua/Spanish migrants to the city of Cuzco, Peru, who were members of two non-profit, non-governmental agencies in 2002 and 2003: the *Asociación Civil, 'Gregorio Condori Mamani' Proyecto Casa del Cargador*, 'Gregorio Condori Mamani Civil Association, House of the Carrier Project' (referred to here as CdC) and *El Centro de Apoyo Integral a la Trabajadora del Hogar*, 'Center for the Integral Support of the Female Home Worker' (referred to as CAITH by the participants themselves). Examples are presented within this work from 17 of the 62 participants who engaged in a role-playing elicitation task in 2002; these 17 participants ranged in age from 10 to 25 years old (mean age 16.5 years old). In 2003, 61 participants completed a certainty-ranking exercise; these participants were between 11 and 58 years of age (mean age 21.5 years old). Those who engaged in spontaneous conversation in 2003 were a subset of the 61 participants who completed the certainty-ranking exercise.

The CdC is a temporary home to primarily adolescent males, the majority of whom earn a living as *cargadores*, 'carriers', by transporting agricultural goods within the large market places of Cuzco.[14] This is a terribly strenuous occupation, as *cargadores* must carry immensely heavy loads on their backs, sometimes reaching weights of over 100 kg or 250 lbs. As many of the *cargadores* are young, this weight may more than double that of their body weight. These large bundles of food, such as potatoes, carrots, tomatoes, or onions, are balanced on the backs of the *cargadores* with rope. The objective of the CdC, as published in the *Manual de Organización y Funciones* by the Public Registry of Cuzco (1996), is to improve the quality of life of the peasant migrant carriers, thereby allowing them to attain respectable levels of health, education, and family well-being.

According to Rofes (2002), the main goal of CAITH is to offer educational support and assistance to female adolescent domestic servants, who come from rural areas outside of the city of Cuzco. CAITH also functions as a temporary home for these female domestic servants.

The majority of the inhabitants of both agencies migrated either seasonally or permanently to the city of Cuzco from mostly surrounding, rural, Quechua-dominant areas within the Department of Cuzco in order to make a living and obtain a higher quality education than would be available to them in their rural communities of origin. Subsistence farming is generally the dominant occupation within all of the participants' home communities and most of the participants spent the early part of their childhood on farms, where they helped to work the fields and herd the sheep, llamas, and alpacas.

Most of the participants began to acquire their second language, Spanish, during childhood and adolescence and also began elementary school within their home communities before migrating to the city of Cuzco. Some of these had received their schooling in Quechua, others had bilingual Quechua-Spanish elementary schooling, while still others received their elementary schooling through the means of Spanish. Therefore, some of these participants began their acquisition of Spanish while still living within their rural communities of origin while others began their L2 acquisition upon their arrival to Cuzco.

6.2 Elicitation Tasks

The data presented below were obtained through the recording of spontaneous conversations among chosen participants in 2003 as well as through the use of two elicitation tasks, a role-playing exercise carried out in 2002 and a certainty-ranking exercise carried out in 2003. Both of these elicitation tasks

---

14   A return visit by the author to the CdC and CAITH in 2009 revealed that both agencies continued to thrive since the data collection for this work took place in 2002 and 2003.

168   MANLEY

are described below. All data collection occurred on the premises of both the
CdC and CAITH, in plain view of all the inhabitants of both agencies.

6.2.1   Role Play Elicitation

Two sources served as motivation for the design of the role play elicitation
task: Chafe's (1980) use of "The Pear Film" and Blum-Kulka, House and Kasper's
(1989) discourse-completion test. Chafe (1980, xii) used a controlled visual
stimulus, "The Pear Film", in order to:

> ... collect examples of different people talking about the same thing ... in
> order to see what similarities and differences emerged between different
> verbalizations of what was, at least to a large extent, the same knowledge.

Chafe (1980, xii) further explains, "It was impossible to imagine how to present
the same 'real' experience to different people in different places at different
times". In lieu of presenting the same 'real' experience to study participants,
Chafe decided that using a film would be a useful compromise.

Blum-Kulka, House, and Kasper investigated "... cross-cultural and intra-
lingual variation in two speech acts: requests and apologies" (1989, 11). The
authors utilized a discourse-completion test in order to obtain "... a large
sample, in seven countries, of two specific speech acts used in the same contexts" (1989, 13). According to Blum-Kulka, House and Kasper (1989, 13–14), the
discourse-completion test:

> ... consists of scripted dialogues that represent socially differentiated sit-
> uations. Each dialogue is preceded by a short description of the situation,
> specifying the setting, and the social distance between the participants
> and their status relative to each other, followed by an incomplete dia-
> logue. Respondents were asked to complete the dialogue, thereby provid-
> ing the speech act aimed at.

Like the methods utilized by Chafe (1980) and Blum-Kulka, House, and Kasper
(1989), the role play elicitation used here allowed for greater comparability
among the participants' responses than would the use of completely naturalistic data alone. Specifically, thirty-one members of the CdC and thirty-one
members of CAITH were asked to respond in Quechua as if they were involved
in a variety of different specific situations. Firstly, each participant was provided with a short description in Spanish of a situation, specifying the relationships among the characters. Edited clip art drawings were used to facilitate the

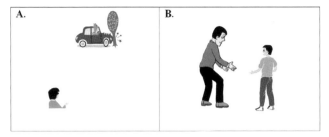

FIGURE 5.1 *Appendix B, item 1*

description of each situation.[15] Two similar sets of nine situations were used, one for the CdC and the other for CAITH, with the main difference being that the protagonist was male for the CdC participants and female for the CAITH participants. The specific situations were designed to present the participants with contexts hypothesized by the author to potentially illustrate differences in use of the Quechua evidential/epistemic/mirative system. Through the utilization of situational descriptions and accompanying drawings, it was possible to impart 'the same knowledge' to each participant as a starting point for his/her response. For example, CdC participants viewed the illustration above while listening to a situational description read aloud in Spanish and Quechua; this description is translated into English below.

> A boy saw that a gentleman crashed his car against the tree in front of his dad's house. Later, his dad asks the boy what happened. What would you say if you were this boy?

In this case, it is clear that the boy had first-hand information regarding the car accident.

6.2.2 Certainty-ranking Exercise

In 2003, members of the CdC and CAITH completed a certainty-ranking exercise in which they were asked to rank a list of six sentences according to the assumed degree of certainty of the speaker; the six sentences differ in terms of their evidential/epistemic/mirative marking. Sixteen CdC participants and

---

15   Appendices B and C include the role play situations and accompanying drawings, corresponding to the examples presented in this chapter. See Feke (2004) for the complete role play instruments, including situations for which examples are not provided in this work.

sixteen CAITH participants completed version 1 below, while fifteen CdC participants and fourteen CAITH participants completed version 2 below;[16] these two versions differ only in terms of the order in which the six sentences are listed. The six sentences of version 1 and version 2 below include all of the possible combinations of the evidential enclitics, *-mi/-n* and *-si/-s*, and the past verb tenses, *-r(q)a-* and *-sqa-*, in addition to the absence of an evidential enclitic, represented here as '∅'.[17] Table 5.2 lists these six possible combinations:

TABLE 5.2 *Certainty ranking morphemic combinations*

(1)	∅	+	-rqa-
(2)	-mi/-n	+	-rqa-
(3)	-si/-s	+	-rqa-
(4)	∅	+	-sqa-
(5)	-mi/-n	+	-sqa-
(6)	-si/-s	+	-sqa-

For both versions, each participant was shown the list of six sentences as the author read these aloud and then was asked to rank them in terms of certainty, with '1' meaning that the speaker is more sure and '6' meaning that the speaker is less sure. The base meaning for all of the sentences is: 'The young men and women were unearthing the potatoes.' Without any evidential/epistemic/mirative marking, the expression would be glossed in the present tense as in (1):

(1) *Wayna-sipas-kuna*   *papa-ta*   *alla-sha-nku*
     Young.man-young.woman-PL   potato-ACC   unearth-PROG-3PL
     'The young men and women are unearthing the potatoes.'

Version 1:
_____ *Waynasipaskuna papata__n__ allashasqaku.*
_____ *Waynasipaskuna papata__n__ allasharqanku.*

---

16   The participants were presented with the six sentences for each version as they appear here, in the same order and with bold and underlined font marking the evidential/ epistemic/mirative morphemes.

17   The conjecture evidential, *-chá*, was not included as there is less debate in the literature regarding this morpheme.

MARKERS OF EVIDENTIAL, EPISTEMIC AND MIRATIVE STANCE

_____ *Waynasipaskuna papata allasharqanku.*
_____ *Waynasipaskuna papata allashasqaku.*
_____ *Waynasipaskuna papatas allasharqanku.*
_____ *Waynasipaskuna papatas allashasqaku.*

Version 2:
_____ *Waynasipaskuna papatan allashasqaku.*
_____ *Waynasipaskuna papatas allasharqanku.*
_____ *Waynasipaskuna papata allashasqaku.*
_____ *Waynasipaskuna papatas allashasqaku.*
_____ *Waynasipaskuna papata allasharqanku.*
_____ *Waynasipaskuna papatan allasharqanku.*

The design of this certainty-ranking exercise effectively isolates for analysis the epistemic dimension of four of the five Cuzco Quechua multidimensional markers of stance studied here; as such, this experimental design is useful in combination with observed naturalistic speech. In naturalistic speech, the evidential, epistemic and mirative dimensions of these morphemes are simultaneously available as frames of reference, often making it difficult for the researcher to determine which dimension(s) are being accessed by the speaker with any specific use of each morpheme. Similarly, Hanks (2005, 209) has noted in the case of Wilkins' (1999) work:

> This simultaneous availability of multiple frames of reference is precisely ruled out by experimental design which reduces the deictic field to one parameter, such as space in the questionnaire developed by Wilkins (1999).

7 Results

The following subsections present the data and results of this work. The results of the certainty-ranking exercise are presented first, since they inform the results of both the role play elicitation and the data obtained through the recording of spontaneous conversation.

7.1 *Certainty-ranking Exercise Results*

As mentioned under Methodology above, 61 participants completed either version 1 or version 2 of the certainty-ranking exercise; 32 participants completed version 1 and 29 participants completed version 2. The six sentences presented to the participants in both versions include all of the possible combinations of the evidential enclitics, *-mi/-n* and *-si/-s*, and the past verb tenses, *-r(q)a-* and

-*sqa*-, in addition to the absence of an evidential enclitic, represented as '∅'. As mentioned above, for both versions, each participant was shown the list of six sentences as the author read these aloud and then was asked to rank them in terms of certainty, with '1' meaning that the speaker is more sure and '6' meaning that the speaker is less sure. A calculation of the average rank scores assigned to each of the six sentences by the participants revealed that, on average, all participants ranked the six sentences in the following way for both version 1 and version 2:[18]

1. *Waynasipaskuna papata allasharqanku.*
2. *Waynasipaskuna papatan allasharqanku.*
3. *Waynasipaskuna papatas allasharqanku.*
4. *Waynasipaskuna papata allashasqaku.*
5. *Waynasipaskuna papatan allashasqaku.*
6. *Waynasipaskuna papatas allashasqaku.*

In table 5.3, the average rankings and standard deviations of the rankings for these six sentences are listed; the sentences numbered 1 through 6 correspond to those found immediately above. In other words, the order in which the sentences are referenced below corresponds to the way in which all participants ranked the sentences for certainty on average. Therefore, as displayed in table 5.3, on average, all participants ranked sentence '1', which contains no evidential enclitic (∅) and the -*r(q)a*- past tense morpheme, as indicating the highest

TABLE 5.3 *Average rankings and standard deviations for the six sentences*

Sentence	Version 1 Avg. Rankings	Version 1 St. Dev.	Version 2 Avg. Rankings	Version 2 St. Dev.
1.	2.41	1.46	2.62	1.74
2.	2.84	1.59	3.14	1.60
3.	3.16	1.14	3.31	1.47
4.	3.88	1.56	3.66	1.72
5.	4.00	2.05	3.83	1.69
6.	4.72	1.33	4.45	1.59

*'1' = more sure, '6' = less sure

---

18 This ranking corresponds to the order in which the possible combinations are presented above in table 5.2.

certainty level. Thus, the average certainty rankings for this sentence have the lowest average value (closest to '1' for highest certainty).

In order to determine whether the results for version 1 and version 2 represent any significant differences between the sentence rankings, a Oneway Analysis of Variance (ANOVA) was performed for each set of results at alpha = 0.05: $(F(5, 186) = 9.71, p < .001)$ for version 1 and $(F(5, 168) = 4.26, p = .001)$ for version 2. Therefore, both Oneway ANOVA test procedures reveal that there are indeed statistically significant differences among the averages for the six sentences in both versions.

In order to investigate these statistically significant differences further, Tukey's HSD Post Hoc Tests for Homogeneous Subsets were conducted at alpha = 0.05 on both data sets. Table 5.4 and table 5.5 below present the mean

TABLE 5.4 *Tukey's HSD Post Hoc Test for Homogeneous Subsets for version 1*

Sentence	N	1	2	3	4
1	32	2.4063			
2	32	2.8438	2.8438		
3	32	3.1563	3.1563	3.1563	
4	32		3.8750	3.8750	3.8750
5	32			4.0000	4.0000
6	32				4.7188
Sig.		.380	.086	.250	.250

TABLE 5.5 *Tukey's HSD Post Hoc Test for Homogeneous Subsets for version 2*

Sentence	N	1	2
1	29	2.6207	
2	29	3.1379	
3	29	3.3103	3.3103
4	29	3.6552	3.6552
5	29	3.8276	3.8276
6	29		4.4483
Sig.		.061	.092

certainty rankings within their homogeneous subsets. Each of the numbered columns in tables 5.4 (columns '1' through '4') and 5.5 (columns '1' and '2') represents a homogeneous subset; mean rankings appearing within the same column are not statistically different from each other.

Table 5.4 above shows that the rankings for sentences 1, 2, and 3 of version 1 (appearing together in column '1'), corresponding to the (1) $\varnothing$ + -$r(q)a$-, (2) -mi/-n + -$r(q)a$-, and (3) -si/-s + -$r(q)a$- morpheme combinations, are statistically different from those of sentences 4, 5, and 6 (appearing together in column '4'), corresponding to the (4) $\varnothing$ + -sqa-, (5) -mi/-n + -sqa-, and (6) -si/-s + -sqa- morpheme combinations. In other words, the mean certainty rankings for sentences 1, 2, and 3 are not found within the same homogeneous subset as are the mean certainty rankings for sentences 4, 5, and 6. Furthermore, in table 5.4, both sentence 1, corresponding to the $\varnothing$ + -$r(q)a$- morpheme combination, and sentence 6, corresponding to the -si/-s + -sqa- morpheme combination, are not found in more than one homogeneous subset. Table 5.5 above shows that the rankings for sentences 1 and 2 of version 2, corresponding to the $\varnothing$ + -$r(q)a$- and -mi/-n + -$r(q)a$- morpheme combinations, are statistically significantly different from that of sentence 6, corresponding to the -si/-s + -sqa- morpheme combination. In other words, sentences 1 and 2 are not found in the same homogeneous subset as sentence 6.

Therefore, these data provide evidence for the notion that the past tense morphemes, -$r(q)a$- and -sqa-, may be used with epistemic extension of their meaning, as they may communicate higher and lower levels of certainty, respectively. As mentioned above, the present work is the first to propose epistemic meanings for -$r(q)a$- and -sqa-. Secondarily, these data suggest that the lack of an evidential enclitic, '$\varnothing$', followed by -mi/-n, followed by -si/-s, express higher to lower levels of certainty, respectively. Therefore, these findings also indicate that the evidential enclitics, -mi/-n, and -si/-s, carry epistemic meaning.

It is important to note, however, that while this certainty-ranking exercise effectively isolates the epistemic dimension of these multidimensional markers of stance for analysis, it does not rule out for the participants the other possible simultaneous frames of reference (evidential and mirative). In other words, in ranking these six sentences for certainty, the participants were attuned to the epistemic dimension of the morphemes but may also have, simultaneously, interpreted the sentences with the possible evidential and/or mirative frames of reference. For this reason, it is not possible to conclude from these results which dimension should be considered as primary for each of the morphemes (evidential, epistemic or mirative). In any case, these signifi-

MARKERS OF EVIDENTIAL, EPISTEMIC AND MIRATIVE STANCE

cant results regarding the epistemic dimension of these morphemes are not diminished, since one would expect to find no significant results, had these morphemes not carried epistemic meaning for the participants. The findings of this certainty-ranking exercise are applied below to the analysis of data obtained through both the role play elicitation and spontaneous recorded conversation in Quechua.

7.2   Role Play Analysis

As mentioned above, participants were engaged in a role-play activity in which they were asked to respond as if they were involved in a variety of different specific situations after first listening to a short description of each situation and viewing accompanying clip art drawings.[19] As presented in the examples below, there is a high degree of variation in the participants' responses; this variation may be accounted for by the following reasons: (1) while the role play activity controlled the general situation and context for discussion for the participants, it was not possible to control the participants' background knowledge pertaining to the situations as well as their personal attitudes regarding each of the situations, and (2) the role play activity did not isolate any of the three possible dimensions for the multidimensional markers of stance (evidential, epistemic and mirative). In other words, in responding to each role play situation, each participant was free to utilize the multidimensional markers of stance examined here with primary reference to either their evidential, epistemic or mirative dimension, as he/she saw fit.

In the sub-sections that follow, the claims of this work, supported by the results of the certainty-ranking exercise presented above, are applied to the analysis of the role play responses obtained. As metapragmatic commentary was not gathered from the participants regarding their attitudes, perspectives and intended messages within their role play responses, it is not possible to draw firm conclusions regarding their use of *-mi/-n*, *-si/-s*, *-r(q)a-* and *-sqa-*; however, given the contexts of the role play situations as well as other linguistic clues produced by the participants, it is possible to arrive at likely hypotheses regarding their use of the morphemes of interest.

---

19   Appendices B and C contain the role play situations and accompanying drawings corresponding to the examples presented here. Within this section, abbreviated descriptions of each situation are included. See Feke (2004) for the complete role play instruments, including situations for which examples are not provided here.

176   MANLEY

7.2.1   Role Play Situation: Causing a Car Crash

In one role play situation, CAITH participants were asked to play the role of a girl who, while driving her mother's car, accidentally crashes into another car (see Appendix C, number 1). Later, when this girl's mother asks what happened, three participants responded in the following three ways:[20]

(2)   *Noqa*   *perdi-ra-ni*   *control-ta*   *awtu-manta.*
      I $lose-PST1-1 $control-ACC $car-ABL
      'I lost control of the car.'

(3)   *Ñaha*   *maneha-ni-q*[21]   *karru-ta*   *y*   *huq*   *awtu-man*
      before $drive-1-AG $car-ACC $and   a $car-ILLA

      tupa-ra-ni.
      hit-PST1-1
      'Earlier, I was driving the car and hit into another car.'

(4)   *Noqa-n*   *karru-ta*   *maneha-sha-ra-ni*   *hinaspa*   *mana*
      I-DIREV $car-ACC $drive-PROG-PST1-1   then   no

      allin-ta-chu   *qhawa-sqa-ni*   *y*   *qonqa-y-manta*
      good-ADVL-NEG   see-PST2-1 $and   careless-1POSS-ABL

      qhawa-qti-y-qa   *choka-sqa-ni*   *karru-wan.*
      see-SEQ-1POSS-TOP $crash-PST2-1 $car-INS
      'I was driving the car, then I didn't see well and (drove) carelessly, then I saw I crashed the car.'

Both (2) and (3) above include *-r(q)a-*. Following the claims of this work, this past tense morpheme may serve as an evidentiality strategy, communicating a direct information source. Also, according to the results of the certainty-ranking exercise, *-r(q)a-* may have epistemic extension, indicating a higher certainty level. As the situation here involves a speaker talking about an event

---

20   Some of the Quechua statements contain Spanish loan words, marked with '$' in the glosses. These Spanish loans have been fully integrated into Quechua as the matrix language; for this reason, these Spanish loans are written with an orthography that intends to reflect the Quechua pronunciation.

21   This form is ungrammatical in Quechua; this speaker may have meant instead to state, *'maneha-ni'* ('I drive/drove') or *'maneha-q ka-ni'* ('I used to drive').

MARKERS OF EVIDENTIAL, EPISTEMIC AND MIRATIVE STANCE

in which she participated, her use of -r(q)a- may reflect both a direct information source and a high level of certainty regarding the event under discussion.

At the start of example (4), the participant uses -mi/-n and -r(q)a- while stating 'I was driving the car'; this is similar to examples (2) and (3) in which the participants speak from the perspective of having a direct information source and a high level of certainty. However, when the speaker in (4) begins to tell of the difficulty she had, 'then I didn't see well and (drove) carelessly, then I saw I crashed the car', there is a switch to the -sqa- past tense morpheme. In this work, it is claimed that -sqa- may function as an evidentiality strategy, used to communicate an indirect information source, and also that -sqa- may have epistemic extension, indicating doubt; in (4), neither meaning would apply, as such meanings would conflict with the prior use of -mi/-n and -r(q)a- to indicate a direct information source and a high certainty level in the first part of this utterance. However, the third claim of this work regarding -sqa-, a mirative reading, is likely in the case of (4), indicating the speaker's surprise at her loss of control of the vehicle. Therefore, in the case of (4), this speaker appears to use the -sqa- past tense with sole reference to its mirative dimension.

7.2.2   Role Play Situation: Observing a Car Crash

CdC participants were asked to play the role of a boy who saw a man crash his car against the tree in front of the boy's father's house (see Appendix B, number 1). Later, when his father asks what happened, one participant responded:

(5) *Huq   carro-n   choca-ra-pu-sqa   huq   mallki-man.*
     A $car-DIREV $crash-SUD-MAL-PST2   one   tree-ILLA
     'A car crashed into a tree.'

In (5), -mi/-n is used along with -sqa-. This use of -mi/-n may simultaneously reference both the evidential and the epistemic dimensions, thereby indicating both a direct information source and a high level of certainty regarding the message conveyed, since the role play character was a direct witness to the event in question. Since this participant's use of -mi/-n establishes his information source and level of certainty, as in (4), the subsequent use of -sqa-, rather than serving as an evidentiality strategy, indicating an indirect information source, or with epistemic extension, indicating doubt, may also likely have been used here as a mirativity strategy, indicating surprise; the fact that this participant uses the infix, -ra (SUD for 'sudden'),[22] lends further support to this hypothesis. According to Aráoz and Salas (1993, 154), -ru, which is realized as

---

22   This morpheme also functions as the hortative in Cuzco Quechua.

-ra before *-pu*, expresses the sudden and recent realization of an action; a sudden and recent action is also likely to be surprising or startling.

Another participant describing the same situation used the following verb:

(6) *Choka-ra-pu-**ra**-n*
     $crash-SUD-MAL-PST1-3
     'He crashed.'

In (6), *-r(q)a-*, rather than *-sqa-*, is used along with the 'sudden' infix, *-ru*. In the case of (6), in contrast with (5), there is no utterance content prior to this verb, indicating evidential and/or epistemic stance. Therefore, in (6), *-r(q)a-*, alone, may be used to communicate information on both the evidential and epistemic dimensions, namely, a direct information source and a high level of certainty. The infix, *-ru*, then, without the additional support of mirative *-sqa-*, functions to communicate the suddenness of the event. Interpreted in this way, (6) may be taken as somewhat of a more concise version of (5), with both examples communicating a direct information source (evidential dimension), high certainty level (epistemic dimension), and surprise/suddenness (mirative dimension).

7.2.3   Role Play Situation: Falling Asleep on the Job

In another role play situation, CdC participants were asked to play the role of a boy who fell asleep on the job. While the boy was sleeping, his colleague/friend fell down from a ladder. Later, when the boy's boss asks the boy what happened, the boy doesn't want to tell the boss that he was sleeping, in fear of losing his job (see Appendix B, number 2). One participant responded:

(7) *Llank'a-sha-qti-y-**mi***   *qonqa-lla-manta*   *khumpa-y*
     work-PROG-SEQ-1POSS-DIREV   careless-LIM-ABL $friend-1POSS

     *pasa-ya-mu-sha-**sqa**.*
     move-DIR-CIS-PROG-PST2
     'While I was working, my friend was carelessly falling down.'

In (7), *-mi/-n* is used along with *-sqa-*. Since this work claims that *-mi/-n* is used as a direct evidential and also with epistemic extension to indicate a high level of certainty, this participant's use of *-mi/-n* as a role play character works to create the false impression for his boss that he was working and did, in fact, witness his friend's fall from the ladder. Since *-mi/-n* establishes a direct information source and/or a high level of certainty, this participant's use of *-sqa-*

MARKERS OF EVIDENTIAL, EPISTEMIC AND MIRATIVE STANCE 179

may be interpreted as a mirativity strategy, indicating surprise at the fact that his friend fell.

Another participant responded to the same situation in the following way:

(8) *Mana-n*   *ri-ku-ni-chu*   *porque*   *mana-n*   *noqa*   *chay*
no-DIREV   see-REFL-1-NEG $because   no-DIREV   I   that

     ratu   *ka-sha-rqa-ni-chu.*
     $while   be-PROG-PST1-1-NEG
     'I didn't see it because I wasn't there at that moment.'

In (8), *-mi/-n* is used along with *-r(q)a-*; this participant's use of these morphemes here may indicate a direct information source and a high level of certainty regarding his not seeing and not being present at the time of his colleague's fall. However, as the boy in this role play situation was indeed there and sleeping at that moment, the use of these morphemes may also work to create a false impression, thereby convincing his boss that he was not there at that moment.

7.2.4   Role Play Situation: Information from a Trusted Person

In another situation, both CdC and CAITH participants were asked to play the role of a boy or girl who was told by his/her mother or father that his/her grandfather won one thousand *soles* in the lottery. The next day, the boy/girl wants to tell his/her friend about this good news (see Appendix B, number 3 and Appendix C, number 2). Two participants responded in the following ways:

(9) *Hatun*   *papa-y-mi*   *qolqe-ta*   *gana-ku-n*
big $father-1POSS-DIREV   money-ACC $win-REFL-3

     waranqa-ta   *gana-ra-n.*
     thousand-ACC $win-PST1-3
     'My grandfather won money, won a thousand.'

(10) *Abuelo-cha-y-mi*   *qayni*   *unchay*   *huq*   *loteria-pi*
$grandfather-DIM-1POSS-DIREV   past   day   a $lottery-LOC

     gana-ra-n   *mil*   *soles-ta.*
     $win-PST1-3 $thousand $soles-ACC
     'Yesterday, my dear grandfather won a thousand soles in a lottery.'

In both (9) and (10), *-mi/-n* and *-r(q)a-* are used although the protagonist does not have a direct information source. Therefore, here, rather than serving as a direct evidential and evidentiality strategy, respectively, these morphemes can be analyzed as being used with epistemic extension, indicating a high certainty level. Since the protagonist of this role play was given this information by his/her parent, who is likely to be a trusted person, both *-mi/-n* and *-r(q)a-* may be interpreted as indicating a high certainty level. Therefore, in the case of (9) and (10), the epistemic dimension of these morphemes, alone, may be accessed by the speakers.

In response to this same situation, two other speakers responded in the following ways:

(11) *Huh p'unchay, abuelu-cha-y   loteria-ta   horqo-ru-sqa.*
     one   day $grandfather-DIM-1POSS $lottery-ACC take-SUD-PST2
     'One day, my dear grandfather took/won the lottery.'

(12) *Papa-y-mi   gana-ra-mu-sqa   loteria-pi   mil*
     $father-1POSS-DIREV $win-SUD-CIS-PST2 $lottery-LOC $thousand

     soles-ta.
     $soles-ACC.
     'My father won a thousand soles in the lottery.'

In (11), *-sqa-* is used and in (12), *-mi/-n* is used along with *-sqa-*. Given the role play context, in the case of (11), it is possible to interpret *-sqa-* along all three dimensions: as an evidentiality strategy (indicating an indirect information source), with epistemic extension (indicating doubt), and/or as a mirativity strategy (indicating surprise). The presence of *-ru*, indicating suddenness, supports a mirative interpretation in (11).

Since *-mi/-n* appears in (12) along with *-sqa-*, the use of these two morphemes together, given this role play context, may be interpreted as communicating epistemic extension in the form of a high level of certainty in the case of *-mi/-n* and an indirect information source and/or surprise in the case of *-sqa-*. The epistemic extension of *-sqa-*, indicating doubt, is ruled out in this case by the use of *-mi/-n* with epistemic extension, indicating certainty. As *-ru* also appears on the verb along with *-sqa-*, a mirative interpretation for *-sqa-* is supported.

7.2.5   Role Play Situation: Widespread Knowledge

Three other role play situations were created with the aim of presenting the participants with real-life information assumed to be widespread, common

MARKERS OF EVIDENTIAL, EPISTEMIC AND MIRATIVE STANCE   181

knowledge among all Peruvians. It is argued here, based on the linguistic choices of the participants, that this assumption was false. In the first of these three situations, CdC and CAITH participants were asked to play the role of a boy or girl who read in a history book that the Spaniards trapped Atahuallpa. The next day, the child's father asks him/her what the Spaniards did (see Appendix B, number 4a and Appendix C, number 3a). Two participants responded in the following ways:

(13) *Atahuallpa-ta   kaptura-**ra**-nku   Cajamarca-pi.*
      Atahuallpa-ACC $capture-PST1-3PL   Cajamarca-LOC
      'They captured Atahuallpa in Cajamarca.'

(14) *Tawa   kaballu-wan   sipi-**ra**-nku,   sipi-y-ta-**n**   muna-**ra**-nku.*
      four $horse-INS   kill-PST1-3PL   kill-INF-ACC-DIREV   want-PST1-3PL
      'They killed (him) with four horses, they wanted to kill (him).'

In both (13) and (14), the participants reveal that they had some prior knowledge regarding the fate of Inca Atahuallpa by responding to the role play situation with added information; however, in the case of (14), the information provided is not historically accurate.[23] In this situation, the participants were told only that the boy or girl whose role they were playing had read that the Spaniards had trapped Atahuallpa. Nothing was told to these participants about where the capture took place or that the Inca was murdered. Therefore, it is obvious that the participants applied their background knowledge in fashioning their responses to the role play situation. In (13), the participant uses -*r(q)a*- and in (14), the participant uses -*mi/-n* and -*r(q)a*-. Since a direct information source would not apply in this role play, these two morphemes may be interpreted along the epistemic dimension only, with epistemic extension, indicating a high level of certainty regarding this information.

In another situation, participants were asked to play the role of a boy or girl who heard on the radio that there had been a terrorist attack in the United States against the Twin Towers. The following day, the child's father asks the child what he/she heard on the radio (see Appendix B, number 4b and Appendix C, number 3b). Two participants responded in the following ways, using both -*si/-s* and -*sqa*-:

---

23   It is general knowledge that Atahuallpa was captured in Cajamarca and later garroted by the Spaniards; Túpac Amaru II, an indigenous leader of the late eighteenth century, was quartered.

(15) *Estados* *Unidus-pi-s*   *terrorista-kuna* *sipi-ra-pu-sqa*[24]
     $states $united-LOC-INDEV $terrorist-PL   kill-SUD-MAL-PST2

soldado-kuna-ta.
$soldier-PL-ACC
'In the United States, the terrorists killed the soldiers.'

(16) *Noqa* *uyari-ni* *Estados* *Unidos-pi-s*   *pasa-sqa*   *huq*
     I   hear-1 $states $united-LOC-INDEV $happen-PST2   a

accidente *pasa-mu-sqa*   *television-pi*   *kay-lla-ta*   *riku-ni.*
$accident   happen-CIS-PST2 $television-LOC   this-LIM-ACC   see-1
'I heard in the United States happened, an accident happened, I saw
only this on TV.'

In both (15) and (16), there is incorrect uptake of the information in the situation by the participants. Although the participants were told that there was a terrorist attack in the United States against the Twin Towers, example (15) states, 'In the United States, the terrorists killed the soldiers'. This incorrect uptake suggests that this participant was unfamiliar with the information contained within this situation. If this participant had already learned of the attack, he would likely have been able to access this information in his memory and use it to fashion an appropriate response to this situation. Therefore, although this participant is playing the role of a boy who has heard this information on the radio, his own unfamiliarity with the topic colors his response. In (16), the participant reports having gathered the information from watching television, although the boy in the situation was described as hearing the information on the radio.

For both (15) and (16), the use of *-si/-s* and *-sqa-* may be interpreted along all three dimensions, the evidential dimension (indicating an indirect information source), the epistemic dimension (indicating doubt) and the mirative dimension (indicating surprise/newsworthiness). Having heard information on the radio or through the means of television may be interpreted as indirect. Also, since both participants provided information that did not conform to the role play situation provided, it is likely that both participants were uncertain or unfamiliar with the message content that they were conveying during the role play. Additionally, both participants may have felt the information to be

---

24   This verb was inflected by the participant for third person singular rather than third person plural, *-sqa-ku*.

MARKERS OF EVIDENTIAL, EPISTEMIC AND MIRATIVE STANCE   183

surprising and/or newsworthy; *-ru* in (15), indicating suddenness, supports a mirative interpretation for *-sqa-*.

In response to this same situation, yet another participant answered in the following way:

(17) *Huq   noticia-ta   uyari-ni   que   Estados   Unidus-pi-n,*
      A $news-ACC   hear-1 $that $states $united-LOC-DIREV

      terrorista-kuna   bombarea-sqa-ku   torre-kuna-ta.
      $terrorist-PL $bomb-PST2-3PL $tower-PL-ACC
      'I heard news that in the United States, terrorists bombed the towers.'

In (17), *-mi/-n* and-*sqa-* are used. In this case, since the protagonist heard the information over the radio rather than having been a direct witness, *-mi/-n* may be interpreted as indicating a high level of certainty; perhaps for this participant, radio news are considered trustworthy in general. Another possibility is that this participant had already learned of this information and, for that reason, was certain. In (17), *-sqa-* may be interpreted as an evidentiality strategy, indicating an indirect information source, and/or as a mirativity strategy, indicating surprise/newsworthiness; both of these meanings for *-sqa-* are possible within the context of this role play.

In another role play situation, participants were asked to play the role of a boy or girl who saw on television that a mall in Lima, Peru, called *Mesa Redonda*, was burning up in flames. Later, his/her father asks the child what he/she saw on television (see Appendix B, number 4c and Appendix C, number 3c). Two participants responded as follows:

(18) *Mesa   Redonda-pi   askha   runa-kuna   incendio-pi*
      $Mesa $Redonda-LOC many   people-PL $fire-LOC

      wañu-pu-sqa-ku.
      die-MAL-PST2-3PL
      'Many people died in the fire at Mesa Redonda.'

(19) *Television-pi   riku-ni   haqay   Lima   llaqta-pi-n   nina*
      $television-LOC see-1   that   Lima   city-LOC-DIREV   fire

      rupha-ra-pu-sqa   vende-kuna-ta.
      burn-SUD-MAL-PST2 $sell-PL-ACC
      'I saw on TV that the fire burned the goods/merchants in the city of Lima.'

In (18), -*sqa*- is used and in (19), -*mi/-n* and -*sqa*- are used together. For both (18) and (19), given this role play context, -*sqa*- may be interpreted as an evidentiality strategy, indicating an indirect information source (the television), and as a mirativity strategy, indicating surprise. The use of -*ru* in (19) supports a mirative interpretation for -*sqa*-. An additional possible interpretation for -*sqa*- in the case of (18) is with epistemic extension, indicating doubt. Since -*mi/-n* is used along with -*sqa*- in (19), an epistemic interpretation of -*sqa*- is ruled out by a contrary interpretation of high certainty for -*mi/-n*; an evidential reading for -*mi/-n* would be contrary to the role play context in this case.

In response to the same situation, another participant replied:

(20) | *Noqa* | *riku-ni* | *television-pi* | *chay* | *Mesa* | *Redonda* | *ni-sqa* |
|---|---|---|---|---|---|---|
| I | see-1 | $television-LOC | that | $Mesa | $Redonda | say-PP |

suntur-cha-sqa	*lugar-mi*	*rupha-ya-pu-sha-rqa-n*	*nina-wan.*
round-DIM-PP	$place-DIREV	burn-INT-MAL-PROG-PST1-3	fire-INS

'I saw on television that the round place they call Mesa Redonda was burning up in flames.'

In (20), this participant uses -*mi/-n* and -*r(q)a*-. Given the role play context that included the television as an indirect information source, these morphemes may be interpreted along the epistemic dimension only, indicating a high level of certainty.

7.2.6 Role Play Situation: Dreams

Lastly, in another role play situation, participants were asked to play the role of a speaker who dreamt that a cow was flying in the sky. The following day, the speaker wants to tell his father about the dream (see Appendix B, number 5). Three participants responded in the following manner:

(21) | *Waka* | *seqa-sha-sqa* | *altu-n-mi.*[25] |
|---|---|---|
| $cow | ascend-PROG-PST2 | $high-PERL-DIREV |

'The cow was ascending (through) the heavens.'

(22) | *Mosqho-ku-ni* | *huq* | *waka* | *vola-sha-sqa* | *altu-nta-n.* |
|---|---|---|---|---|
| dream-REFL-1 | a | $cow | $fly-PROG-PST2 | $high-PERL-DIREV |

'I dreamt a cow was flying through the heavens.'

---

25   This instance of *altu-n-mi* is ungrammatical; rather, this speaker may have meant to produce *altu-nta-n* as in (22).

MARKERS OF EVIDENTIAL, EPISTEMIC AND MIRATIVE STANCE 185

(23) *Waka-ta   riku-sha-sqa;   sueño   ka-sha-sqa.*
   $cow-ACC   see-PROG-PST2 $dream   be-PROG-PST2
   'I was seeing a cow; it was a dream.'

In both (21) and (22), -*mi*/-*n* and -*sqa*- are used and in (23), -*sqa*- is used. The use of -*mi*/-*n* in (21) and (22) may indicate a direct information source (one's own dream) or a high level of certainty regarding the contents of the dream; therefore, contrary readings for -*sqa*- along the evidential and epistemic dimensions are ruled out and surprise remains as the only possible interpretation for -*sqa*- in (21) and (22). In the case of (23), epistemic and mirative interpretations are possible for -*sqa*-, indicating doubt and surprise, respectively. Since cows do not fly, it is likely that all three participants would find this information to be surprising or unexpected. Additionally, by default, dreams may be spoken of in Quechua using the mirative -*sqa*-, as a dream state could be considered as indicating an unprepared mind; as mentioned above, Cusihuamán (2001, 161) recognizes the use of -*sqa*- in describing dreams.

7.2.7   Summary

For each of the role play responses analyzed above, possible interpretations are provided for the use of -*mi*/-*n*, -*si*/-*s*, -*r*(*q*)*a*- and -*sqa*- based on the claims of this work. It is argued here that these interpretations likely correspond to the original intent and perspectives of the participants, as the constraints of each given situational context are known and additional linguistic clues support these interpretations. As mentioned above, without metapragmatic commentary from the participants themselves, it is not possible to draw firm conclusions regarding their use of these morphemes.

In the following section, examples obtained through the recording of spontaneous conversations are presented that also support the claims of this work.

7.3   *Analysis of Spontaneous Conversations*

This section includes recorded examples gathered from two spontaneous, informal conversations in Quechua that also support the claims of this work. The conversational participants of the first informal conversation are the author and two young, female inhabitants of CAITH, referred to here as 'S' and 'D'; these are not the first initials of their names. The second conversation is between the author, 'M', and two male inhabitants of the CdC. In this second conversation, examples are presented that were spoken by only one of these CdC inhabitants, referred to here as 'G'; this is not the first initial of this participant.

186   MANLEY

During the conversation with the CAITH participants, 'S' asked 'D':

(24) S: *Qayna*   *unchay,*   *ima-ta*   *ruwa-ra-nki*
          past   day   what-ACC   do-PST1-2
          'What did you do yesterday?'

(25) D: *Noqa*   *waqa-yu-sha-ra-ni.*
          I   cry-INT-PROG-PST1-1
          'I was crying a lot.'

Both (24) and (25) include -*r(q)a*-. As 'S' would expect for 'D' to have had a
direct information source and a high level of certainty regarding her activities of the preceding day, this use falls in line with the claims of this work for
-*r(q)a*-, as an evidentiality strategy with epistemic extension. Thus, in asking
the question in (24), 'S' shifted perspective to the addressee, 'D'; this is often
referred to in the literature as shifting the deictic center. The use of -*r(q)a*- in
'D's' response may also be interpreted along both the evidential and epistemic
dimensions. 'S' and 'D' continued to discuss their activities of the previous day
by using verbs such as the following:

(26) *uyari-ra-ni*
      listen-PST1-1
      'I listened.'

(27) *pinta-ku-ra-ni*
      $paint-REFL-PST1-1
      'I painted.'

(28) *dibuha-ra-nchis*
      $draw-PST1-1PL.INCL
      'We drew.'

(29) *qelqa-yu-ra-ni*
      draw-INT-PST1-1
      'I drew a lot.'

In examples (26) through (29), the speakers were agents of the actions in question and, as such, had a direct information source and a high level of certainty
regarding the information.

    Below, 'D' reminds 'S' of an experience they both shared the previous year:

MARKERS OF EVIDENTIAL, EPISTEMIC AND MIRATIVE STANCE

(30) D: *Qayna   wata   ri-ra-yku,   chay-manta   huq*
        past   year   go-PST1-1PL.EXCL   that-ABL   one

    chinka-ru-ku-sqa   wathiya-ta   ruwa-sha-qti-yki
    get.lost-SUD-REFL-PST2   wathiya-ACC   do-PROG-SEQ-1S2O
    'We went last year, and then one got lost while I was making the
    wathiya for you.'[26]

In (30), both -*r(q)a*- and -*sqa*- are used. First, 'D' uses -*r(q)a*- while stating, 'We
went last year'. In line with the claims of this work -*r(q)a*- may be used here
since 'D' was an agent in the activity and therefore had a direct information
source and a high level of certainty regarding the information. Then, 'D' uses
-*sqa*- as she continues to say that 'one got lost while I was making the *wathiya*
for you'. As 'D's' use of -*r(q)a*- had already established the appropriate evidential and epistemic interpretations, this subsequent use of -*sqa*- may be interpreted only along the mirative dimension, indicating surprise. As getting lost
is generally unexpected, and since -*ru* is also used, indicating suddenness, this
interpretation is supported for -*sqa*-.

The following exchange occurred during the conversation with the two CdC
inhabitants:

(31) M: *Ima-ta-n   ruwa-rqa-nki   kunan   p'unchay,   tutamanta-pi?*
        what-ACC-DIREV   do-PST1-2   now   day   morning-LOC
        'What did you do this morning?'

(32) G: *Noqa-taq   ichaqa,   trabajo-y-pi   tarea*
        I-EMP   however $work-1POSS-LOC $homework

    completa-na-y-ta,   completa-mu-sha-ra-ni;
    $complete-NMLZ-1POSS-ACC $complete-TRANS-PROG-PST1-1

    tuku-pa-mu-sha-ra-ni.
    finish-BEN-TRANS-PROG-PST1-1
    'And I, however, at my work, had to complete, was completing my
    homework; I was finishing it.'

---

26 A *wathiya* is a traditional, Andean oven made of pieces of dry earth; potatoes are most
    commonly baked within this type of earth-oven.

While (31) includes both *-mi/-n* and *-r(q)a-*, 'G' responds in (32), using *-r(q)a-*. Since 'G' was the agent of the event described, his use of *-r(q)a-* may be interpreted as communicating both a direct information source and a high level of certainty regarding the information.

The following exchange continues on the topic of the activities of the previous day:

(33) M: *Chay-manta,*   *Sacsayhuaman-man-chu*   *ri-rqa-nkichis*   *Inti*
         that-ABL   Sacsayhuaman-ILLA-INTR   go-PST1-2PL   Inti

Raymi-paq?
Raymi-DAT
'So, did you go to Sacsayhuaman for Inti Raymi?'

(34) G: *Ri-yku-n,*   *arí.*   *Askha*   *runa-kuna*   *ka-sqa.*
         go-1PL.EXCL-DIREV   yes   a.lot   person-PL   be-PST2
'We went, yes. A lot of people were there.'

In (34), 'G' uses *-mi/-n* in stating, 'We went, yes'; here, since 'G' was an agent in this activity, *-mi/-n* may be interpreted along the evidential dimension, as indicating a direct information source, and also along the epistemic dimension, communicating a high level of certainty regarding the information. As he continues, in stating 'A lot of people were there', he uses *-sqa-*; in order not to contradict the evidential and epistemic interpretations for his prior use of *-mi/-n*, only a mirative reading remains for *-sqa-*, indicating surprise or newsworthiness.

'G' goes on to describe the scene at *Inti Raymi*, a sun-worshipping ceremony/celebration/reenactment, in the following way:

(35) G: *Puri-nku,*   *uyari-nku,*   *hoq*   *lado-kuna-manta*   *runa-kuna*
         walk-3PL   listen-3PL   other $place-PL-ABL   people-PL

hamu-q-pas   *chay-pi*   *ka-sha-ra-nku*   *Inti*   *Tayta-ta*
come-AG-ADD   that-LOC   be-PROG-PST1-3PL   sun   god-ACC

qhawa-ri-spa.
look-INCH-GER
'They walk, they listen, and people coming from other places were also there, looking toward the sun god.'

MARKERS OF EVIDENTIAL, EPISTEMIC AND MIRATIVE STANCE 189

In (35), 'G' uses -*r(q)a*-, as he directly participated in the event under discussion and so gathered this information firsthand and had a high level of certainty regarding the information.

Another exchange with 'G' went as follows:

(36) M: *Macchu   Pichu-man   ri-rqa-ni,   huq   khumpa-y-wan.*
Macchu   Pichu-ILLA   go-PST1-1   a $friend-1POSS-COM
'I went to Macchu Pichu with a friend of mine.'

(37) G: *Riki,   allin-mi.   Allin-chu   ka-sqa?*
Of course   good-DIREV   good-INTR   be-PST2
'Of course, that's good. Was it great?'

In (37), 'G' first responds to (36) with an expression containing -*mi/-n*, followed by a question containing -*sqa*-. It so happens that 'G' had not been to Macchu Pichu before this exchange. Therefore, his use of -*mi/-n* may be interpreted along the epistemic dimension, as indicating a high level of certainty; his use of 'of course' supports an interpretation of a high certainty level. In order not to contradict the previous epistemic reading for -*mi/-n*, his subsequent use of -*sqa*- may be interpreted as a mirativity strategy, indicating surprise, with the perspective shifted to the listener (the author in this case). 'G' may have assumed that the experience of going to Macchu Pichu would have been new and/or surprising.

Finally, in another exchange with 'G', the topic of conversation is the time that he prepared stuffed peppers for some tourists hiking the Inca Trail:

(38) M: *Chay   rocoto-q   uhu-n-pi,   ima-n?*
that $pepper-GEN   inside-3POSS-LOC   what-DIREV
'What was inside that pepper?'

(39) G: *Relleno   verduras-pi   ka-sqa,   habas,   zanahoria*
$filling $vegetables-LOC   be-PST2 $fava.beans $carrots

chay-mi.
that-DIREV
'In the vegetables' filling were fava beans, carrots, that's all.'

In (39), 'G' uses -*mi/-n* and -*sqa*-. In this case, as 'G' prepared the stuffed peppers, he had a direct information source and a high level of certainty regarding the information. Since 'G' produced (39) in response to a question, his use of *-sqa-* may also be interpreted as a mirativity strategy with the perspective shifted to the listener; for the author, the contents of the stuffed peppers were a surprise.

For each of the spontaneous conversational examples analyzed above, possible interpretations are provided for the use of *-mi/-n, -si/-s, -r(q)a-* and *-sqa-* based on the claims of this work. As for the role play situations described in the previous section, it is argued here that these interpretations likely correspond to the original intent and perspectives of the participants, given the topics of conversation as well as additional linguistic clues in support of these interpretations.

8 Discussion and Conclusion

In conclusion, this chapter has sought to fill important gaps in the broader literature on stance and deixis as well as in the study of Quechua evidentiality, epistemics and mirativity specifically. As discussed above, based on the groundbreaking work of both Du Bois (2007), in his conceptualization of the stance triangle, and Hanks (2005, 2011), in his practice approach to deixis, the Cuzco Quechua enclitics, *-mi/-n, -chá* and *-si/-s*, and the past-tense morphemes, *-r(q)a-* and *-sqa-*, are referred to here as multidimensional markers of stance, which may simultaneously communicate evidentiality (information source), epistemology (degree of certainty/doubt) and, in the case of *-sqa-*, mirativity (surprise or newsworthiness). Section 2, above, examined the multidimensional nature of stance and deixis across all languages. One gap that this work has aimed to fill is to add to the overall number of studies that recognize evidential, epistemic and mirative markers as markers of stance/deixis, anchoring utterances to the context of speech. Additionally, since the majority of existing work on stance/deixis across languages has examined free morphemes, the examination of bound morphemes here represents another way in which this work has sought to address gaps in the broader literature on stance and deixis. As the participants of this work used the five Cuzco Quechua morphemes of interest to engage in evidential, epistemic and mirative stance acts, they fulfilled the demands of Du Bois' (2007) stance triangle in: (1) evaluating an object along the evidential, epistemic and mirative dimensions, (2) positioning a subject in relation to the evaluated object, and (3) aligning with other subjects. As mentioned above, in his practice approach to deixis, Hanks (2005, 2011) also recognizes that evaluation is central to deictic expression. Furthermore, following the Introduction to this volume, in finding

Hanks (2005, 2011) to describe deictics in a way that is consistent with Du Bois' stance triangle, this work supports the unification of the concepts of stance and deixis, with deixis being considered as a subclass of stance that serves a specifically referential function.

As discussed in section 3, there continues to be a great deal of disagreement in the cross-linguistic literature regarding the definitions of evidentiality and epistemology. By employing key terminological concepts from Aikhenvald (2004) and Aikhenvald and Storch (2013), as described in section 4, it has been possible to describe the ways in which the five bound morphemes of interest here function strategically within Cuzco Quechua discourse; the analysis of these five morphemes put forth here falls in line with what Aikhenvald (2004) has observed cross-linguistically, in her analysis of evidential/epistemic/ mirative systems in 500 different languages from around the globe.

As outlined in section 5, there is much debate among investigators of Quechua language varieties regarding the communication of evidentiality, epistemology and mirativity and the analysis put forth in this work offers a coherent, multifaceted, inclusive compromise to this debate. Specifically, based on a review of the relevant literature as well as the results and analyses of the original data presented above, this work claims: (1) -*mi/-n* is a direct evidential which may be utilized with epistemic extension to indicate certainty, (2) -*chá* is a conjecture evidential which may be utilized with epistemic extension to communicate doubt, (3) -*si/-s* is an indirect evidential which may be utilized with epistemic extension to indicate doubt, (4) -*r(q)a-* may be utilized as an evidentiality strategy to communicate direct information source and also with epistemic extension to indicate certainty, and (5) -*sqa-* may be utilized as an evidentiality strategy to communicate indirect information source, with epistemic extension to indicate doubt, and as a mirativity strategy, indicating surprise and newsworthiness. This work is the first to claim epistemic extensions for -*r(q)a-* and -*sqa-*, indicating certainty and doubt, respectively. Thus, as described here, each of these five morphemes is multidimensional and allows the speaker to simultaneously take more than one type of stance, including evidential stance, epistemic stance and mirative stance.

As described above, the data for this work were gathered from two bilingual Quechua/Spanish communities in Cuzco, Peru in recorded, spontaneous conversations as well as in response to two elicitation tasks: role playing and a certainty-ranking exercise. The statistically significant findings of the certainty-ranking exercise were applied above to the analysis of spontaneous conversation as well as examples elicited through role play.

Specifically, the data obtained from the certainty-ranking exercise provide evidence for the claim that the past tense morphemes, -*r(q)a-* and -*sqa-*, may be used with epistemic extension of their meaning, as they may communicate higher and lower levels of certainty, respectively. Secondarily, these data suggest that the lack of an evidential enclitic, '∅', followed by -mi/-n, followed by -si/-s, express higher to lower levels of certainty, respectively. Therefore, these findings also indicate that the evidential enclitics, -mi/-n, and -si/-s, carry epistemic meaning.

For each of the role play responses analyzed above as well as for each of the examples obtained through the recording of spontaneous conversations, possible interpretations were provided for the use of -mi/-n, -si/-s, -r(q)a- and -sqa- based on the findings and claims of this work. It is argued that these interpretations likely correspond to the original intent and perspectives of the participants, based on the constraints of each given role play context, the topics of spontaneous conversation and additional linguistic clues to support these interpretations.

Upon examination of the examples obtained through the recording of spontaneous conversations as well as those elicited through role play, it is clear that these speakers of Cuzco Quechua use their evidential, epistemic and mirative resources, the evidential enclitics and past tense morphemes, in complex and subtle ways in order to communicate a wide variety of intended perspectives. While the evidential enclitics, -mi/-n, -chá and -si/-s, stand in paradigmatic contrast to each other, as do the -r(q)a- and -sqa- past tense morphemes, the enclitics may be combined with the past tense morphemes within single utterances, thereby creating additional shades of meaning. More specifically, table 5.6, below, summarizes the interpretations that were provided for five of the six possible combinations of the relevant morphemes within the examples obtained through the role play elicitation as well as in spontaneous conversation. The participants did not produce -si/-s in combination with -r(q)a-. In table 5.6, the dimensions appearing in bold for each combination represent interpretations that were consistently possible in every use of that combination across all role play and spontaneous conversation examples; those dimensions that are not in bold represent interpretations that were ruled out in at least one role play or spontaneous conversation example of the given combination. Following are summaries for each combination produced by the participants.

For example, in the case of the '∅ + -r(q)a-' combination, all but one of the examples allowed a two-dimensional interpretation of both a direct information source and a high certainty level (examples 2, 3, 6, 24–29, 32, 35); in example (13), it was possible to rule out an evidential reading of direct information source, based on the role play context provided, leaving only an epistemic reading of high certainty as a possibility.

MARKERS OF EVIDENTIAL, EPISTEMIC AND MIRATIVE STANCE 193

TABLE 5.6 *Multidimensionality of the combinations exemplified in this work*

		Evidential dimension	Epistemic dimension	Mirative dimension
(1) ∅	+ -r(q)a-	direct information source	**high certainty**	N/A
(2) -mi/-n	+ -r(q)a-	direct information source	**high certainty**	N/A
(3) -si/-s	+ -r(q)a-	N/A	N/A	N/A
(4) ∅	+ -sqa-	indirect information source	doubt	**surprise/ newsworthiness**
(5) -mi/-n	+ -sqa-	(in)direct information source	**high certainty**	**surprise/ newsworthiness**
(6) -si/-s	+ -sqa-	**indirect information source**	**doubt**	**surprise/ newsworthiness**

*Bold text represents interpretations that were consistently possible across all examples.

In the case of the '-*mi/-n* + -*r(q)a*-' combination, examples (4) and (8) allowed a two-dimensional interpretation of both a direct information source and a high certainty level, while a direct information source interpretation was ruled out for examples (9), (10), (14) and (20), leaving an epistemic reading (high certainty) as the only possibility.

For the '∅ + -*sqa*-' combination, the mirative dimension remained as a possibility for all examples: examples (11) and (18) allowed for a three-dimensional interpretation (indirect information source, doubt, surprise/newsworthiness); example (23) permitted a two-dimensional interpretation (doubt and surprise/newsworthiness); a one-dimensional, mirative interpretation only was applied in the case of example (4).

Regarding the '-*mi/-n* + -*sqa*-' combination, the epistemic value of -*mi/-n* (high certainty) and the mirative interpretation of -*sqa*- (surprise/newsworthiness) were possible in all examples: in examples (5), (7), (21), (22), (34) and (39), it was possible to interpret -*mi/-n* two-dimensionally (direct information source and high certainty) along with a mirative reading for -*sqa*-; examples (12), (17) and (19) allowed a one-dimensional, epistemic interpretation for -*mi/-n* (high certainty) and a two-dimensional interpretation for -*sqa*- (indirect information source and surprise/newsworthiness); example (37) permitted an epistemic reading for -*mi/-n* (high certainty) along with a mirative reading for -*sqa*- (surprise/newsworthiness).

Finally, as regards the '-*si*/-*s* + -*sqa*-' combination, three-dimensional interpretations were possible for both examples (15) and (16) (indirect information source, doubt and surprise/newsworthiness) and no examples were produced with any of the three dimensions as ruled out due to the situational context.

Based on table 5.6 and the examples of this work, it may be tempting to conclude that the epistemic dimension is primary for -*mi*/-*n* and -*r(q)a*-, since an evidential reading was sometimes ruled out for these morphemes and an epistemic reading was never precluded. Likewise, one might interpret these results as suggesting that the mirative dimension is primary for -*sqa*-, given that a mirative reading was consistently possible in all examples and at times both the accompanying evidential and epistemic readings were ruled out. It is argued here that such conclusions cannot be supported, given limitations in the design of the role play elicitation instrument; the role play situations provided to the participants isolated only some of the possible interpretations for the morphemes. For example, while some role play scenarios were designed such that the protagonist received information secondhand, thus precluding a direct information source interpretation, no role play situations specified that the protagonist was doubtful, which would have precluded an interpretation of a high certainty level. Therefore, while these data effectively demonstrate the multidimensional nature of these morphemes, it is not possible to determine primacy of any of the three dimensions (evidential, epistemic, and mirative) based on this work.

Since each of the Quechua stance markers examined here is multidimensional and carries multiple meanings, not all of which are necessarily applied with each use of these morphemes, and also since the evidential enclitics may be combined with the past tense morphemes, Quechua's stance-marking/deictic possibilities may be considered similar in complexity to those of other languages with complex evidential/epistemic/mirative systems, such as the Northern Iroquoian languages, as described by Mithun (1986), and Kashaya, as examined by Oswalt (1986). For example, Mithun (1986, 90–91) found that in Cayuga, the same evidential particle meaning, 'it seems', may be used to indicate that the information being conveyed is based on appearance, to hedge both precision and certainty, and as a marker of courtesy.

In the case of Quechua language varieties as well as for other languages with complex evidential/epistemic/mirative systems, the ethnography of these systems, committed to avoid oversimplification and focused on the discovery of the multiple meanings (semantics) and multiple uses (pragmatics) of these morphemes, continues to be a fruitful, future direction for research. Such investigations will continue to uncover these languages' rich possibilities for expression.

Appendix A

1	first person singular	GEN	genitive
1PL.INCL	first person plural inclusive	GER	gerund
		ILLA	illative
1PL.EXCL	first person plural exclusive	INCH	inchoative
		INDEV	indirect evidential
1POSS	first person possessive	INF	infinitive
1S2O	first person subject to second person object	INS	instrumental
		INT	intensifier
2	second person singular	INTR	interrogative
2PL	second person plural	LIM	limitative
3	third person singular	LOC	locative
3PL	third person plural	MAL	malefactive
3POSS	third person possessive	NEG	negative
ABL	ablative	NMLZ	nominalizer
ACC	accusative	PERL	perlative
ADD	additive	PL	plural
ADVL	adverbalizer	PP	past participle
AG	agentive	PROG	progressive
BEN	benefactive	PST1	simple past
CIS	cislocative	PST2	narrative past, perfective
COM	comitative		
DAT	dative	REFL	reflexive
DIM	diminutive	SEQ	sequential
DIR	directional	SUD	sudden
DIREV	direct evidential	TOP	topic
EMP	emphatic	TRANS	translocative

Appendix B

Role Play: **Casa del Cargador**

In each situation presented below, the Spanish and Quechua text read aloud by the author to the participants appears along with the English translation. Larger versions of the accompanying clip art drawings were shown to each participant as he/she listened to the verbal description of each situation.

1. You witnessed first-hand:

Un joven vio que un señor chocó su carro contra el árbol de la casa de su papá. Más tarde, su papá le pregunta al joven qué pasó. ¿Qué dirías si tú fueras este joven? Hacemos el diálogo como si tú fueras el joven y como si yo fuera tu papá. Yo, como tu papá te pregunto, "¿Qué pasó rato antes?" Kunanmi, kikin respuestata runasimipi qowanki. "Iman kunachallan pasaran?"

'A boy saw that a gentleman crashed his car against the tree in front of his dad's house. Later, his dad asks the boy what happened. What would you say if you were this boy? Let's do the dialogue as if you were the boy and as if I were your dad. I, as your dad, ask you "What just happened?" Now, give me the same answer in Quechua. "What just happened?"'

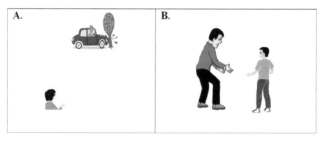

FIGURE 5.1 *Appendix B, item 1*

2. You want them to think you witnessed first-hand:

Un joven se durmió mientras trabajaba con su compañero. Cuando el joven estaba durmiendo, su compañero de trabajo se cayó de unas gradas. Más tarde, el jefe del joven le pregunta qué pasó. El joven no quiere decirle a su jefe que estaba durmiendo. Entonces, como si tú fueras el joven, ¿qué le dirías a tu jefe? Ahora, como si yo fuera tu jefe, te pregunto, "¿Qué le pasó a tu compañero?" Kunanmi, kikin respuestata runasimipi qowanki. "Iman khumpaykita pasaruran?"

'A boy fell asleep while he was working with his friend/colleague. When the boy was sleeping, his friend/colleague fell down from a ladder. Later, the boy's boss asks him what happened. The boy doesn't want to tell his boss that he was sleeping. So, as if you were the boy, what would you tell your boss? Now, as if I

MARKERS OF EVIDENTIAL, EPISTEMIC AND MIRATIVE STANCE 197

FIGURE 5.2 *Appendix B, item 2*

were your boss, I ask you, "What happened to your friend/colleague?" Now, give me the same answer in Quechua. "What happened to your friend?"'

3. Family told you:

Un día, un papá le dice a su hijo, "Tu abuelo ganó mil soles en la lotería." Al día siguiente, el hijo quiere contar eso a su amiga. Ahora, hacemos el diálogo, como si yo fuera tu amiga y como si tú fueras este joven. Como si yo fuera tu amiga, te pregunto, "¿Cómo está tu familia?" Kunanmi, kikin respuestata runasimipi qowanki. "Imaynallan familiayki kashan?"

'One day, a dad says to his son, "Your grandfather won one thousand soles in the lottery." The next day, the son wants to tell this to his friend. Now, let's do the dialogue as if I were your friend and as if you were this boy. As if I were your friend, I ask you, "How's your family?" Now, give me the same answer in Quechua. "How is your family doing?"'

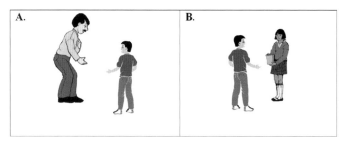

FIGURE 5.3 *Appendix B, item 3*

4. Widespread knowledge:

   a. *Un joven leyó en un libro de historia que los españoles le atraparon a Atahuallpa. Al día siguiente, su papá le pregunta qué hicieron los españoles. Ahora, como si yo fuera tu papá y como si tú fueras este joven, ¿qué me dirías? Haciendo el diálogo, te pregunto, "¿Qué hicieron los españoles?" Kunanmi, kikin respuestata runasimipi qowanki. "Imatan españolkuna ruwaranku?"*

   'A boy read in a history book that the Spaniards trapped Atahuallpa. The next day, his dad asks him what the Spaniards did. Now, as if I were your dad and as if you were this boy, what would you tell me? Doing the dialogue, I ask you, "What did the Spaniards do?" Now, give me the same answer in Quechua. "What did the Spaniards do?"'

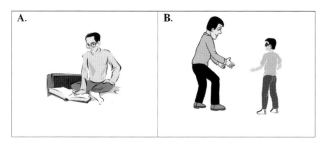

FIGURE 5.4 *Appendix B, item 4a*

b. *Un joven escuchó en la radio que hubo un atentado terrorista en los EE.UU. contra las torres gemelas. Al día siguiente, su papá le pregunta al joven qué escuchó en la radio. Ahora, como si yo fuera tu papá y como si tú fueras este joven, ¿qué me dirías? Te pregunto, "¿Qué escuchaste en la radio?" Kunanmi, kikin respuestata runasimipi qowanki. "Imatan radiopi uyariranki?"*

'A boy heard on the radio that there was a terrorist attack in the United States against the Twin Towers. The next day, his dad asks the boy what he heard on the radio. Now, as if I were your dad and as if you were this boy, what would you tell me? I ask you, "What did you hear on the radio?" Now, give me the same answer in Quechua. "What did you hear on the radio?"'

FIGURE 5.5 *Appendix B, item 4b*

c. *Un joven vio en la televisión que un centro comercial, llamado Mesa Redonda, de la ciudad de Lima estaba encendiéndose, quemándose en llamas. Más tarde, su papá le pregunta qué vio en la televisión. Ahora, como si yo fuera tu papá y como si tú fueras este joven, ¿qué me dirías? Te pregunto, "¿Qué viste en la televisión?" Kunanmi, kikin respuestata runasimipi qowanki. "Imatataq television-piri rikuranki?"*

'A boy saw on television that a mall, called Mesa Redonda, of the city of Lima, was burning up in flames. Later, his dad asks him what he saw on television. Now, as if I were your dad and as if you were this boy, what would you tell me? I ask you, "What did you see on television?" Now, give me the same answer in Quechua. "And what did you see on television?"'

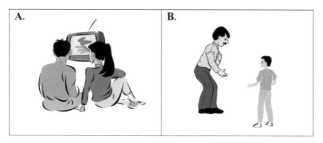

FIGURE 5.6 *Appendix B, item 4c*

5. Sleeping:

Una noche, un joven estaba soñando. En su sueño, (muy claro vio que) (recordaba un poco no más que), una vaca estaba volando en el cielo. Al día siguiente, el joven quiere contarle a su papá sobre su sueño. Ahora, hacemos el diálogo, como si yo fuera tu papá y como si tú fueras este joven. Te pregunto, "¿Qué soñaste anoche?" Kunanmi, kikin respuestata runasimipi qowanki. "Imatan ch'isi mosqokuranki?"

'One night, a boy was dreaming. In his dream, (very clearly, he saw that) (he remembered only a little bit that) a cow was flying in the sky. The next day, the boy wants to tell his dad about his dream. Now, let's do the dialogue, as if I were your dad and as if you were this boy. I ask you, "What did you dream last night?" Now, give me the same answer in Quechua. "What did you dream last night?"'

FIGURE 5.7 *Appendix B, item 5*

Appendix C

Role Play Investigation: CAITH

In each situation presented below, the Spanish and Quechua text read aloud by the author to the participants appears along with the English translation. Larger versions of the accompanying clip art drawings were shown to each participant as he/she listened to the verbal description of each situation.

1. You witnessed first-hand:

   Una joven estaba manejando el carro morado de su mamá y chocó con otro carro. Más tarde, su mamá le pregunta a la joven qué pasó. La joven quiere decirle a su mamá lo que pasó. ¿Qué dirías tú si fueras esta joven? Hacemos el diálogo como si tú fueras la joven y como si yo fuera tu mamá. Yo, como tu mamá te pregunto, "¿Qué pasó?" Kunanmi, kikin respuestata runasimipi qowanki. "Iman pasaruran?"

   'A girl was driving her mom's purple car and crashed into another car. Later, her mom asks the girl what happened. The girl wants to tell her mom what happened. What would you say if you were this girl? Let's do the dialogue as if you were the girl and as if I were your mom. I, as your mom, ask you, "What happened?" Now, give me the same answer in Quechua. "What just happened?"'

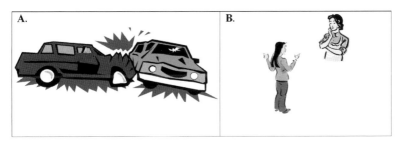

FIGURE 5.8 *Appendix C, item 1*

2. Family told you:

   Un día, una mamá le dice a su hija, "Tu abuelo ganó mil soles en la lotería." Al día siguiente, la hija quiere contar eso a su amiga. Ahora, hacemos el diálogo, como si yo fuera tu amiga y como si tú fueras esta joven. Como si yo fuera tu amiga, te pregunto, "¿Cómo está tu familia?" Kunanmi, kikin respuestata runasimipi qowanki. "Imaynallan familiayki kashan?"

'One day, a mom says to her daughter, "Your grandfather won one thousand soles in the lottery." The next day, the daughter wants to tell that to her friend. Now, let's do the dialogue, as if I were your friend and as if you were this girl. As if I were your friend, I ask you, "How's your family doing?" Now, give me the same answer in Quechua. "How is your family doing?"'

FIGURE 5.9 *Appendix C, item 2*

3. Widespread knowledge:

   a. *Una joven leyó en su libro de historia que los españoles le atraparon a Atahuallpa. Al día siguiente, su amiga le pregunta qué hicieron los españoles. Ahora, como si yo fuera tu amiga y como si tú fueras esta joven, qué me dirías. Haciendo el diálogo, te pregunto, "¿Qué hicieron los españoles?" Kunanmi, kikin respuestata runasimipi qowanki. "Imatan españolkuna ruwaranku?"*

   'A girl read in her history book that the Spaniards trapped Atahuallpa. The next day, her friend asks her what the Spaniards did. Now, as if I were your friend and as if you were this girl, what would you tell me? Doing the dialogue, I ask you, "What did the Spaniards do?" Now, give me the same answer in Quechua. "What did the Spaniards do?"'

MARKERS OF EVIDENTIAL, EPISTEMIC AND MIRATIVE STANCE 203

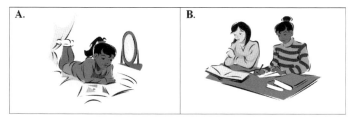

FIGURE 5.10   Appendix C, item 3a

b. *Una joven escuchó en la radio que hubo un atentado terrorista en los EE.UU. contra las torres gemelas. Al día siguiente, su papá le pregunta a la joven qué escuchó en la radio. Ahora, como si yo fuera tu papá y como si tú fueras esta joven, ¿qué me dirías? Te pregunto, "¿Qué escuchaste en la radio?" Kunanmi, kikin respuestata runasimipi qowanki. "Imatan radiopi uyariranki?"*

'A girl heard on the radio that there was a terrorist attack in the United States against the Twin Towers. The next day, her dad asks the girl what she heard on the radio. Now, as if I were your dad and as if you were this girl, what would you tell me? I ask you, "What did you hear on the radio?" Now, give me the same answer in Quechua. "What did you hear on the radio?"'

FIGURE 5.11   Appendix C, item 3b

c. *Una joven vio en la televisión que un centro comercial, llamado Mesa Redonda, de la ciudad de Lima estaba encendiéndose, quemándose en llamas. Más tarde, su papá le pregunta qué vio en la televisión. Ahora, como si yo fuera tu papá y como si tú fueras esta joven, ¿qué me dirías? Te pregunto, "¿Qué viste en la televisión?" Kunanmi, kikin respuestata runasimipi qowanki. "Imatan televisionpi rikuranki?"*

'A girl saw on television that a mall, called Mesa Redonda, of the city of Lima, was burning up in flames. Later, her dad asks her what she saw on television. Now, as if I were your dad and as if you were this girl, what would you tell me? I ask you, "What did you see on television?" Now, give me the same answer in Quechua. "What did you see on television?"'

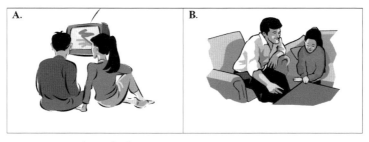

FIGURE 5.12   *Appendix C, item 3c*

Appendix D

Certainty-ranking Exercise

For both versions below, participants were shown the list of six sentences as the author read these aloud and then asked to rank them in terms of certainty, with "1" meaning that the speaker is more sure and "6" meaning that the speaker is less sure. The base meaning for all of the sentences is: 'The young men and women were unearthing the potatoes.'

Version 1:
____ *Waynasipaskuna papata<u>n</u> allasha<u>sqa</u>ku.*
____ *Waynasipaskuna papata<u>n</u> allasha<u>rqa</u>nku.*
____ *Waynasipaskuna papata allasha<u>rqa</u>nku.*
____ *Waynasipaskuna papata allasha<u>sqa</u>ku.*
____ *Waynasipaskuna papata<u>s</u> allasha<u>rqa</u>nku.*
____ *Waynasipaskuna papata<u>s</u> allasha<u>sqa</u>ku.*

Version 2:

____ *Waynasipaskuna papata<u>n</u> allasha<u>sqa</u>ku.*

____ *Waynasipaskuna papata<u>s</u> allasha<u>rqa</u>nku.*

____ *Waynasipaskuna papata allasha<u>sqa</u>ku.*

____ *Waynasipaskuna papata<u>s</u> allasha<u>sqa</u>ku.*

____ *Waynasipaskuna papata allasha<u>rqa</u>nku.*

____ *Waynasipaskuna papata<u>n</u> allasha<u>rqa</u>nku.*

Bibliography

Adelaar, Willem F.H. 2013. "A Quechuan mirative?" In *Perception and cognition in language and culture*, edited by Alexandra Y. Aikhenvald and Anne Storch. 95–110. Leiden/Boston: Brill.

Aikhenvald, Alexandra Y. 2004. *Evidentiality*. Oxford: Oxford University Press.

Aikhenvald, Alexandra Y. and Anne Storch, eds. 2013. *Perception and cognition in language and culture*. Leiden/Boston: Brill.

Anderson, Lloyd B. 1986. "Evidentials, paths of change, and mental maps: Typologically regular asymmetries." In *The linguistic coding of epistemology*, edited by Wallace Chafe and Johanna Nichols. 273–312. Norwood, NJ: Ablex.

Aráoz, Dora, and Américo Salas. 1993. *Manual de gramática quechua, pautas fundamentales*. Cuzco, Peru: Instituto de Pastoral Andina.

Asociación Civil 'Gregorio Condori Mamani'. 1996. "Asociación Civil 'Gregorio Condori Mamani' Proyecto Casa del Cargador, Manual de organización y funciones". Manuscript. Cuzco, Peru.

Bendix, E.H. 1993. "The grammaticalization of responsibility and evidence: Interactional potential of evidential categories in Newari." In *Responsibility and evidence in oral discourse*, edited by Jane H. Hill and Judith T. Irvine. 226–247. Cambridge/New York: Cambridge University Press.

Blum-Kulka, Shoshana, Juliana House and Gabriele Kasper. 1989. *Cross-cultural pragmatics: Requests and apologies*. Norwood, New Jersey: Ablex.

Brugman, Claudia and Monica Macaulay. 2010. "Characterizing evidentiality." Paper presented at the annual meeting for the Linguistic Society of America, Baltimore, Maryland, January 9.

Bühler, Karl. 1934. *Sprachtheorie*. Jena-Stuttgart: Gustav Fischer.

Chafe, Wallace. 1986. "Evidentiality in English conversation and academic writing." In *The linguistic coding of epistemology*, edited by Wallace Chafe and Johanna Nichols. 261–272. Norwood, NJ: Ablex.

———, ed. 1980. *The pear stories, cognitive, cultural, and linguistic aspects of narrative production*, Norwood, NJ: Ablex.

Chafe, Wallace and Johanna Nichols, eds. 1986. *Evidentiality: The linguistic coding of epistemology.* Norwood, NJ: Ablex.

Cusihuaman, Antonio. 2001. *Gramática Quechua, Cuzco Collao, 2nd edition.* Cuzco, Peru: Centro de Estudios Regionales Andinos "Bartolomé de Las Casas".

DeLancey, Scott. 1997. "Mirativity: The grammatical marking of unexpected information." *Linguistic Typology* 1:33–52.

———. 2001. "The mirative and evidentiality." *Journal of Pragmatics* 33:369–82.

Escobar, Anna María. 2000. *Contacto social y lingüístico, El español en contacto con el quechua en el Perú,* Lima, Peru: Pontificia Universidad Católica del Perú Fondo Editorial.

Faller, Martina. 2002. "Semantics and pragmatics of evidentials in Cuzco Quechua." PhD diss., Stanford University.

———. 2004. "The deictic core of 'non-experienced past' in Cuzco Quechua." *Journal of Semantics* 21(1):45–85.

Feke, Marilyn. 2004. "Quechua to Spanish cross-linguistic influence among Cuzco Quechua-Spanish bilinguals: The case of epistemology." PhD diss., University of Pittsburgh.

Floyd, Rick. 1999. *The structure of evidential categories in Wanka Quechua.* Dallas: Summer Institute of Linguistics and University of Texas at Arlington.

Giorgi, Alessandra. 2010. *About the speaker: Towards a syntax of indexicality.* Oxford: Oxford University Press.

Hardman, Martha James. 1986. "Data-source marking in the Jaqi languages." In *The linguistic coding of epistemology,* edited by Wallace Chafe and Johanna Nichols. 113–136. Norwood, NJ: Ablex.

Hill, Jane H. and Judith T. Irvine, eds. 1993. *Responsibility and evidence in oral discourse.* New York: Cambridge University Press.

Hintz, Daniel. 2011. *Crossing aspectual frontiers: Emergence, evolution, and interwoven semantic domains in South Conchucos Quechua discourse.* Berkeley: University of California Press.

———. 2007. "Past tense forms and their functions in South Conchucos Quechua." PhD diss., University of California, Santa Barbara.

Howard, Rosaleen. 2012. "Shifting voices, shifting worlds: Evidentiality, epistemic modality and speaker perspective in Quechua oral narrative." *Pragmatics and Society* 3(2):243–269.

Hurtado de Mendoza Santander, William. 2001. *Pragmática de la cultura y la lengua quechua.* Cuzco, Peru: Centro de Estudios Regionales Andinos "Bartolomé de Las Casas" and Lima, Peru: Universidad Nacional Agraria La Molina.

Jackobson, Roman. 1957. *Shifters, verbal categories and the Russian verb.* Cambridge: MIT Press.

Jespersen, Otto. 1923/1959. *Language: Its nature, development and origin*. London: Allen and Unwin.

Lee, Tae Yoon. 1997. *Morfosintaxis amerindias en el español americano: Desde la perspectiva del quechua*. Madrid: Ediciones Clásicas, Universidad Complutense de Madrid.

Levinson, Stephen C. 1997. *Pragmatics*. Cambridge: Cambridge University Press.

Lucey, Kenneth G., ed. 1996. *On knowing and the known, introductory readings in epistemology*. Amherst, NY: Prometheus Books.

Manley, Marilyn S. 2007. "Cross-linguistic influence of the Cuzco Quechua epistemic system on Andean Spanish." In *Spanish in contact: Policy, social, and linguistic inquiries*, edited by Kim Potowski and Richard Cameron. 191–209. Philadelphia: John Benjamins.

Mushin, Ilana. 2000. "Evidentiality and deixis in narrative retelling." *Journal of Pragmatics* 32:927–957.

Nuckolls, Janis B. 1993. "The semantics of certainty in Quechua and its implications for a cultural epistemology." *Language in Society* 22:235–255.

———. 2008. "Deictic selves and others in Pastaza Quichua evidential usage." *Anthropological Linguistics* 50(1):67–89.

———. 2012. "From quotative other to quotative self: Evidential usage in Pastaza Quichua." *Pragmatics and Society* 3(2):226–242.

Rofes Chávez, Maite. 2002. *¿Estás bien? CAITH: La cultura del afecto con trabajadoras del hogar*. Cuzco, Peru: CAITH.

Sidnell, Jack. 2005. *Talk and practical epistemology*. Amsterdam/Philadelphia: John Benjamins.

Torero, Alfredo. 1964. "Los dialectos quechuas." *Anales Científicos de la Universidad Agraria* 2:446–478.

Weber, David. 1989. *A grammar of Huallaga (Huanuco) Quechua*. Berkeley: University of California Press.

Weissenborn, Jürgen and Wolfgang Klein, eds. 1982. *Here and there: Cross-linguistic studies on deixis and demonstration*. Philadelphia: John Benjamins.

Wilkins, David P. 1999. "Demonstrative questionnaire: 'THIS' and 'THAT' in comparative perspective." In *Manual for the 1999 field season*, edited by David. P. Wilkins. Nijmegen: Max Planck Institute for Psycholinguistics.

CHAPTER 6

Discourse Deixis in Southern Quechua: A Case Study on Topic and Focus

Antje Muntendam

1 Introduction

This paper examines discourse deixis in Southern Quechua. Specifically, it investigates the syntactic, morphological and prosodic marking of focus, and to some extent, topic, in the variety of Quechua spoken in the department of Cochabamba, Bolivia. While there are several studies on discourse deixis (in particular topic and focus) in Peruvian varieties of Quechua (i.e. Muysken 1995, Sánchez 2010), Bolivian varieties have not been studied extensively.

In 2009, the number of Quechua speakers in Bolivia was estimated at 2,530,985 (Ministerio de Asuntos Exteriores y Cooperación, FUNPROEIB Andes and UNICEF 2009, 517). Bolivian Quechua forms part of Quechua IIC in Torero's classification, which also includes Ayacucho Quechua and Cuzco Quechua (Torero 1964). Phonologically, Bolivian Quechua is similar to Cuzco Quechua; importantly, both varieties have glottalized and aspirated consonants. Morphologically, however, Bolivian Quechua is quite different from Cuzco Quechua (Adelaar and Muysken 2004, 188). A distinction is sometimes made between a northern and a southern variety of Bolivian Quechua, which are spoken in non-contiguous areas (Landerman 1991). The variety of Quechua spoken in the department of Cochabamba belongs to the southern Bolivian variety.

Discourse deixis refers to the use of expressions that signal a relationship between an utterance and the prior or subsequent discourse (Levinson 1983, 2004). According to Levinson (1983, 2004), discourse deixis includes temporal deictic terms (*next, before, last week*), spatial deictic terms (*in the last paragraph*), utterance initial expressions that indicate a relationship with the preceding discourse (*but, however, in conclusion, well*), and the use of demonstratives (*this, that*) to refer to the preceding or following discourse. In Quechua, a variety of morphemes encode reference to the prior or preceding discourse, such as topic markers, focus markers and relational markers (see Introduction). This work specifically focuses on topic and focus markers. According to Levinson (1983, 88), topic markers can be classified as discourse deictic elements, as

---

© KONINKLIJKE BRILL NV, LEIDEN, 2015 | DOI 10.1163/9789004290105 _007

> ... a major function of topic marking is precisely to relate the marked utterance to some specific topic raised in the prior discourse, i.e. to perform a discourse-deictic function.

Levinson (1983, 2004) does not specifically mention focus markers as discourse deictic elements, but like topic markers, focus markers draw the attention to an element and establish a relationship between that element and the prior discourse. Specifically, a focus marker indicates the new or non-presupposed information of the sentence, and in the case of contrastive focus, it contrasts an element in the utterance with some other element in the prior discourse or context.

This relationship that morphological topic and focus markers establish between an utterance and the prior discourse can also be encoded through other means in different languages, such as syntactic or prosodic means. As Levinson (1983) points out, changes in word order in English have a similar function as morphological topic markers in some other languages. In the following example, the left-dislocated element is the topic of the sentence:

(1)   *That blouse, it's simply stunning* (Levinson 1983, 89).

Moreover, in some languages a particular prosody is associated with topic or focus (see below). As pointed out in the Introduction, Quechua speakers have different morphological, syntactic and prosodic means to encode topic and focus, thus relating an utterance to the prior discourse or context.

Topic and focus marking are briefly mentioned in grammars of Bolivian Quechua (e.g. Solá and Lastra 1964). However, to my knowledge, there have not been any in depth studies of the different strategies used to encode the discourse deictic notions of focus and topic in this variety.

This chapter mainly addresses focus, but topic is also briefly discussed. Topic is what the sentence is about; the rest of the sentence expresses what is said about the topic (Rizzi 1997). Following Chomsky (1971) and Jackendoff (1972), focus is defined in this work as the new information in a sentence while the rest of the sentence is presupposed. The focus structure of a sentence can be examined by means of question-answer pairs, where there is a clear relation between an utterance and the prior discourse. The focus of a sentence is the part of that sentence that replaces the *wh*-phrase in the corresponding question. There are different types of focus. A first distinction is made in the literature between broad focus and narrow focus. In broad focus, the entire sentence is new information, as in (2) below. In narrow focus, on the other hand, one constituent is focused, e.g. the subject (as in (3)) or the object.

(2) a. *What happens?*
(2) b. [*_FJohn reads a book.*]

(3) a. *Who reads a book?*
(3) b. [*_FJohn*] *reads a book.*

A second distinction is made between neutral (or non-contrastive) focus, as in the question-answer pair in (3), and contrastive focus, as in (4) below. In contrastive focus, information is negated and new information is given. In (4), the subject is in contrastive focus; that is, there is a contrast between Mary and John. The relation between the utterance in (b) and the prior discourse (i.e. the question in (a)), is one of contrast.

(4) a. *Does Mary read a book?*
(4) b. *No.* [*_FJohn*] *reads a book.*

Cross-linguistically, different strategies are employed to encode topic and focus: they can be expressed via morphological strategies (via topic/focus markers), syntactic strategies (via changes in word order), prosodic strategies or a combination of those. By means of these different strategies, the attention is drawn towards a particular utterance and a relation is established between that utterance and the prior or subsequent discourse.

It has been shown that topic and focus are marked morphologically and syntactically in many varieties of Quechua (i.a. Cerrón-Palomino 1987, Muysken 1995, Sánchez 2010). Less is known about the prosodic marking of topic and focus in Quechua. In this work, peak alignment, downstep, Fo, duration and intensity are examined.

The alignment of peaks (within the stressed syllable or in the posttonic syllable) has been found to be correlated with focus in different languages. For instance, for Spanish, it has been argued that non-final peaks fall in the posttonic syllable in broad focus, whereas they fall within the stressed syllable in contrastive focus (e.g. De la Mota 1997, Face, 2001, 2002, Prieto, van Santen and Hirschberg 1995, Vanrell, Stella, Gili-Fivela and Prieto 2013). One question addressed by this work is whether in Quechua there is a difference between broad and contrastive focus with respect to peak alignment.

In this work, downstep and upstep are also studied, because differences between broad and narrow focus have been observed with respect to this feature for different languages. For instance, in English, peaks are downstepped in broad focus sentences, that is, peaks are lower with respect to the previous

DISCOURSE DEIXIS IN SOUTHERN QUECHUA 211

peaks (Liberman and Pierrehumbert 1984). In narrow focus sentences in English, however, the peak associated with the focused word is raised. This means that for instance in an SVO sentence with narrow focus on the object, the peak on the object is upstepped (i.e. higher than the previous peak) instead of downstepped, giving more prominence to the object. Furthermore, in languages such as English, peaks after a focused word are lower (Liberman and Pierrehumbert 1984). This work examines whether in Quechua broad focus and narrow contrastive focus differ with respect to downstep/upstep; that is, is downstep/upstep used to give more prominence to focused constituents?

Finally, in different languages, contrastive focus is associated with a higher Fo (Face 2001, 2002 for Madrid Spanish), a higher intensity (Kim and Avelino 2003 for Mexican Spanish), and an increased duration of the stressed syllable of the focused word (De la Mota 1997 for Peninsular Spanish, Face 2001 for Madrid Spanish, Kim and Avelino 2003 for Mexican Spanish). This work investigates whether, in Quechua, differences in focus are correlated with differences in Fo, duration and intensity as well.

Therefore, this study contributes to the understanding of topic and focus marking as discourse deictics in Bolivian Quechua. It also shows that there are important dialectal differences among varieties of Quechua. The chapter is organized as follows. In section 2, previous studies on topic and focus in Quechua are discussed. In section 3, the methods used for the data collection are presented. Section 4 presents the results of the study and discusses the morphological, syntactic and prosodic strategies that are used to encode focus and topic in this variety of Bolivian Quechua. Section 5 provides some conclusions.

2 Topic and Focus in Quechua

2.1 *Quechua Morphosyntax, Topic and Focus*
Quechua languages (or language varieties) are agglutinative. The canonical word order of Quechua is SOV, but in main clauses the word order is relatively free and other word orders are possible for discourse-pragmatic reasons (Cerrón-Palomino 1987).

In most Quechua varieties, topic and focus can be morphologically marked. Specifically, the suffix *-qa* is used to mark the topic of the sentence or discourse. Moreover, the language has a system of evidential suffixes, which can also be used for focus marking. An evidential suffix such as *-mi* (*-n* after a vowel),[1] which in its evidential meaning expresses direct experience, can appear on the focused constituent or on the first constituent in a sentence.[2] In sentence-initial position, the constituent marked with -*mi/-n* can be interpreted as either expressing focus (5a) or as conveying an evidential meaning (5b). In other positions in the sentence, the constituent marked with -*mi/-n* is necessarily interpreted as focused (6) (Muysken 1995). The evidential suffixes can also be used to mark the constituent that answers the corresponding *wh*-question; that is, it is used to mark the new information of a sentence.

(5) *Pidru-n   wasi-ta   ruwa-n.*
    Pedro-DIREV   house-ACC   make-3
    (a)   'It is Pedro that builds a house.'
    (b)   'Pedro builds a house.' (Muysken, 1995, 381)

(6) *Pidru   wasi-ta-n   ruwa-n.*
    Pedro   house-ACC-DIREV   make-3
    'It is a house that Pedro builds.' (Muysken, 1995, 380)

The suffixes -*mi/-n* and -*qa* appear at the end of a phonological word, and are mutually exclusive, meaning they cannot appear together on the same word. There can only be one phrase marked with -*mi/-n* per clause (Muysken 1995), as is evident from the ungrammaticality of (7). There can be multiple phrases marked with -*qa* in a single sentence: in (8), both the subject and the object are marked with -*qa*:

(7) **Papa-ta-m   miku-n-mi   Mariya-m.*
    $potato-ACC-DIREV   eat-3-DIREV   Maria-DIREV
    'They are potatoes that María eats.' (Sánchez 2010, 48)

---

1   There are three evidential suffixes: -*mi/-n* (direct experience), -*si/-s* (hearsay) and -*chá* (dubitative) (Muysken 1995) (see Manley this volume for an overview of their meanings). Of these three suffixes, -*mi/-n* is used most to express focus.

2   Throughout this paper, I use the Cuzco Quechua -*mi/-n*, -*si/-s* and -*chá* to refer to the evidential suffixes. In the variety of Quechua spoken in the department of Cochabamba, the forms are -*min/-n*, -*sis* and -*chá* (Solá and Lastra 1964, 46). The topic marker is -*qa* in both Cuzco Quechua and Bolivian Quechua.

DISCOURSE DEIXIS IN SOUTHERN QUECHUA

(8) *Runa-qa*   *wasi-ta-qa*   *ruwa-rqa-n.*
     man-TOP   house-ACC-TOP   build-PST1-3
     'As for the man, he built the house.' (Sánchez 2010, 45)

According to Muysken (1995), the topic marker *-qa* and the focus marker *-mi/-n* can occur in the same sentence, as in (9). According to the pattern in (9), there can be between zero and two phrases marked with *-qa* at the beginning of the sentence. The *-qa* marked phrase(s) can be followed by a verb or a constituent marked with *-mi/-n*, and after the verb there can be up to three phrases marked with *-qa*. An example of a sentence in which *-qa* and *-mi/-n* co-occur is given in (10).

(9) $\{X\text{-}qa^{0\text{-}2}\}$ $\{V/XP\}$-DIREV … $\{Z\text{-}qa^{0\text{-}3}\}$ (Muysken 1995, 385)

(10) *Chay*   *runa-qa*   *Ayakuchu-ta-n*   *ri-n.*
      that   man-TOP   Ayacucho-ACC-DIREV   go-3
      'That man is going to Ayacucho.' (Muysken 1995, 385)

Topics or focused elements can remain *in situ*, see (11) and (12). In both (11) and (12), the canonical word order SOV is used. In (11), the direct object is marked for focus, and in (12) it is marked as the topic of the sentence.

(11) *Pidru*   *wasi-ta-n*   *ruwa-n.*
      Pedro   house-ACC-DIREV   make-3
      'It is a house that Pedro builds.' (Muysken 1995, 380)

(12) *Pidru-m*   *wasi-ta-qa*   *ruwa-rqa-n.*
      Pedro-DIREV   house-ACC-TOP   make-PST1-3
      'It was Pedro who built the house.' (Sánchez 2010, 71)

According to Sánchez (2010), the canonical order SOV has the syntactic representation that is given in (13). The subject is in the specifier of vP, the object is displaced from its original position to the specifier of VP, and the verb is in VP (Sánchez 2010).

(13) *Mariya*   *papa-ta*   *ranti-chka-n.*
      Mariya $potato-ACC   buy-PROG-3
      $[_{vP}$ Mariya $[_{v'}$ v $[_{VP}$ papata$_i$ $[_{v'}$ rantichkan t$_i$ $]]]]$.
      'Mariya is buying potatoes.' (Sánchez 2010, 14)

Topic and focus elements can also be preposed to the left-periphery of the sentence, resulting in a change in word order: see (14) and (15).

(14) *T'anta-ta-**m***   *Huwan*   *miku-ru-n.*
      bread-ACC-DIREV   Juan   eat-PST2-3
      'It was bread that Juan ate.' (Sánchez 2010, 65)

(15) *Wasi-ta-**qa***   *Pirdu-m*   *ruwa-rqa-n.*
      house-ACC-TOP   Pedro-DIREV   build-PST1-3
      'The house, Pedro built it.' (Sánchez 2010, 71)

In most varieties of Quechua, preposed elements are morphologically marked. In (14) the preposed direct object *t'anta* 'bread' is marked with *-mi/-n* expressing focus, and in (15) the preposed direct object *wasi* 'house' is marked with *-qa* for topic. In these examples, object fronting gives rise to OSV order, but it can also result in OVS order. In the case of OSV, the object is moved over the subject. To derive OVS, the object and the verb are moved above the subject. Subject fronting and verb fronting are also possible in Quechua, giving rise to SOV,[3] and VOS or VSO respectively. The order VSO is illustrated in (16).

(16) *Upya-ru-n-mi*   *warma*   *yaku-ta.*
      drink-PRF-3-DIREV   boy   water-ACC
      'The boy drank the water.' (Sánchez 2003, 35)

Finally, SVO is derived from SOV by moving the subject and verb above the object. These fronted focus/topic elements are located in the left-periphery or the CP-domain (Cinque 1990, Rizzi 1997).

Topics can also be moved to a postverbal position, but focused elements cannot (Cerrón-Palomino 1987, Muysken 1995, Sánchez 2010): see (17)–(18).

(17) *Mariya-m*   *Xwana-man*   *qu-n*   *libru-ta-**qa**.*
      Maria-DIREV   Juana-DAT   give-3 $book-ACC-TOP
      'As for the book, Maria gives it to Juana.' (Sánchez 2010, 94)

---

3 Given that SOV is also the canonical order in Quechua, in SOV sentences the subject can either be in its canonical position (in the specifier of vP) or in fronted position (in the CP-domain).

DISCOURSE DEIXIS IN SOUTHERN QUECHUA 215

(18) *Mariya*   *Xwana-man*   *qu-n*   *libru-ta-n.*
Maria   Juana-DAT   give-3 $book-ACC-DIREV
'It is the book that Maria gives to Juana.' (Muysken 1995, 383)

In (17), right adjunction of the direct object results in the order SIOVO. Subjects can also appear in the right periphery as topic, resulting in OVS. As shown by Sánchez (2010, this volume), right-adjoined topics can be morphologically marked or unmarked. In sum, different morphosyntactic means are used in Quechua to establish a relation between the focused element or topic of an utterance and the prior discourse.

2.2   *Quechua Prosody, Topic and Focus*
In the majority of Quechua language varieties, primary stress falls on the penultimate syllable of the word (Landerman 1991, 51). An exception is formed by words that are marked with an emphatic or exclamatory suffix attracting ultimate stress, e.g. *Achacháy*! 'Wow, it's hot!'

Previous studies on the intonation of Cuzco Quechua (Cusihuamán 2001, O'Rourke 2005, 2009) and Ayacucho Quechua (Parker 1963) showed that declarative sentences end in a low tone. O'Rourke (2005, 2009) studied declarative intonation in Cuzco Quechua more in detail, using experimental measures. The results of her study revealed that final peaks were aligned within the stressed syllable. The majority of non-final peaks were also aligned within the stressed syllable, but there were some non-final peaks that were aligned in the post-tonic syllable. The majority of the peaks were downstepped, that is, lower than the previous peak. However, there were also some even and upstepped (i.e. higher) peaks. It was not clear whether these peaks carried a different pragmatic meaning (O'Rourke 2005, 65). Most declarative sentences ended in a low tone, which was in line with Cusihuamán (2001) and Parker (1969).

Most studies on Quechua II varieties (Cusihuamán 2001, O'Rourke 2005, Parker 1969) suggest that topic and focus are not marked prosodically in these varieties. O'Rourke (2005, 2009) did not find differences between sentences with and without *-mi/-n* with respect to peak alignment and downstepped and upstepped peaks, which led her to tentatively conclude that focus is not expressed phonologically in Cuzco Quechua (O'Rourke 2005). O'Rourke (2009) showed that words marked with *-mi/-n* had the highest peak, indicating prominence, but no evidence was found for lower peaks after the *-mi/-n* marked word. O'Rourke (2005, 2009) only included verb-final sentences with broad and narrow neutral focus. Contrastive focus was not included in O'Rourke's (2005, 2009) investigations of Quechua. Therefore, it has not been clear whether contrastive focus is marked in prosody in Cuzco Quechua. Also, it remains unknown whether utterances with different word orders are marked differently. Cole (1982) argues that in Imbabura Quechua, which is a QIIB variety spoken in Ecuador, contrastive focus is associated with a higher peak on the focused element.

There have been a few studies on prosody in Quechua I varieties. Hintz (2003, 63–64) found that in South Conchucos Quechua a 'newsworthy element' in postverbal position is often marked by a rise in pitch or intensity, or a pause. A 'newsworthy element' is defined as an element that is salient, for instance because it contains new information or it expresses a contrast in the discourse.

There is very little information available on the prosody of Bolivian Quechua. Solá and Lastra (1964) mention a falling contour for Cochabamba Quechua, as was found for the other varieties mentioned above. These authors do not mention the use of prosody to encode focus or topic.

2.3 *Summary*

In sum, in many varieties of Quechua, focus is encoded in syntax (via changes in word order) and morphology (via topic and focus particles), but possibly not in phonology. That is, no specific contour has been found for focus and topic. To date, detailed studies of contrastive focus have not been conducted.

This chapter examines topic and focus in the Quechua variety spoken in the department of Cochabamba, Bolivia and addresses the syntactic, morphological and prosodic strategies that are used to encode the discourse deictics, topic and focus, in this variety of Quechua. The research questions of this study are: (a) Which strategies are used to encode topic and focus in this variety of Quechua? and (b) If focus is encoded prosodically in this variety of Quechua, which prosodic features are involved?

It will be shown that topic and focus in this variety of Quechua can be marked *in situ* and in fronted position, as in other varieties of Quechua. The topic marker is infrequent and morphological focus markers are obsolete; that is, there is a loss of morphological marking. It will be shown that there are differences between broad and contrastive focus for downstep. Also, some speakers infrequently use differences in Fo, duration and intensity to distinguish broad focus and contrastive focus.

This work is the first to address morphological, syntactic and prosodic aspects of focus (and to a lesser extent topic) in Bolivian Quechua. It reveals important dialectal differences with respect to the marking of the topic and focus (two aspects of discourse deixis). In many varieties of Quechua, focus is encoded in syntax and morphology. In this variety, however, focus seems to be encoded only in syntax and to a limited extent in prosody, but not in morphol-

DISCOURSE DEIXIS IN SOUTHERN QUECHUA

ogy. Topic is infrequently marked in morphology. Individual differences with respect to topic/focus marking and the possibility of Spanish influence are also briefly addressed.

3 Methodology

The aim of this study was to analyze morphological, syntactic and prosodic strategies for encoding focus and, to some extent, topic. Most research on prosody is laboratory-based and involves reading tasks. One of the strengths of reading tasks is that the researcher has more control over the data; the researcher has control over, for instance, the number of syllables, the presence of voiceless consonants, and the position of the target word in the sentence. Reading tasks also allow the researcher to collect a large amount of comparable data (Post and Nolan 2012, Xu 2010). Moreover, speech elicited by a reading task can be analyzed semi-automatically, unlike (completely) spontaneous speech, which needs to be labeled and analyzed by hand, causing the analysis to be more laborious and sensitive to errors.

Although reading tasks have strengths as a tool to collect data on prosody, they also have weaknesses. Speech elicited by a reading task is to a certain extent artificial, and it is unknown to what extent it reflects naturally occurring speech. Previous studies of prosody have in fact shown differences between read speech and spontaneous speech (Face 2003). Moreover, in some cases reading tasks are not culturally appropriate. Reading tasks are especially not appropriate for use in indigenous communities, considering the relatively low levels of literacy and the sometimes also relatively low levels of education of the participants. The participants for this study were relatively highly educated (see section 3.1), but the majority of them were low literate in Quechua. For the purpose of the current study, reading tasks would also not have allowed the examination of syntactic and morphological strategies. Therefore, different tasks were used. Specifically, the data for this study come from a picture-story task and an elicitation task with question-answer pairs.

3.1 *Participants*

A sociolinguistic questionnaire was used to select the participants. In this questionnaire,[4] participants were asked their age, place of birth, age of acquisition of Quechua and Spanish, the frequency and domains of use for Quechua

---

4 The questions were asked in conversations to create an informal setting. Also, many participants were low literate.

and Spanish, their education, occupation and family background. Only adult participants who were originally from the area (Tarata and Huayculí), who acquired Quechua in early childhood, who reported a high proficiency in Quechua, and who frequently used the language were included in this study. The information obtained by means of the questionnaire is also used to account for variability in the results.

The participants of this study were six adult Quechua speakers from Tarata and the nearby community Huayculí, in the department of Cochabamba, Bolivia. Four of the participants were male and two were female. Their ages ranged between 50 and 67 years, with a mean of 56.5 years (SD = 7.2). All of the participants were native speakers of Quechua. Five participants acquired Spanish simultaneously with Quechua. The other participant learned Spanish when he entered school at the age of 5. All participants used Quechua on a daily basis and as a home language and reported a high level of proficiency in Quechua. Four of the participants received some sort of higher education after secondary school. The other two participants did not continue their education after elementary or secondary school. The main characteristics of the participants are summarized in table 6.1.[5]

TABLE 6.1 *Characteristics of the participants*

Spk	Sex	Age	Education	Occupation
1	M	50	university (civil engineering); unfinished	municipal employee
2	M	67	teacher training college	retired school principal
3	M	63	school of music	music teacher
4	M	57	elementary school	potter
5	F	52	teacher training college	elementary school teacher
6	F	50	secondary education	restaurant owner

3.2 *Picture-story Task*

The data for this study come from a picture-story task and an elicitation task consisting of question-answer pairs. For the first task, pictures were created for three traditional Andean stories: *La zorra y la lora* 'The fox and the parrot',

---

5 The participants are listed in an order that is convenient for the discussion of the results (see section 4).

DISCOURSE DEIXIS IN SOUTHERN QUECHUA 219

La zorra y el gallo 'The fox and the rooster', and *La zarigüeya y el utuskuru*[6] 'The opossum and the bug' (Martínez Parra 1999). These stories were selected because the majority of the participants were familiar with these or similar stories, whose action takes place in the Andes and includes local animals. In the task, the participants narrated a story based on a sequence of pictures. The participants saw all the pictures before narrating the story and had the opportunity to ask clarification questions. There was no time limit for the narration.

The pictures created for the story *La zorra y la lora* 'The fox and the rooster' are provided in figure 6.1 in appendix B. In this story, a fox approaches a condor and asks him to take him to the moon. The condor agrees, upon which the fox ties himself to the condor with a rope. When they are flying in the sky, they come across a little parrot that starts laughing upon seeing the fox and the condor. The fox gets upset with the parrot for making fun of him and starts insulting him. The little parrot in turn gets upset for being offended and cuts the rope that ties the fox to the condor. The fox then starts falling down to the earth while screaming for help. The reader is referred to Muntendam (2009) for the other stories and the corresponding pictures.

This picture-story task was used to examine topic and focus strategies as aspects of discourse deixis in relatively spontaneous speech and to compare the data from the elicitation task with that of a more spontaneous form of speech. Some pictures from the picture-story task were also used in the elicitation task involving question-answer pairs, which is explained below.

3.3 Elicitation Task Involving Question-Answer Pairs

Question-answer pairs provide information regarding the strategies that are used to encode focus in a particular language: the focus of a sentence is that part of the sentence that replaces the *wh*-phrase in the corresponding question (Rooth 1992, Zubizarreta 1998). For the elicitation task including question-answer pairs, eighteen pictures were used with seven questions eliciting broad focus, narrow neutral focus on the subject, the object and the VP, and contrastive focus on the subject, object and the VP, in addition to distractor questions. The questions eliciting different focus types are explained below. The pictures depicted simple actions and served as a semantic context for the questions, which were read aloud to the participants.[7] An example of a picture is given in figure 6.2 (appendix B). The questions corresponding to this picture are presented in (19)–(25):

---

6 According to an anonymous reviewer, an *utuskuru* is a bug that attacks maize-plants.
7 Six pictures came from the materials created for the picture-story task. The other pictures came from Soto (1993).

(19) *Ima-taj   pasa-sa-n?*   (broad focus)
    what-CONTR $happen-PROG-3
    'What is happening?'

(20) *Ima-ta-taj   runa   ruwa-sa-n?*   (narrow focus on the VP)
    what-ACC-CONTR   man   do-PROG-3
    'What is the man doing?'

(21) *Pi-taj   llama-ta   q'ati-sa-n?*   (narrow focus on the subject)
    who-CONTR $llama-ACC   drive-PROG-3
    'Who is driving the llama?'

(22) *Ima-ta-taj   runa   q'ati-sa-n?*   (narrow focus on the object)
    what-ACC-CONTR   man   drive-PROG-3
    'What is the man driving?'

(23) *Warmi-chu   llama-ta*
    woman-INTR $llama-ACC

    q'ati-sa-n?   (contrastive focus on the subject)
    drive-PROG-3
    'Is the woman driving the llama?'

(24) *Runa   khuchi-ta-chu   q'ati-sa-n?*   (contrastive focus on the object)
    man   pig-ACC-INTR   drive-PROG-3
    'Is the man driving a pig?'

(25) *Runa   llama-man   qara-sa-n-chu?*   (contrastive focus on the VP)
    man $llama-DAT   feed-PROG-3-INTR
    'Is the man feeding the llama?'

The participants heard the questions and answered them based on the pictures. The question in (19) elicits broad focus; that is, the entire sentence is new information. The questions in (20)–(22) elicit focus on only one constituent (i.e. the subject NP, the object NP, or the VP), which contains new information. The questions in (23)–(25) contain incorrect information; the target answers negate the information in the question and provide new information. These questions thus elicit contrastive focus on one constituent (i.e. the subject NP, the object NP, or the VP). The questions provided some sort of prior discourse for the answers.

DISCOURSE DEIXIS IN SOUTHERN QUECHUA

The target answer corresponding to the questions in (19)–(25) is presented in (26). In the case of questions (23)–(25), the target answer in (26) is preceded by *mana* 'no'.

(26) *Runa   llama-ta   q'ati-sa-n.*
     man $llama-ACC   drive-PROG-3
     'The man is driving the llama.'

The participants were instructed to answer in complete sentences, but they were free to use different word orders and morphological markers. The target sentences were all transitive sentences with a subject, a verb and a direct object, and the majority of the target subjects (17 out of 18, or 94.4%) and objects (16 out of 18, or 88.9%) were two-syllable words. The direct objects were generally marked with the accusative marker -*ta*, adding an additional syllable to the words. The majority of the stressed syllables of the subjects (16 out of 18, or 88.9%) and of the objects (15 out of 18, or 83.3%) were open syllables (that is, syllables ending in a vowel). Given that the participants gave spontaneous answers, there was variability in the data.

In addition to the questions above, there were distractor questions, which added variation to the task and ensured the participants paid attention to the specific questions. Both the pictures and the questions were randomized to avoid order effects. Two versions of the task were used, which only differed in the order in which the pictures and questions were presented. Participants were randomly (and evenly) assigned to one of the two versions. The sessions started with instructions about the picture-story task and the question-answer task. Subsequently, there was a practice session for the question-answer task with three pictures. The sessions were recorded with a Shure head-worn microphone and a Sony MZ 200 minidisc recorder and later transferred to a computer. The sessions lasted one hour or an hour and a half and were held in an informal setting.

The design of the study led to some limitations. The task elicited relatively spontaneous speech, but because the participants used different word orders, lexicon and morphology, the amount of comparable data across conditions was relatively small. For the study of prosodic strategies, a task eliciting a fixed word order (such as the one reported in Van Rijswijk and Muntendam 2012) could lead to less loss of data. Also, the number of speakers was relatively small.

4 Results

The data were analyzed with respect to the morphological, syntactic and prosodic strategies that were used to encode focus, and to some extent, topic. The data from the picture-story tasks were transcribed and the utterances elicited in the question-answer task were coded according to the speaker, use of morphological markers, word order, and focus condition. This chapter presents the preliminary findings of the analysis of the subject and object in broad focus and contrastive narrow focus; neutral (or non-contrastive) narrow focus is not discussed here. To examine the use of prosodic strategies to encode topic and focus, the contours of the sentences were studied. Furthermore, Fo, intensity and duration were examined in *Praat* (Boersma and Weenink 2010). As explained above, the participants gave spontaneous answers to the questions asked in the elicitation task and there was no restriction on the use of different word orders and morphological markers. Because there was variation between the speakers in the use of different morphological, syntactic and prosodic strategies, the results are not only discussed for the entire group of speakers but also per speaker.

4.1 *Morphological Strategies*

The data from the elicitation task with question-answer pairs were analyzed for the use of morphological, syntactic and prosodic strategies to mark focus and topic. This section focuses on the morphological strategies used to mark focus and topic, whereas the syntactic and prosodic strategies are discussed in sections 4.2 and 4.3 below.

The results of the elicitation task involving question-answer pairs revealed that none of the participants used the suffix *-mi/-n* or either of the other evidential suffixes to mark the focus of the sentence. In many varieties of Quechua (e.g. Cuzco Quechua), morphological markers are obligatory on a focused element when it is fronted, but not so in this variety. These data thus suggest that focus is not morphologically marked in this variety of Quechua. These results are also confirmed by the data from the picture-story task, in which no evidential suffixes appeared.

As discussed in section 2, the suffix *-mi/-n* and the two other evidential suffixes do appear in dictionaries and grammars of Bolivian Quechua (e.g. Solá and Lastra 1964). Speaker 2 was familiar with *-mi/-n, -si/-s* and *-chá*, although he claimed to not ever use them. According to this speaker, the use of these suffixes is considered to be archaic. This suggests that the suffixes *-mi/-n, -si/-s* and *-chá* are currently obsolete in this variety of Quechua. However the fact

DISCOURSE DEIXIS IN SOUTHERN QUECHUA

that Speaker 2 was familiar with them suggests that their loss is relatively recent. Although these suffixes may not be found in the Quechua spoken in the department of Cochabamba, it cannot be assumed that they are not still used in other varieties of Bolivian Quechua. The loss of these suffixes could be due to influence from Spanish, in which focus and evidentiality are not morphologically marked. Interestingly, in other varieties of Southern Quechua (e.g. Cuzco Quechua), the evidential suffixes are still in use and *-mi/-n* is used as a morphological focus marker (Sánchez 2010, van Rijswijk and Muntendam 2012).

The majority of the participants did not use a morphological marker to mark the topic of the sentence either. Only one of the participants (Speaker 1) infrequently used the suffix *-qa* to mark the topic of the sentence, establishing a relationship between that utterance and the prior discourse. In particular, this speaker used *-qa* on the subject to mark it for topic in sentences with SOV order when the object was in contrastive focus. This is illustrated in (27b) below, which is an answer to the question in (27a). The suffix *-qa* in (27b) marks the subject as the topic of the sentence, and establishes a link with the prior discourse, that is, the question in (27a). I will come back to the use of *-qa* marked topics in the following sections.

(27) a. *Runa-kuna*   *qolqe-ta-chu*   *h'api-sa-nku?*
      man-PL   money-ACC-INTR   grab-PROG-3PL
      'Are the men grabbing the money?'

(27) b. *Mana.*   *Runa-kuna-qa*   *suwa-ta*   *h'api-sa-nku.*
      no   man-PL-TOP   thief-ACC   grab-PROG-3PL
      'No. The men are grabbing the thief.'

Speaker 1 also used the topic marker *-qa* in the picture-story task, although infrequently. Speaker 4 used *-qa* once to mark topic in the picture-story task, but he did not use it in the elicitation task including question-answer pairs. None of the other speakers used the topic marker, and similarly to *-mi/-n*, the use of this suffix is considered by all participants to be archaic. Therefore, the suffix *-qa* may be gradually disappearing from this variety of Quechua. However, it is still frequently used in Cuzco Quechua, and possibly also in other varieties of Bolivian Quechua.

In sum, these data suggest that focus, and to a lesser extent, topic, are generally not expressed morphologically in this variety of Bolivian Quechua. The question that remains is what role syntactic and prosodic strategies play in focus and topic marking in this variety. The loss of morphological marking could possibly result in a more prominent role for syntax and prosody. In the following sections, syntactic and prosodic strategies for encoding focus are examined, as well as their interaction.

4.2 Syntactic Strategies

The data from the elicitation task involving question-answer pairs were analyzed for the use of different word orders in answer to the questions eliciting broad focus, contrastive focus on the subject (contrS) and contrastive focus on the object (contrO). Table 6.2 shows the use of different word orders per condition in counts and percentages for all participants combined. Answers that contained only one word or a different description of the situation were excluded from the analysis. Table 6.12 in appendix C shows the results per speaker.

TABLE 6.2   *Frequencies and percentages of different word orders in three conditions: broad focus, contrastive focus on the subject (contrS) and contrastive focus on the object (contrO)*

	broad		contrS		contrO	
	N	%	N	%	N	%
SOV	56	64.4	51	54.3	39	43.3
SVO	23	26.4	39	41.5	13	14.4
OSV	0	0	0	0	2	2.2
OVS	0	0	1	1.1	4	4.4
VSO	1	1.2	0	0	0	0
VOS	0	0	0	0	0	0
OV	2	2.3	0	0	29	32.2
VO	4	4.6	0	0	3	3.3
SV	1	1.2	3	3.2	0	0
VS	0	0	0	0	0	0
Total	87		94		90	

Table 6.2 shows that for broad focus, the basic order SOV was used most frequently (64.4%). The order SVO, however, was also frequent (26.4%). There appears to be no relationship between the use of SOV or SVO in this variety of Bolivian Quechua and the semantics of the verb, unlike in the Quechua of

DISCOURSE DEIXIS IN SOUTHERN QUECHUA 225

North Junín in which SVO is used with motion verbs and SOV with other action verbs (Fuqua 1992). In these data on Bolivian Quechua, both word orders were used with motion verbs and other action verbs.

There was variability among speakers, as is evident from table 6.12 (see appendix C). Although all participants used both SOV and SVO for broad focus, some differences can be observed. In particular, Speakers 1, 2, 5 and 6 had a preference for SOV (16, 6, 11 and 15 cases, respectively), whereas Speaker 3 had a slight preference for SVO (3 cases), and Speaker 4 used both orders equally (7 cases each).

Given that all participants for this study were bilingual in Quechua and Spanish, the high frequency of SVO for broad focus could be due to an influence from Spanish, which has the canonical word order of SVO. A high frequency of the SVO order has also been reported for other varieties of Southern Quechua, possibly due to influence from Spanish (see Sánchez 2003).

For contrastive focus on the subject, the orders SOV and SVO were also the most frequently used (54.3% and 41.5%, respectively). In these cases, the focused subject appears in preverbal position. Speakers 1, 2 and 6 showed a preference for SOV (13, 10 and 11 cases, respectively), whereas Speakers 3, 4 and 5 used SVO more frequently (6, 11 and 11 cases, respectively). The order OVS, where the focused subject appears at the end of the sentence, was used once (1.1%) by Speaker 3.

For contrastive focus on the object, different orders were used. The canonical order SOV, in which the focused object appears *in situ*, was most frequent (43.3%). This percentage includes 5 utterances with a topic-marked subject (S-*qa* OV). The order SVO, in which the focused element appears post-verbally, was less frequent (14.4%). In this condition, the focused direct object was frequently fronted, appearing in sentence-initial position, resulting in the orders OV (32.2%), OSV (2.2%) and OVS (4.4%).

As shown in table 6.12 (appendix C), there was inter-speaker variability for contrastive focus on the object as well. Speaker 1 mostly used SOV (10 cases) and S-*qa* OV (5 cases), in which the subject is marked with -*qa* and the object appears in preverbal position. This strategy only occurred in the condition of contrastive focus on the object and with the order SOV. Speaker 2 mostly used SOV (9 cases), but also some SVO (4 cases), OV (2 cases) and VO (1 case). Speakers 5 and 6 mostly used SOV (4 and 9 cases, respectively) and OV (11 and 7 cases, respectively). For Speaker 3 the order OV (4 cases) was most frequent, but he also used SOV (2 cases), SVO (2 cases), OSV (1 case) and VO (1 case). Finally, Speaker 4 used SVO (4 cases), OV (5 cases), OVS (4 cases) and OSV (1 case); this speaker used a fronting strategy resulting in OVS and OSV more frequently than the other speakers.

The data discussed above suggest a difference between the focus conditions with respect to the use of SOV and SVO. These two orders, which were the most frequent, are examined in more detail below. Table 6.3 shows the counts and percentages for SOV and SVO per focus condition.

TABLE 6.3   *Frequencies and percentages of SOV and SVO in three conditions: broad focus, contrastive focus on the subject (contrS) and contrastive focus on the object (contrO)*

	SOV		SVO	
	N	%	N	%
broad	56	70.9	23	29.1
contrS	51	56.7	39	43.3
contrO	39	75	13	25

As presented in table 6.3, in the three focus conditions, the order SOV was more frequent than SVO. However, in the condition of contrastive focus on the subject, the order SVO is more frequent (43.3%) than in broad focus and contrastive focus on the object (29.1% and 25%, respectively), suggesting a relation between word order and focus condition. A Fisher's exact test revealed a non-significant trend indicating that contrastive focus on the subject occurred more frequently with SVO than contrastive focus on the object ($p = .031$).[8]

The elicitation task did not specifically elicit topics, that is, questions of the type, "What about the X?", were not included in the task. Therefore, the discussion of topic is preliminary. The data presented in table 6.2 above, show that the topic appeared in initial position, as in SOV or SVO sentences with contrastive focus on the object. As stated in section 4.1, there were five instances of SOV and contrastive focus on the object in which the subject was morphologically marked for topic. The topic can also appear *in situ*, as is evident from the cases with OSV and contrastive focus on the object. Finally, the cases of OVS with contrastive focus on the object showed that the topic also appeared in post-verbal position.

In sum, these results reveal that different word orders are used in this variety of Quechua. The focused element can appear *in situ* or in fronted position,

---

8   A Bonferroni adjusted alpha level of .0167 (.05/3) was used for all statistical tests.

DISCOURSE DEIXIS IN SOUTHERN QUECHUA 227

as in other Quechua varieties. In particular, the use of SOV for all focus conditions indicates that the focused element can appear *in situ*. The orders OVS and OSV for contrastive focus on the object are examples of cases in which the object is fronted for focus reasons. In some cases, it is not clear whether the focus element appears *in situ* or in fronted position, as in SOV with contrastive focus on the subject or OV with contrastive focus on the object.

The data revealed that the orders SOV and SVO are the most frequent. The order SVO was relatively frequent for contrastive focus on the subject, but the difference between this focus condition and the other focus conditions was not significant. The high frequency of SVO could be due to convergence towards Spanish. I come back to the possibility of Spanish influence in section 5.

There was variability among the speakers with respect to the encoding of focus in syntax. The results showed that both Speaker 2 and Speaker 4 made use of syntactic strategies to mark focus. For instance, Speaker 2 used OVS for contrastive focus on the subject and OSV for contrastive focus on the object, and Speaker 4 used OSV and OVS for contrastive focus on the object. Speakers 1, 3, 5 and 6 frequently used the same word order (SOV and/or SVO) for different focus types. Given that no morphological markers are used to mark focus, the question that now remains is whether focus is marked prosodically in addition to syntactically. The prosody of Bolivian Quechua and the use of prosodic strategies to encode focus are addressed in the next section.

4.3   *Prosodic Strategies*

In this section, the prosody of Bolivian Quechua is discussed. Specifically, peak alignment (section 4.4.1), downstep and upstep (section 4.4.2), and Fo, intensity and duration (section 4.4.3) are discussed. As explained in section 1, the peaks associated with the stressed syllables in an utterance can fall within the stressed syllable (early peak alignment) or in the posttonic syllable (late peak alignment). In some languages (e.g. some varieties of Spanish), non-final peaks in broad focus are aligned late, whereas they are aligned early in contrastive focus; in other words, peak alignment is used to distinguish broad and contrastive focus (e.g. Face 2001, 2002). The question that remains is whether peak alignment plays a role in focus marking in Bolivian Quechua.

Downstep and upstep refer to the relative height of the peaks in an utterance. This work examines the relationship between downstep/upstep and focus in Bolivian Quechua. The question is whether contrastive focus is associated with a more prominent peak. Finally, Fo, duration and intensity are studied as acoustic correlates of focus. As discussed in section 1, in different languages (e.g. English and some varieties of Spanish), contrastive focus is associated with a higher Fo, a higher intensity and a longer duration of the stressed syllable of the focused word. These features are studied for Bolivian Quechua here as well. This section mainly concerns focus, and topic is only briefly discussed.

4.3.1 Peak Alignment

Peak alignment of the three peaks in sentences with the order SOV and SVO was analyzed. The other word orders did not occur with sufficient frequency to allow for a thorough quantitative analysis. As explained above, a peak or Fo maximum can be found within the stressed syllable (early peak) or in the post-tonic syllable (late peak) of a word. For some languages (e.g. Spanish), it has been argued that peak alignment is correlated with focus. Specifically, peaks in non-final words fall on the post-tonic syllable in broad focus, whereas they fall within the stressed syllable when they are in contrastive focus (see Face 2002). The question here is whether non-final and final peaks fall within the stressed syllable or in the posttonic syllable in Quechua and whether a difference can be observed between focus conditions, as has been argued for Spanish. Table 6.4 below shows the alignment of the peaks in sentences with the order SOV. Peak 1 is the Fo maximum on the subject, peak 2 the Fo maximum on the object, and peak 3 the Fo maximum on the verb. For peak 1, the results are also given per speaker. Some sentences in which the alignment of the peak could not be perceived due to the presence of voiceless consonants and breaks in the pitch contour were excluded from the analysis.

TABLE 6.4   *Alignment of peak 1, peak 2, and peak 3 in SOV sentences*

Position	Speakers	N	Fo max within the stressed syllable		Fo max in the posttonic syllable	
Peak 1 (subject)	All	142	90	63.4%	52	36.6%
	Spk 1	44	15	34.1%	29	65.9%
	Spk 2	24	16	66.7%	8	33.3%
	Spk 3	7	5	71.4%	2	28.6%
	Spk 4	12	8	66.7%	4	33.3%
	Spk 5	21	20	95.2%	1	4.8%
	Spk 6	34	26	76.5%	8	23.5%
Peak 2 (object)	All	133	133	100%	0	0
Peak 3 (verb)	All	110	110	100%	0	0

DISCOURSE DEIXIS IN SOUTHERN QUECHUA

In SOV sentences, the peak on the object (peak 2) and the peak on the sentence final verb (peak 3) were always aligned within the stressed syllable of the word (100% for both peaks—see table 6.4). The peak on the subject (peak 1) was mostly aligned within the stressed syllable (63.4%), but late alignment also occurred (36.6%). Closer inspection of the data revealed inter-speaker variability. As presented in table 6.4, for Speaker 1, most sentence initial peaks were aligned in the posttonic syllable (65.9%), whereas for the other speakers they were more frequently aligned within the tonic syllable. For Speaker 5, 95.2% of the initial peaks were aligned within the stressed syllable.

Table 6.5 below shows the counts and percentages of early versus late peak alignment for peak 1 in sentences with SOV for the three focus conditions: broad focus, contrastive focus on the subject and contrastive focus on the object. As shown in table 6.5, the initial peak fell mostly within the stressed syllable in the three focus conditions. Early peak alignment was somewhat more frequent for broad focus and contrastive focus on the subject than for contrastive focus on the object, but a Fisher's exact test revealed no statistically significant differences between the three focus conditions.

Table 6.6 below shows the alignment of peaks in SVO sentences. Peak 1 refers to the Fo maximum on the subject, peak 2 to the Fo maximum on the verb, and peak 3 to the Fo maximum on the object. The results for sentences with SVO order shown in table 6.6 are similar to those for sentences with SOV order. In particular, the peak on the verb (peak 2) and the peak on the object (peak 3) fell within the stressed syllable in all cases (100% for both peaks). Most initial peaks were aligned early (76.1%), but there were also late peaks (23.9%). The speaker-by-speaker analysis showed that late peaks occurred for all

TABLE 6.5   *Frequencies and percentages of early versus late peak alignment for peak 1 in SOV sentences in three focus conditions: broad focus, contrastive focus on the subject (contrS) and contrastive focus on the object (contrO)*

	Fo max within the stressed syllable		Fo max in the posttonic syllable	
	N	%	N	%
broad	37	67.3	18	32.7
contrS	31	63.3	18	36.7
contrO	22	57.9	16	42.11
Total	90		52	

TABLE 6.6   *Alignment of peak 1, peak 2 and peak 3 in SVO sentences*

Position	Speakers	N	Fo max within the stressed syllable		Fo max in the posttonic syllable	
Peak 1 (subject)	All	67	51	76.1%	16	23.9%
	Spk 1	5	2	40%	3	60%
	Spk 2	4	6	60%	4	40%
	Spk 3	10	8	80%	2	20%
	Spk 4	21	15	71.4%	6	28.6%
	Spk 5	14	14	100%	0	0
	Spk 6	7	6	85.7%	1	14.3%
Peak 2 (verb)	All	66	66	100%	0	0
Peak 3 (object)	All	59	59	100%	0	0

TABLE 6.7   *Frequencies and percentages of early versus late peak alignment for peak 1 in SVO sentences in three conditions: broad focus, contrastive focus on the subject (contrS) and contrastive focus on the object (contrO)*

	Fo max within the stressed syllable		Fo max in the posttonic syllable	
	N	%	N	%
broad	15	68.2	7	31.8
contrS	27	81.8	6	18.2
contrO	9	75	3	25
Total	51		16	

speakers except for Speaker 5. Speaker 5 consistently used early peak alignment in SVO sentences.

Table 6.7 shows the counts and percentages of early versus late peak alignment of peak 1 in SVO sentences for the three focus conditions. The majority of the peaks were aligned early in all focus conditions. Early peak alignment was somewhat more frequent in the condition of contrastive focus on the subject (81.8%) than in the other conditions. However, a Fisher's exact test showed no statistically significant differences between the focus conditions.

DISCOURSE DEIXIS IN SOUTHERN QUECHUA 231

Late peak alignment was thus observed in the three focus conditions, that is, it was not limited to broad focus. This suggests that peak alignment is not used to distinguish broad and contrastive focus in this variety of Bolivian Quechua. The pragmatic meaning of this difference in peak alignment is not clear. Some late peaks occurred in compounds, e.g. *warmi wawa* 'little girl' (lit. 'woman child'), but there were also other cases of late peaks. Some late peaks could possibly be analyzed as high boundary tones, indicating a difference in phrasing.

Figure 6.3 in appendix D shows an example of a high boundary tone on the posttonic syllable. This sentence was uttered by Speaker 1 in answer to a question eliciting contrastive focus on the object (see (28)).

(28) a. *Runa-kuna   qepi-ta-chu   wata-sa-nku?*
       man-PL   load-ACC-INTR   tie-PROG-3PL
       'Do the men tie the load?'

(28) b. *Mana.   Runa-s-qa   yunta   wata-sa-nku.*
        no   man-$PL-TOP $yoke   tie-PROG-3PL
        'No. The men are tying the yoke.'

In this SOV sentence, the subject is marked for topic with *-qa*. In Quechua, the topic marker *-qa* does not attract stress and the stress is on the penultimate syllable. The contour of this sentence is similar to that of other SOV sentences but there is a high boundary tone on the posttonic syllable of the subject, and there is a short pause after the topic-marked subject. It is interesting to note that the direct object in (28b) is not marked with the accusative marker *-ta*. Moreover, although most Quechua words bear penultimate stress, it is the final syllable of the object that is stressed here. According to Solá and Lastra (1964, 25), the morpheme *-ta* in Cochabamba Quechua has two allomorphs: *-ta* and ultimate stress on the noun. These two allomorphs occur in free variation when the direct object noun is not in utterance-final position, as is the case in (28). I will come back to this below.

As shown in tables 6.4 and 6.6 above, 63.4% of the initial peaks in SOV sentences were aligned early, whereas the percentage was 76.1 for initial peaks in SVO sentences. Although early peaks were somewhat more frequent in SVO sentences than in SOV sentences, the difference between SOV and SVO was not statistically significant.

In sum, all non-initial peaks (i.e. peaks 2 and 3 on the object and the verb) were aligned early in both SOV and SVO sentences. Most of the initial peaks (i.e. on the subject) were aligned early, but there were also instances of late peak alignment. Peak alignment did not seem to be correlated with focus; all non-initial peaks were aligned early, regardless of focus type. For initial peaks (i.e. on the subject), there was more variation, but this variation did not seem to be related to focus. Some late peaks could be analyzed as high boundary tones, but more research is needed to understand the meaning of late peaks in Quechua.

These results for peak alignment are in tune with O'Rourke (2005, 2009), who found that the majority of initial peaks and all non-initial peaks were aligned early in Cuzco Quechua. O'Rourke's (2005, 2009) study was limited to verb-final utterances, the majority of which were analyzed as broad focus sentences. Although her study included some utterances with *-mi/-n*, which she analyzed as narrow focus sentences, there were no cases of contrastive focus. The present study includes three focus conditions and different word orders, and shows that peak alignment is not used to distinguish broad and contrastive focus in Bolivian Quechua.

4.3.2   Downstep and Upstep

In this section, the frequencies of downstepped, even and upstepped peaks are presented. Following O'Rourke (2005), a downstepped peak is defined in this work as a drop in pitch of greater than 7 Hz, and in the case of upstepped peaks there is an increase of more than 7 Hz. Even peaks refer to cases in which there is a difference of less than 7 Hz between subsequent peaks, also following O'Rourke (2005). The relationship between downsteps/upsteps and focus is discussed here as well: the question examined here is whether there is more prominence on the focused element, and reduced or downstepped peaks after the focused element. The discussion here focuses on the two most frequent word orders in the data, SOV and SVO. These orders occurred with sufficient frequency in the three focus conditions (broad focus, contrastive focus on the subject and contrastive focus on the object) to make a quantitative analysis possible. The other word orders are briefly discussed at the end of this section. Table 6.8 below shows the frequencies and percentages of downstepped, even, and upstepped peaks in SOV sentences. Results are shown for the comparison between the first peak and the second peak, and the comparison between the second and the third peak.

As shown in table 6.8, the majority of the middle and final peaks in SOV sentences was downstepped, that is, lower than the previous peak. Specifically, 78.3% of all middle peaks and 69.2% of all final peaks were downstepped. There were also even and upstepped peaks. The results presented in table 6.8 reveal a difference between the three focus conditions for the middle peak.

DISCOURSE DEIXIS IN SOUTHERN QUECHUA   233

TABLE 6.8   *Downstepped, even, and upstepped peaks in SOV sentences, comparing peak 1–2 and peak 2–3*

| | Peak 1 → 2 | | | Peak 2 → 3 | | |
	Downstep	Even	Upstep	Downstep	Even	Upstep
broad	45/55	8/55	2/55	35/50	11/50	4/50
	(81.8%)	(14.5%)	(3.6%)	(70%)	(22%)	(8%)
contrS	45/52	6/52	1/52	34/50	11/50	5/50
	(86.5%)	(11.5%)	(1.9%)	(68%)	(22%)	(10%)
contrO	18/31	9/31	4/31	21/30	7/30	2/30
	(58.1%)	(29%)	(12.9%)	(70%)	(23.3%)	(6.7%)
Total	108/138	23/138	10/138	90/130	29/130	11/130
	(78.3%)	(16.7%)	(5.1%)	(69.2%)	(32.3%)	(12.2%)

In particular, when comparing peak 1 and 2, the highest percentage of even and upstepped peaks was found for sentences with a contrastive focus on the object; in these sentences, 29% of the middle peaks were even and 12.9% were upstepped, whereas these percentages are lower for sentences with broad focus (14.5% and 3.6%, respectively) and sentences with contrastive focus on the subject (11.5% and 1.9%, respectively). A Fisher's exact test revealed significantly more even and upstepped middle peaks in the condition of contrastive focus on the object than in the condition of contrastive focus on the subject (p = .006). The difference between contrastive focus on the object and broad focus was marginally significant (p = .022). There thus appeared to be a relation with focus such that contrastive focus on the object was more frequently associated with an even or upstepped peak. In these sentences, the object received more prominence than in broad focus and contrastive focus on the subject. When the subject was in contrastive focus, the subsequent peaks received less prominence as indicated by the higher frequency of downstepped peaks.

Figure 6.4 (appendix D) shows a typical downstepped contour of a sentence with SOV order and broad focus, whereas figure 6.5 (appendix D) shows an upstepped peak on the object in the context of contrastive focus on the object. Although there are breaks in the pitch contour due to the presence of voiceless consonants, it is clear that the peak on the object is upstepped and higher than in the other focus conditions.

TABLE 6.9 *Downstepped, even, and upstepped peaks in SVO sentences, comparing peak 1–2 and peak 2–3*

	Peak 1 → 2			Peak 2 → 3		
	Downstep	Even	Upstep	Downstep	Even	Upstep
broad	18/22	4/22	0/22	11/20	6/20	3/20
	(81.8%)	(18.2%)		(55%)	(30%)	(15%)
contrS	36/39	3/39	0/39	28/37	6/37	3/37
	(92.3%)	(7.7%)		(75.7%)	(16.2%)	(8.1%)
contrO	10/13	3/13	0/13	5/11	5/11	1/11
	(76.9%)	(23.1%)		(45.5%)	(45.5%)	(9.1%)
Total	64/74	10/74	0/74	44/68	17/68	7/68
	(86.5%)	(13.5%)		(64.7%)	(25%)	(10.3%)

Note that in the sentence corresponding to figure 6.5 (appendix D), the accusative marker on the direct object is missing (as in (28b) above) and the final syllable of the object is stressed. The stressed syllable is marked with capitals in (29):

(29) *Runa   chukchuKA   apa-sa-n.*
     man   pick   bring-PROG-3
     'The man is bringing a pick.'

Table 6.9 above shows the frequencies and percentages of downstepped, even, and upstepped peaks in SVO sentences. The results for SVO sentences showed that over eighty percent (86.5%) of the middle peaks were downstepped, whereas 13.5% were even; there were no instances of upstepped middle peaks. Regarding the final peak, 64.7% were downstepped, 25% were even and 10.3% were upstepped. Downstepped middle and final peaks were most frequent in sentences with a contrastive focus on the subject, suggesting that peaks after the focused word receive less prominence. This has also been found for other languages, such as Spanish (e.g. Hualde 2005). Moreover, even and upstepped peaks together were more frequent than downstepped peaks in sentences with a contrastive focus on the object, suggesting that the object is given more prominence when it is in contrastive focus. However, the differences between the focus conditions were not statistically significant.

Tables 6.13 and 6.14 in appendix C show the results per speaker for SOV and SVO sentences, respectively. As shown in table 6.13, there was some inter-speaker variability for SOV sentences. Speakers 5 and 6 used downstepped middle peaks more frequently than the other speakers. These speakers used downstepped middle peaks in over eighty percent of the cases (86.4% and 81.8%, respectively). These speakers used only downstepped middle peaks for contrastive focus on the subject (and no upstepped and even peaks). The few cases of upstepped peaks corresponded to contrastive focus on the object (see table 6.13). The sentence in figure 6.5 (appendix D) was uttered by Speaker 5. For Speakers 1 and 3, downstepped middle peaks were less frequent than for the other speakers (71.8% and 71.4%, respectively). In other words, Speakers 1 and 3 used even and upstepped peaks more frequently than the other speakers. Regarding the final peak, the percentage of downstepped peaks was relatively low for Speaker 2 (45.8%). For this speaker, a substantial number of even peaks (45.8%) were observed. The speech of Speaker 2 was characterized by a relatively flat contour, which could explain the high frequency of even peaks (see figure 6.6 in appendix D).

The results for SVO are similar (see table 6.14 in appendix C). Speakers 2 and 3 used a substantial number of even peaks. For Speaker 2, 30.8% of the middle peaks and 46.2% of the final peaks were even, whereas for Speaker 3, 40% of the middle peaks and 54.5% of the final peaks were even. The even peaks did not seem to be correlated with focus type in these speakers and the cases of even peaks occurred in the three focus conditions in these speakers. The even peaks could be due to the relatively flat contour both speakers used: that is, there were relatively small differences in Fo in these cases.

As stated above, the other word orders were not sufficiently frequent for a thorough quantitative analysis. The contours of these orders (OSV, OVS, VSO, OV, VO, SV) were generally downstepped as well. For OVS, there were two instances where the final peak was even. For VO, there were three instances of even peaks and one instance with a higher peak on the object. These were all cases of contrastive focus on the object.

In sum, most peaks were downstepped, but there were also even and upstepped peaks. The even and upstepped peaks were correlated with focus type, especially in SOV sentences: even and upstepped peaks were most frequent in contrastive focus on the object. In the condition of contrastive focus on the subject, downstepped peaks were most frequent, indicating lower peaks after the focused element. Given that even upstepped peaks occurred in the other conditions, more research is needed to examine the function of even peaks and upsteps in Quechua.

4.3.3 Fo, Intensity and Duration

In this section, Fo, intensity and duration as possible prosodic correlates of focus are discussed. The question here is whether Fo, intensity and duration are used to mark contrastive focus in this variety of Quechua. Given that there was inter- and intra-speaker variability with respect to the word order, lexicon (e.g. *qhari* 'young man' for *runa* 'man') and morphology (*runa-kuna* man-PL 'men' with the Quechua plural marker versus *runa-s* man-$PL 'men' with the Spanish plural marker) used in the elicitation task with question-answer pairs, the data were analyzed per speaker. Due to the design of the task, there were few comparable data points. Therefore, the findings presented in this section are preliminary.

Sentences with the same word order, morphology, and lexicon were examined for differences in Fo, intensity and duration between the focus conditions.[9] Prominence is a relative measure; that is, an element may be more prominent in comparison to another. Therefore, for these sentences, differences in the maximum Fo, maximum intensity and duration of the stressed syllable of the subject and of the object were measured. In broad focus sentences, the Fo and intensity tend to be higher at the beginning of the sentence and lower towards the end. If Fo, intensity and duration are used to mark contrastive focus, the largest difference between the subject and the object is expected in the condition of contrastive focus on the subject, indicating a relatively high Fo and intensity and a relatively long duration of the subject compared to the object. The smallest difference between the subject and the object is expected for the condition of contrastive focus on the object, indicating a relatively high Fo and intensity and a relatively long duration of the object (in comparison with the subject).

In general, Speakers 1, 2, 3 and 4 made very limited use of these prosodic features to encode focus. That is, for these speakers, very few instances were observed in which contrastive focus on the subject or the object was associated with an increased Fo, intensity or duration. For Speaker 1, there were three SOV sentences that were comparable across the three conditions. In these sentences, the difference between the maximum intensity of the subject and the maximum intensity of the object was largest for contrastive focus on the subject (mean = 6.7 dB) and smallest for contrastive focus on the object (mean = 3.05 dB). That is, the maximum intensity of the subject was relatively high when it was in contrastive focus. In these cases, the maximum intensity of the object was relatively low. Conversely, when the object was in contrastive focus,

---

9 As stated above, morphology played a very limited role in topic and focus marking. The prosody of the sentences marked with *-qa* is discussed below.

DISCOURSE DEIXIS IN SOUTHERN QUECHUA

the maximum intensity of the subject was relatively low and that of the object was relatively high. The difference between the focus conditions for intensity is small. Moreover, no differences between the conditions were found for duration and Fo for Speaker 1.

The speech of Speaker 2 was characterized by a relatively flat contour that was identical across focus conditions (as in figure 6.6 in appendix D). Similarly, Speakers 3 and 4 generally did not use prosody to mark focus. That is, no significant differences in Fo, intensity and duration were observed. As stated above, Speaker 3 used the order OVS once in answer to a question eliciting contrastive focus on the subject. In this case, the subject received prominence, as reflected in a rise in pitch and intensity on the subject. The maximum intensity of the subject and that of the object was almost identical (80 dB for the object and 79.8 dB for the subject). Furthermore, there was a pitch rise of 35.7 Hz on the stressed syllable. Unfortunately, there was no OVS sentence in broad focus that this sentence could be compared to.

The instances in which contrastive focus was associated with a higher Fo or intensity or a longer duration in Speakers 1, 2, 3 and 4 seemed to be isolated in nature. In other words, generally these speakers did not use these prosodic strategies to mark focus.

Speaker 5 seemed to make more use of prominence-lending features to encode focus. For example, Speaker 5 used prosody to distinguish between SOV sentences with broad and contrastive focus on the object. In Speaker 5's broad focus sentences, the contour was falling and the highest pitch and intensity were on the subject. However, in several sentences with contrastive focus on the object, the highest pitch and intensity were on the object for Speaker 5. This is evident when comparing figure 6.5 (contrastive focus on the object) with figure 6.7 (broad focus) (see appendix D). This strategy for encoding focus is consistent with Cole's (1982) finding that in Imbabura Quechua, the highest peak is on the focused element. Similar strategies were observed for other word orders, such as SVO and VO. Although Speaker 5 made use of prosody to encode focus in several instances, she did not always use it, suggesting that the use of prosody to convey focus was not a stable characteristic of her speech.

For Speaker 6, some cases were also observed in which she employed prosody to encode contrastive focus. Table 6.10 below shows the means of the duration (in milliseconds) of the stressed syllable of the subject and the object in the three focus conditions for Speaker 6. The last column shows the difference between the duration of the stressed syllable of the subject and the duration of the stressed syllable of the object. These results are based on six sentences that occurred with the same word order (SOV), lexicon and morphology in the three conditions and that can thus be compared for the use of prosody.

238   MUNTENDAM

TABLE 6.10 *Means of the duration of the subject, the object and the duration difference*
(subject – object) (in ms) in the three focus conditions for Speaker 6 (N = 6)

	Subject	Object	Difference (subject – object)
broad	251.8	161.8	90
contrS	279.7	171.9	107.8
contrO	250.1	183.5	66.6

Sentences in which other words (e.g. *qhari* 'young man' instead of *runa* 'man') or other morphemes (Spanish plural -*s* instead of Quechua plural -*kuna*) were used were excluded from this analysis.

Table 6.10 shows that the duration of the stressed syllable of the subject was longer when the subject was in contrastive focus (279.7 ms) than when it was in broad focus (251.8 ms) or when the object was in contrastive focus (250.1 ms). Furthermore, the stressed syllable of the object was longer when the object was in contrastive focus (183.5 ms) than when the sentence was in broad focus (161.8 ms) or when the subject was in contrastive focus (171.9 ms). Importantly, the difference between the duration of the stressed syllable of the subject and that of the stressed syllable of the object was the largest when the subject was in contrastive focus (107.8 ms), and the smallest when the object was in contrastive focus (66.6 ms). These results suggest that Speaker 6 used duration in these cases to distinguish contrastive focus from broad focus. Given that this analysis is based on a small data set and the differences are relatively small, the results need to be interpreted with caution.

Table 6.11 shows the means of the maximum intensity (in decibels) of the subject and the object and the difference between the maximum intensity of the subject and the maximum intensity of the object for the same six sentences in the three focus conditions for Speaker 6.

These results revealed minimal differences between the three conditions for the maximum intensity of the subject, that is, these differences are not salient. Similarly, the differences between the three conditions for the maximum intensity of the object are small. However, some more substantial differences are observed while comparing the maximum intensity of the subject and that of the object. This difference was larger in sentences with a contrastive focus on the subject (3.3 dB) than in sentences with broad focus (1.3 dB) and sentences with contrastive focus on the object (0.7 dB). This indicates that,

DISCOURSE DEIXIS IN SOUTHERN QUECHUA

TABLE 6.11 *Means of the maximum intensity of the subject, the object and the difference (subject – object) (in dB) in the three focus conditions for Speaker 6 (N = 6)*

	Subject	Object	Difference (subject – object)
broad	70.2	68.9	1.3
contrS	71	67.7	3.3
contrO	69.5	68.8	0.7

for Speaker 6, the decline in intensity was in fact larger when the subject was in contrastive focus.

There were seven sentences that were comparable across the conditions of broad focus and contrastive focus on the subject. For these sentences, the difference in the Fo maximum was larger in contrastive focus on the subject (mean = 37.6 Hz) than in broad focus (mean = 13.4 Hz). No differences in Fo were found between broad focus and contrastive focus on the object. In sum, these data suggest that Speaker 6 used some prosody (duration, intensity, Fo) to encode focus in Quechua. However, not all instances of contrastive focus for Speaker 6 were associated with an increased Fo, intensity or duration.

To summarize, these preliminary findings for Fo, intensity and duration suggest that, in general, these features are not used to encode a difference between broad focus and contrastive focus. However, some speakers (in particular Speakers 5 and 6) made some use of acoustic correlates of focus, but there was intra-speaker variability. Their use of prosody could possibly be due to an influence from Spanish, but more research on the local variety of Spanish is needed to support this hypothesis.

4.3.4   Summary

In this section, peak alignment, downstep and upstep, and the use of prominence-lending features such as Fo, intensity and duration to encode focus were examined. The majority of peaks for all speakers were aligned early in all focus conditions, indicating that alignment was not used to mark focus. Late peaks were found for some speakers, but the exact pragmatic meaning was not clear. The analysis of downstepped, even and upstepped peaks revealed that most peaks were downstepped. Upstepped and even peaks were most frequent in the condition of contrastive focus on the object, suggesting more prominence on the object. Furthermore, in the condition of contrastive focus on the subject, there were relatively many downstepped peaks. The analysis of the use of prosodic features showed inter-speaker variability. Four speakers made very limited use of prosodic features to convey focus, whereas the other two speakers made slightly more use of prosody.

This inter-speaker variability could be due to a variety of factors. First, it could be that speakers who use more morphological or syntactic strategies to express focus use fewer prosodic strategies. None of the speakers used focus particles, but Speakers 1 (in both tasks) and 4 (in the picture-story task) infrequently used -*qa* to mark the topic of the sentence. In this respect, their Quechua was more conservative than that of the other speakers. Speaker 4 also used more alternative word orders to encode focus. Speakers 5 and 6 frequently used the same word order with downstepped peaks in all conditions. This might motivate the use of prosodic strategies. Given that there was not sufficient data for a thorough quantitative analysis of the use of Fo, intensity and duration, these findings need to be interpreted with caution.

The question that follows is to what extent the use of prosodic strategies to mark focus is due to an influence from Spanish. The two speakers who made more use of prosody to encode focus in Quechua are simultaneous bilinguals, meaning that these speakers acquired Quechua and Spanish at the same time in their childhood. Both speakers reported a high proficiency in Quechua and Spanish and frequently interact in both languages. Speaker 5 received her higher education in Spanish and works as an elementary school teacher. At her work she mostly uses Spanish, but also some Quechua. Moreover, she frequently speaks Quechua at home, with friends and with relatives. Speaker 6 has not received any higher education and works as a restaurant owner. In her work, she frequently interacts in both languages. Speaker 4 acquired Quechua before Spanish and is more proficient in Quechua than in Spanish. Like Speakers 5 and 6, Speakers 1, 2 and 3 acquired both Quechua and Spanish in their early childhood at home. Given that these speakers are also proficient in Spanish and frequently interact in Spanish, there does not seem to be a direct correlation between language proficiency and use and a transfer of prominence-lending features from Spanish to Quechua. An analysis of these speakers' Spanish could provide more information on cross-linguistic influence.

5 Conclusion

This study examined the use of morphological, syntactic and prosodic strategies in the expression of focus and topic as discourse deictics in a variety of Bolivian Quechua. The results showed that topic and focus in this variety of

DISCOURSE DEIXIS IN SOUTHERN QUECHUA

Quechua can be marked *in situ* and in fronted position, as in other varieties of Quechua. The topic marker is less frequent than in other varieties and morphological focus markers have been lost; that is, there is a loss of morphological marking to relate utterances to the prior discourse.

The prosodic analysis revealed that peak alignment is not used to encode differences in focus. The majority of peaks were aligned early, regardless of focus type. Some initial peaks were aligned late, which is in agreement with O'Rourke's (2005, 2009) findings for Cuzco Quechua. However, it was shown here that the difference in early versus late peak alignment is not correlated with focus in this variety of Bolivian Quechua.

The analysis of relative peak height showed that most peaks were downstepped but some were even or upstepped. O'Rourke (2005, 2009) also found some even and upstepped peaks for Cuzco Quechua. This work furthermore shows a correlation between even peaks/upsteps and focus. In particular, even peaks/upsteps are more frequent with contrastive focus on the object, indicating a more prominent peak on the focused word.

A preliminary analysis of Fo, intensity and duration differences showed that most participants did not use these prominence-lending features to convey focus. However, particularly with two participants, contrastive focus was in some cases associated with a higher Fo maximum, a higher intensity and an increased duration of the stressed syllable. Research with more speakers and more comparable data points is needed to explore this issue further.

Some individual differences with respect to topic and focus marking were found. Speaker 1 used the morphological marker *-qa* to mark topic and used more late peaks. Speaker 4 used an object fronting strategy or a strategy in which the focused object appeared in preverbal position more than the other speakers. Speakers 5 and 6 used some prosodic strategies. For Speakers 2 and 4, no differences were found between the focus conditions.

Given that some speakers did not seem to use morphological nor prosodic strategies to encode focus, an important question is whether they perceive the difference between sentences with the same word order in different focus conditions. A perception study is needed to study this issue. If the speakers do perceive differences in focus structures, other prosodic features may be involved in focus marking.

Another important question is to what extent focus marking in this variety of Bolivian Quechua has been affected by contact with Spanish. Spanish has affected other areas of the local Quechua variety. First, the high frequency of SVO order could be due to an influence from Spanish. Second, plurality of nouns is frequently marked with the Spanish plural marker *-s* instead of the Quechua plural marker *-kuna* (see for instance (25) above). There is inter- and intra-speaker variability with respect to plural marking. That is, the same speakers used the Quechua and the Spanish plural markers interchangeably; for instance, *runa-kuna* (man-PL 'men') and *runa-s* (man-$PL 'men') were found for the same speaker. It should be noted that these allomorphs for the plural morpheme are also mentioned for Cochabamba Quechua in Solá and Lastra (1964, 21), in addition to the allomorphs *-es, -skuna* and *-kunas*.

Third, Quechua traditionally does not make use of indefinite articles, but in bilingual speech the Quechua numeral *uk* [ux] 'one' is frequently used as an indefinite article, see (30):

(30) *Uk runa uk khuchi-ta q'ati-sa-n.*
one man one pig-ACC drive-PROG-3
'A man is driving a pig.'

This phenomenon has also been found for other varieties of Southern Quechua and has been attributed to Spanish influence (see Sánchez 2003). As with plural marking, there was inter- and intra-speaker variation with respect to the use of *uk*.

Fourth, the accusative case marker *-ta* was not always used to mark the direct object, see (28)–(29). Interestingly, in these cases the stress was on the final syllable of the direct object noun. As with the other phenomena, there is inter- and intra-speaker variability, which means that the accusative case marker has not been completely lost. As mentioned above, according to Solá and Lastra (1964) the accusative case marker *-ta* and final stress on the noun occur in free variation when the noun is not in utterance-final position. It is not clear to what extent the less frequent use of *-ta* is related to an influence from Spanish:

(31) *Runa-s-qa yunTA wata-sa-nku.* (contrO)[10]
man-$PL-TOP $yoke tie-PROG-3PL
'The men are tying the yoke.'

Finally, lexical influence from Spanish to Quechua is also frequent in this variety.

In order to gain a better understanding of a possible Spanish influence in the area of focus marking in this variety of Quechua, the strategies used by these speakers to mark focus in Spanish need to be examined as well.

---

10 The sentence in (31) was uttered in the context of contrastive focus on the object, but this phenomenon also occurred in other focus conditions.

DISCOURSE DEIXIS IN SOUTHERN QUECHUA

Overall, this study has revealed variation between varieties of Southern Quechua. In many varieties of Quechua, focus is encoded in syntax and morphology. In the Quechua spoken in the department of Cochabamba, Bolivia, however, focus seems to be encoded in syntax and to some extent in prosody, but not in morphology. In addition, the use of the topic -qa as a discourse deictic seems to be reduced compared to other varieties of Quechua. This shows that the findings for one variety of Quechua cannot be generalized to other varieties of Quechua. Moreover, contact between Quechua and Spanish may result in different linguistic outcomes in different regions.

The loss of morphological marking of topic and focus could signal a decline in the use of the language. In this respect, it is interesting to note that Kalt (this volume) found that Cuzco Quechua children use all of the directional morphemes that are used by adult speakers of Quechua, indicating continued longevity of Quechua morphemes. On the other hand, and as a reviewer pointed out, the loss of morphological topic and focus marking could also be a standard case of language change, comparable to the loss of gender marking in Dutch. Future research on Bolivian Quechua morphology is needed to determine whether the loss of topic/focus morphemes is an isolated phenomenon, or whether it extends to other morphemes (such as the directional morphemes). The answer to this question could shed more light on Quechua language change in Bolivia.

Regarding why this variety of Quechua in some respects seems to have more influence from Spanish than other varieties (e.g. other Bolivian Quechua varieties and Cuzco Quechua), several explanations are possible. One explanation for the difference between this variety and other Bolivian Quechua varieties could be the proximity of the communities studied here to the city of Cochabamba and the relatively high geographic mobility: some inhabitants of Tarata work in Cochabamba, and vice versa. Moreover, inhabitants of Tarata and nearby communities frequently visit Cochabamba to go shopping. These Quechua speakers are therefore frequently in contact with Spanish. The Quechua varieties spoken in some other areas of Bolivia are more conservative, and to my knowledge the morphological, discourse deictic, topic and focus markers are still in use in the Quechua spoken in more isolated communities in the department of Potosí.

Proximity to a city and geographic mobility cannot be the only explanations, given that the morphological topic and focus markers are still in use in varieties of Cuzco Quechua (see e.g. Sánchez 2010, van Rijswijk and Muntendam 2012). Some differences can be observed between the communities studied here and Quechua communities in the department of Cuzco. Firstly, the number of simultaneous bilinguals in Tarata and Huayculí is relatively high, meaning that most people acquired Spanish in addition to Quechua in their early childhood. Moreover, there are some Spanish monolinguals and very few (if any) monolingual Quechua speakers in Tarata and Huayculí. In the community near Cuzco studied by van Rijswijk and Muntendam (2012), on the other hand, there are relatively many consecutive bilinguals, who acquired Quechua prior to Spanish. Also, there are still some monolingual Quechua speakers in town, which could contribute to the maintenance of Quechua.[11] Secondly, the presence of the *Academia Mayor de la Lengua Quechua* in Cuzco and the perceived higher status of Cuzco Quechua compared to Bolivian Quechua could contribute to the maintenance of a slightly more conservative variety of Quechua. It should be noted, however, that although the morphological topic and focus markers are still used in the department of Cuzco, Cuzco Quechua is influenced by Spanish in other areas, as is evident for instance from the lexical influence from Spanish in Quechua and the decline in use of the accusative marker *-ta*. More research is needed to address the differences between the Quechua varieties.

Acknowledgements

This research has been funded by Middlebury College, the Royal Netherlands Academy of Arts and Sciences (KNAW) and the ERC project 'Traces of Contact' (grant number 230310). I would like to thank Clodoaldo Soto Ruiz and Instituto de Estudios Peruanos for their permission to use drawings from Soto (1993), and Editorial San Marcos for permission to use the stories and drawings from Martínez Parra (1999). I am grateful to the participants from Tarata and Huayculí for their hospitality, time and patience. Finally, I would like to thank the reviewers for their valuable comments. All errors are my own.

Appendix A

ACC	accusative	INTR	interrogative
CONTR	contrastive	PL	plural
DAT	dative	PROG	progressive
DIREV	direct evidential	PST1	past

---

11 Unfortunately I do not know the exact number of monolingual Spanish speakers, monolingual Quechua speakers, consecutive bilinguals and simultaneous bilinguals in the different areas. The information provided here is based on fieldwork conducted between 2001 and the present in both areas.

PST2	perfective	1, 2, 3	first, ... person
TOP	topic	$	loan word

Appendix B

FIGURE 6.1 *Example of a sequence of pictures, used in the picture-story task (adapted from Martínez Parra 1999)*

FIGURE 6.2 *Example of a picture used in the question-answer task (Soto Ruiz 1993)*

TABLE 6.12 *Frequencies of the word orders used in the three focus conditions in the elicitation task (broad focus, contrastive focus on the subject (contrS) and contrastive focus on the object (contrO)), per speaker*

	Speaker 1			Speaker 2			Speaker 3			Speaker 4			Speaker 5			Speaker 6		
	broad	contrS	contrO	broad	contrS	contrO	broad	contrS	contrO	broad	contrS	contrO	broad	contrS	contrO	broad	contrS	contrO
SOV	16	13	10	6	10	9	1	4	2	7	6	0	11	7	4	15	11	9
S-*qa* OV	0	0	5	0	0	0	0	0	0	0	0	0	0	0	0	0	0	0
SVO	1	3	1	4	5	4	3	6	2	7	11	4	5	11	1	3	3	1
OSV	0	0	0	0	0	0	0	0	1	0	0	1	0	0	0	0	0	0
OVS	0	0	0	0	0	0	0	1	0	0	0	4	0	0	0	0	0	0
VSO	0	0	0	0	0	0	1	0	0	0	0	0	0	0	0	0	0	0
VOS	0	0	0	0	0	0	0	0	0	0	0	0	0	0	0	0	0	0
OV	0	0	0	1	0	2	1	0	4	0	0	5	0	0	11	0	0	7
VO	0	0	0	3	0	1	1	0	1	0	0	0	0	0	1	0	0	0
SV	0	0	0	1	2	0	0	1	0	0	0	0	0	0	0	0	0	0
VS	0	0	0	0	0	0	0	0	0	0	0	0	0	0	0	0	0	0
Other	1	2	2	3	1	2	11	8	6	4	1	4	2	0	1	0	4	1

TABLE 6.13 Downstepped, even, and upstepped peaks for SOV sentences, comparing peak1–2 and peak2–3, per speaker and condition

| | | Peak 1 → 2 | | | | | | | Peak 2 → 3 | | | | | | |
| | | N | Downstep | | Even | | Upstep | | N | Downstep | | Even | | Upstep | |
			N	%	N	%	N	%		N	%	N	%	N	%
Spk 1	broad	16	12	75	3	18.7	1	6.3	16	11	68.8	2	12.5	3	18.8
	contrS	13	11	84.6	2	15.4	0	0	13	6	46.2	4	30.8	3	23.1
	contrO	10	5	50	1	10	4	40	10	6	60	3	30	1	10
	Total	*39*	*28*	*71.8*	*6*	*15.4*	*5*	*12.8*	*39*	*23*	*59*	*9*	*23.1*	*7*	*17.9*
Spk 2	broad	6	4	66.7	2	33.3	0	0	6	2	33.3	3	50	1	16.7
	contrS	12	11	91.7	1	8.3	0	0	12	7	58.3	5	41.7	0	0
	contrO	6	4	66.7	2	33.3	0	0	6	2	40	3	40	1	20
	Total	*24*	*19*	*79.2*	*5*	*20.8*	*0*	*0*	*24*	*11*	*45.8*	*11*	*45.8*	*2*	*18.2*
Spk 3	broad	1	1	100	0	0	0	0	1	0	0	1	100	0	0
	contrS	4	3	75	0	0	1	25	4	4	100	0	0	0	0
	contrO	2	1	50	1	50	0	0	2	1	50	1	50	0	0
	Total	*7*	*5*	*71.4*	*1*	*14.3*	*1*	*14.3*	*7*	*5*	*71.4*	*2*	*28.6*	*0*	*0*
Spk 4	broad	7	7	100	0	0	0	0	6	4	66.7	2	33.3	0	0
	contrS	6	3	50	3	50	0	0	5	4	80	1	20	0	0
	contrO	0	0	0	0	0	0	0	0	0	0	0	0	0	0
	Total	*13*	*10*	*76.9*	*3*	*23.1*	*0*	*0*	*11*	*8*	*72.7*	*3*	*27.3*	*0*	*0*

TABLE 6.13 *Downstepped, even, and upstepped peaks for SOV sentences, comparing peak 1– 2 and peak 2–3, per speaker and condition (cont.)*

		Peak 1 → 2							Peak 2 → 3						
		N	Downstep		Even		Upstep		N	Downstep		Even		Upstep	
			N	%	N	%	N	%		N	%	N	%	N	%
Spk 5	broad	11	11	100	0	0	0	0	8	6	75	2	25	0	0
	contrS	7	7	100	0	0	0	0	6	4	66.7	1	16.7	1	16.7
	contrO	4	1	25	1	25	2	50	4	4	100	0	0	0	0
	Total	*22*	*19*	*86.4*	*1*	*4.6*	*2*	*9.1*	*18*	*14*	*77.8*	*3*	*16.7*	*1*	*5.6*
Spk 6	broad	14	10	71.4	3	21.4	1	7.1	13	12	92.3	1	7.7	0	0
	contrS	10	10	100	0	0	0	0	10	9	90	0	0	1	10
	contrO	9	7	77.8	1	11.1	1	11.1	8	8	100	0	0	0	0
	Total	*33*	*27*	*81.8*	*4*	*12.1*	*2*	*6.1*	*31*	*29*	*93.6*	*1*	*3.2*	*1*	*3.2*
All	broad	55	45	81.8	8	14.5	2	3.6	50	35	70	11	22	4	8
	contrS	52	45	86.5	6	11.5	1	1.9	50	34	68	11	22	5	10
	contrO	31	18	58.1	9	29	4	12.9	30	21	70	7	23.3	2	6.7
	Total	*138*	*108*	*78.3*	*23*	*16.7*	*7*	*5.1*	*130*	*90*	*69.2*	*29*	*32.2*	*11*	*12.2*

		Peak 1 → 2							Peak 2 → 3						
		N	Downstep		Even		Upstep		N	Downstep		Even		Upstep	
			N	%	N	%	N	%		N	%	N	%	N	%
Spk 1	broad	1	1	100	0	0	0	0	1	1	100	0	0	0	0
	contrS	3	3	100	0	0	0	0	3	2	66.7	1	33.3	0	0
	contrO	1	1	100	0	0	0	0	1	0	0	1	100	0	0
	Total	*5*	*5*	*100*	*0*	*0*	*0*	*0*	*5*	*3*	*60*	*2*	*40*	*0*	*0*
Spk 2	broad	4	2	50	2	50	0	0	4	2	50	2	50	0	0
	contrS	5	4	80	1	20	0	0	5	3	60	1	20	1	20
	contrO	4	3	75	1	25	0	0	4	1	25	3	75	0	0
	Total	*13*	*9*	*69.2*	*4*	*30.8*	*0*	*0*	*13*	*6*	*46.2*	*6*	*46.2*	*1*	*7.7*
Spk 3	broad	2	1	50	1	50	0	0	3	1	33.3	2	66.7	0	0
	contrS	6	4	66.7	2	33.3	0	0	6	3	50	3	50	0	0
	contrO	2	1	50	1	50	0	0	2	1	50	1	50	0	0
	Total	*10*	*6*	*60*	*4*	*40*	*0*	*0*	*11*	*5*	*45.5*	*6*	*54.5*	*0*	*0*
Spk 4	broad	7	7	100	0	0	0	0	4	2	50	0	0	2	50
	contrS	11	11	100	0	0	0	0	11	10	90.9	1	9.1	0	0
	contrO	4	3	75	1	25	0	0	2	2	100	0	0	0	0
	Total	*22*	*21*	*95.5*	*1*	*4.5*	*0*	*0*	*17*	*14*	*82.4*	*1*	*5.9*	*2*	*11.8*

TABLE 6.14 *Downstepped, even, and upstepped peaks for SVO sentences, comparing peak 1-2 and peak 2–3, per speaker and condition (cont.)*

| | | Peak 1 → 2 | | | | | | | Peak 2 → 3 | | | | | | |
| | | N | Downstep | | Even | | Upstep | | N | Downstep | | Even | | Upstep | |
			N	%	N	%	N	%		N	%	N	%	N	%
Spk 5	broad	5	5	100	0	0	0	0	5	3	60	1	20	1	20
	contrS	11	11	100	0	0	0	0	9	7	77.8	0	0	2	22.2
	contrO	1	1	100	0	0	0	0	1	0	0	0	0	1	100
	Total	*17*	*17*	*100*	*0*	*0*	*0*	*0*	*15*	*10*	*66.7*	*1*	*6.7*	*4*	*26.7*
Spk 6	broad	3	2	66.7	1	33.3	0	0	3	2	66.7	1	33.3	0	0
	contrS	3	3	100	0	0	0	0	3	3	100	0	0	0	0
	contrO	1	1	100	0	0	0	0	1	1	100	0	0	0	0
	Total	*7*	*6*	*85.7*	*1*	*14.3*	*0*	*0*	*7*	*6*	*85.7*	*1*	*14.3*	*0*	*0*
All	broad	22	18	81.8	4	18.2	0	0	20	11	55	6	30	3	15
	contrS	39	36	92.3	3	7.7	0	0	37	28	75.7	6	16.2	3	8.1
	contrO	13	10	76.9	3	23.1	0	0	11	5	45.5	5	45.5	1	9.1
	Total	*74*	*64*	*86.5*	*10*	*13.5*	*0*	*0*	*68*	*44*	*64.7*	*17*	*25*	*7*	*10.3*

Appendix D

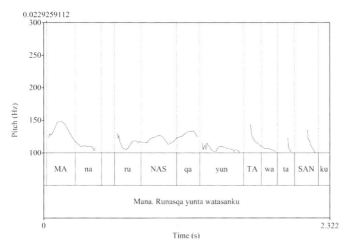

Mana.	Runa-s-qa	yunta	wata-sa-nku.
no	man-PL-TOP	yoke	tie-PROG-3PL

'No. The men are tying the yoke.' (Speaker 1)

FIGURE 6.3 *Utterance with SOV order and contrastive focus on the object*
Note: There is a high tone of 133.3 Hz on the topic marker -qa.

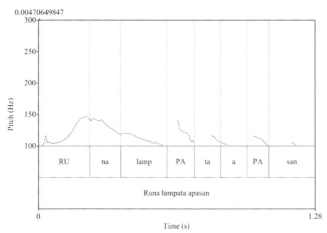

Runa	lampa-ta	apa-sa-n.
man	pick-ACC	bring-PROG-3

'The man is bringing a pick.' (Speaker 1)

FIGURE 6.4 *Utterance with SOV order in broad focus*
Note: The Fo maximum of the stressed syllable of the subject is 146.7 Hz, that of the object 124.8 Hz, and that of the verb 115.3 Hz.

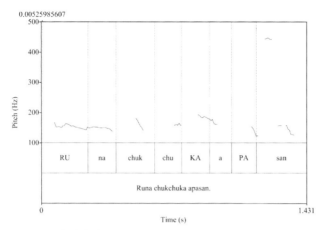

Runa   chukchuka   apa-sa-n.
Man   pick   bring-PROG-3
'The man is bringing a pick.' (Speaker 5)

FIGURE 6.5 *Utterance with SOV order and contrastive focus on the object*
Note: *The F0 maximum of the stressed syllable of the subject is 162.9 Hz, and that of the object 186.7 Hz. There are perturbations in the F0 contour, but the F0 maximum of the stressed syllable of the verb is clearly lower than that of the object. The maximum intensity is 69.8 dB for the subject, 76.6 dB for the object, and 68.2 dB for the verb.*

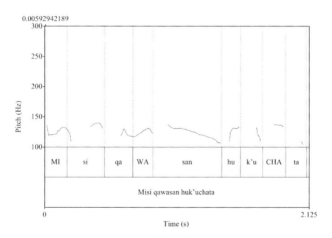

Misi   qawa-sa-n   huk'ucha-ta.
cat   watch-PROG-3   mouse-ACC
'The cat is watching the mouse.' (Speaker 2)

FIGURE 6.6 *Utterance with SVO order in broad focus*
Note: *The F0 maximum of the stressed syllable of the subject is 132.9 Hz, that of the verb 130.9 Hz, and that of the object 136.8 Hz.*

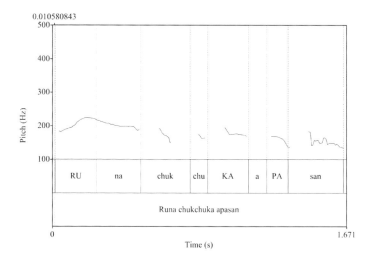

Runa   chukchuka   apa-sa-n.
Man   pick   bring-PROG-3
'The man is bringing a pick.' (Speaker 5)

FIGURE 6.7   *Utterance with SOV order in broad focus*
Note. *The F0 maximum of the stressed syllable of the subject is 224.6 Hz, that of the object 176.8 Hz, and that of the verb 168.9 Hz. The maximum intensity is 80 dB for the subject, 77.6 dB for the object, and 76.1 dB for the verb.*

Bibliography

Adelaar, Willem and Pieter Muysken. 2004. *The Languages of the Andes*. Cambridge: Cambridge University Press.

Boersma, Paul and David Weenink. 2010. *Praat: doing phonetics by computer.* Version 5.1.44. http://www.praat.org/.

Cerrón-Palomino, Rodolfo. 1987. *Lingüística Quechua*. Cuzco, Peru: Centro de Estudios Rurales Andinos Bartolomé de las Casas.

Chomsky, Noam. 1971. "Deep structure, surface structure and semantic interpretation." In *Semantics: An interdisciplinary reader in philosophy, linguistics and psychology*, edited by Danny D. Steinberg and Leon A. Jakobovits. 183–217. Cambridge: Cambridge University Press.

Cinque, Guiglielmo. 1990. *Types of A'-dependencies*. Cambridge, MA: MIT Press.

Cole, Peter. 1982. *Imbabura Quechua*. Amsterdam: North-Holland Publishing Company.

Cusihuamán, Antonio. 2001. *Gramática Quechua. Cuzco-Collao*. Cuzco, Peru: Centro de Estudios Rurales Andinos Bartolomé de las Casas.

De la Mota, Carme. 1997. "Prosody of sentences with contrastive new information in Spanish." In *Intonation: theory, models and applications. Proceedings of an ESCA workshop*, edited by Antonis Botinis, Georgios. Kouroupetroglou, and George Carayiannis. 75–78.

Face, Timothy. 2001. "Focus and early peak alignment in Spanish intonation." *Probus* 13: 223–246.

———. 2002. "Local intonational marking of Spanish contrastive focus." *Probus* 14: 71–92.

———. 2003. "Intonation in Spanish declaratives: differences between lab speech and spontaneous speech." *Catalan Journal of Linguistics* 2: 115–131.

Fuqua, Ronald. 1992. "Word order in discourse of North Junin Quechua." MA thesis. University of Texas at Arlington.

Hintz, Diane. 2003. "Word order in Southern Conchucos Quechua." Unpublished MA thesis. University of California Santa Barbara.

———. 2006. "Stress in South Conchucos Quechua: a phonetic and phonological study." *International Journal of American Linguistics* 72: 477–521.

Hualde, José Ignacio. 2005. *The sounds of Spanish*. Cambridge: Cambridge University Press.

Jackendoff, Ray. 1972. *Semantic interpretation in generative grammar*. Cambridge, MA: MIT Press.

Kim, Sahyang and Avelino, Heriberto. 2003. "An intonational study of focus and word order variation in Mexican Spanish." In *La tonía: dimensiones fonéticas y fonológicas*, edited by Esther Herrera and Pedro Martín Butragueño. 357–374. Mexico City, Mexico: El colegio de México.

Landerman, Peter Nelson. 1991. "Quechua dialects and their classification." PhD diss., University of California at Los Angeles.

Levinson, Stephen. 1983. *Pragmatics*. Cambridge: Cambridge University Press.

———. 2004. "Deixis." In *The handbook of pragmatics*, edited by Laurence Horn and Gregory Ward. 97–121. Oxford: Blackwell.

Liberman, Mark and Janet Pierrehumbert. 1984. "Intonational invariance under changes in pitch range and length. In *Language, sound, structure: Studies in phonology presented to Morris Halle by his teacher and students*, edited by Mark Aronoff and Richard Oehrle. 157–223. Cambridge, MA: MIT Press.

Martínez Parra, Reynaldo. 1999. *La fábula quechua*. Lima: Editorial San Marcos.

Ministerio de Asuntos Exteriores y Cooperación, FUNPROEIB Andes and UNICEF, 2009. *Atlas Sociolingüístico de Pueblos Indígenas de América Latina*, Vol. 2. Cochabamba, Bolivia.

Muntendam, Antje. 2009. "Linguistic transfer in Andean Spanish: syntax or pragmatics?" PhD diss., University of Illinois at Urbana-Champaign.

Muysken, Pieter. 1995. "Focus in Quechua." In *Discourse Configurational Languages*, edited by Katalin É Kiss. 375–393. New York: Oxford University Press.

O'Rourke, Erin. 2005. "Intonation and language contact: A case study of two varieties of Peruvian Spanish." PhD diss., University of Illinois at Urbana-Champaign.

———. 2009. "Phonetics and phonology of Cuzco Quechua declarative intonation: An instrumental analysis." *Journal of the International Phonetic Association* 39, 3: 291–312.

Parker, Gary. 1969. *Ayacucho Quechua grammar and dictionary*. The Hague, Paris: Mouton.

Post, Brechtje and Francis Nolan. 2012. "Data collection for prosodic analysis of continuous speech and dialectal variation" In *The Oxford handbook of laboratory phonology,* edited by Abigail C. Cohn, Cécile Fougeron and Marie K. Huffman. 538–547. Oxford: Oxford University Press.

Prieto, Pilar, Van Santen, Jan and Julia Hirschberg. 1995. "Tonal alignment patterns in Spanish." *Journal of Phonetics* 23: 429–451.

Rizzi, Luigi. 1997. "The Fine Structure of the Left Periphery." In *Elements of Grammar*, edited by Liliane Haegeman. 281–337. Dordrecht: Kluwer Academic Press.

Rooth, Mats. 1992. "A theory of focus interpretation" *Natural Language Semantics* 1: 75-116.

Sánchez, Liliana. 2003. *Quechua-Spanish Bilingualism. Functional Interference and Convergence in Functional Categories*. Amsterdam: John Benjamins.

———. 2010. *The Morphology and Syntax of Topic and Focus: Minimalist Inquiries in the Quechua Periphery*. Linguistik Aktuell Series. Amsterdam: John Benjamins.

Solá, Donald and Yolanda Lastra. 1964. "The structure of Cochabamba Quechua." *Quechua Language Materials Project*. Cornell University, Ithaca.

Soto Ruiz, Clodoaldo. 1993. *Manual de Enseñanza*. Lima, Peru: Instituto de Estudios Peruanos.

Torero, Alfredo. 1964. "Los dialectos quechuas." *Anales Científicos de la Universidad Agraria* 2: 446–478.

Vanrell, María del Mar, Stella, Antonio, Gili-Favela, Barbara, and Pilar Prieto. 2013. "Prosodic manifestations of the Effort Code in Catalan, Italian and Spanish contrastive focus." *Journal of the International Phonetic Association* 43(2): 195–220.

Van Rijswijk, Remy and Antje Muntendam. 2012. "The prosody of focus in the Spanish of Quechua-Spanish bilinguals: a case study on noun phrases" *International Journal of Bilingualism.* DOI: 10.1177/1367006912456103.

Xu, Yi. 2010. "In defense of lab speech" *Journal of Phonetics* 38: 329–336.

Zubizarreta, María Luisa. 1998. *Prosody, Focus, and Word Order.* Cambridge, MA: MIT Press.

CHAPTER 7

From Nominal Predicate to Deictic Clausal Highlighter: The Development of *hina* 'like'

Pieter Muysken

1 Introduction

The element 'like' holds a special position in the literature on grammaticalization in English, where it has developed as a hedge and as a quotative or reportative marker, among other uses, in addition to its original meaning of marking similarity (Meehan 1991; Romaine and Lange 1991). I will return to this below. In the Quechua of Puno (Southern Peru, almost on the border with Bolivia), the element *hina* 'like' similarly has undergone a number of changes in its distribution and grammatical use, which are however quite different from what has happened in English. This paper outlines these changes. To give just one example, the use of *hina* as a deictic clausal highlighter is illustrated in (1). A deictic clausal highlighter points to the content of a specific clause in the context of a larger construction.

(1) *Para-chun- pis*   *hina*   *llank'a-lla-saq.*
     rain-HORT.3SG-ADD   LIKE   work-LIM-FUT.1SG
     'Even if it rains I will work.'

Here *hina* functions as a subordinating element following the conditional clause, which has full inflection.

The form *hina*'s spectacular extension in meanings goes much beyond that of its English counterpart 'like', but it has not developed into a quotative like its English counterpart. A first approach to understanding the range of uses for *hina* analyzed here is the consideration of the fact that many lexical items in Quechua are multifunctional; however, the range of uses of *hina* exceeds that of most other items, as far as I can establish, and includes adopted functions of marking discourse deixis, in terms of marking relations between references to states of affairs in succeeding clauses.

Puno Quechua is a variety of Southern Peruvian Quechua, and as far as I know, it is mutually intelligible with the well-known and prestigious variety spoken in Cuzco, as well as with the varieties spoken in Bolivia. All these varieties share a number of Quechua II morphological characteristics, but have as a special feature the series of ejective and aspirated stops, which set them apart from Quechua I varieties, and also from Ayacucho Quechua (Adelaar and Muysken 2004, 183–191). The varieties spoken in Puno and Arequipa are characterized by a high number of morphological and lexical borrowings from Aymara (Adelaar and Muysken 2004, 187). This is the result of the fact that in this area Aymara was spoken as a dominant language until fairly recently. The present paper will also explore the possibility that the changes in the distribution of *hina* are related to the strong Aymara substrate in Puno Quechua, and compare *hina* with the Cuzco Quechua complementizer / clausal highlighter *chay-qa* 'that-TOP'.

The present paper is based on unpublished fieldwork data from the town of Lampa (near Juliaca), published data from nearby Ayaviri (Muysken 1985), and published Puno Quechua textual data (Büttner, Cointet & Chuquimamani 1984).[1] I worked with fifteen speakers in Lampa, the large majority of them teenagers (six were members of a local soccer team that I sponsored with a new ball, several others were girls from the local secondary school, and a few young adults were members of a local study and discussion group). In Ayaviri I worked with three adult males.[2] The methodology employed was a combination of elicited translations from Spanish, elicited appropriateness judgments of examples constructed by me or provided by others, and elicited translations to Spanish of examples offered by me. Both in Lampa and in Ayaviri, Quechua is used very frequently in daily life, by people with an indigenous ethnicity as well as *mestizos*, and therefore there were no problems in terms of working on the language.

2 The Grammaticalization of 'like' in English

Meehan (1991) and Romaine and Lange (1991), apparently independently from one another, have drawn attention to the fact that English 'like' has developed from a preposition marking similarity to a 'marker of reported speech and thought', to use Romaine and Lange's term. In the model proposed by Romaine and Lange, there is a chain of developments, roughly as in figure 7.1. The meaning of 'like' develops from a propositional preposition ('someone like Mary') to a textual conjunction ('Winston tastes good like a cigarette should.'),

---

1 Examples cited from Büttner, Cointet & Chuquimamani (1984) are marked in the text as YA with a page number.

2 Their assistance is gratefully acknowledged here.

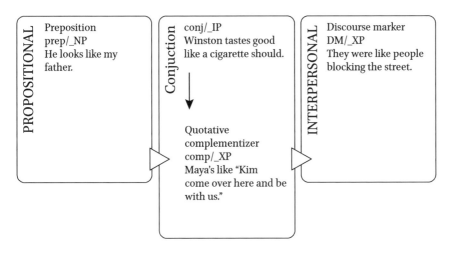

FIGURE 7.1 *Schematic overview of the grammaticalization path of 'like' as proposed in Romaine and Lange (1991, 261)*

to an interpersonal discourse marker ('They were like very happy to see me'). The quotative use and meaning (as in 'Maya's like "Kim come over here and be with us".' in figure 7.1) is assumed to have developed out of the textual function.

Romaine and Lange's observations have been further developed and incorporated into a theory of grammaticalization by Traugott (1997). In this theory, a series of unidirectional changes was proposed, i.e. steps in the grammaticalization process, whereby each new meaning developed from a previous one, step by step.

Subsequently, Buchstaller (2004) has interpreted the broad findings regarding the different functions of 'like' into a 'radial structure' model, shown in figure 7.2, inspired by Lakoff (1987). In this model the original meaning of 'like', involving approximation, similarity, and comparison, remains the core from which the other meanings and uses, such as focus, quotative, and pragmatic hedge, are dynamically 'radiated', i.e. synchronically derived in language use. A focus reading would be involved since the quoted part of an utterance is automatically the focus. The pragmatic hedge comes in since the quotation reported is always approximative, as in 'I'd be like "yes you can, just [say 'hello']".' The narrator has a reduced responsibility with respect to what was said and how.

Buchstaller argues that it is more appropriate to think of this radial structure as a network of related meanings which remain in continuous interaction than as a chain of unidirectional changes, in which older meanings disappear.

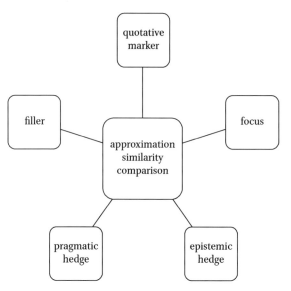

FIGURE 7.2 *The radial structure model for 'like' as proposed in Buchstaller (2001)*

In addition to directionality, another way in which a radial structure model may differ from a grammaticalization chain model as given in figure 7.1 is that often there is only one central meaning linked to any two other meanings of the form, while in the grammaticalization chain model there is no such restriction.

3   Quechua Information Structure and Clausal Highlighters

In the Quechua languages, word order tends to be SOV, but is fairly flexible, depending on the information structure of the utterance. In addition, there are a number of suffixal particles that are centrally involved in information structure. Clausal subordination is primarily marked through suffixes on the (clause-final) verb, but particularly in the Southern Peruvian varieties, separate particles may also play a role as clause linkers.

The suffixal particles involved in Quechua information structure are the topic marker *-qa* and the focal/evidential set *-mi/-m; -si/-s; -cha/-ch* (e.g. Muysken 1995). A main clause may have the following overall structure:

(XP-TOPIC)....   V-INFLECTION-EVIDENTIAL   ....(XP-TOPIC)

FROM NOMINAL PREDICATE TO DEICTIC CLAUSAL HIGHLIGHTER 263

Typically, a clause may contain one or more topicalized constituents in initial position, other material, an inflected verb with evidential marking, as in (2a) below, and some element following as afterthoughts, optionally also marked as topics (2b). If another element than the predicate is in focus, evidential marking occurs on that element (2c). However, evidential marking may not appear on a post-verbal element (2d) (2a–2d are constructed examples).

(2) a. *Mariya-qa*   *sara-ta*   *qu-n-mi*   *Xwan-man.*
     Maria-TOP   corn-ACC   give-3-EVI   Juan-ALL
     'Maria gives corn to Juan.'

     b. *Mariya-qa*   *sara-ta*   *qu-n-mi*   *Xwan-man-qa.*
     Maria-TOP   corn-ACC   give-3-EVI   Juan-ALL-TOP
     'Maria gives corn, to Juan.'

     c. *Mariya-qa*   *sara-ta-n*   *qu-n*   *Xwan-man.*
     Maria-TOP   corn-ACC-EVI   give-3   Juan-ALL
     'It is corn that Maria gives to Juan.'

     d. *Mariya-qa   *sara-ta*   *qu-n*   *Xwan-man-mi.*
     Maria-TOP   corn-ACC   give-3   Juan-ALL-EVI

Clause subordination is mostly marked through suffixes on the subordinate verb: nominalizers such as *-sqa* 'realized action' and *-na* 'unrealized action', or adverbial subordinators such as *-spa* 'same subject' and *-qti* 'different subject'. The subordinate clauses often precede the main verb, but this is not obligatory. As just noted, adverbial subordinators can also mark co-reference (using the subordinator *-spa*, as in (25) below) or disjoint reference (using the subordinator *-qti*, as in (11) below) of the subjects of the main and subordinate clauses.

     Sometimes, a lexical subordinator marks a subordinate or co-subordinate clause. I will return to this towards the end of this paper.

4   Basic Functions of *hina* 'like' in Southern Peruvian Quechua

In some of the dictionaries of the Southern Peruvian Quechua varieties, there are many entries for *hina* and derived forms, covering between two and three pages, with Lira (n.d.) being the most detailed source. Parker (1969, 15) reconstructs *hina* for Proto-Quechua with the meaning 'manner, condition', which I will take as the basic meaning and use of *hina*. In Ecuadorian Quechua,

264 MUYSKEN

hina has lost this nominal meaning, and functions mainly as a postposition, as in *warmi-shina* 'like a woman, woman-ish'.[3]

Table 7.1 presents a brief selection of the entries for *hina* in three dictionaries: Cusihuamán G. (1976), Lira (n.d.), and Herrero and Sánchez (1978), including some of the fixed expressions in which it occurs. Some specific meanings are listed in addition to the general key meaning of similarity mentioned by all authors. Cusihuamán G. (1976) and Lira (n.d.) are dictionaries of Cuzco Quechua (Peru), while Herrero and Sánchez (1978) is a dictionary of Cochabamba Quechua (Bolivia).

TABLE 7.1   *The entries for* hina *in three dictionaries; (-) marks when a particular usage is not found*

	Cusihuamán G. (1976, 55–6)	Lira (n.d., 78–80)	Herrero and Sánchez (1978, 394–5)
Predicative nominal *hina*	*en el mismo estado* [in the same state], *lo mismo* [the same]	*acostumbradamente* [customarily]	*desocupado* [unoccupied]
Fixed *hina-pura*	–	–	*igual ... u otro* [equal among each other]
Fixed *hina-ntin*	–	*todo entero* [entirely], *todo completo* [completely]	–
Adverb *hina*	*aproximadamente* [approximately], *igualmente* [equally]	–	*igual que* [equal to], *lo mismo que* [the same as], *tan ... como ...* [as ... as ...]
Postposition *hina*	*como* [like]	*en calidad de* [in the capacity of]	*como* [like]

---

3   I will return to the specificities of the form *shina* below.

	Cusihuamán G. (1976, 55–6)	Lira (n.d., 78–80)	Herrero and Sánchez (1978, 394–5)
Verb *hina-y*	*hacer o ser* (*así o asá*) [do or be like this or that]	–	–
Connector *hina-spa*	*y así* [and thus], *entonces* [then], *de esta manera* [in this way], *de ese modo* [in that fashion]	–	–
Adverb *hina-sti-n*	*todas partes* [(on) all sides], *en distintas direcciones* [in different directions]	–	–
Conjunction *hina*	–	*tan luego como* [as soon as], *al punto que* [at the point that]	–
Adverb *a-hina*	–	–	*ajina-lla-pi* 'cuando esto te cuento' [while I am telling this]
Adverb *u-hina*[4]	–	–	–
Fixed *kay hina*	–	–	*que es así, de esta manera o modo* [which is like this, in this way or fashion]

---

4 This entry, meaning 'in a different way', does not appear in any of the dictionaries, only in the data discussed in the paper. I have added it to emphasize this.

All authors agree that *hina* can function as a noun/adjective (i.e. a nominal element with predicative function), an adverb, a postposition taking a complement, and a verb taking the full range of inflections. I will illustrate these different uses in the next section with examples from Puno Quechua.

Notice that the postposition *hina* does not take the place of the case marker, necessarily, as shown in the following example from Cusihuamán (1976, 55):

(3) *Pisi-ta   hina-lla   apa-mu-nki.*
    little-ACC   LIKE-LIM   take-CIS-2SG
    'Bring just a little.'

A single case of *hina* used as a conjunction is found in Lira (n.d., 79), but combined with a suffixal subordinator, -*qti* 'different subject' (original spelling in example):

(4) *Hina-s*[5]   *hamu-kkti-ki...*
    LIKE-ADD   come-DS-2SG
    'As soon as you come, ...'

I will now turn to a description of the uses of *hina* in Puno Quechua and discuss its development.

5   Developments in the use of *hina* in the Quechua of Puno

I will illustrate the different uses of *hina*, starting with the predicative nominal, illustrated in (5):

(5) *Ka-chun   hina-lla!*
    COP-HORT.3SG   LIKE-LIM
    'Let it be like this!'

---

5 One reviewer wonders whether the -*s* in this and other examples should not be glossed as reportative, rather than additive. Note, however, that reportative -*s*/-*si* does not occur elsewhere in this corpus, and the example is not from a traditional narrative. Also -*s* in (4) is clearly not reportative. I assume -*s* to be a reduced form of -*pis*/-*pas*.

FROM NOMINAL PREDICATE TO DEICTIC CLAUSAL HIGHLIGHTER 267

The very frequent adverbial use is illustrated in (6) and (7), where *hina* is used
to refer back to an anterior situation in the preceding clause.

(6) *Chaqra-ta*   *allin-ta*   *ruwa-n-ku,*   *hina-lla-taq*
    field-ACC   good-ACC   make-3-PL   LIKE-LIM-EMP

    uywa-kuna-ta   *uywa-n-ku.*
    beast-PL-ACC   raise-3-PL
    'They work their fields well, and in the same way they raise their animals.'
    (YA20)

(7) *Llaki-sqa*   *llaki-sqa-lla*   *huk*   *sama*
    be.sad-NMLZ   be.sad-NMLZ-LIM   one   rest

    puri-yka-sha-rqa-ni.   *hina-n*   *huk*
    walk-INT-PROG-PST1-1SG   LIKE-EVI   one

    p'unchay   *kay*   *llaqta-pi*
    day   this   town-LOC

    livru-ta   *tari-ni.*
    $book-ACC   find-1SG
    'Very sadly I was walking around in this town one day of rest, and thus
    I find a book.' (YA14)

From this adverbial it is a small step to an initial clausal discourse connector,
where *hina* refers back to a situation in the discourse context. In this case it is
not the preceding coordinated clause, but an earlier sentence. In the previous
discourse for (8) a disease was described in the community, which then leads
to the situation in (8).

(8) *Hina-s*   *wawa-kuna-qa*   *huk-manta*   *huk*
    like-ADD   child-PL-TOP   one-ABL   one

    unqu-sqa   *ikhuri-n-ku.*
    fall.ill-NMLZ   turn.out-3-PL
    'Thus the children turn out to be ill one after the other.' (YA24)

Another very frequent use of *hina* is that of postposition, in an [NP P[like]]
construction, as in (9) and (10):

268   MUYSKEN

(9) *Hatun   ka-ni   tura-y   <u>hina.</u>*
    tall   COP-1SG   brother-1SG   LIKE
    'I am tall like my brother.'

(10) *Mama-y   <u>hina</u>   mana-n   wayk'u-q   ka-n-man-chu.*
     mother-1SG   LIKE   not-EVI   cook-AG   COP-3-POT-NEG
     'S/he could not cook like my mother.'

What is striking in Puno Quechua is the incorporation of an anaphoric element, as in (11)–(12):

(11) *A-<u>hina</u>   ka-qti-n-qa   kay   unu   phuhu   qhilli-chari.*
     DA-LIKE   COP-DS-3-TOP   this   water   spring   dirty-DUB
     'If it is like that, this water source is perhaps dirty.' (YA24)

(12) *A-<u>hina</u>-ta   astawan   allin-ta   kawsa-sun-man.*
     DA-LIKE-ACC   more   good-ACC   live-FUT.1PL-POT
     'Like this we could live better.'

It is not clear what the etymology is of this element *a-* in *a-hina*.[6] It could be sound-symbolically related to the vowel /a/ in the demonstratives *kay* 'this' and *chay* 'that', but this is pure speculation. Example (13) shows that the combination of *a-hina*, with an anaphoric element, may not be used as a modifier.

(13) *A-<u>hina</u>   papa-ta   ranti-rqa-ni.*
     DA-LIKE   potato-ACC   buy-PST1-1SG
     'I bought potatoes in this way.'
     *'I bought this class of potatoes.'

The latter meaning has to be conveyed periphrastically:

(14) *Ka-sqa-n   papa-ta   ranti-rqa-ni.*
     COP-NMLZ-3   potato-ACC   buy-PST1-1SG
     'I bought this (same) class of potatoes.'

---

6 One suggestion by a reviewer would be that it could be related to *así* in Spanish. However, Spanish influence on Quechua in this region is very limited; such partial morphological copying is rarely found elsewhere in Spanish-Quechua language contact. Manley (2007) suggests that the elongated [s] and the use of words containing [s] or [si] in some Andean Spanish variants in evidential contexts may be linked to Spanish *sí*, a possible semantic calque of the Quechua evidential *-mi*.

FROM NOMINAL PREDICATE TO DEICTIC CLAUSAL HIGHLIGHTER 269

While the combination *a-hina* was mentioned by Herrero and Sánchez (1978, 349) in a single example, the incorporation of an element with separate reference, resulting in *(h)u-hina*, has not been documented to my knowledge. It is illustrated in (15)–(17):

(15) *Lampa*   *iglisiya*   *hu-hina*   *Juliaca*   *iglisiya-manta.*
      Lampa $church   DD-LIKE   Juliaca $church-ABL
      'The church of Lampa is other than/different from the church of Juliaca.'
      (Ayaviri)

(16) *Qan*   *rura-nki*   *u-hina(-ta)*   *ladu-manta.*
      you   do-2SG   DD-LIKE-ACC $side-ABL
      'You do it differently.'

(17) *Qan*   *hu-hina(-ta)*   *rura-nki.*
      you   DD-LIKE-ACC   do-2SG
      'You do it differently.' (Ayaviri)

Possibly the etymology of the *(h)u-* in *(h)u-hina* is the numeral [hoq] /huq/ 'one, other'.[7]

Just like many other nominal roots, *hina* may also function as a verbal root, 'be like, do like'. A standard example would be (18), implying agentivity:

(18) *Ama*   *hina-y-chu!*
      PROH   LIKE-IMP-NEG
      'Don't act/be like that!'

In many cases, there is a stative meaning, as in (19):

(19) *Arí,*   *hina-n-mi*   /   *hina-n-puni.*
      yes   LIKE-3-EVI   LIKE-3-EMP
      'Yes, it is (always) like that.'

---

7   One reviewer notes that the pair *u-hina* / *a-hina* exhibits a striking parallelism with the Aymara demonstratives *aka* 'this' and *uka* 'that' and their derived forms *ak"ama* 'like this' and *uk"ama* 'like that'.

Example (20) shows that verbal *hina-* can sometimes be paraphrased as *hina ka-* 'be like this':[8]

(20) *Hina*   *ka-qti-n-qa,*   ...   /   *hina-qti-n-qa,*   ...
     LIKE   COP-DS-3-TOP   LIKE-DS-3-TOP
     'If it were like this, ...'

Interestingly, verbal *hina-* can also incorporate disjoint *u-* and anaphoric *a-*:

(21) *U-hina*   *ka-qti-n-qa,*   ...   /   *u-hina-qti-n-qa,*   ...
     DD-LIKE   COP-DS-3-TOP   DD-LIKE-DS-3-TOP
     'If it were differently, ...'

(22) *A-hina*   *ka-qti-n-qa,*   ...   /   *a-hina-qti-n-qa,*   ...
     DA-LIKE   COP-DS-3-TOP   DA-LIKE-DS-3-TOP
     'If it were like this, ...'

There is a very slight difference in meaning between (20) and (22), with a more specific situation implied in (22) than in (20), since *a-hina* is specifically anaphoric.

The contrast between (23) and (24) shows that verbal *hina-*, though agentive, cannot be transitive:

(23) * *Chay-ta*   *hina-sha-ni.*
       that-ACC   LIKE-PROG-1SG
       'I am doing that like this.'

(24) *Chay-ta*   *hina*   *rura-sha-ni.*
     that-ACC   LIKE   do-PROG-1SG
     'I am doing that like this.'

As mentioned by Cusihuamán (1976) (cf. table 7.1), the fixed expression *hina-spa* 'LIKE-SS' involving verbal *hina-* may function as a discourse connector:

(25) *P'inka-ku-rqa-ni*   *qhiswa*   *simi*
     shame-REFL-PST1-1SG   Quechua   language

     qhiswa   *simi*   *rima-y-ta-qa*
     Quechua   language   speak-INF-ACC-TOP

---

8 One reviewer notes that apparently, *hina ka-* is not simply a paraphrase of *hina-*, for *hina-* can also mean 'to act like that'(cf. example 18), whereas *hina ka-* cannot have that meaning.

FROM NOMINAL PREDICATE TO DEICTIC CLAUSAL HIGHLIGHTER 271

rima-y-ta,	*hina-spa-taq*
speak-INF-ACC	LIKE-SS-EMP

qunqa-ra-pu-sqa-ni.
forget-INT-BEN-PST2-1SG
'I felt ashamed of speaking Quechua, and being that way I forgot how to speak Quechua.' (YA21)

So far, the uses of *hina* in Southern Quechua/Puno Quechua correspond roughly to the wide range found in the literature for related varieties. I now turn to the innovations that characterize the varieties spoken in the Puno region, but that to my knowledge are not documented elsewhere. From being a postposition used with nouns, *hina* has developed into a clausal complementizer with nominalized clauses, and then to a postposition with finite clauses. It has also developed into a highlighter with adverbial (switch reference) clauses, and a highlighting complementizer with some finite clauses, as I will show in the examples (26) through (31) that follow.

The structure closest to one of an ordinary postposition is [IP-nominalizer P[like]], as in (26) and (27):

(26) | *Wayna* | *ka-sqa-n* | *hina-n,* | *kunan-pis* | *hina-lla-taq.* |
|---|---|---|---|---|
| boy | COP-NMLZ-3 | LIKE-EVI | now-ADD | LIKE-LIM-EMP |

'The way he was as a boy, like that he is now as well.'

(27) | *Pay* | *ka-sqa-n* | *hina* | *ñuqa-pis* |
|---|---|---|---|
| 3SG.PRO | COP-NMLZ-3 | LIKE | 1SG.PRO-ADD |

ka-y-ta	*muna-yman.*
COP-INF-ACC	want-POT.1SG

'I would like to be like s/he is.'

Similar to these cases, but with an event rather than a predicate as the element in the scope of the postposition, is (28):

(28) | *Qhawari-sqa-yku* | *hina,* | *Huninsaya* | *ayllu* |
|---|---|---|---|
| look-NMLZ-1PL | LIKE | Huninsaya | ayllu |

ayllu-kuna-pas	*ñawpaq-man*	*puri-ri-n-ku.*
ayllu-PL-ADD	ahead-ALL	walk-INC-3-PL

Hanansaya	*ayllu*	*wak*
Hanansaya	ayllu	other

'As we have seen, the ayllu Huninsaya, the ayllu Hanansaya, and the other ayllus are moving forward.' (YA21)

While examples (26)–(28) involved a case-less nominalized clause, *hina* also occurs with fully inflected main tense clauses, in the structure [IP P/C[like]], as in (29)–(31):

(29)
Kay	*yacha-y*	*wasi*	*qaylla*
this	know-INF	house	near

hina	*wawa-kuna-pas*	*uywa-kuna-pas*
LIKE	child-PL-ADD	beast-PL-ADD

unu	*phuhu-manta-qa*	*ni-sha-rqa-nchis*
water	spring-ABL-TOP	say-PROG-PST1-1PL.INCL

ka-sqa-lla-n-manta-s	*unu-ta*	*uha-n-ku.*
COP-NMLZ-LIM-3-ABL-ADD	water-ACC	drink-3-PL

'This school is very close to a water well, like we said, and both children and animals drink the water.' (YA24)

(30)
Irqi-lla	*ka-rqa-nki*	*hina*	*ka-q-lla*	*ka-sha-nki.*
boy-LIM	COP-PST1-2SG	LIKE	COP-AG-LIM	COP-PROG-2SG

'The way you were as a little boy, that same way you are now.'

(31)
T'impu-ta	*haywari-n-ku*	*hina*	*sinchi*	*sumaq-mi.*
timpu-ACC	serve-3-PL	LIKE	very	good-EVI

'The way they serve the timpu here is very good.'

In all cases (5)–(31) listed so far for Puno Quechua, the basic meaning of *hina* involving sameness or similarity is maintained. However, in a number of cases meanings and uses are encountered which depart from that of expressing similarity. A first case involves *hina* as an enumerative nominal conjunction. In (32) it is used with NPs without case marking:

FROM NOMINAL PREDICATE TO DEICTIC CLAUSAL HIGHLIGHTER   273

(32)   *Yanamayu*   *runa-kuna*   *urqu-kuna-pi*   *hina*   *papa*
      Yanamayu   people-PL   mountain-PL-LOC   LIKE   potato

      <u>*hina*</u>   *isañu*   <u>*hina*</u>   *siwara*   <u>*hina*</u>
      LIKE   isaño   LIKE   barley   LIKE

      <u>*hina*</u>   *uqa*   <u>*hina*</u>   *illaku*
      LIKE   oca   LIKE   illaco

      kiwna   *allin-ta*   *uri-chi-n-ku*
      quinoa   good-ACC   grow-CAUS-3-PL
      'The people of Yanamayu grow potatoes, ocas, illaco, isaño, barley, and quinoa in the mountains, and very well.' (YA 20)

However, it can also occur with case-marked NPs:

(33)   *Wawa-kuna-qa*   <u>*hina*</u>   *simi-n-ta*   <u>*hina*</u>
      child-PL-TOP   LIKE   mouth-3-ACC   LIKE

      siki-n-ta-s   *puri-chi-pu-n-ku.*
      back.side-3-ACC-ADD   run-CAUS-BEN-3-PL
      'The children let it run through their mouth as well as their backside.' (YA25)

(34)   <u>*Hina*</u>   *papa-ta*   <u>*hina*</u>   *lisas[9]-ta*   <u>*hina*</u>   *uka-ta*   *tarpu-ni.*
      like   potato-ACC   LIKE $lisa-ACC   LIKE   oca-ACC   sow-1SG
      'I sow potato on one side, lisa on another, and oca on yet another.'

What examples (32)–(34) have in common is that the enumerated NPs are part of a scenario in similar ways. Enumeration where this similarity is not implied is less well accepted, as in (35), where the two, Juan and Maria, do not form a natural pair:

(35)   ??   <u>*Hina*</u>   *Xwan-ta*   <u>*hina*</u>   *Mariya-ta*   *riku-rqa-ni.*
           LIKE   Juan-ACC   LIKE   Maria-ACC   see-PST1-1SG
           'I saw Juan and Maria.'

---

9   The Spanish adjective *lisa* is borrowed as a plural noun (from *papas lisas* 'smooth potatoes').

Thus the first meaning extension of *hina* is from direct similarity to having a similar role in a scenario as another element, and hence enumeration.

The second extension of *hina* was already mentioned by Lira (n.d.) and involves temporal identity or similarity, and hence semi-simultaneity: 'as soon as'. Examples (36)–(38) illustrate this semi-simultaneity with fully inflected Main Tense subordinate clauses:

(36) *Qulqi-ta*   *gana-saq*   *<u>hina</u>*   *chhika-raq*
money-ACC $earn-FUT.1SG   LIKE   just-CONT

rura-saq   *wasi-ta.*
make-FUT.1SG   house-ACC
'If I will earn money, only then will I build a house.'

(37) *Chhika-raq*   *hamu-sha-q*   *ka-ni*   *<u>hina</u>,*
just-CONT   come-PROG-AG   COP-1SG   LIKE

mana *kay* *ayllu-pi* *yacha-ku-q-chu* *ka-ni.*
not this village-LOC know-REFL-AG-NEG COP-1SG
'When I was just arriving, I did not feel at home in this village.'

(38) *Yanamayu yacha-y* *wasi-ta* *tata* *mama* *hunu-ku-n-ku*
Yanamayu know-INF house-ACC father mother gather-REFL-3-PL

<u>hina</u>-s *tata* *Mayta-qa* *a-<u>hina</u>-ta* *rima-n*
LIKE-ADD father Mayta-TOP DA-LIKE-ACC speak-3
'When the parents gather in the Yanamayu school, father Mayta talks like this.' (YA26)

While in (36) and (37) the subjects of the main and subordinate clause are identical (the proximate construction), in (38) they are disjoint (the obviative construction).

In the next example, (39), the subordinate clause is inflected with the proximate (same subject) subordinator -*spa*, in the structure [IP-*spa* C[like][prox]]:

(39) *Hamu-spa* *<u>hina</u>* *llank'a-saq.*
come-SS LIKE work-FUT.1SG
'When I come, I will work.'

FROM NOMINAL PREDICATE TO DEICTIC CLAUSAL HIGHLIGHTER   275

However, there can also be an inflected verb in this construction:

(40) *Qulqi-ta   gana-nqa   hina-s   wasi-ta   rura-nqa.*
     money-ACC $earn-FUT.3SG   LIKE-HS   house-ACC   make-FUT.3SG
     'When he will earn money, they say he will build a house.'

In a similar way, *hina* can combine with the disjoint subject (obviative) subordinator *-qti*, in the structure [IP-*qti* C[like][obv]]:

(41) *Hamu-qti-n   hina   mikhu-sun.*
     come-DS-3   LIKE   eat-FUT.1PL
     'We will eat when he comes.'

However, it is not clear that *hina* always implies semi-simultaneity of the type
'as soon as'. In the following [IP C[like][prox]] structure, it seems like temporal
coincidence:

(42) *Lima-ta   ri-ni   hina   qhapaq   ka-rqa-ni.*
     Lima-ACC   go-1SG   LIKE   rich   COP-PST1-1SG
     'When I went to Lima I was rich.'

The same holds in the obviative counterpart, [IP C[like][obv]]:

(43) *Yanamayu   ayllu-ta   karu-manta   qhawari-nchis   hina-qa,   yuraq*
     Yanamayu   ayllu-ACC   far-ABL   see-1PL.INCL   LIKE-TOP   white

     kapilla-n   riku-ku-n.
     $chapel-EVI see-REFL-3
     'When we watch Yanamayu ayllu from afar, the white chapel is seen.'
     (YA 19)

Sometimes the main clause is absent:

(44) *Tata   kura   phista   p'unchay   hamu-n   hina-lla.*
     father $priest $feast   day   come-3   LIKE-LIM
     'Only when the priest comes to the fiestas.'

The simultaneous reading may come close to a structure where a temporal
relative interpretation is given, [IP C[like][relative]], as in (45):

(45) *Chay   p'unchay   chiri-n   <u>hina</u>   ka-rqa-n   dumingu.*
      that   day   be.cold-3   LIKE   COP-PST1-3 $Sunday
      'That day that it was cold was Sunday.'

Another clausal particle *-pas/-pis* is glossed as 'additive' since that may be its basic meaning, but it often has an indefinite meaning as well.[10] It may appear either on *hina*, as in (46), or on an element in the subordinate clause, as in (47):

(46) *Qulqi-ta   gana-saq   <u>hina</u>-pas,   ...*
      money-ACC $earn-FUT.1SG   LIKE-ADD
      'Although I will earn a lot of money, ...'

(47) *Para-chun-<u>pis</u>   <u>hina</u>   llank'a-lla-saq.*
      rain-HORT.3SG-ADD   LIKE   work-LIM-FUT.1SG
      'Even if it rains I will work.'

In these cases, *-pas/-pis* helps to create a contrast between the two clauses; in (47) the condition contrasts with the resulting statement. The fact that the clausal particle can appear inside of the clause marked with *hina* suggests that the latter is not a true subordinator.

The same conclusion can be drawn from cases where *hina* is combined with Spanish borrowing *si* 'if', in a [C IP C[like][obv]] structure:

(48) *<u>Si</u>-chus   chiri-sha-n   <u>hina</u>   mana   hamu-saq-chu.*
      $if-DUB   be.cold-PROG-3   LIKE   not   come-FUT.1SG-NEG
      'If it is cold I will not come.'

The historical development of *hina* as can be reconstructed from the texts and grammars since 1560 still needs to be charted. Likewise, a cross-linguistic, pan-Quechuan survey still needs to be carried out. However, my impression is that in no other language in the family does *hina* have the same range of meanings.

6 Comparing *hina* to Cuzco Quechua *chay(qa)*

The extension of *hina* to a role as deictic clausal highlighter needs to be seen in the light of overall Quechua co-subordination patterns. First of all, it should be noted that sometimes coordinate structures, without any overt subordination marking, will get a subordinate interpretation:

---

10   In the same way, Dutch *ook* / German *auch* can be both additive and indefinite.

FROM NOMINAL PREDICATE TO DEICTIC CLAUSAL HIGHLIGHTER

(49) *Muna-y-pis   ka-y,   mana qan-wan kasara-ku-y-man-chu.*
    love-INF-ADD COP-INF not   you-with marry-REFL-1SG-POT-NEG
    'Even if you were lovely, I would not marry you.'

Here the first conjunct is marked infinitive, and the second has potential or irrealis mood.

Second, particularly in the southern Quechua varieties, question words may introduce embedded questions without nominalization marking on the embedded verb, as in (50):

(50) *Yacha-nki-chu   <u>hayk'aq</u>   chaya-mu-nqa   mama-y?*
    know-2SG-Q   when   arrive-CIS-FUT.3SG   mother-1SG
    'Do you know when my mother will arrive?'

The 'embedded' question word may carry a discourse marker suggestive of main clause status:

(51) *Yacha-nki-chu   <u>hayk'aq-chus</u>   chaya-mu-nqa   mama-y?*
    know-2SG-Q   when-DUB   arrive-CIS-FUT.3SG   mother-1SG
    'Do you know when my mother may arrive?'

Importantly, however, in the southern varieties, the distal demonstrative *chay* 'that' is frequently used as a clause linker. A first use, common in all Quechua varieties, is as the introducer of a second clause, here combined with the case marker or suffixal postposition *-rayku*:

(52) *Sinchi-ta   qasa-n,   <u>chay-rayku</u>   mana*
    strong-ACC   freeze-3   that-CAUS   not

    allin-ta-chu .   qaspi-sun.
    good-ACC-NEG   harvest-FUT.1PL
    'It freezes hard, and therefore we will not harvest well.'

However, *chay* also occurs frequently as a deictic clausal highlighter or conditional marker in post-IP position, just like *hina,* see (53)–(54):

(53) [*Hamu-nki   <u>chay</u>*]   *kusi-ku-saq.*
    come-2SG   that   happy-REFL-FUT.1SG
    'If you come I will be happy.'

(54) [*Para-sha-n* <u>*chay*</u>] *mana* *hamu-ni-chu.*
rain-PROG-3 that not come-1SG-NEG
'If it rains I do not come.'

The conjunction *chay* can also be an alternative (55b) to nominalization (55a) in factive complements, both meaning 'I know that Juan has built a house.'

(55) a. *Yacha-ni* *Xwan* *wasi-ta* *rura-<u>sqa-n-ta.</u>*
know-1SG Juan house-ACC make-NMLZ-3-ACC

b. *Yacha-ni* *Xwan* *wasi-ta* *rura-rqa-n* <u>*chay-ta.*</u>
know-1SG Juan house-ACC make-PST1-3 that-ACC

c. * *Yacha-ni* *Xwan* *wasi-ta* *rura-rqa-n* *hina-ta.*
know-1SG Juan house-ACC make-PST1-3 LIKE-ACC

Notice that *hina* cannot be used in this context, as shown in (55c). *Hina* in Puno Quechua has the meaning of *chay* in Southern Quechua (among other meanings). *Chay* exists in Puno Quechua, but not with the same meanings as in Cuzco Quechua, and many of its uses have been taken over by *hina*.[11]

7   Possible Aymara Influence

Given the strong Aymaran presence in the Puno area, it would be natural to explore possible Aymaran influence on the development of *hina*. Currently, Aymara speakers are concentrated in the border zone between Peru and Bolivia (with a large Aymara-speaking group, of over one million speakers, crossing the border on the Bolivian altiplano), and in pockets in the area between Puno and Arequipa. However, it is assumed that in earlier times, the Puno area was Aymara speaking. The extent and degree of Aymara-Quechua bilingualism in the border region is not known, and merits further investigation. Information about the grammar of Aymara is less easily accessible than that about Quechua, and therefore I have to be somewhat careful with claims about possible links with Aymara.

Cerrón (2000, 211) discusses the comparative particle *-hama*, which functions as a suffix in expressions such as *qala-hama* 'like a stone', and hypothetically postulates *-hamu* as the Proto-Aymaran form. There is no suggestion that

---

11   We do not know, however, how the varieties are related historically.

FROM NOMINAL PREDICATE TO DEICTIC CLAUSAL HIGHLIGHTER 279

-hamu/-hama has other uses. An example from Bolivian Aymara of this form (spelled *-jama* in the source text but having undergone vowel reduction) is (56) (Gallego 1994, 268):

(56) *Pedro-x   Pabl-jam   suma-wa.*
     Pedro-TOP   Pablo-LIKE   good-EVI
     'Pedro is good like/just as Pablo.'

This form also occurs in a compound expression (Gallego 1994, 49):

(57) *kun-jama-(ru-)-ti-x*
     what-LIKE-ALL-Q-TOP
     'just like ...'

The most explicit treatment of subordination is Dedenbach-Salazar Sáenz and de Dios Yapita (1994). Two examples in their description may be relevant. First of all, they draw attention to the use of the demonstratives *uka* 'that (distal)' and *uk^ha* (with an aspirated pronunciation) 'that (distal) so much' as a subordinator and suggest that the use of Quechua *chay* 'that (distal)' as a subordinator may derive from this form (1994, 148). This is plausible given the fact that the territory of the Quechua varieties that use *chay* as a subordinator— Cuzco, Puno, Bolivia—coincides with the territory where Aymara is or was spoken. The following are some examples of the use of *uka* in this way (Gallego 1994, 292):

(58) *Tiempo-niya   uka-xa,   llamayu-ñ   yant'a-:.*
     $time-POSS   that-TOP   harvest-INF.ACC   try-FUT.1SG
     'If I (will) have time, I will try to harvest.'

(59) *Domingö-n   uka-xa,   fiesta-ru-w   sara-:.*
     $Sunday-LOC   that-TOP $fiesta-ALL-EVI   go-FUT.1SG
     'If it were Sunday, I would go to the party.'

The subordinator *uka* may also be combined with *-jama* (Gallego 1994, 303):

(60) *Juma-x   mun-k-ta   uk-jama-w   lura-:.*
     you-TOP   want-PROG-2SG   that-LIKE-EVI   do.-FUT.1SG
     'I will do it like you want.'

The other possibly relevant point is the use of *-sina* as a clausal subordinator in Aymara, which is used when the subject of the main and subordinating clause are identical just like Quechua *-spa*. Of course, *-sina* is not *hina*, but the two fricatives are related to each other in Quechua. The form *hina* appears as *shina* in Ecuadorian Quechua (through a process of more general though not quite regular sound changes). It is not impossible that the formal similarity to *-sina* has inspired the extension of *hina* to a subordinator in the clausal domain. However, *shina* does not have the function of subordinator in Ecuadorian Quechua; it is only used as a nominal predicate, adverb, and postposition.[12]

There is also a separate element *ina* (Gallego 1994, 111) in Aymara, with a whole range of contradictory meanings, both positive and negative: 'very, no/without/nothing, perhaps/never, inefficiently/without trying, enough'. An example would be (61) (Gallego 1994, 112):

(61) *Qullqi-x   ina-w   bolsillu-xa-n   utj-itu.*
      money-TOP   enough-EVI $pocket-1SG.POSS-LOC   be-3SG.SUBJ>1SG.OBJ
      'I have enough money in my pocket.'

Clearly this form *ina* merits further investigation, but the link with Quechua *hina*, if any, is far from clear, also because it occupies a different position in the sentence. Quechua *hina* as a clausal highlighter typically occurs in final or initial position, while this form occurs after the initial topic in (61).

In sum, as far as I can tell, there is no direct parallel to *hina* in Aymara with the same range of meanings and uses, but there is the possibility of indirect influence through the presence of *-sina*. The use of *chay* as a subordinator in Southern Quechua varieties has a much more direct source of inspiration in Aymara *uka*.

8   Conclusions: The Map of *hina*

In conclusion, we can state that the already polyfunctional form *hina* has increased its range of meanings as a deictic clausal highlighter extensively in Puno Quechua.

---

12   One reviewer notes that the form *hina* appears as *china* in Southern Quechua I, and argues that a relation with the distal demonstrative *chay* 'that' is likely.

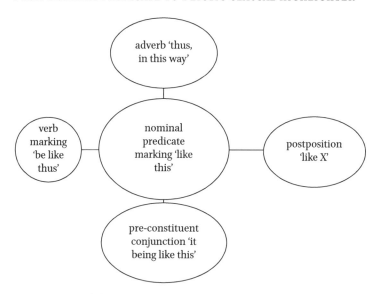

FIGURE 7.3 *Radial structure model for* hina

Returning to the grammaticalization debate regarding English 'like' at the beginning of this paper, I conclude that there is no absolute directional change with absolute semantic change. All original meanings are preserved, as far as I can see (and co-exist). Nonetheless, the meanings of *hina* need to be modeled in a complex network with several links in the chain. In the first instance, the predicate nominal could develop radially in a number of directions, as portrayed in figure 7.3.

In all instances, the original meaning remains, as illustrated in (62).

(62) a. nominal > adverb > conjunction
   b. nominal > postposition > incorporated postposition
   c. nominal > postposition > postposition with nominalized clauses > similarity complementizer with main clauses > temporal adverbial complementizer with main clauses
   d. nominal > verb > deverbal conjunction
   e. nominal > enumerative conjunction

Radiality (a network of meanings rather than a meaning change) may be considered as being linked to pluri-directionality: since the original meaning is preserved, various developments remain possible.

A question that remains, of course, is why 'like' has undergone such very different developments in English versus Quechua. Recall that in English the uses of 'like' went mostly from adposition to conjunction to quotative and hedge-marker. In the literature on English, these developments are discussed as natural extensions. We find similar developments in other European languages. However, if they are so natural, why did they not occur in Quechua?[13] I will discuss several possibilities regarding the diverging developments in English and Quechua.

I do not know of detailed studies of multi-functionality in the Quechua lexicon (this is in fact a worthwhile research project), but many nominals in Quechua can also function as verbs. This possibility also explains the ease with which *hina* could be verbalized. Examples include (Cerrón-Palomino 1994, 79):

(63) a. *t'ika*   'flower'   *t'ika-*   'flourish'
     b. *pirqa*   'wall'   *pirqa-*   'build a wall'
     c. *ñawi*   'eye'   *ñawi-*   'look'
     d. *q'uñi*   'warm'   *q'uñi-*   'heat'

Thus *hina* as a verb has acquired new uses, and this was subsequently the basis for its use as a verbal conjunction and discourse linker.

In terms of morphological possibilities, as far as I am aware, English 'like' cannot be inflected. In contrast, as we have seen, *hina* can carry case marking, limitative suffixes, as well as verbal person and subordination marking. Interestingly enough, *hina* cannot carry nominal personal inflection, as far as I have seen, as shown in (64a). However, it is possible to have a nominal person marker after a subordinator when it is used as a verb, as in (64b), showing there is no absolute restriction.

(64) a. * *hina-yki*
        LIKE-2SG
        'like you', 'your resemblance', ...

     b.   *hina-qti-yki*
        LIKE-DS-2SG
        'if you are like this'

---

13   A systematic cross-linguistic survey of different grammaticalization developments of 'like' has not been carried out, to my knowledge, although Fleischmann and Yaguello (2004) are a step in that direction. Of course Spanish *como* has a wide range of meanings, including 'like', 'as', and 'since'. In Chilean Spanish, *igual* is also used as a discourse marker (San Martin 2004–5), and in French *genre* has functions somewhat similar to 'like'.

FROM NOMINAL PREDICATE TO DEICTIC CLAUSAL HIGHLIGHTER

The ungrammaticality of (64a) requires further study, and a deeper understanding of nominal person marking, since for all intents and purposes *hina* is nominal in nature. The ungrammaticality of (64a) is all the more surprising since we do have forms such as (65):

(65) *sapa-yki*
      alone-2SG
      'you alone'

Here another relational nominal is felicitously used with person marking.

Possibly one of the reasons that *hina* did not develop into a quotative, as in English, is that there is a productive semi-grammaticalized quotative marker already available in Quechua, namely *ni-spa* [say-SS] 'saying'.[14]

One of the things that likewise may have extended the range of possibilities for *hina* is its positioning possibilities. The element 'like' in English necessarily precedes its complement, except in compound phrases such as 'the mayor of New York-like' and possibly in colloquial expressions such as 'that is really interesting, like', where 'like' functions like a post-clausal hedge marker. The element *hina* has developed pre-complement [X __] uses in addition to its post-complement functions [__X].

Altogether, it is striking that the form *hina* has undergone so many developments, as has English 'like', but in different semantic and pragmatic directions: not so much a hedge-marker and a quotative as a deictic clausal linker. The fact that many of the Quechua speakers involved may have been bilingual with Aymara may have stimulated this development, but the functional expansion of *hina* from a postposition to a clausal highlighter had its own logic, as I have tried to argue in this paper.

Acknowledgements

This paper was presented originally in a very different form in Spanish at the International Conference of Americanists at the Free University Amsterdam in 1988, under the title *Historia de hina*, inspired by the title of Vargas Llosa's novel *Historia de Mayta*. I am grateful to my colleagues present at that meeting, particularly Willem Adelaar, and to the people of Lampa (Puno, Peru) for their

---

14   In some other South American languages, such as Kwaza, there are grammaticalized quotatives as well (van der Voort 2002).

contributions and reflections on the special features of Quechua. I also want to thank both of the editors, Isabelle Buchstaller, and three anonymous readers for very helpful comments.

Appendix A

ABL	ablative	INT	intensifier
ACC	accusative	LIM	limitative
ADD	additive	LOC	locative
AG	agentive	NEG	negation
ALL	allative	NMLZ	nominalizer
BEN	benefactive	PST1	past
CAUS	causative	PST2	perfective
CIS	cislocative	PL	plural
CONT	continuative	PL.INCL	inclusive plural
COP	copula	POSS	possessive
DA	deictic anaphoric	POT	potential
DD	deictic disjoint	PRO	pronoun
LIM	limitative	PROG	progressive
DS	different subject	PROH	prohibitive
DUB	dubitative	PROX	proximate
EMP	emphatic	Q	question word
EVI	evidential	REFL	reflexive
FUT	future	SG	singular
HORT	hortative	SS	same subject
HS	hearsay	TOP	topic
IMP	imperative	1,2,3	first, ... person
INC	incoative	$	loan word
INF	infinitive		

Bibliography

Adelaar, Willem F.H., and Pieter C. Muysken. 2004. *The Languages of the Andes*. Cambridge University Press.

Buchstaller, Isabelle. 2004. The Sociolinguistic Constraints on the Quotative System— US English and British English Compared. Unpublished PhD diss., University of Edinburgh.

Büttner, Marie-Magdaleine, Cointet, Françoise, and Nonato R. Chuquimamani Valer. 1984. *Yanamayu Ayllu 1. Ahinata astawan allinta kawsasunman*. Puno. Cuzco: Centro de estudios rurales andinos 'Bartolomé de las Casas'.

Cerrón Palomino, Rodolfo. 1994. *Quechumara: Estructuras paralelas de las lenguas quechua y aimara*. La Paz: Centro de Investigación del Campesinado (CIPCA).

———. 2000. *Lingüística Aimara*. Lima/Cuzco: Centro de Estudios Andinos 'Bartolomé de las Casas'.

Cusihuamán G., Antonio. 1976. *Diccionario Quechua Cuzco-Collao*. Lima, Peru: Ministerio de Educación/Instituto de Estudios Peruanos.

Dedenbach-Salazar Sáenz, Sabine, and Juan de Dios Yapita. 1994. "Las oraciones compuestas en Aymara—aproximaciones para su comprensión y su estudio." In *Language in the Andes*, edited by Peter Cole, Gabriela Hermon and Mario Daniel Martín, 126–150. Newark, Delaware: Latin American Studies Program.

Fleischman, Suzanne and Marina Yaguello. 2004. "Discourse markers across languages. Evidence from English and French." In *Discourse Across Languages and Cultures*, edited by Carol Lynn Moder and Aida Martinovic-Zic, 129–148. Amsterdam: Benjamins.

Gallego, Saturnino fsc. (1994). *Kisimira 1—Gramática viva de la lengua aymara*. La Paz: Bruño/hisbol.

Herrero, Joaquín S.J. and Federico Sánchez de Lozada. 1978. *Método práctico para la enseñanza y aprendizaje de la lengua quechua*. Cochabamba, Bolivia: Imprenta Visión.

Lakoff, George. 1987. *Women, fire, and dangerous things: what categories reveal about the mind*. Chicago: University of Chicago Press.

Lira, Jorge A. n.d. [1941, 1988]. *Breve diccionario kkechuwa español*. Cuzco, Peru: Edición popular.

Manley, Marilyn S. 2007. "Cross-linguistic influence of the Cuzco Quechua epistemic system on Andean Spanish." In *Spanish in Contact: Policy, Social and Linguistic Inquiries*, edited by Kim Potowski and Richard Cameron, 191–209. Philadelphia, Pennsylvania: John Benjamins Publishing Company.

Meehan, Teresa. 1991. "It's Like, 'What's Happening in the Evolution of Like?': A Theory of Grammaticalization." *Kansas Working Papers in Linguistics* 16: 37–52.

Muysken, Pieter. 1985. Field notes, Lampa, Peru.

———. 1995. "Focus in Quechua." In *Discourse-Configurational Languages*, edited by Katalin E. Kiss, 375–393. New York: Oxford University Press.

Parker, Gary J. 1969. "Comparative Quechua Phonology and Grammar III: Proto-Quechua Lexicon." *Hawaii Working Papers in Linguistics* 1(4): 1–61.

Romaine, Suzanne, and Deborah Lange. 1991. "The Use of *like* as a Marker of Reported Speech and Thought: A Case of Grammaticalization in Progress." *American Speech* 66(3): 227–279.

San Martín, Abelardo. 2004–2005. "*Igual* como marcador discursivo en el habla de Santiago de Chile: función pragmática-discursiva y estratificación social de su empleo." *Boletín de Filología* 40: 201–232.

Traugott, Elizabeth C. 1997. "The role of the development of discourse markers in a theory of grammaticalization." Paper originally presented at ICHL XII, Manchester 1995.

Voort, Hein van der. 2002. "The quotative construction in Kwaza and its (de-)grammaticalisation." In *Current Studies on South American Languages* [Indigenous Languages of Latin America, 3, edited by Mily Crevels, Simon van de Kerke, Sérgio Meira and Hein van der Voort, 307–328. Leiden: Research School of Asian, African, and Amerindian Studies (CNWS).

CHAPTER 8

Right Peripheral Domains, Deixis and Information Structure in Southern Quechua*

Liliana Sánchez

1 Introduction

In many languages, the linguistic expression of information structure (new, old, shared information and the current topic of discourse in a sentence) may be grammaticalized at the phonology/syntax interface (Donati and Nespor 2003, Nespor and Vogel 1986, Pereltsvaig 2004, Selkirk 1984, Zubizarreta 1998), at the syntax component (Horvath 1986, Vallduvi 1995), or at the syntax/morphology interface (Cinque 1999, Sánchez 2010, Speas 2004). In Southern Quechua varieties spoken in Peru, there are overt morphological markers that indicate whether a constituent is a main topic in discourse, new information (focus) and/or provides the hearer with the source of information (direct evidence or hearsay), a grammatical characteristic also known as evidentiality. These markers appear mostly on constituents at the left edge of sentences (Cerrón Palomino 1987, Muysken 1995, Sánchez 2010) and very rarely on constituents at the right edge of sentences (Sánchez 2010). In this paper, I analyze the information status and syntactic status of right margin or right dislocated constituents (RDCs) in Southern Quechua, a verb final language characterized by a canonical Subject Object Verb (SOV) word order. I also analyze the deictic nature of RDCs in discourse.

The following examples illustrate two types of sentences in Southern Quechua: (1) a sentence with canonical SOV word order and (2) one with a left margin, morphologically marked constituent and an RDC.[1]

Canonical SOV sentence:

---

* I use the term Southern Quechua to refer to the Quechua varieties spoken in the Southern Andes of Peru that belong to the Quechua II subgroup (Torero 1964).
1 Following Sánchez (2010) I use PST.REP and PST.ATT for the reportative past and the attested past respectively to indicate that these are tenses that express syncretism in tense and evidentiality values.

© KONINKLIJKE BRILL NV, LEIDEN, 2015 | DOI 10.1163/9789004290105_009

(1) *Mariya*   *papa-ta*   *ranti-chka-n.*[2]
     Maria   potato-ACC   buy-PROG-3
     'Maria is buying potatoes.'
     (Sánchez 2010, 13)

Sentence with left and right margin constituents:

(2) *Hina*   *chay-si*   *rima-paya-sqa*   [*pichinku-cha-ta*].[3]
     like   that-INDEV.FOC   talk-ITER-PST.REP   bird-DIM-ACC
     'That way (they say) (she) talked to the birdy.'
     (Sánchez 2010, 185)

In sentence (1), no constituent is morphologically marked as a topic, as focus or as having hearsay or direct evidentiality values. In sentence (2), the constituent *chay-si* 'that way' at the left margin of the sentence, namely outside the SOV domain, is marked with the suffix -*si* that has a focus and a second hand or reportative information interpretation. The constituent *pichinkuchata* 'the birdy' appears in a postverbal position at the right margin of the sentence and also outside the SOV domain. Notice that it is not morphologically marked to indicate its information status as the topic of discourse or as new information.

In Sánchez (2010), the issue of the discourse role of these RDCs was raised and the hypothesis was put forth that, while left margin constituents are morphologically marked because in Quechua there is a high degree of grammaticalization of discourse and speaker-oriented aspects of the sentence such as topic, focus and evidentiality, right margin constituents are not morphologically marked because they do not fulfill those specific grammaticalized discourse functions. Instead, they serve the functions of disambiguating between potentially competing topics or referring to a previously mentioned element that is not the main topic of discourse. In order to find further evidence for that initial proposal and to develop a better understanding of the types of RDCs found in Quechua, in this paper I explore the following research questions:

---

2 The spelling in this chapter follows the standardization efforts proposed in Cerrón-Palomino (1994). Cerrón-Palomino proposes a more conservative approach to Quechua spelling using the form -*chka* in writing for the progressive suffix, which is pronounced differently across Southern varieties.

3 Throughout the paper, right dislocated constituents will appear bracketed.

1. What types of constituents (subjects, direct/indirect/oblique objects, adverbs) appear as morphologically unmarked RDCs in Quechua?[4]
2. What is their interpretation in discourse?

Before I present some background information on the distinction between the left and right peripheries of sentences across languages, I would like to sketch some of the main syntactic assumptions I make. I assume a modular approach to language, one in which syntax is independent from phonological expression or Phonological Form (PF) (Chomsky 2000). These two levels may interact but are, in principle, independent from each other. Furthermore, I assume a syntactic analysis of sentences according to which verbs project into Verb Phrases (VPs) that contain their arguments. These are mostly Determiner Phrases or Noun Phrases (DPs) that have the grammatical functions of subjects, direct objects or indirect objects. VPs may also include non-argumental phrases such as DPs that are locative expressions or benefactive expressions. I also assume the projection of an Inflectional or Tense Phrase (IP or TP) to be the equivalent of the main sentence that has a canonical SOV word order in Quechua, as in (1). In addition to an IP projection, I assume a Complementizer Phrase (CP), which is the highest projection.[5] Cross-linguistically, the CP projection is known to host constituents with the information status of focus (new information), topic (old information or theme of discourse) and/or evidentiality (Cinque 1999, Rizzi 1997). The CP area is also known as the left periphery (Rizzi 1997). Following Sánchez (2010), I assume that constituents such as *Hina chaysi* 'that way (they say)' in (2) are on the left periphery or CP area in Quechua. Notice that this constituent is synchretically marked for focus and reportative evidentiality.[6] In the view I adopt here, I follow Sánchez (2010) in assuming that these markers are the morphological expression of a basic syntactic operation, Agree (Chomsky 2008), that takes place in the left periphery of Southern Quechua between a Focus feature and a left peripheral constituent.[7] This operation takes place with focus and evidentiality, topic or other speaker-oriented features and generates left margin constituents. I also assume that

---

4 I assume that verbs select internal and external arguments. I will use the term subject to refer to external arguments and direct object and indirect object to refer to internal arguments. Other arguments that are not selected by the verb will be labeled oblique objects. These include locatives and benefactives, among others.
5 For a detailed presentation of these standard assumptions, see Carnie (2013).
6 Not all sentences in Quechua have left peripheral constituents marked for topic, focus or evidentiality.
7 The basic syntactic operations are Merge and Agree (Chomsky 2008).

material to the right of the verb, such as *pichinkuchata* 'little birdy' in (2), is adjoined to the right of the TP projection and is dislocated from its original VP internal position.

Having sketched my syntactic assumptions, I proceed now to provide the context of previous research on the left and right margins. The relationship between information structure and marginal or peripheral positions in a sentence has been abundantly explored for the left periphery in null subject SVO languages, such as Italian (Cinque 1990, Rizzi 1997), and to some extent for SOV languages in subordinate clauses, such as German (Finselow and Lenertová 2011). However, the right periphery in canonical SOV languages has been less explored than the left periphery in languages such as Dutch (assumed to be underlyingly SOV by Barbiers 2000) or Tamil (Herring 1994), and its contribution to information structure and discourse coherence has not been analyzed in depth, especially in null subject languages. Even less analyzed has been the deictic nature of the right margin material.

In this paper, I propose that RDCs in Southern Quechua serve the function of drawing the addressee's attention to a new object present in the situational context but not previously mentioned. This is precisely the type of deictic function described by Cornish (2008, 999) according to whom deixis:

> Serves prototypically to draw the addressee's attention focus to a new object of discourse (or to a new aspect of an existing one) that is derived by default via the situational context of utterance—whose center point is the 'here and now' of the speaker's verbal and non-verbal activity.

This type of deictic use of RDCs in discourse is illustrated by sentences such as (3), uttered by a participant in this study while narrating a story based on a series of pictures inspired by Mayer and Mayer (1992) and used in previous research (Sánchez 2003, 2006, 2010). In this sentence, the RDC *unu ukhuta* 'inside the water' refers to an element present in the context, that is, observable in the picture, but not mentioned in the previous discourse:

(3) *Hina-spa   waqa-yu-spa   maskha-chka-nku,   [unu   ukhu-ta].*
     like-GER   cry-INT-GER   search-PROG-3.PL   water   inside-ADVL
     'Then while crying they looked for (him), in the water.'

In sentence (3), the water is not a main element of the story and will not become one in the subsequent utterances in the narration. It is referenced by the speaker as present in the picture but it will not play a central role in discourse.

RIGHT PERIPHERAL DOMAINS   291

In addition to the above type of RDC, I will also discuss RDCs that serve a different deictic function; they refer back to an element previously mentioned in discourse that does not play a central role in the particular segment of discourse in which the RDCs appear. This is the case in the fragment of discourse presented in sentences (4a–c). In sentence (4a), the subject and topic of discourse is a group of characters who are looking for a little frog. Their actions are being described as going down a hill and at the same time wondering where the little frog is. The subject is expressed via a third person plural agreement marker on the main verb *ninku* 'say' and the subordinate nominalization *urayamuspankuña* 'coming down the hill.' In sentence (4b), a different subject *ch'iqllacha* 'the little frog' is introduced with third person singular subject agreement on the verb and as an RDC, not as a preverbal subject and not as a left margin topic. In (4c) (same as sentence 1 above), the subject is the same as in (4a) and is not an overt pronoun or a DP (Determiner Phrase or Noun Phrase); it is only marked by third person plural subject agreement on the verb:

(4) a. *Uraya-mu-spa-nku-ña*   *ni-nku:*   *may-taq*   *chay*
        go.down-CIS-GER-3.PL-DISC   say-3.PL   where-EMP   that

        ch'iqlla-cha-ri   *ni-spa.*
        frog-DIM-TOP2   say-GER
        'Coming down (the hill) (they) said: Where is the little frog?'

     b. *Mana*   *ka-n-chu,*   [*ch'iqlla-cha*].
        not   be-3-NEG   frog-DIM
        'The little frog is not (here).'

     c. *Hina-spa*   *waqa-yu-spa*   *maskha-chka-nku,*   [*unu*   *ukhu-ta*].
        like-GER   cry-INT-GER   search-PROG-3.PL   water   inside-ADVL
        'Then while crying they looked for (him), in the water.'

This pattern of discourse in which a null subject has the same referent and is the topic of discourse in sentences (4a) and (4c) while there is a morphologically unmarked postverbal intervening subject with a different referent in (4b) appears to indicate that RDCs that are morphologically unmarked as topics are not involved in the computation of discourse topic relationships in the same way as the null subjects are. Basically, RDCs are not discourse topics.

In this respect, morphologically unmarked RDCs differ crucially from morphologically marked left peripheral material that is related to a different notion of deixis, one that is based on the speaker perspective and anchors the speaker's point of view. In Quechua, morphologically marked left-margin topics indicate that the speaker is highlighting a constituent as the topic of discourse, whereas an RDC can be used merely to resolve a potential ambiguity arising from a sequence of null pronominal or DP subjects or to refer to shared knowledge that is not the main topic of discourse. As noted by Giorgi (2010, 7) for Italian, left peripheral constituents are speaker-oriented and syntactic in nature:

> There is a syntactic position in the left-most periphery of the clause, and precisely in the Complementizer layer, that encodes the temporal -and presumably spatial as well- coordinates of the speaker.

In Southern Quechua too, the left periphery involves the perspective of the speaker regarding what constitutes new or contrastive information (focus) and the theme of discourse (topic). It also includes what Mushin (2000) labels 'epistemological deixis', expressed in evidential markers that primarily involve the assessment of the source of information by the speaker. The right periphery, on the other hand, involves a different type of discourse deixis that does not include the main elements of the speaker's perspective regarding what constitutes the topic of discourse but is meant to help the addressee identify new elements that are not central to the narration or not presented as the main topic.

In this paper, I present the results of a study of the distribution of morphologically unmarked right margin constituents in Southern Quechua oral narrations according to their argumental status, namely according to whether they are arguments of the verb (subjects, direct objects or indirect objects) or not (oblique objects, adverbs or other elements). The argumental status is relevant because it is revealing of the level of potential topicality of the constituent, since it has been shown that preverbal and null subjects are more likely than other arguments to be topics of discourse cross-linguistically (Taboada and Wiesemann 2010).

The data for this study come from the picture-based narratives of 19 native speakers (9 males and 10 females, aged 18–33) of three Southern Quechua varieties (Apurimac, Arequipa and Cuzco) who also speak Spanish.[8] In addition to identifying the type of constituents that may appear at the right margin of sentences in these narratives, I will also discuss the deictic nature of RDCs. All

---

8 While it is likely that their knowledge of Spanish may have some impact on the distribution of RDCs and on the patterns found, the main goal of this paper is to provide a description of the RDCs as they occur in these speech samples. The issue of cross-linguistic influence will be left aside for future studies.

three Southern Quechua varieties have null pronominal or null DP subjects, subject agreement morphology on the verb and canonical SOV word order.

The paper is organized as follows. In section 2, a brief introduction to the syntactic and morphosyntactic properties of peripheral domains and their relationship to information structure in Southern Quechua is presented as well as the expected frequencies of RDCs in the data analyzed, given the previous proposals discussed. In section 3, the present study and its results are presented and the results are discussed in section 4. Some concluding remarks are presented in section 5.

2   Peripheral Domains and Information Structure in Southern Quechua

Before presenting previous proposals on peripheral domains in Southern Quechua varieties, I present some of the basic characteristics of Southern Quechua varieties that become relevant in understanding constituents in the right periphery of the sentence. Quechua consists of agglutinative language varieties with very regular suffixation and head final word order (Adelaar and Muysken 2004, Cerrón-Palomino 1987). Verbs are marked for person agreement and sentences may have overt or null subjects and objects, as exemplified in sentence (3) above, where both the subject and the direct object of the verb *maskha-chka-nku* '(they) searched for (him)' are not overtly present as independent DPs and only the subject is morphologically marked on the verb (Sánchez 2010).[9] Main sentences with overt constituents with wide focus have an SOV canonical word order.

Another characteristic of most Quechua language varieties, and this is the case for Southern Quechua varieties, is that DPs are morphologically marked for case (accusative, dative and oblique cases). This characteristic will become relevant in the explanation of how RDCs are interpreted in discourse because it is revealing of their argumental or non argumental status. Quechua DPs lack overt definite determiners but have demonstratives and, in some forms of Quechua-Spanish bilingual speech, the numeral *huk* 'one' has emerged as an indefinite determiner (Sánchez 2003).

The variety of speech analyzed in this study comes from speakers who are fluent in Southern Quechua and are bilingual in Spanish. They were born in

---

9   Some sentences and discourse fragments analyzed in this paper were previously presented in Sánchez (2010). The whole data set, which was collected in 2005, was not analyzed in that book.

the southern regions of Cuzco, Apurimac and Arequipa in Peru. At the time of data collection, they were all living in the city of Cuzco. The characteristics already mentioned (agglutinative suffixation, head final word order, null subjects and objects, and lack of overt definite determiners) have all been documented for Southern Quechua (Cerrón-Palomino 1987, Cusihuamán 2001). All of these varieties have been classified as belonging to the same sub-branch, labeled Quechua IIC by Torero (1964).

Previous work on right peripheral constituents in SVO languages, such as Romance languages, has analyzed them as focus positions (Belletti 2005). The availability of a sentence-internal focus position was first proposed by Jayaseelan (2001) for Malayalam, an SOV language. In Malayalam, *wh*-words must appear in immediate preverbal position (Jayaseelan 2001, 40), as shown in the following examples:

(5)   *Ninn-e*   *aarc*   *aTiccu?* (sic)[10]
      you-ACC   who   beat-PST
      'Who beat you?'

(6)   **aarc*   *Ninn-e*   *aTiccu?* (sic)
      who   you-ACC   beat-PST
      'Who beat you?'

The obligatory nature of this preverbal position led Jayaseelan (2001, 41) to propose that there is a focus projection available immediately above the VP (Verbal Phrase) and right below the IP (Inflectional Phrase), as in:

(7) $[_{IP} \, I \, [_{FP} \, F \, [_{vP} \, v \, [_{VP} \, V \, DO]]]]$

In Jayaseelan's analysis, this IP-internal focus position in Malayalam is occupied by *wh*-expressions. Cecchetto (1999) and Belletti (2005) propose to extend this focus analysis to right dislocated objects in Romance languages such as Italian, especially those occurring in clitic right dislocation structures as in examples (8) and (9):

(8)   *Io*   *l=ho*   *visto,*   *[Gianni].*
      I   3.SG.ACC-have   seen   Gianni
      'I saw Gianni.'
      (Cecchetto 1999, 49)

---

10   There are no dashes between the roots and the suffixes in the original paper.

RIGHT PERIPHERAL DOMAINS 295

(9) *Gianni*   *ve-rrà*   *lui.*
Gianni   come-FUT.3   he
'Gianni himself will come'
(Belletti 2005, 10)

Belletti (2005) proposes a structure parallel to the one proposed for the C-domain by Rizzi (1997) for IP-internal focalized and topicalized constituents that contain a Topic and a Focus position, as shown in (10):

(10) [TopP Top [FP Foc [TopP Top [VP]]]]

The right dislocated elements in sentences such as (8) or (9) move to the specifier of an IP-internal position over the VP and remain in that position after subsequent movement of other VP material.

This proposal has been extended to Quechua language varieties (Sánchez 2010), despite the fact that they have a canonical SOV word order, mainly because they account for right margin constituents that are morphologically marked as topics, as shown in (11). This example illustrates the case of a right margin constituent marked with a topicalization particle. The verb is transitive and there is only one constituent in the right margin:

(11) *Pidru-m*   *ruwa-rqa-n*   *[wasi-ta-qa]*.[11]
Pedro-DIREV.FOC   build-PST.ATT-3   house-ACC-TOP
'It is Pedro who built the house.' (first hand information)
(Muysken 1995, 383)

Some speakers may even accept two right margin constituents morphologically marked for topic, as in example (12) that illustrates a sentence with a ditransitive verb:

(12) *Qayna punchaw-qa*   *tayta-n-qa*   *qu-rqa-n-mi*
past day-TOP   father-3-TOP   give-PST.ATT-3-DIREV.FOC

[wasi-ta-qa   *churi-n-man-(qa)]*.
house-ACC-TOP   son-3-DAT-TOP
'Yesterday, the father, GAVE the house to his son.'
(Sánchez 2010, 179)

---

11   Interestingly, constituents marked for focus and evidentiality are banned from postverbal positions. Sánchez (2010) accounts for this as a lack of an IP-internal evidentiality projection.

As mentioned before, these are not the only cases of right margin constituents possible in Southern Quechua. As noted by Muysken (1995) for Cuzco Quechua and by Sánchez (2010) for Southern Quechua, some RDCs that are morphologically unmarked as topics are possible, as in the following example with a transitive verb and one right margin constituent:

(13) Mariya   Huwana-man   qu-n   [libru-ta].
     Maria   Juana-DAT   give-3 $book-ACC
     'Maria gives the book to Juana.'
     (Muysken 1995, 383)

In previous work (Sánchez 2010), it has also been noted that it is possible to find two right edgepositions with a transitive verb, as illustrated by the following example in which we see a clear case of a direct object discontinuous DP *pajaruchata* 'little bird', marked with accusative case, followed by an adjectival phrase *qilluchata* 'yellow' which is also marked for accusative case:

(14) Hina-spa-n   tari-ru-spa   ka-rqa-n,
     like-GER-DIREV.FOC   find-INT-GER   be-PST.ATT-3

     [paharu-cha-ta],   [qillu-cha-ta].
     $bird-DIM-ACC   yellow-DIM-ACC
     'Then (she) had found a yellow bird.'
     (Sánchez 2010, 38)

Sánchez (2010) also notes that with some ditransitive verbs, it is possible to find two edge positions with a special phonological property, namely, creaky voice:

(15) Hina-spa wasi-n-man apa-pu-sqa,   [chay biyiha-cha],
     like-GER house-3-DAT bring-REG-PST.REP   that $old.woman-DIM

     [chay   pichingu-cha].
     that   little.bird-DIM
     'Then the old woman took the little bird to her house.'
     Sánchez (2010, 38)

On the basis of this distinction, Sánchez (2010) proposes the following generalization. There are two types of right-edge elements: a) Morphologically marked topics that enter an Agree relationship with the lower topic head, as

RIGHT PERIPHERAL DOMAINS

proposed by Belletti (2005), and move to its specifier. Constituents marked with focus and evidentiality features (such as the subject *Pidru* in sentence (11)) are banned from that position because the paradigm of morphemes *-mi*, *-si*, *-chá* is syncretic for focus and evidentiality and there is only one evidentiality projection per clause and it is in the C-domain, and b) Unmarked elements are outside the intonational unit (characterized by creaky voice vowels in some dialects).[12]

One important aspect of these unmarked elements is that while they appear in discourse, they are not accepted as grammatical by native speakers in isolated sentences. Thus, while a sentence such as (16) can be found embedded in speech, it is not accepted as grammatical as an isolated sentence by native speakers:

(16) *Chay-manta*   *phiña-ri-ku-n*   [*warma*].
     that-ABL   upset-INCH-REFL-3   boy
     'Then the boy got upset.'

In principle, all constituents should be able to appear as RDCs, irrespectively of their argumental or non-argumental status in Quechua. However, the proposal made here is that RDCs are non-topical in nature and refer to either a non-central element present in the discourse context or to a previously-introduced element that is not the main topic of discourse.

The task used to test this proposal is a picture-based, story-telling task in which there is a limited number of animated characters that interact in various ways (see section 3.2), which limits the number of potential main agentive topics in discourse. Given the nature of the task with a limited number of characters, which does not require the constant introduction of new topics of discourse that are engaged in the actions portrayed in the pictures, a high frequency of null subjects as continuing topics is expected. This assumes that, in the case of intransitive verbs, RDCs would tend to be either oblique objects referring to elements present in the context but non-topical, or non-topical subjects. In the case of transitive and ditransitive verbs, RDCs could be non-topical subjects, direct objects and indirect objects (only with ditransitive verbs) as well as oblique objects referring to elements present in the context but non-topical or not previously mentioned. In general, it is expected that argumental and non argumental RDCs are treated neither as topics of

---

12   For a more detailed discussion of prosodic and intonational properties of the right margin, see Sánchez (2010). Other important aspects of phonological properties of Southern Quechua can be found in O'Rourke (2009).

discourse nor as focalized elements, given that discourse topics and focalized constituents appear in the left margin of sentences. RDCs introduce a reference to elements present in the context but not previously mentioned in discourse or to elements not central to the topic structure of discourse. Since this is the case, as presented below, the idea that material in the right margin of the sentence in Southern Quechua varieties serves discourse context-sensitive deictic functions is supported.

3   Methods

3.1   *Participants*
Participants in this study were 19 adult Southern Quechua speakers from Peru (9 males and 10 females). Seven participants had Quechua as their first language and the other twelve were bilingual in Quechua and Spanish from birth. Their ages at the time of data collection ranged from 18–33 with a mean age of 24. Five had attained high school-level education and fourteen college-level education. Ten participants were born in Cuzco, seven in Apurimac, one in Arequipa, and one in Ayacucho. At the time of data collection, all of them were living in the city of Cuzco and declared that they had relatives or friends with whom they interacted in Quechua.

3.2   *Materials*
Participants were asked to narrate a story from a sequence of pictures based on the book '*Frog where are you?*' (Mayer and Mayer 1992) and modified for previous studies (Sánchez 2003, 2006). The stories were recorded and transcribed using the CHILDES transcription system.

The sequence of pictures starts with the image of a child surrounded by some animals (a dog, a toad and a turtle) who opens a box and finds a little frog inside. The following pictures show the animosity of the big toad towards the little frog as the group formed by the child and the animals embarks on a series of adventures, such as walking towards the mountains and traveling on a raft in a river. At each point, the big toad shows his jealousy either by biting the little frog or kicking it out of the raft. The turtle lets the child know about this state of affairs. After the little frog has fallen into the water, all of the characters look for it. They return to what appears to be the boy's house and sit down at the door to cry for the lost animal. In the end, the little frog returns and all of the characters appear happy once again. As is shown in the next subsection, the sequence of pictures contains a fixed number of events that allows a certain regularity in the production of verbs by the speakers.

RIGHT PERIPHERAL DOMAINS

3.3 Data Analysis

In the following section, I present the data from the narratives involving RDCs according to their syntactic status (DPs or non-DPs) and in the case of DPs according to their argumental or non-argumental status. Then the frequency of RDCs is presented according to the type of verb in the main sentence in which they appear (intransitive or transitive verbs), and in each case the type of antecedents of the RDCs in discourse is presented and discussed. The narratives comprised a total of 480 sentences, of which 202 had at least one morphologically unmarked RDC. Argumental (subject, direct object and indirect object) and non-argumental (oblique) DPs, adverbial phrases, and some adjectival and quantificational phrases (the latter two labeled as 'other') were coded for this study. Arguments of intransitive and transitive verbs were coded separately in order to distinguish between verbs with only subjects as a potential argumental topic and verbs with either a subject or an object as potential topics. Sentential RDCs were not included in the coding because they might have a different type of relationship with the main clause and have an independent nominalized verb.

4 Results

4.1 Types of RDCs According to Syntactic Projection

There were 54 sentences with more than one RDC. Sentences with one RDC referenced postverbal subjects, direct objects and oblique objects as illustrated in (17), (18) and (19) (previously introduced as example (4c), adverbial RDCs, and other RDCs such as numerals:

Subject RDC:

(17) *Mana*   *ka-n-chu*   [*ch'iqlla-cha*].
      not   be-3-NEG   frog-DIM
      'The little frog is missing.'

Direct Object RDC:

(18) *Kay warma-cha qucha pata-pi   diha-yku-n   [hatun hamp'atu-ta].*
      this boy-DIM   lake   near-LOC $leave-INT-3 big   toad-ACC
      'This boy left the big toad near the lake.'

Oblique RDC:

(19) *Hina-spa*   *waqa-yu-spa*   *maskha-chka-nku,*   [*unu*   *ukhu-ta*].
like-GER   cry-INT-GER   search-PROG-3.PL   water   inside-ADVL
'Then while crying they looked for (him), in the water.'

Adverbial RDC:

(20) *Hina-spa-y*   *chay*   *chiku-cha*   *kida-ka-pu-n*   [*allin*].
like-GER-DISC   that $boy-DIM $stay-REFL-REG-3   well.ADVL
'Then that boy stays there well.'

Other RDC:

(21) *Chay-manta-s*   *yaku-pi*   *puri-sqa-ku*   [*tawa-nku*].
that-ABL-INDEV.FOC   water-LOC   walk-PST.REP-3.PL   four-3.PL
'Then they walked in the water, the four of them.'

The overall frequencies of right dislocated constituents in the Quechua narratives is shown in figure 8.1. These numbers include cases in which there was more than one RDC per sentence. The majority of postverbal right peripheral constituents corresponds to subjects, followed by direct objects and oblique objects.

The high frequency of subject RDCs shown in figure 8.1 can be explained by the type of sentences used in the stories. Of the total of 202 sentences with RDCs, 100 had intransitive verbs, 86 had transitive verbs, 14 had presentational intransitive verbs and only 2 had ditransitive verbs (see figure 8.2). These frequencies are relevant in order to understand the way in which discourse in the narratives was structured, given the limited number of characters involved in the story. As mentioned above, subject and oblique RDCs were expected with intransitive verbs, whereas transitive and ditransitive verbs would also include direct and indirect object RDCs. Preverbal subjects are more likely to be topical while direct and indirect objects in canonical positions are less likely to be topics, and therefore as RDCs they should not be as frequent as subject RDCs. As figure 8.2 shows, the narratives had a high frequency of intransitive verbs which might be responsible for the subject RDCs as the most frequent of all RDC types as shown in figure 8.1.

In terms of the number of RDCs per sentence, the highest frequency corresponded to sentences with only one RDC (150), followed by those with two RDCs (27), and those with three RDCs (13). There were five sentences with four RDCs and only four sentences with five RDCs. Lastly, there were only three

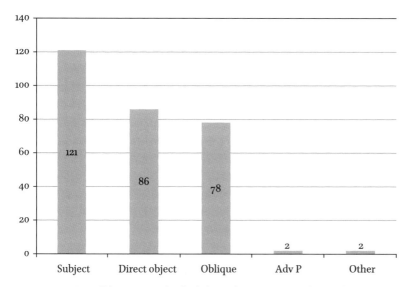

FIGURE 8.1 *Overall frequencies of right dislocated constituents in the Quechua narratives*

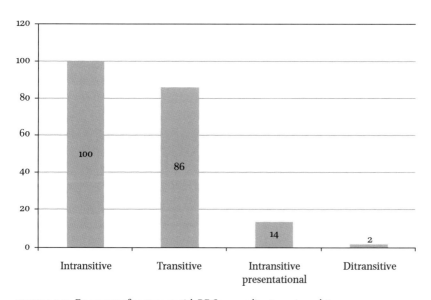

FIGURE 8.2 *Frequency of sentences with RDCs according to main verb type*

sentences with six RDCs (see fig. 8.3). This is also consistent with an overall higher frequency of intransitive verbs.

Examples of sentences with two or more RDCs showed a variety of DP types according to case marking and syntactic position. Example (22) shows a DP marked as illative, an oblique case, and one marked as accusative,

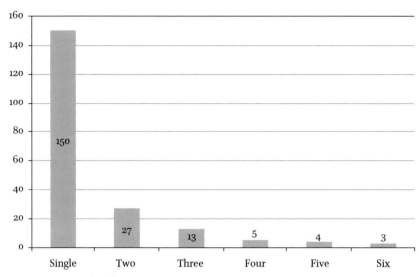

FIGURE 8.3 *Number of RDCs per sentence*

indicating it is a direct object. Example (23) shows a sequence of DPs that have the default lack of marking that characterizes nominative subject DPs, and example (24) shows a sequence of DPs marked as comitative and illative, both cases characteristic of oblique objects:

(22) *Hina-spa*   *chay-manta-pis*   *kacha-ru-n*   [*mayu*
     like-GER   that-ABL-ADD   send-INT-3   river

   ukhu-man]   [*taksa*   *hamp'atu ta*].
   inside-ILL   medium   toad-ACC
   'Then after that, (he) sent the medium sized toad to the river.'

(23) *Pay-pa*   *ka-sqa*   [*animal-kuna*]   [*huq*   *allqu*]
     he-GEN   be-PST.REP $animal-PL   one   dog

   [*hamp'atu*],   [*tortuga*]
   toad $turtle
   'There were his animals, a dog, (a) toad, (a) turtle.'

RIGHT PERIPHERAL DOMAINS 303

(24) *Huwan-mi*   *lluqsi-sqa,*   [*amigu-n-wan*],   [*kampu-man*]
Juan-DIREV.FOC leave-PST.REP $friend-3.POSS-COM $field-ILL

[*sapu-n-wan*]   [*allqu-n- wan*],   *y*   [*tortuga-cha-n-wan*],
$toad-3-COM   dog-3-COM $and $turtle-DIM-3.POSS-COM

[*kampu-man*].
$field-ILL
'Juan left with his friend, to the field, with his dog, with his toad and with his turtle, to the field.'

It is worth noting that out of the 52 sentences with more than one RDC, 27 examples involved constituents differently marked for case, as in sentence (22), one with an oblique marking such as illative and one with the accusative marker that direct objects receive. Sentences with three or more RDCs involved some form of juxtaposition or coordination of constituents with the same argumental or non-argumental status as in:

(25) *Huq*   *kuti-n-si*   *huq*   *chiku-cha*
one   time-3-INDEV.FOC one $boy-DIM

kampu-pi   *puri-ku-sqa*   [*allqu-cha-n-wan*]   [*huk*
$field-LOC   walk-REFL-PST.REP dog-DIM-3.POSS-COM one

sapu-cha-puwan] [*huk*   *tortuga-cha-puwan*].
$toad-DIM-COM   one $turtle-DIM-COM
'Once, there was a boy walking in the fields with his little dog, his little toad and his little turtle.'

As is described further in the discussion section below, the fact that these RDCs are unmarked for topic and do not appear to enter into Agree relationships with functional features in the CP area does not mean that there is no access to the information coming from the sentence level, given that these DPs in the right margin are appropriately marked for case.

4.2   *RDCs According to Verb Type*
Sentences with a single RDC were divided in terms of the verb types as follows: 75 had intransitive verbs, 68 had transitive verbs, 5 had intransitive

presentational verbs, and only 2 had ditransitive verbs. The distribution is shown in figure 8.4:

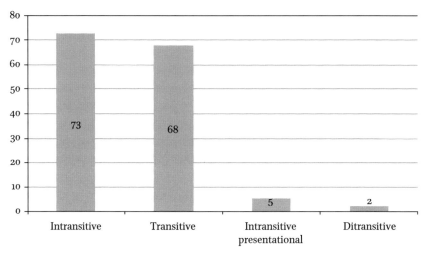

FIGURE 8.4 *RDCs according to verb type*

The high frequency of RDCs with intransitive verbs may be an effect of the task, as the stories involved many actions involving only an agent. At the same time, their high frequency is revealing because as presented below, they could be indicative of a high frequency of non topical subjects and oblique objects that refer to elements not previously mentioned in discourse but present in the situational context.

4.2.1   RDCs in Sentences with Intransitive Verbs

Intransitive presentational verbs with RDCs involved cases in which the RDC referred to an element that was not the subject and not the agent of the actions described by the speaker, as shown in the following sequence of discourse:

(26) *Hina-spa   kay   kampu-ta   lluqsi-sqa   chiku-cha*
     like-GER   this $field-ACC   leave-PST.REP $boy-DIM

   animal-cha-n-kuna-ntin   huk   kaha-ta   tari-ku-n.
   $animal-DIM-3.POSS-PL-INCL   one $box-ACC   find-REFL-3
   'Then, having left for this field, the young boy with his animals found a box.'

RIGHT PERIPHERAL DOMAINS 305

(27) *Hina-spa   chay   kaha-cha-pi   ka-sqa   [huchuy   sapu-cha].*
     like-GER   that $box-DIM-LOC   be-PST.REP little $toad-DIM
     'Then in the little box, there was the little toad.'

(28) *Chay-manta,   huk,   chay   huk   sapu-cha-ta   sumaq-ta*
     that-ABL   one   that   one $toad-DIM-ACC nice-ADVL

     urqu-spa   uywa-ku-chka-ra-n.
     take-GER   raise-REFL-PROG-PST.ATT-3
     'Then taking the little toad nicely (from the box), (he) was caring for
     (him).'

In sentences (26) and (28), the subject of the sentence is the boy. Sentence (27)
has an intransitive presentational verb that introduces the frog as a postverbal
subject. In sentence (28), the frog is the object. Notice that the subject in (26)
(the boy) continues to be the agentive topic of discourse. The introduction of
the frog as a postverbal subject with a presentational intransitive is followed by
the continuation of the agentive topic as a subject in the next sentence.

In the case of non-presentational intransitive verbs, a similar pattern is
observed in examples (2)a–c, repeated here as (29)–(31):

(29) *Uraya-mu-spa-nku-ña   ni-nku: may-taq   chay*
     go.down-CIS-GER-3.PL-DISC   say-3.PL   Where-EMP   that

     ch'iqlla-cha-ri   ni-spa.
     frog-DIM-TOP2   say-GER
     'Coming down (the hill) (they) said: Where is the little frog?'

(30) *Mana   ka-n-chu,   [ch'iqlla-cha].*
     not   be-3-NEG   frog-DIM
     'The little frog is not (here).'

(31) *Hina-spa   waqa-yu-spa   maskha-chka-nku,   [unu   ukhu-ta].*
     like-GER   cry-INT-GER   search-PROG-3.PL   water   inside-ADVL
     'Then while crying they looked for (him), in the water.'

In sentence (29), the subject is plural and its referent is the group formed by a
boy and some of his animals that have noted that the little frog was missing. In
sentence (30), the intransitive verb *kay* 'to be' appears as an existential verb in
the scope of negation and its subject is postverbal. Importantly, the subject is

not the topic of the discourse. In the following sentence in discourse (31), the null subject refers back to the group formed by the boy and his other animals.

In the case of RDCs in sentences with transitive verbs, there is also a similar pattern. In sentence (32), Juanito is the subject/topic of the sentence; then in sentence (33) the direct object *huq uchuy ch'iqllachata* 'the little frog' appears in postverbal position and in (34) the main subject is the child's friends, but the subject is introduced in reference to the boy in the form of an overt pronoun with a genitive marker *paypa* 'he-GEN'. Clearly, the main topic of the fragment is the boy:

(32) *Huwanito,   huq   kaha-cha-n-pi,   kaha-cha-n   ka-sqa.*
 Juanito   one $box-DIM-3POSS-LOC $box-DIM-3.POSS   be-PST.REP
 'Juanito, in his box, (there) was his box/he had a box.'

(33) *Chay   ukhu-pi   uywa-sqa   [huq   huch'uy   ch'iqlla-cha-ta].*
 that   inside-LOC   raise-PST.REP   one   little   frog-DIM-ACC
 'Inside (he) had raised a little frog.'

(34) *Chay-manta   pay-pa   amigu-cha-n-kuna   hina*
 that-ABL   he-GEN $friend-DIM-3.POSS-PL   so

 ka-lla-sqa-taq   huq   hamp'atu,   hatun
 be-LIM-PST.REP-CONTR   one   toad   big

 hamp'atu,   huq   tortuga,   huq-taq   allqu- cha- n.
 toad   one $turtle   one-CONTR   dog-DIM-3.POSS
 'Then his friends were just there (like that), a toad, a big toad, another his dog.'

The interpretation of one of the sentences with a ditransitive verb is part of a complex sequence of events described in sentences (35)–(38) below. In this case, I will focus on the RDC in sentence (37) below. In the first image described by the speaker who uttered this segment of discourse, the whole group formed by the boy and his animals is boarding a raft and getting in the river, hence, the plural null subject in sentence (35). In a subsequent event portrayed in the pictures, one can see the big toad kicking the small frog into the river. The speaker utters (36), using a third person singular null subject with two subordinate clauses as RDCs. Sentence (37) is uttered to refer to a picture in which the turtle appears to be calling the boy's attention to the recent event. It is in the context of this picture that the speaker utters sentence (37) with the turtle as

RIGHT PERIPHERAL DOMAINS   307

a preverbal subject, a null object and the indirect object *chikuchaman* 'the boy'
in postverbal position. In the next utterance, sentence (38), the agentive topic
of discourse goes back to the whole group as in sentence (35), and the sentence
has a third person plural null subject.

(35) *Chay-manta-taq*   *ri-sqa-ku,*   [*balsa-pi*],   [*balsa-pi*],   [*mayu-ta*].
     that-ABL-CONTR   go-PST.REP-3.PL $raft-LOC $raft-LOC   river-ADVL
     'Then (they) went on the raft in the river.'

(36) *Chay-pi*   *igual*   *urma-chi-rqa-n*   *hayt'a-spa*
     that-LOC $same   fall-CAUS-PST.ATT-3PL   kick-GER

     mayu-man   *mana*   *kuwinta-ta*   *qu-ku-spa.*
     river-ILL   not $realization-ACC   give-REFL-GER
     'Right there (he) made him fall, kicking (him) intó the river, without real-
     izing it.'

(37) *Tortuga*   *willa-sqa*   [*chiku-cha-man*].
     $turtle   tell-PST.REP.3 $boy-DIM-DAT
     'The turtle had told the boy (this).'

(38) *Maskha-rqa-nku.*
     search-PST.ATT-3.PL
     '(They) searched (for him).'

As in the previous example with the transitive verb, the RDC *chikuchaman* 'the
boy' in (37) is not the central topic of the fragment, as the group is the agentive
topic of this segment.

   As mentioned above, sentences with intransitive verbs were more frequent
than those with transitive verbs. This frequency could be indicative of high frequencies of non-topical subject and oblique RDCs. In fact, in figure 8.5 oblique
RDCs are the most frequent, closely followed by subject RDCs, with only one
adverb RDC.

   Oblique RDCs appeared in the narratives of 16 out of the 19 participants in
the study and ranged from one to four occurrences per participant. I take this
to indicate that these were not random occurrences that took place only with
a limited number of speakers. The next fragment of discourse illustrates the
case of an oblique RDC with an intransitive verb. In the first sentence (39), a
third person plural null subject is the topic of discourse and refers to the group
formed by the boy and his animals. It is followed by a sentence (40) with a

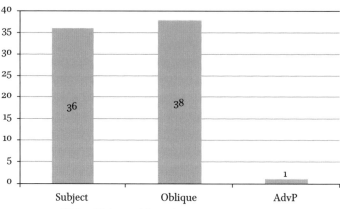

FIGURE 8.5 *RDCs with intransitive verbs*

different overt subject *chiqllacha* 'the little frog' and an oblique RDC *bote-manta* 'off the boat' that appears in the pictures but has not been mentioned in discourse before. The RDC instantiates a case of deixis in which the referent is present in the situational context and not in discourse. Sentence (41) repeats the predicate now with a null subject referring to the little frog and in sentence (42) the subject goes back to a third person plural null subject that has the same referent as the subject in sentence (39):

(39) *Chay-manta,   ri-chka-nku,   ri-chka-nku.*
 that-ABL   go-PROG-3.PL   go-PROG-3.PL
 'Then, (they) are going, (they) are going.'

(40) *Hina-spa   uña   chiqlla-cha   salta-ra-mu-chka-n-taq*
 like-GER   tiny   frog-DIM $jump-INT-CIS-PROG-3-EMP

 [*bote-man(ta)*].[13]
 $boat-ABL
 'Then the tiny froggy is jumping off the boat.'

---

13   The parentheses indicate that in the audio the last syllable (*-ta*) is hardly audible.

RIGHT PERIPHERAL DOMAINS 309

(41) *Salta-ra-mu-n*   [*bote-man(ta)*].
     $jump-INT-CIS-3 $boat-ABL
     '(He) jumps off the boat.'

(42) *Hina,*   *ri-chka-nku,*   *ri-chka-nku.*
     SO   go-PROG-3.PL   go-PROG-3.PL
     'So, (they) are going, (they) are going.'

The RDC in example (40) introduces an element not previously mentioned in discourse but present in the situational context, namely in the pictures.[14]

Support for the notion that oblique RDCs have a deictic function regarding elements not previously present in discourse comes from the distribution of the antecedents of oblique RDCs. As can be seen in figure 8.6, although there are some oblique RDCs with previously mentioned oblique RDCs as anteced- ents and one with a subject antecedent, most of the oblique RDC antecedents appear in the context (pictures) and have not been previously mentioned in the discourse. This answers the question of what discourse functions they fulfill and supports the view that they are non-topical and mostly deictic in nature.

The second most frequent type of RDC with intransitive verbs are subjects. They appeared in the narratives of 14 of the 19 participants in the study and ranged from one to eight occurrences per narrative. The following fragment (43)–(46) illustrates the types of contexts in which they appear. In sentence (46), the subject RDC *sapo* 'the toad' has as its most immediate antecedent a null subject in sentence (44), which had been introduced in a previous sen- tence (43). Notice that in the intervening sentence (45) *Huwan-qa* is reintro- duced in discourse as a topic that appears on the left margin of the sentence and is morphologically marked with *-qa*. It is after that reintroduction of *Huwan* as the discourse topic that, in the next sentence, the null subject must be disambiguated with a postverbal subject that is morphologically unmarked for topic:

(43) *Qucha-man*   *chaya-ru-spa-nku-taq-mi*   *chay*   *sapu*
     lake-ILL   arrive-INT-GER-3.PL-CONTR-DIREV.FOC   that $toad

     riniga-sqa   *ri-chka-ra-n.*
     $upset-PST.REP.3   go-PROG-PST.ATT-3
     'As they arrived to the lake they left with the upset toad.'

---

14   In sentence (41), the predicate of sentence (40) is repeated and I do not count it as a new instance.

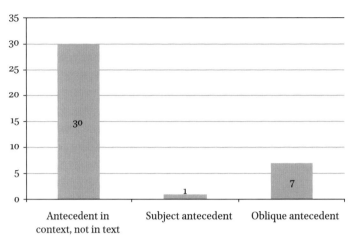

FIGURE 8.6 *Antecedents of oblique RDCs*

(44) *Hina-spa-n-mi huk rumi-pi kida-ru-ku-n.*
like-GER-3-DIREV.FOC one rock-LOC $stay-INT-REFL-3
'Then he (= the toad) stayed on a rock.'

(45) *Chay-manta-taq-mi Huwan-qa kuti-ra-mu-spa*
that-ABL-CONTR-DIREV.FOC Juan-TOP come-INT-CIS-GER

advirti-ru-n.
$warn-INT-3
'Then as Juan was coming back, he warned him (= the toad).'

(46) *Advirti-sqa-n-manta-taq-mi siqara-pu-n [sapo].*
$warn-PP-3-ABL-CONTR-DIREV.FOC leave-REG-3 $toad
'After he was warned, the toad went back.'

In this respect, subject RDC antecedents presented a somewhat different distribution than oblique RDCs, since their most frequent antecedents were other subjects previously mentioned in discourse, as shown in figure 8.7 below. However, as presented in the discussion of the previous fragment, in 14 out of the 20 occurrences in which their antecedent was a subject, there was an intervening subject with a different referent between the RDC and its most immediate previous mention. This indicates that these subject RDCs were nontopical.

There were some cases of subject RDCs in which there was no intervening subject, but these were not full DPs. Rather, they were cases in which there was an adjectival phrase referring to a subject in a context in which there

RIGHT PERIPHERAL DOMAINS

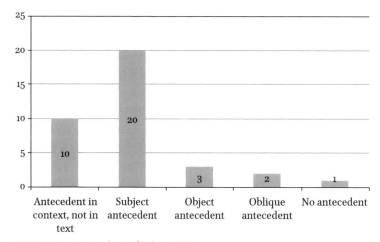

FIGURE 8.7 *Antecedents of Subject RDCs*

was ambiguity as to whether the speaker was referring to the big toad or the small toad:

(47) *Chay-manta,   phiña,   phiña   ka-sqa   [hatun].*
     that-ABL   upset   upset   be-PST.REP.3 big
     'Then, the big (one) was upset.'

There were also cases in which the antecedent was present in the context but not in the text as in the mention of the whole story at the end of the narrative in sentence (48). The reference to the story is part of the discourse context, but was not mentioned before in the text:

(48) *Chay-pi   tuku-ku-n   [chay   kuwinto].*
     that-LOC   end-REFL-3   that $story
     'There ends this story.'

There were also cases that introduced a quantifier to refer to the participants in the story, as in (49):

(49) *Mana-n   kuwinta-ta   qu-pu-sqa-ku-chu*
     not-DIREV.FOC $realization-ACC   give-REG-PST.REP-3.PL-NEG

     [kinsa-nti-nku].
     three-INCL-3.PL
     'The three of them did not realize.'

4.2.2 RDCs in Sentences with Transitive Verbs

In the case of single RDCs in sentences with transitive verbs, the highest frequency was that of direct object RDCs, 52 in total, followed by subject RDCs with a much lower frequency, nine, as shown in figure 8.8. Object RDCs appeared in the narratives of 17 out of the 19 speakers, ranging from one to seven occurrences per narrative.

Unlike oblique RDCs and subject RDCs with intransitive verbs, the distribution of direct object RDCs according to their antecedent showed a more even distribution across categories. Out of the 52 object RDCs, 19 had another object previously mentioned in discourse as their antecedent, 17 had a previously-mentioned subject and 12 had an antecedent present in discourse but not previously mentioned. The distribution is shown in figure 8.9.

Object RDCs with object antecedents were found in the narratives of 11 out of the 19 speakers, ranging from one to three cases per narrative. Given the sequence of pictures in which there is a big toad who is jealous of the little frog and interacts with it, it is not surprising that 17 out of the 19 object RDCs with object antecedents refer to the toad or the frog. As in the case of some RDCs with intransitive verbs, some sentences with object RDCs and object antecedents are preceded by a sentence with an intervening subject, as shown in the following fragment:

(50) *Chay-qa   pay-kuna   qhawa-sqa-ku   [taksa   hamp'atu-cha-ta].*
     that-TOP   3-PL   see-PST.REP-3.PL   medium   toad-DIM-ACC
     'Then they saw the medium sized toad.'

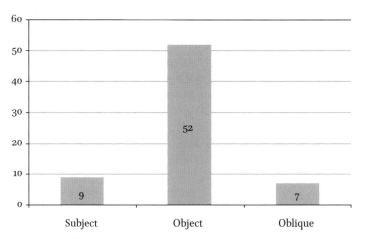

FIGURE 8.8 *RDCs with transitive verbs*

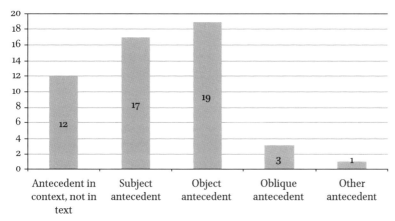

FIGURE 8.9 *Direct Object RDCs according to antecedent*

(51) | *Hina-spa* | *kusi* | *ka-sqa-ku.* |
     | like-GER | happy | be-PST.REP-3PL |

'Then they were happy.'

(52) | *Pero* | *hatun* | *hamp'atu* | *millay-ta* | *qhawa-yu-n* |
     | $but | big | toad | ugly-ADVL | see-INT-3 |

| [*taksa* | *hamp'atu-ta*]. |
| medium | toad-ACC |

'But the big toad gave the medium sized toad a mean look.'

It is important to highlight that the speaker who produced (52) also had preverbal direct objects, indicating that the speaker does use the SOV word order in sentences in which the whole sentence is new information, namely, sentences with canonical word order. In fact, the speaker produced preverbal direct objects in the same narrative, as shown by this sentence uttered at the beginning of the story:

(53) | *Chay-si-si* | *huk* | *kaha-cha-ta* | *tariku-sqa-ku.*[15] |
     | then-INDEV.FOC-INDEV.FOC | one | $box-DIM-ACC | find-PST.REP-3.PL |

'Then they found a box.'

---

15 It appears to be the case that in *chaysisi,* the first instance of *–si* has been lexicalized and requires a *-si* marker.

314   SÁNCHEZ

This indicates that at least in the speech of this speaker, pre-verbal and post-verbal objects appear to have a different distribution in discourse. While preverbal objects are part of the whole sentence as new information, postverbal ones are not new information.[16]

The following fragment of discourse illustrates the case of an object RDC with a distant subject antecedent:

(54) *Hina-spa-y*　　　　*uña*　　*ch'iqlla-cha-s*　　　　*sayk'u-ru-n.*
　　　like-GER-DISC　　tiny　　frog-DIM-INDEV.FOC　　tire-INT-3
　　　'Then the little frog got tired.'

(55) *Machu*　　*hamp'atu-pis*　　*sayk'u-ru-lla-n-taq.*
　　　old　　　toad-ADD　　　　tire-INT-LIM-3-CONTR
　　　'The old toad also got tired.'

(56) *Hina-spa*　　*tortuga*　　*pata-man*　　*siqayu-spa-nku*　　*ri-nku.*
　　　like-GER　　$turtle　　above-ILL　　climb-GER-3.PL　　go-3.PL
　　　'Having climbed on top of the turtle, they went/walked.'

(57) *Hina-spa*　*chay-manta*　*allin-ta*　　*ri-chka-ya-qti-nku*[17]　　*machu*
　　　like-GER　after-ABL　　good-ADVL　go-PROG-AUG-SEQ-3.PL　old

　　　hamp'atu hayta-spa, wiqchu-yu-n, [*na-ta*],　　[*uña ch'iqlla-cha-ta*].
　　　toad　　　kick-GER　　throw-INT-3　FILLER-ACC　tiny　frog-DIM-ACC
　　　'Then after they had nicely left, kicking (him), (the old toad) threw, uh, the tiny frog.'

The object RDC in (57) has as its antecedent the distant subject in (54) and there are three intervening subjects. The first one is *machu hamp'atu* 'the old toad' in (55), and in (56) the subject is a third person plural null subject. In sentence (57), there are two subordinate clauses: the first one with a third person plural subject that is marked with a different subject switch reference marker

---

16　This difference was found in other speakers as well. One could argue that postverbal direct objects could be the result of crosslinguistic influence from Spanish. I would like to argue that while that is a possibility, the existence of preverbal objects in sentences with canonical word order indicates that there is a difference in discursive functions between preverbal and postverbal direct objects.

17　The gloss selected for -*ya* (AUG) is that assigned to the augmentative suffix -*yu* by Cusihuamán (2001). An allomorph of -*yu* is -*ya* and it adds an affective meaning to the action.

RIGHT PERIPHERAL DOMAINS

-*qti*, and the second one with *machu hamp'atu* 'the old toad' as an overt subject, a null object and the verb marked with the gerund that is also a same subject switch reference marker *-spa*. The main clause in (57) has a third person singular null subject with the old toad as a referent and the object RDC *uña ch'iqllacha* 'the tiny frog.' Notice that the RDC in this last sentence is preceded by the word *na-ta*, formed by the root *na*, a lexical filler in speech, and the accusative marker *-ta*. This seems to indicate that the speaker was looking for the lexical item to which the RDC refers. This particular fragment has a high complexity of null subjects and objects as well as one different subject (*-qti*), also known as sequential, and one same subject switch reference marker (the gerund *-spa*). It seems plausible that the object RDC is added by the speaker to help the hearer find the reference for the object of the second subordinate clause and the main clause.

There were also cases of object RDCs with an antecedent in context but not in discourse:

(58) *Hina-spa-n-mi*   *kaha-manta*   *urqu-mu-n* [*chay* *chiqlla-ta*].
like-GER-3-DIREV.FOC $box-ABL   take-CIS-3 that   frog-ACC
'Then (he) took that frog from the box.'

In this case, the frog has not been previously mentioned in discourse but is present in the pictures.

The following examples illustrate one of the nine subject RDCs with a transitive verb:

(59) *Hina-pti-n*   *tortuga-cha*   *willa-n* [*sapu-ta*].[18]
like-SEQ-DIREV.FOC $turtle-DIM   tell-3 $toad-ACC
'Then the turtle told about the toad.'

(60) *Rana-cha-ta*   *wikapa-rpari-n*   [*sapu*].
$frog-DIM-ACC   throw-INTL-3 $toad
'The toad intentionally threw the froggy.'

The RDC subject in sentence (60) refers back to the object in sentence (59) and is different from the subject of (59). Again in this case, the postverbal subject allows the hearer to choose between the subject and the object of

---

18   The use of an accusative marker *-ta* instead of the ablative marker *-manta* in this case is peculiar.

sentence (59) as potential antecedents of the null subject or the subject agreement marker in (60).

4 Discussion

The qualitative and quantitative analyses of the data presented indicate that, in order to understand the role of RDCs in discourse, it is necessary to consider their referents in discourse beyond the sentence level and to do so paying attention to the situational context. As presented in the previous sections, RDCs occurring in sentences with intransitive verbs do not refer to the main agentive topic of a particular fragment of discourse. Oblique RDCs in sentences with intransitive verbs tend to have referents not previously mentioned in discourse although present in the situational context, and subject RDCs have referents that are not immediately preceding subjects. In the case of transitive verbs, direct object RDCs also occur in contexts in which their referent is present in the situational context and not previously mentioned in discourse, and in contexts in which there are intervening subjects that may compete as potential antecedents for a null object.

The frequencies presented in the previous section of this chapter support the view that, unlike left margin constituents that are morphologically marked as topic or focus and unlike right margin constituents marked for topic, all of which are selected as part of the initial numeration of the sentence (Chomsky 2000), RDCs are the result of a discourse level strategy that allows for the construal of deictic relations outside the scope of narrow syntax where Agree relationships take place. For this strategy to work, there must be access to syntactic information relevant for case marking. In fact, such a strategy has been proposed by Safir (2008) to account for a subgroup of relationships (antecedent-anaphor and bound-variable relations) that cannot be fully accommodated within the domain of narrow syntax operations such as Agree or Move but correspond to the interpretive component. The interpretive component can establish these relationships on the basis of the structures built in syntax. In Safir's view, the distribution of bound readings for pronouns can only be understood as taking place outside the realm of the basic tree-building operations of the narrow syntax.

There is no Agree relationship between RDCs that are morphologically unmarked for focus, evidentiality and topic and the relevant features in the C-domain, nor between RDCs and any possible TP-internal projection of such features. Unmarked RDCs do not enter Agree relations with functional features in the C-domain and therefore lack the spellout markings that left-margin

RIGHT PERIPHERAL DOMAINS   317

topics and focused constituents have. The contrast can be seen in sentence (61) and sentence (35), repeated here as (62):

(61) *Hina-taq-mi,*   *ultimu-pi-qa*   *taksa*   *hamp'atu*
     like-CONTR-DIREV.FOC $last-LOC-TOP   medium   toad

     rikhu-ri-mu n.
     see-INCH-CIS-3
     'Then, at the last moment, the medium sized toad shows up.'

(62) *Chay-manta-taq*   *ri-sqa-ku,*   *[balsa-pi],*   *[balsa-pi],*
     that-ABL-CONTR   go-PST.REP-3.PL $raft-LOC $raft-LOC

     [mayu-ta].
     river-ACC
     'After that (they) went on the raft in the river.'

Whereas the left margin constituent *ultimu-pi-qa* in (61) has an oblique *-pi* case marker and a topic marker *-qa*, the postverbal phrase *balsa-pi* is only marked for locative and not for topic. *Ultimupiqa* 'at the last moment' is interpreted as a relevant topic from the perspective of the speaker, whereas *balsapi* 'on the raft' is provided as information that might be needed by the hearer but is not relevant to the speaker's perspective.

As Southern Quechua allows for null arguments (null subjects and null objects), the availability of their overt counterparts in the right margin in a non-canonical, postverbal position is compatible with an analysis in which RDCs may occupy clause-external positions. As pointed out in Sánchez (2010), they also lack intervention effects, namely, they are not rendered ungrammatical if there is an intervening constituent between them and their antecedent and they are not accepted as grammatical in isolated sentences. Therefore, given their lack of C-related marking and the fact that RDCs involve deictic relations that take place beyond the sentential level, I would like to propose that RDCs are not part of the initial numeration. Morphologically unmarked RDCs are cases of 'post-clausal' deixis. This is consistent with the definition of deixis proposed by Cornish (2008) (cited in the introduction), according to which deictic elements draw the attention of the addressee to a new object of discourse via the situational context of utterance. In the view I adopt here, RDCs unmarked for focus or topic do not enter the realm of deixis based on the speaker's perspective of the central elements of a narrative (Frascarelli 2007) or of the evaluation of the source of information by the speaker and are not part of the C-domain (Giorgi 2010). As mentioned above, in Quechua, most of these speaker-oriented features and C-domain features are grammaticalized features such as focus, evidentiality, tense and topic (Hintz 2007, Sánchez 2010) and they receive morphological markings. Morphologically unmarked RDCs do not form part either of the co-construction of mutual knowledge as suggested for a subtype of evidentials, as proposed by Hintz (2012). The type of deixis exemplified by RDCs is a secondary level of deixis, one that does not refer to main topics of discourse and that does not highlight the relevance of the constituent for the speaker's construction of the central aspects of the narrative. It is instead a strategy that allows either the introduction of information not central to the main structure of topics in discourse, or the disambiguation among previous antecedents in order to assist the hearer.

In that respect, morphologically unmarked RDCs are a repair strategy that helps to facilitate comprehension by the addressee. They are adjoined to the clause, possibly at the PF level, but do not violate the argumental structure of the verb in that they are appropriately marked for case. In that sense, the speaker can add them by accessing the structural relations already created in the narrow syntax, but since RDCs are added to the clause after the sentence has been constructed, they cannot enter into proper syntactic relations such as Agree with features in the C-domain. So, RDCs are added at the PF component with appropriate case marking and are interpreted appropriately via means of a deictic relationship established in the situational or in the discourse contexts.

5   Concluding Remarks

The results obtained in this study show that the Southern Quechua narratives analyzed make transparent the distinction between syntactic representation at the sentence level and the gradual construction of sequences of sentences in a narrative. This gradual construction requires repair strategies such as the one analyzed here. The Southern Quechua left periphery is morphologically marked because it is constructed as part of the syntactic representation; the right periphery hosts phrases that are not part of the narrow syntax. This accounts for why sentence-level grammaticality judgments differ greatly in Quechua, as noticed in Sánchez (2010), from what has been observed here at the narrative level in oral production. In grammaticality judgments, no postverbal subjects are accepted without -qa markers, whereas in oral production, postverbal subjects are found as well as other oblique DPs and even objects. This cannot be directly observed in SVO languages with no overt morphological marking for topic, focus and evidentiality, such as Spanish or Italian with postverbal subjects that can be interpreted as bearing focus in isolated sentences, as proposed by Belletti (2005). Southern Quechua RDCs in the narratives analyzed show a link between post-syntactic PF strategies and deictic functions that are available to the interpretive component that involve introducing discourse referents present in the situational context and strategies oriented to helping the addressee. In this respect, they show evidence of the articulation of syntax and the PF level in discourse such that PF utilizes the products of the syntactic component to satisfy interpretive needs.

Appendix A

3	third person	INCH	inchoative
ABL	ablative	INCL	inclusive
ACC	accusative	INDEV.FOC	indirect evidential.focus
ADD	additive	INT	intensifier
ADVL	adverbial	ITER	iterative
AUG	augmentative	LOC	locative
CIS	cislocative	NEG	negative
COM	comitative	PL	plural
CONTR	contrastive	POSS	possessive
DAT	dative	PROG	progressive
DIM	diminutive	PST.ATT	past attested
DIREV.FOC	direct evidential.focus	PST.REP	past reported
DISC	discourse marker	REFL	reflexive
EMP	emphatic	REG	regressive
FUT	future	SEQ	sequential
GEN	genitive	TOP	topic
GER	gerund	TOP2	topic*
ILL	illative		

* This is used for –*ri* (a type of contrastive topic), not for -qa, a non-contrastive one.

Bibliography

Adelaar, Willem and Pieter Muysken. 2004. *The Languages of the Andes*. Cambridge: Cambridge University Press.

Barbiers, Sjef. 2000. "The right periphery in SOV Languages. English and Dutch." In *The derivation of VO and OV*, edited by Peter Svenonius, 181–218. Amsterdam: John Benjamins.

Belletti, Adriana. 2005. "Extended doubling and the VP periphery." *Probus* 17: 1–35.

Carnie, Andrew. 2013. *Syntax*. Oxford: Wiley-Blackwell.

Cecchetto, Carlo. 1999. "A comparative analysis of left and right dislocation in Romance." *Studia Linguistica* 53, 1: 40–67.

Cerrón-Palomino, Rodolfo. 1987. *Lingüística quechua*. Cuzco, Perú: Bartolomé de las Casas.

———. 1994. *Quechua sureño diccionario unificado*. Lima, Perú: Biblioteca Nacional del Perú.

Chomsky, Noam. 2000. Minimalist Inquiries: The Framework. In *Step by Step: Essays on Minimalist Syntax in honor of Howard Lasnik*, edited by Roger Martin, David Michaels and Juan Uriagereka, 89–155. Cambridge, Massachusetts: MIT Press.

———. 2008. On phases. In *Foundational Issues in Linguistic Theory*, edited by Robert Freidin, Carlos Otero, and María Luisa Zubizarreta, 133–166. Cambridge, Massachusetts: MIT Press.

Cinque, Guiglielmo. 1990. *Types of A'-dependencies*. Cambridge, Massachusetts: MIT Press.

———. 1999. *Adverbs and Functional Heads: A Cross-linguistic Perspective*. New York: Oxford University Press.

Cornish, Francis. 2008. "How indexicals function in texts: Discourse, text, and one neo-Gricean account of indexical reference." *Jounal of Pragmatics* 40: 997–1018.

———. 2011. "'Strict' anadeixis, discourse deixis and text structuring." *Language Sciences* 33: 753–767.

Cusihuamán, Antonio. 2001. *Gramática quechua. Cuzco-Collao*. Centro de Estudios Regionales Andinos Bartolomé de las Casas.

Donati, Caterina and Marina Nespor. 2003. "From focus to syntax." *Lingua* 113: 1119–1142.

Finselow, Gisbert and Denisa Lenertová. 2011. "Left peripheral focus: mismatches between syntax and information structure." *Natural Language and Linguistic Theory* 29: 169–209.

Frascarelli, Mara. 2007. "Subjects, topics and the interpretation of referential pro." *Natural Language and Linguistic Theory* 25: 691–734.

Giorgi, Alessandra. 2010. *About the speaker. Towards a syntax of indexicality*. Oxford: Oxford University Press.

Herring, Susan. 1994. "Afterthoughts, antitopics and emphasis: The syntactization of postverbal position in Tamil." In *Theoretical Perspectives on Word Order in South Asian Languages*, edited by Miriam Butt, Tracy Holloway King and Gillian Ramchand, 119–150. CSLI Lecture Notes.

Hintz, Diane M. 2007. "Past tense forms and their functions in South Conchucos Quechua: time, evidentiality, discourse structure and affect." PhD diss., University of California at Santa Barbara.

——— 2012. "The evidential system in Sihuas Quechua: personal vs. shared knowledge." Paper presented at The Nature of Evidentiality Conference, University of Leiden, The Netherlands, June 14–16.

Horvath, Judith. 1986. *Focus in the Theory of Grammar and the Syntax of Hungarian*. Dordrecht: Foris Publications.

Jayaseelan, K. A. 2001. "IP-internal Topic and Focus Phrases." *Studia Linguistica* 55, 1: 39–75.

Mayer, Mercer and Marianna Mayer. 1992. *One Frog Too Many*. New York, NY: Dial. Press.

Mushin, Ilana. 2000. "Evidentiality and deixis in narrative retelling." *Journal of Pragmatics* 32: 927–957.

Muysken, Pieter. 1995. "Focus in Quechua." In *Discourse Configurational Languages*, edited by Katalin É Kiss, 375–393. New York: Oxford University Press.

Nespor, Marina and Irene Vogel. 1986. *Prosodic Phonology*. Dordrecht: Foris Publications.

Pereltsvaig, Aysa. 2004. "Topic and focus as linear notions: Evidence from Italian and Russian." *Lingua* 114: 325–344.

Rizzi, Luiggi. 1997. "The Fine Structure of the Left Periphery." In *Elements of Grammar*, edited by Liliane Haegeman, 281–337. Dordrecht: Kluwer Academic Press.

O'Rourke, Erin. 2009. "Phonetics and phonology of Cuzco Quechua declarative intonation: An instrumental analysis." *Journal of the International Phonetic Association* 39, 3: 291–312.

Safir, Ken. 2008. Coconstrual and narrow syntax. *Syntax* 11, 3: 330–355.

Sánchez, Liliana. 2003. *Quechua-Spanish Bilingualism. Functional Interference and Convergence in Functional Categories*. Amsterdam: John Benjamins.

———. 2006. Kechwa and Spanish Bilingual Grammars: Testing Hypotheses on Functional Interference and Convergence. *International Journal of Bilingual Education and Bilingualism* 9, 5: 535–556.

———. 2010. *The Morphology and Syntax of Topic and Focus: Minimalist Inquiries in the Quechua Periphery*. Linguistik Aktuell Series. Amsterdam: John Benjamins.

Selkirk, Elisabeth. 1984. *Phonology and syntax*. Cambridge, Massachusetts: MIT Press.

Speas, Margaret. 2004. "Evidentiality, logophoricity and the syntactic representation of pragmatic feature." *Lingua* 114: 255–276.

Taboada, Maite and Loreley Wiesemann. 2010. "Subjects and topics in conversation." *Journal of Pragmatics* 42, 7: 1816–1828.

Torero, Alfredo. 1964. "Los dialectos quechua." *Anales científicos de la Universidad Agraria* 2: 446–478.

Vallduvi, Enric. 1995. "Structural Properties of Information Packaging in Catalan." In *Discourse Configurational Languages*, edited by Katalin É. Kiss, 122–152. New York: Oxford University Press.

Zubizarreta, María Luisa. 1998. *Prosody, Focus, and Word Order*. Cambridge, Massachusetts: MIT Press.

Index

acquisition 19, 42–43, 62, 101–102, 104, 124, 136, 138–139, 167
adverb 11, 20, 31, 78, 107n, 119, 263–267, 271, 280–281, 289, 292, 299–300, 307
adverbial subordinator 263
aesthetics 26, 41–42, 59
affect 13–14, 27–28, 31, 39–40, 55, 148, 162n11, 314n17
affix order 27
anaphor/anaphora 10, 12, 75, 77, 82, 87–88, 93, 268, 270, 316
aspect 11, 11n6, 18, 26, 39–40, 42, 53, 62, 159, 162
    continuous 16, 36, 38, 40–41, 53–54
    perfective 16, 27, 39, 54, 57, 154
attention 10, 14–15, 27, 39, 45, 49, 55–56, 58, 61, 76, 80–81, 93
Aymara 20, 260, 269n, 278–280, 283

benefactive 13–14, 31–33, 40, 43–44, 55–58, 60–61, 289
bilingual 19, 29, 62, 112, 147, 166–167, 225, 240, 242–244, 278, 283, 293, 298
borrowing 50, 260, 276

cislocative 10, 13–14, 28–29, 33–38, 51–54, 59–62
clausal highlighter 20, 259–260, 271, 276–277, 280, 283
clusters 26–31, 43, 47–50, 55, 62, 71–72, 110
complementizer 20, 260–261, 271, 281, 289, 292
conditional 128, 131–132, 135, 259, 277
co-reference 263
co-subordination 276
CP domain 214, 214n, 289, 303

deictic center 3–4, 10–11, 17, 19, 33–34, 37–38, 59, 78, 84, 88, 103, 109, 111, 126, 139, 186
deictic shift/transposition 3–6, 17, 19, 37–38, 43, 126–128, 139, 151, 186, 189–190
    speaking self vs. the other 17, 109–110, 126, 165

deictic theory
    interactionist approach to deixis 3–6, 149
    practice approach to deixis 2–5, 18, 145, 148–149, 190
    spatialist approach to deixis 3–4, 149
deixis
    discourse deixis 5, 7, 11, 14–16, 20–21, 208–210, 215–216, 220, 223, 241, 243, 259, 292
    epistemological deixis/stance 2, 16–17, 19–21, 43, 78, 103, 108–109, 113, 118–124, 136–137, 139, 150–151, 262
    evidential deixis/stance 7, 26, 33–34, 37, 40–43, 45, 50–53, 57–63, 103, 150–151, 222–223, 263–264
    multidimensional nature of 6, 19–20, 145, 147–150, 171, 174–175, 190–191, 193–194
    nonreferential deixis 5–6
    person deixis 5, 7–10, 18, 21, 32–34, 38, 40, 59, 75, 145
    place/spatial deixis 5, 7, 10–11, 16, 18–19, 21, 25–62, 76–89, 93–94, 103, 145, 149, 160, 208, 292
    propositional deixis 103, 138
    referential deixis 2, 5–6, 76, 146, 191
    social deixis 5, 12–14, 18, 27, 39–41, 43, 58, 61–62
    spatio-temporal deixis 102, 110, 123, 138
    temporal/time deixis 5, 7, 10–12, 18, 21, 32, 35–40, 61, 75, 81, 103, 110, 126, 145
delayed mandate 116, 137
demonstratives 1, 5, 10–11, 18–19, 33, 52, 59–60, 75–81, 84–86, 88, 90–95, 208, 268, 269n, 277, 279, 280n, 293
directional morphemes 10–11, 18, 26–43, 47–62, 243
discourse marker 75, 261, 277, 282
disjoint reference 263, 275–276
distal 10, 18, 33, 52, 76–78, 81, 86–89, 93, 277, 279, 280n
drama 42, 59
dynamic 19, 27, 29–31, 61, 63, 110, 123, 138

elsetime   32, 35, 40

elsewhere   29, 31, 33, 35, 37, 40, 54

emergence   3, 36, 38, 54

enumerative conjunction   272, 281

epistemic extension   11n4, 11n5, 16–17, 19–20, 27, 30, 36, 152–155

epistemic modality vs. evidentiality   102–104, 108–109, 139

evaluation   2–3, 5, 13, 30, 61, 149, 151–152, 317

evidential enclitics

    conjecture (inference)   19, 102, 106–108, 113, 114n, 128, 140, 147, 152, 160–166, 191

    direct evidence   17, 19, 53, 60, 102, 104–109, 115, 124, 129, 133, 137–140, 147, 152, 159–163, 166, 178, 180, 191, 287

    report (hearsay)   104–108, 116, 116n, 128, 138, 140, 158, 160, 287–288

    See also delayed mandate

evidentiality strategy   11n4, 11n5, 19–21, 152–155

experienced past *–ra-*   19, 52, 102, 110–111, 117, 120, 124, 126, 128–129, 131, 138

focus   1, 14–15, 17, 19–20, 102, 104, 106–107, 113–115, 137–138, 208–255, 261–263, 287–289, 292–295, 297, 316–318

    broad focus   209–211, 215–216, 219–220, 224–234, 236–239, 248–251, 253–255

    contrastive focus   20, 107, 114, 209–211, 215–216, 220, 223–239, 241, 242n, 248–251, 253–254

    equi-statement   107, 107n, 113–114

    narrow focus   209–211, 215, 219–220, 232

    neutral focus   210, 215, 219

    non-contrastive focus   107, 114, 210

    sentence focus   102, 106–107

    wh-question   107–108, 113, 131, 140, 209, 212, 219

    wide focus   293

focus marker   14–15, 17, 20, 102, 104, 107, 138, 208–213, 216, 223, 241, 243–244

fronted/preposed (position)   15, 20, 214, 216, 222, 225–227, 241

gesture   10, 59–61, 75, 79

gradience   84, 86

grammaticalization   40, 146, 260–262, 281–283

hedge   259, 261–262, 282–283

honorifics   5, 12–13, 43, 58, 75

illocutionary force   17, 33

implicature   90, 93, 165

indexical   2, 5–6, 40, 75

inflectional marking   7–10, 13, 26

information structure   262, 287, 290, 293

in situ   15, 20, 213, 216, 225–227, 241

intensity   27–29, 39, 49–52, 55–56, 58, 60–61, 63, 67–69

irrealis (mood)   13, 277

joint attention   61, 76, 80–81, 94

language vitality   43, 50

left-dislocated element   209

malefactive   31–32, 43, 49–50, 57–58, 61

manner   18, 26–27, 31, 39–40, 62, 263

maturation   62, 124

middle voice   31

mirativity   16, 21, 90, 93, 95, 110, 122, 145–147

mirativity strategy   11n5, 20, 152–155

mood   11, 18, 26–27, 34, 39–40, 55–56, 62, 153, 277

movement   10–11, 18, 25–27, 29, 32–35, 37–38, 49, 52–57

multiple storytellers   41–42

Nahuatl   41

naturalistic/spontaneous speech   19, 101, 104, 112–118, 138–139, 147, 171, 190–192, 217, 219

nominalizer   263, 271

nominal predicate   280–281

non-experienced past *–sqa-*

    mirative ("sudden discovery")   110, 122

    resultative   117, 153

non-past   111, 126, 128–132, 135

null   1, 8–9, 21, 290–294, 297, 306–309, 314–317

object

    direct object   213–215, 221, 225, 231, 234, 242, 289, 292–293, 296, 299–303, 306, 312–316

    indirect object   289, 292, 297, 299–300, 307

INDEX

oblique 289, 292–293, 297, 299–304, 307–313, 316–318
objective meaning 25, 62
origo 41, 78, 81

parallelism 49
Paruro children 111–112
periphery
  left periphery 214, 289–290, 292–293
  right periphery 15, 215, 290, 292–293, 318
person marking 7, 153, 282–283
phatic communication 83
poetics 49
postposition 20, 264, 266–267, 271, 277, 280–281, 283
potential mood 277
prenominal 78
pronominal 5, 7–9, 292–293
prosody/prosodic 15, 20, 209–211, 215–217, 221–223, 227, 236–240, 243, 297n12
  boundary tone 231–232
  contour 216, 231, 233, 235, 237
  downstep 210–211, 215–216, 227, 232–240, 249–252
  duration 20, 76, 211, 216, 227–228, 236–241
  Fo 20, 211, 216, 227–230, 235–241, 253–255
  intensity 20, 211, 216, 227–228, 236–241, 254–255
  intonation 75–76, 215, 297
  pause 83, 88, 216, 231
  peak 20, 210–211, 215–216, 227–235, 237, 239, 241, 249–252
    final peak 215, 228, 232–235
    middle peak 232–235
    non-final peak 210, 215, 227–228
  peak alignment 20, 210, 215, 227–232, 239, 241
  stress 215, 231, 234, 242
  upstep 210–211, 215, 227, 232–235, 239, 241, 249–252
proximal 3, 18, 33, 60, 76–78, 86, 92–93

Quechua/Quichua varieties
  Bolivian Quechua 145n1, 163n12, 208–209, 222–225, 231–232, 241, 243–244, 264

Cuzco Quechua 1, 13–14, 17–20, 26, 31, 38, 101, 107–108, 110, 114n3, 145–147, 157–159, 161–165, 171, 177n22, 190–192, 208, 215, 222–223, 232, 241, 243–244, 260, 264, 276, 278, 296
Ecuadorian Quichua 1, 11n6, 17–18, 75n, 76, 165, 263, 280
Huamalíes Quechua 157, 163–164
Paruro Quechua 114–115
Pastaza Quichua 1, 18, 21, 75n1, 76, 164–165
Puno Quechua 1, 20, 259–260
Quechua I 26, 156–157, 216, 260, 280n12
Quechua II 1n, 145n1, 156–157, 208, 215–216, 260, 287n*
South Conchucos Quechua 40, 157, 161–163, 216
Southern Quechua 1, 7, 15, 17, 20, 26, 30, 145, 208, 223, 225, 242–243, 271, 277–278, 280, 287, 289–290, 292–294, 296, 297n, 298, 317–319
Tarma Quechua 107, 157–158
Tena Quichua 1, 18, 75–76
Wanka Quechua 107, 157, 159–161
quotative 259, 261–263, 282–283

radial structure model 261–262, 281
reflexive 13, 25, 31, 56–58, 62
regressive 32–34, 49, 58, 60–61
relational marker 14–15, 40, 208
reported speech 78–79, 132, 260
right dislocated constituent (RDC) 1, 20, 287–319

same reference vs. switch reference 20, 133–134, 271, 314–315
semantic
  overlap 13, 25–27, 27n1, 32–33, 62, 81, 152
  range 18, 25, 43, 45, 51, 61
source monitoring 104–105
specification marker 14–15
stance triangle 1–3, 5, 18, 145, 148, 190–191
stative 32–34, 49, 58, 61
subject 1, 7, 21, 32, 39–42, 52, 57, 106, 107n, 118, 133, 139, 209–210, 212–215, 219–240, 248, 253–255, 289–293, 297, 299–318
subjective 13, 25–26, 41–42, 56, 62, 76, 161
substrate 20, 260

theory of mind   101–102, 104, 124, 139
Tibetan   104–106, 124, 140
topic   1, 14–15, 20–21, 77–78, 80, 82–83, 93,
    208–217, 223, 225–226, 231, 240–241,
    243–244, 253, 262–263, 280, 287–289,
    291–292, 295–300, 303–310, 316–318
translocative   11, 29, 33–36, 38, 54, 62
Turkish   102, 104–105, 140

verb
    borrowed   50
    intransitive   9, 12, 32–33, 36, 38, 54, 297,
        299–312, 316
    ± motion   10–11, 27, 29, 32–38, 40, 49,
        52–55, 225
    of communication   37, 52
    suppletive   12
    transitive   9, 28n3, 32–33, 38, 50–55, 57,
        221, 270, 295–312

word order   209–211, 213–214, 216, 225–227,
    262, 287, 289, 293–295, 313–314
    OSV   214, 224–227, 235, 248
    OV   224–225, 227, 235, 248
    OVS   214–215, 224–227, 235, 237, 248
    SOV   211, 213–214, 223–229, 231–233,
        235–237, 248–250, 253–255, 262,
        287–290, 293–295, 313
    SV   224, 235, 248
    SVO   211, 214, 224–232, 234–235, 237, 241,
        248, 251–252, 290, 294, 318
    VO   224–225, 235, 237, 248
    VOS   214, 224, 248
    VS   224, 248
    VSO   214, 224, 235, 248

Yucatec Maya   6, 149–150